Lecture Notes in Computer Science 6378

Commenced Publication in 1973
Founding and Former Series Editors:
Gerhard Goos, Juris Hartmanis, and Jan van Leeuwen

Deborah L. McGuinness   James R. Michaelis
Luc Moreau (Eds.)

Provenance and Annotation of Data and Processes

Third International Provenance and Annotation Workshop
IPAW 2010, Troy, NY, USA, June 15-16, 2010
Revised Selected Papers

 Springer

Volume Editors

Deborah L. McGuinness
Tetherless World Constellation
Rensselaer Polytechnic Institute
110 8th Street, Troy, NY 12180, USA
E-mail: dlm@cs.rpi.edu

James R. Michaelis
Tetherless World Constellation
Rensselaer Polytechnic Institute
110 8th Street, Troy, NY 12180, USA
E-mail: michaj6@cs.rpi.edu

Luc Moreau
University of Southampton
School of Electronics and Computer Science
Southampton SO17 1BJ, United Kingdom
E-mail: l.moreau@ecs.soton.ac.uk

Library of Congress Control Number: 2010940987

CR Subject Classification (1998): H.3-4, D.4.6, I.2, H.5, K.6, K.4, C.2

LNCS Sublibrary: SL 3 – Information Systems and Application, incl. Internet/Web and HCI

ISSN   0302-9743
ISBN-10   3-642-17818-9 Springer Berlin Heidelberg New York
ISBN-13   978-3-642-17818-4 Springer Berlin Heidelberg New York

springer.com

© Springer-Verlag Berlin Heidelberg 2010
Printed in Germany

Typesetting: Camera-ready by author, data conversion by Scientific Publishing Services, Chennai, India
Printed on acid-free paper   06/3180

In Memoriam,
Eleanor Louise McGuinness,
1917 - 2010

Preface

Interest in and needs for provenance are growing as data proliferate. Data are increasing in a wide array of application areas, including scientific workflow systems, logical reasoning systems, text extraction, social media, and linked data. As data volumes expand and as applications become more hybrid and distributed in nature, there is growing interest in where data came from and how they were produced in order to understand when and how to rely on them. Provenance, or the origin or source of something, can capture a wide range of information. This includes, for example, who or what generated the data, the history of data stewardship, manner of manufacture, place and time of manufacture, and so on. Annotation is tightly connected with provenance since data are often commented on, described, and referred to. These descriptions or annotations are often critical to the understandability, reusability, and reproducibility of data and thus are often critical components of today's data and knowledge systems.

Provenance has been recognized to be important in a wide range of areas including databases, workflows, knowledge representation and reasoning, and digital libraries. Thus, many disciplines have proposed a wide range of provenance models, techniques, and infrastructure for encoding and using provenance. One timely challenge for the broader community is to understand the range of strengths and weaknesses of different approaches sufficiently to find and use the best models for any given situation. This also comes at a time when a new incubator group has been formed at the World Wide Web Consortium (W3C) to provide a state-of-the-art understanding and develop a roadmap in the area of provenance for Semantic Web technologies, development, and possible standardization.

The Third International Provenance and Annotation Workshop (IPAW 2010) built on the success of previous workshops held in Salt Lake City (2008), Chicago (2006, 2002), and Edinburgh (2003). It was held during June 15–16, in Troy, New York, at Rensselaer Polytechnic Institute. IPAW 2010 brought together computer scientists from different areas and provenance users to discuss open problems related to the provenance of computational and non-computational artifacts. A total of 59 people attended the workshop. These attendees came from the United States (USA), the United Kingdom (UK), the Netherlands, Germany, Brazil, and Japan. We received 36 submissions in response to the initial call for papers. Each of these submissions was reviewed by at least three reviewers. Overall, 7 submissions were accepted as full papers, 11 were accepted as medium-length papers, 7 were accepted as demo papers, and 6 were accepted as short papers. In addition, a follow-up call for late-breaking work in the form of a poster and abstract was issued, which resulted in 10 additional contributions being made.

The workshop was organized as a single-track event with paper, poster, and demo sessions interleaved. Susan Davidson (University of Pennsylvania) presented a keynote address on provenance and privacy.

Prior to IPAW 2010, on June 14, 28 attendees participated in a Provenance Hackathon, organized by Paul Groth. The aim of the Provenance Hackathon was to see whether participants, grouped in teams, could quickly build end-user applications that demonstrate unique benefits of provenance, through leveraging existing infrastructure and provenance models. Each application was evaluated based on provenance usage and usefulness by a panel of three judges. Details of participating teams, as well as provenance strategies and solutions, can be found at http://thinklinks.wordpress.com/2010/06/15/provenance-hackathon/

Immediately following IPAW 2010, a group of 28 researchers met to discuss plans for the fourth and last Provenance Challenge. The Provenance Challenge series was initiated to understand and compare expressiveness of provenance systems; it evolved into an interoperability challenge, in which provenance information is exchanged between systems. The Second Provenance challenge led to the specification of a common provenance model, the Open Provenance Model [1], which was tested in the Third Provenance Challenge. The purpose of the fourth and last Provenance Challenge is to apply the Open Provenance Model to a broad end-to-end scenario, and demonstrate novel functionality that can only be achieved by the presence of an interoperable solution for provenance. The participants successfully identified a scenario and provenance queries as well as a draft schedule. Details can be found at http://twiki.ipaw.info/bin/view/Challenge/FourthProvenanceChallenge

After the challenge planning meeting, a group of 20 researchers met to discuss evolving issues with one provenance Interlingua (PML). The workshop was organized by Paulo Pinheiro da Silva. Applications and tools were presented and use cases were articulated to help motivate and prioritize language extensions.

IPAW 2010 and associated workshops were a very successful event with much enthusiastic discussion and many new ideas generated. We are grateful for the support of STI Innsbruck for sponsoring the Provenance Hackathon, of Microsoft for sponsoring the banquet, and for Rensselaer for providing meeting space and staff support. We also thank the Program Committee members for their thorough reviews.

Reference

[1] Luc Moreau, Ben Clifford, Juliana Freire, Joe Futrelle, Yolanda Gil, Paul Groth, Natalia Kwasnikowska, Simon Miles, Paolo Missier, Jim Myers, Beth Plale, Yogesh Simmhan, Eric Stephan, and Jan Van den Bussche. The open provenance model core specification (v1.1). Future Generation Computer Systems, July 2010. (DOI: 10.1016/j.future.2010.07.005) (URL: http://eprints.ecs.soton.ac.uk/21449/)

Organization

IPAW 2010 was organized by the Tetherless World Constellation at Rensselaer Polytechnic Institute.

Workshop Co-chairs

Deborah L. McGuinness   Rensselaer Polytechnic Institute, USA
Luc Moreau   University of Southampton, UK

Program Committee

Christian Bizer   Freie Universität Berlin, Germany
James Cheney   University of Edinburgh, UK
Richard Cyganiak   DERI, Ireland
Susan Davidson   University of Pennsylvania, USA
Li Ding   Rensselaer Polytechnic Institute, USA
Ian Foster   University of Chicago,USA
Peter Fox   Rensselaer Polytechnic Institute, USA
Juliana Freire   University of Utah, USA
Alyssa Glass   Stanford University, USA
Paul Groth   Vrije Universiteit Amsterdam, The Netherlands
Olaf Hartig   Universität zu Berlin, Germany
Michael Hausenblas   DERI, Ireland
Bertram Ludaescher   University of California, Davis, USA
Marta Mattoso   UFRJ, Brazil
Simon Miles   Kings College, UK
Paolo Missier   University of Manchester, UK
Jim Myers   NCSA, USA
Paulo Pinheiro da Silva   University of Texas, El Paso, USA
Beth Plale   Indiana University, USA
Satya Sahoo   Wright State University, USA
Yogesh Simmhan   Microsoft Research, USA
Kerry Taylor   CSIRO, Australia
Jan Van den Bussche   Universiteit Hasselt, Belgium
Evelyne Viegas   Microsoft Research, USA
Jun Zhao   University of Oxford, UK

Provenance Hackathon Chair

Paul Groth   Vrije Universiteit Amsterdam, The Netherlands

Publication Chair

James R. Michaelis   Rensselaer Polytechnic Institute, USA

Local Organizers

Jacky Carley   Rensselaer Polytechnic Institute, USA
Li Ding   Rensselaer Polytechnic Institute, USA
Alvaro Graves   Rensselaer Polytechnic Institute, USA
Timothy Lebo   Rensselaer Polytechnic Institute, USA
James P. McCusker   Rensselaer Polytechnic Institute, USA

Poster/Demonstration Session Chairs

Stephan Zednik   Rensselaer Polytechnic Institute, USA
Patrick West   Rensselaer Polytechnic Institute, USA

Sponsoring Institutions

Microsoft Corporation, Redmond, WA, USA
Rensselaer Polytechnic Institute, Troy, NY, USA
Springer, New York, NY, USA
STI Innsbruck, Innsbruck, Austria

Table of Contents

On Provenance and Privacy

Susan B. Davidson

University of Pennsylvania

Provenance is a double-edged sword. On the one hand, it enables transparency, understanding the "why" and "where" of data, and reproducibility of results. On the other hand, it potentially exposes intermediate data and the functionality of modules within the workflow. However, a scientific workflow often deals with proprietary modules as well as private or confidential data, such as genomic or medical information. Hence providing exact answers to provenance queries over all executions of the workflow may reveal private information. In this talk we discuss potential privacy issues in a scientific workflow - module privacy, data privacy, and provenance privacy - and frame several natural questions: (i) Can we formally analyze module, data or provenance privacy giving provable privacy guarantees for an unlimited/bounded number of provenance queries? (ii) How can we answer provenance queries, providing as much information as possible to the user while still guaranteeing the required privacy? Then we look at module privacy in detail and propose a formal model. Finally we point to several directions for future work.

D.L. McGuinness, J.R. Michaelis, and L. Moreau (Eds.): IPAW 2010, LNCS 6378, p. 1, 2010.

The Provenance of Workflow Upgrades

David Koop[1], Carlos E. Scheidegger[2], Juliana Freire[1], and Cláudio T. Silva[1]

[1] University of Utah
[2] AT&T Research

Abstract. Provenance has become an increasingly important part of documenting, verifying, and reproducing scientific research, but as users seek to extend or share results, it may be impractical to start from the exact original steps due to system configuration differences, library updates, or new algorithms. Although there have been several approaches for capturing workflow provenance, the problem of managing upgrades of the underlying tools and libraries orchestrated by workflows has been largely overlooked. In this paper we consider the problem of maintaining and re-using the provenance of workflow upgrades. We propose different kinds of upgrades that can be applied, including automatic mechanisms, developer-specified, and user-defined. We show how to capture provenance from such upgrades and suggest how this provenance might be used to influence future upgrades. We also describe our implementation of these upgrade techniques.

1 Introduction

As tools that capture and utilize provenance are accepted by the scientific community, they must provide capabilities for supporting reproducibility as systems evolve. Like any information stored or archived, it is important that provenance is usable both for reproducing prior work and migrating that work to new environments. Just as word processing applications allow users to load old versions of documents and convert them to newer versions and data processing libraries provide migration paths for older formats, provenance-enabled tools should provide paths to upgrade information to match newer software or systems. Furthermore, it is important to capture and understand the changes that were made in order to run a previous computation in a new environment. One goal in documenting provenance is that users can more easily verify and extend existing work. If a given computation cannot be translated to newer systems or software versions, extensions become more difficult.

Workflow systems have made significant strides in allowing users to quickly compose a variety of tools while automatically capturing provenance information during workflow creation and execution [11,8]. Such systems enforce a structure on computations so that each workflow step is easily identifiable. Unfortunately, while these systems provide interfaces to a variety of routines and libraries, they are limited in their ability to upgrade workflows when the underlying routines or their interfaces are updated. It is well-known that software tends to *age* [19].

D.L. McGuinness, J.R. Michaelis, and L. Moreau (Eds.): IPAW 2010, LNCS 6378, pp. 2–16, 2010.

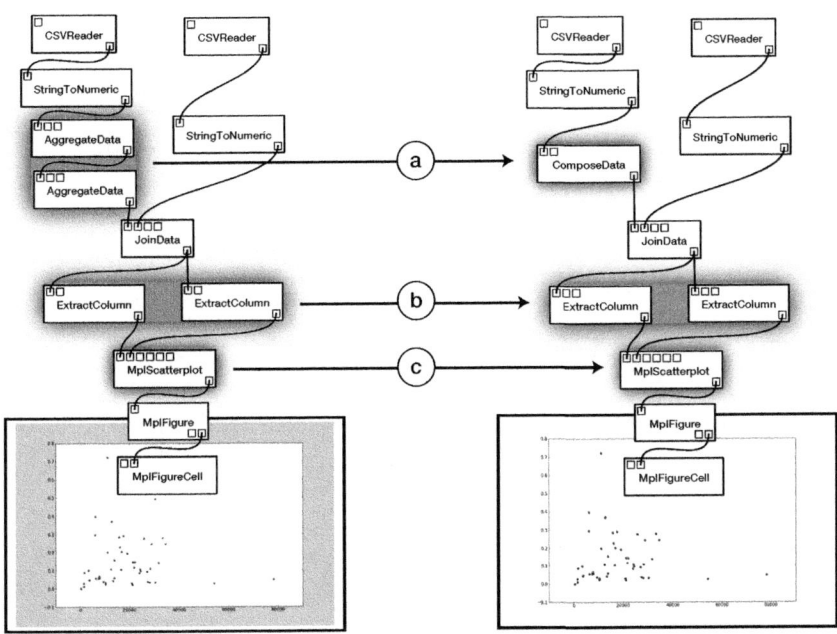

Fig. 1. A workflow comparing road maintenance and number of miles of road by state before and after upgrading two packages. In (a), the `AggregateData` module has been replaced, and the developer has specified an upgrade to combine multiple aggregation steps into a single `ComposeData` module. In (b), the interface of `ExtractColumn` has been updated to offer a new parameter. Finally, in (c), the interface of the plotting mechanism has not changed, but the implementation of that module has, as evidenced by the difference in the background of the resulting plots.

As requirements change, so do implementations and interfaces. This is more starkly obvious in the case of workflows, where different software tools from a variety of different sources need to be orchestrated. Figure 1 shows an example of different modifications that can be applied to workflow modules, including the addition of new parameters, the merger of two modules, and the replacement of the underlying computation. Still, many workflow systems do store information about the versions of routines as provenance. We seek to use this information to design schemes that allow users to migrate their work as newer algorithms and systems are developed.

There are two major approaches when dealing with upgraded software components and the documents or applications that utilize them. It is often important to maintain old versions of libraries and routines for existing applications that rely on them. In this case, an upgrade to a library should not replace the existing version but rather augment existing versions. Such an approach is common in system libraries and Web services where deleting previous versions can render existing code unexecutable. However, when we can safely upgrade the document

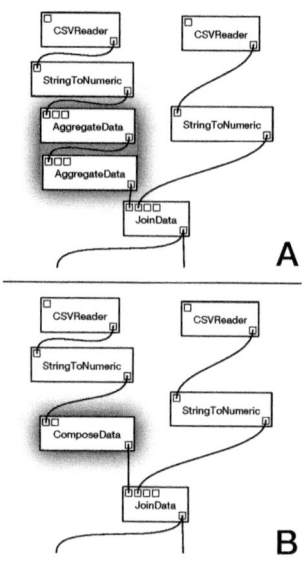

Upgrade Provenance (A → B)
delete connection StringToNumeric → AggregateData
delete connection AggregateData → AggregateData
delete module AggregateData version 1.0.4
delete connection AggregateData → JoinData
delete module AggregateData version 1.0.4
add module ComposeData version 1.1.0
add connection StringToNumeric → ComposeData
add connection ComposeData → JoinData

Execution Provenance (A)
execute module CSVReader version 0.8.0
execute module StringToNumeric version 0.9.0
→ **execute module AggregateData version 1.0.4**
→ **execute module AggregateData version 1.0.4**
execute module CSVReader version 0.8.0
execute module StringToNumeric version 0.9.0
execute module JoinData version 1.0.0
...

Execution Provenance (B)
execute module CSVReader version 0.8.0
execute module StringToNumeric version 0.9.0
→ **execute module ComposeData version 1.1.0**
execute module CSVReader version 0.8.0
execute module StringToNumeric version 0.9.0
execute module JoinData version 1.0.0
...

Fig. 2. On the right, we show the provenance of upgrading workflow (A) to the updated workflow (B). Besides the provenance of the upgrade, here we show the provenance of the executions of both (A) and (B). Note that version information is maintained in both forms of provenance.

or application to match the new interfaces, we might modify the object to utilize the new version. This second approach is more often used for documents than for existing applications or code, because there exists an application that can upgrade old versions. While the first approach is important to to ensure that the original work can be replicated, because workflows are only loosely coupled to their implementations and live in the context of a workflow system, this second approach is sensible for them. Furthermore, as Figure 2 illustrates, by capturing the provenance of the upgrades, we know exactly what has been changed from the original version and how it might be reverted.

In order to accomplish the goal of upgrading an existing workflow, we must solve the challenges of detecting when upgrades are necessary and applicable, as well as dealing with routines (modules) from disparate sources. Because workflow systems often store information about the modules included in workflows, it is possible to detect when the current implementation of a module differs from one that was previously used. However, since they come from different sources, each source may define or release upgrades differently. Thus, we cannot hope to upgrade workflows atomically, without considering specific concerns from each source. Finally, while some upgrades may be automated or specified by a developer, others may require user intervention. When the user needs to be in the loop, it is important to make the process less tedious and error-prone.

Contributions. We propose a routine for detecting when a workflow is incompatible with current installed software and approaches for both automated and user-defined upgrades. Our automated algorithm combines default routines for cases when only implementations changes with developer-defined routines, and uses a piecewise algorithm to process all components from each package at once. This allows complex upgrades, like replacing a subworkflow containing three modules with a single module. For user-defined upgrades, we suggest how a user might define a single upgrade once and apply it automatically to a collection of workflows. Finally, we discuss how upgrades should be considered as an integral part of the information currently managed by provenance-enabled systems. It is critical that we can determine what steps may have led to an upgraded workflow producing different results from the original. We describe our implementation of this upgrade framework in the VisTrails system [26].

2   Workflow Upgrades

2.1   Background

A *workflow* describes a set of computations as well as an order for these computations. To simplify the presentation, we focus on dataflows; but note that our approach is applicable to more general workflow models. In a dataflow, computational flow is dictated by the data requirements of each computation. A dataflow is represented as a directed acyclic graph where nodes are the computational *modules* and edges denote the data dependencies as *connections* between the modules—an edge connects the *output port* of a module to an *input port* of another. Often, a module has a set of associated *parameters* that can control the specifics of one computation. Some workflows also utilize *subworkflows* where a single module is itself implemented by an underlying workflow.

Because workflows abstract computation, there must be an association between the module instances in a workflow and the underlying execution environment. This link is managed by the *module registry* which maps module identifiers to their implementations. For convenience and maintenance, related modules are often grouped together in *packages*. Thus, the module identifier may consist of package identifier, a module name, an optional namespace, and information about the version of the implementation. Version information can serve to inform us when implementations or interfaces in the environment change.

Consider, for example, the VisTrails system [26]. In VisTrails, each module corresponds to a Python class that derives from a pre-defined base class. Users define custom behaviors by implementing a small set of methods. These, in turn, might run some code in a third-party library or invoke a remote procedure call via a Web service. The Python class also explicitly describes the interface of the module: the set of allowed input and output connections, given by the module's *ports*. A VisTrails package consists of a set of Python classes.

Incompatible Workflows. After a workflow is created, changes to the underlying implementation of one or more of its modules may make the workflow *incompatible*. Figure 3 shows an incompatible and a valid version of a workflow. Because

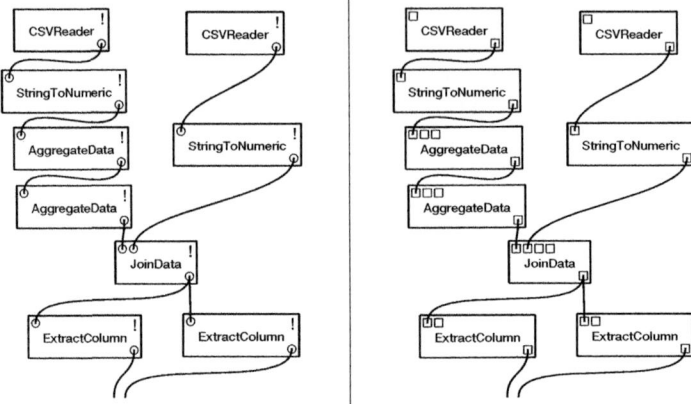

Fig. 3. Incompatible (left) and valid (right) versions of a workflow. In an incompatible workflow, the implementation of modules is missing, and thus, no information is available about the input and output ports of these modules.

module registry information is usually not serialized with each workflow, it can be difficult for users to define upgrades for obsolete workflows. As shown in the figure, although we may lack the appropriate code to execute a module or display the complete set of input and output interfaces for a module, we can display each module with the subset of ports identified by connections in the workflow. This is useful to allow users to edit incompatible workflows in order to make them compatible with their current environment.

Provenance of Module Implementation. Workflow systems offer mechanisms for capturing provenance information both about the evolution of the workflow itself and each execution of a workflow [11,12,21]. Information about the implementations used for each workflow module may be stored together with either evolution or execution provenance (i.e., the execution log). However, note that if the interface for a module changes, it will often require a change in the workflow specification. Thus, while the execution provenance may contain information about the versions used to achieve a result, any change in the interface of a module may make reproducibility via execution provenance alone difficult. By storing information about the implementations (like versions of each module) as evolution provenance, we can connect the original workflow to all upgraded versions.

Workflow evolution can be captured via *change-based provenance* [12], where every modification applied to a workflow is recorded. The set of changes is represented as a tree where nodes correspond to workflow versions and an edge between two nodes corresponds to the difference between the two corresponding workflow specifications.

Any workflow instance can be reconstructed by applying the entire sequence of change operations from the root node to the current version. For upgrades, we can leverage this approach to record the set of changes necessary to update an old workflow to a new version. Note that these changes define the difference between the two versions, so our provenance will maintain an explicit definition of the upgrade for reference and comparison.

2.2   Detecting the Need for Upgrades

To support upgrades, workflow systems must provide developers with facilities to develop and maintain different versions of modules (and packages) as well as detect and process inconsistencies when workflows created with older versions of modules are materialized. First, it is important to have a mechanism for identifying a group of modules (e.g., using a group key), as well as a version indicator or some other method like content-hashing that can be used to identify when module implementations may have changed. Ideally, any version identifier of a module should reflect the version of the code or underlying libraries. In fact, we may be able to aid developers by signaling when their code has changed, alerting them to the need to change the version. Alternately, developers might link version identifiers to revisions of their code as defined in a version control system.

Second, we need to tackle the problem of identifying when and where upgrades might be necessary. Upon opening a workflow, the system needs to check that the modules specified are consistent with the implementation defined by the module registry. As discussed earlier, this usually involves checking version identifiers but could also be based on actual code. If there are inconsistencies, we need to identify the type of discrepancy; the workflow may specify an obsolete version of a module, a newer version, or perhaps the module may not exist in the current registry. In all of these cases, we need to reconcile the workflow to the current environment.

2.3   Processing Upgrades

We wish to allow developers to specify upgrade paths but also provide automated routines when upgrades are trivial and allow users to override the specified paths. The package developer can specify how a specific module is to be upgraded in all contexts. If that is not possible or the information is not available for a given module, we can attempt to automatically upgrade a module by replacing the old version with a new version of the same module. A third method for upgrading a workflow is to display the obsolete modules and let the user replace them directly. Our upgrade framework leverages all three approaches. It starts with developer-specified changes, provides default, automated upgrades if the developer has not provided them, and allows the user to choose to accept the upgrade, modify it, or design their own.

Developer-Defined Upgrades. Because the modules of any workflow may originate from a number of different packages, we cannot assume that a global procedure can upgrade the entire workflow. Instead, we allow developers to specify upgrade

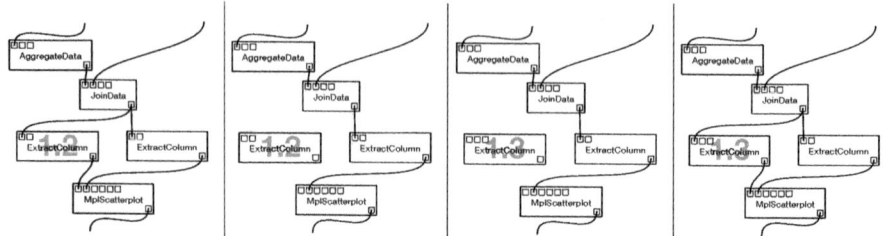

Fig. 4. Upgrading a single module automatically involves deleting all connections, replacing the module with the new version, and finally adding the connections back

routines for each package. Specifically, we allow them to write a method which accepts the workflow and the list of incompatible modules. A module may be incompatible because it no longer exists in the package or its version is different from the implementation currently in the registry. A developer needs to implement solutions to handle both of these situations, but the system can provide utility routines to minimize the effort necessary for some types of changes. In addition, there may be cases where the developer wants to replace entire sub-workflows with different ones. Changes in the specification of parameter values may also require upgrade logic. For example, an old version of module may have taken the color specification as four integers in the [0,255] range, but the new version requires floats in the [0.0, 1.0] range. Such conversions can be developer-specified so that the a user need not modify their workflows in order for them to work with new package versions. Note that developer-specified upgrades may need to be aware of the initial version of a module. For example, if version 0.1 of a module has a certain parameter, version 0.2 removes it, and version 1.0 adds it back, the upgrade from 0.1 to 1.0 will be necessarily different than the upgrade from 0.2 to 1.0.

Automatic Upgrades. We can attempt to automate upgrades by replacing the original module with a new version of the same module. For any module that needs an upgrade, we check the registry for a module that shares the same identifying information (excluding version) and use that module instead. Note that it is necessary to recreate all incoming and outgoing connections because the old module is deleted and a new module is added. If an upgraded module renames or removes a port, it is not possible to complete the upgrade. We can either continue with other upgrades and notify the user, or rollback all changes and alert the user. Also note that if two connected modules both require upgrades we will end up deleting and adding at least one of the connections twice, once for the first module replacement and again for the second module upgrade. Finally, we need to transfer parameters to the new version in a similar procedure as that used with connections. See Figure 4 for an example of an automatic upgrade.

User-Assisted Upgrades. While we hope that automatic and developer-specified upgrades will account for most of the cases, they may fail for complicated situations.

In addition, a developer may not specify all upgrade paths or a user may desire greater control over the changes. In such a scenario, we need to display the old, incompatible pipeline, highlight modules that are out-of-date, and allow the user to perform standard pipeline manipulations. One problem is that, because we may not have access to the version of the package that was used to create the workflow, we may not be able to display the module correctly for the user to interact with. With VisTrails, we can display the basic graph connectivity as shown in Figure 3, but we may not have entire module specification. Our display is therefore a "recovery mode" where the workflow is shown but cannot be executed or interacted with in the same way as a valid version. Once users replace all old modules with current versions, they will able to execute the workflow and interact with it. We can aid users by providing high-level actions that allow them to, for example, replace an incompatible module with a new, valid one.

In addition, while users may be willing to perform one or two upgrades manually, it would be helpful if we are able to aid users by automating future upgrades based on those they have already defined. Workflow analogies provide this functionality by allowing users to select existing actions including upgrades and apply them to other workflows [20]. Because analogies compute a soft matching between starting workflows, they can be applied to a variety of different workflows. Thus, for a large collection of workflows, a user may define a few upgrades and compute the rest automatically using these analogies.

2.4   Provenance Concerns

Given a data product, we cannot hope to reproduce or extend the data product without knowing its provenance—how it was generated. If our provenance information includes information about the versions of the modules used, we can use that to drive upgrades. Note that without version information, we may incorrectly determine which upgrades are necessary. Thus, the provenance of the original workflow is important to define the upgrade.

At the same time, we wish to capture the provenance of the upgrades. When users either run old versions of workflows or upgrade and modify these versions, it is important to track the changes both in the execution provenance and in the workflow evolution provenance. By noting the specific module versions used in the execution provenance, we can better support reproducibility. We need to ensure that the versions recorded are exactly the versions executed, not allowing silent upgrades to happen without being noted in the provenance. Similarly, whenever a user upgrades a workflow, the changes that took place should be noted as evolution provenance so that subsequent changes are captured correctly. See Figure 2 for an example of captured provenance information that is relevant for upgrades.

As a workflow evolves over a number of years and is modified by a number of users, it is important to track the provenance of this evolution. Upgrades may be critical changes in workflow development and often occur when a new user starts to revise an existing result. By keeping track of these actions, we may be able to identify how, for example, inconsistencies in results may have arisen because of an upgrade. In addition, we do not lose links as workflows are refined. Without upgrades, a user may create a (duplicate) workflow rather than re-use an existing one. If that occurs, we lose important provenance of the original workflow and related workflows.

3   Implementation

We have implemented the framework described in Section 2 in the VisTrails system. Below, we describe this implementation.

In VisTrails, when a workflow is loaded (or materialized), it is validated against the current environment: the classes defining the modules and the port types for each module. To detect whether modules have changed, we begin by checking each module and ensuring the requested version matches the registry version. Next, we check each connection to ensure that the ports they connect are also valid. Finally, we check the parameter types to ensure they match those specified by the implementation. If any mismatches are detected, we raise an exception that indicates what the problem is and which part of the workflow it affects. Note that if one problem occurs, we can immediately quit validation and inform the user, but if we wish to fix the problems, it is useful to identify all issues. Thus, we collect all exceptions during validation, and pass them to a handler.

We attempt to process all upgrades at once, with the exception of subworkflows which are processed recursively. To this end, we sort all requests by the packages that they affect, and attempt to solve all issues one package at a time. This way, a package developer can write a handler to process a group of upgrade requests instead of processing each request individually.

Replace, Remap, and Copy. Note that an upgrade that deletes an old module and adds a new version discards information about existing connections, parameters, and annotations. In order to maintain this information as well as its provenance, we extended VisTrails change-based provenance with a new change type (or action) that replaces the original module, remaps the old information, and copies it to a new version of the module. This ensure that we transfer all relevant information to the new version and maintain its provenance. The new action extracts information about connections, parameters and annotations from the old module before replacing it, and then adds that information to the new module. Note that, because interfaces may change, we allow the user to remap parameter, port, or annotation names to match the new module's interface.

Algorithm. Formally, our algorithm for workflow upgrades takes a list of detected inconsistencies between a workflow and the module registry and produces a set of actions to revise the workflow. We categorize inconsistencies as "missing", "obsolete", or "future" modules, and this information is encoded in the exception allowing developers to tailor upgrade paths accordingly. We begin by sorting these errors by package identifier. Then for each package, we check if the package has a handler for all types of upgrades. If it does, we call that handler.

If not, we cannot hope to reconcile "missing" modules. For obsolete modules, we can attempt to automatically reconcile them by replacing them with newer versions. For future modules, we can attempt to downgrade them automatically, but usually we raise this error to the user.

Automatic upgrades work module by module, and for each module, we first check to see if an upgrade is possible before proceeding. An upgrade is possible if the module interface has not changed from the version specified by the workflow and the version that exists on the system. We check that by seeing if each connection and parameter setting can be trivially remapped. If they can, we extract all of the connections and parameters before deleting all connections to the module and the module itself. Then, we add the new version of the module and replace the connections and parameters. All of these operations are encoded as a single action.

For developer-defined upgrades, we pass all of the information about inconsistencies as well as the current state of the workflow to the package's upgrade handler. The handler can make use of several capabilities of the workflow system to minimize the amount of code. Specifically, we have a remap function that allows a developer to specify how to replace a module when interface changes are due to renaming. In addition, developers can replace entire pieces of a workflow, but doing so might require locating subworkflows that match a given template. Many workflow systems already have query capabilities, and these can be applied to facilitate these more complex upgrades. As with automatic upgrades, these operations are encoded as a single action.

If automated and developer-defined upgrades cannot achieve a compatible workflow, a user can define an upgrade path. Most of this process is manual and mirrors how a user might normally update a workflow. Until the workflow is compatible with the current environment, the workflow cannot be executed, giving users a well-defined goal. Upon achieving a valid workflow, we can save the user's actions and use workflow analogies [20] to help automate future upgrades.

Subworkflows. To handle subworkflows, both validation and upgrade handling are performed recursively. Thus, we process any workflow by first recursing on any subworkflow modules, processing the underlying workflows, and then continuing with the rest of the workflow. However, our upgrades must be handled using an extra step; if we update a subworkflow, we must also update the module tied to that subworkflow to reflect any changes. For example, a subworkflow may modify its external interface by deleting inputs or outputs. Thus, we must upgrade a module after updating its underlying subworkflow.

Preferences. While upgrades are important, we wish to add them without interfering with a user's normal work. Besides the choice between upgrading or trying to load the exact workflow with older package versions, a user may also wish to be notified of upgrades and persist their provenance in different ways. Specifically, if old versions exist, a user may wish to always try use them, automatically upgrade, or be prompted for a decision. If not, a user has a similar selection of options: never upgrade, always upgrade, or be presented with the choice to upgrade. When a user wants to upgrade, he may choose to persist the provenance of these upgrades immediately or delay saving these changes until other changes occur. If a user is browsing workflows, it may may reasonable to only persist upgrade provenance when the workflow is modified or run. This way, a user can examine a workflow as it would appear after an upgrade, but the persistence of these upgrades is delayed until something is changed or the workflow is executed. Users might also want to have immediate upgrades where the upgrade provenance is persisted exactly when any workflow is upgraded, even if the user is only viewing the workflow.

4   Discussion

While perfect reproducibility cannot be guaranteed without maintaining the exact system configuration and libraries, we believe that workflow upgrades offer a sensible approach to manage the migration from older workflows to new environments. Note that provenance allows us to always revisit the original workflow, and we can run this version if we can reconstruct the same environment. By storing the original implementations along with workflows, we may be able to reproduce the original run, although changes in the system configuration may limit such runs. Thus, coupling provenance with version control systems could ensure that we users can access previous package implementations. However, when extending prior work in new environments, upgrades also serve to convert older work to more efficient and extensive environments. In addition, managing multiple software versions is a non-trivial task, and even with a modern OS package management system, installing a given package in the presence of conflicts is actually known to be NP-Complete [9]. Thus, we cannot expect in general to easily run arbitrarily old library versions. Because workflows abstract the implementation from the computational structure, the results of upgrades are more likely be valid.

Some workflow systems use Web services or other computational modules that are managed externally. In these cases, we may not know if the interface or implementation may have changed so it is harder to know when upgrades are necessary. However, the services may make version information available or the workflow system may be able to detect a change in the interface [5]. In this case, we are not able to leverage developer-specified upgrade routines, but we should be able to accomplish automatic or user-specified upgrades.

When using change-based provenance to track upgrades, a user can see both the original evolution as well as the upgrades and progress after the upgrades. See Figure 5 for an example. It may be useful to upgrade an entire collection of related workflows while retaining the original provenance of exploration, but adding the upgraded versions may lead to a complex interface. We believe that restructuring the tree to display the original history but with links to the upgrades might be useful. Finally, we emphasize that the change-based model for the workflows provenance in VisTrails is an attractive medium in which to incorporate the upgrading data. Since the upgrades as represented as actions, they are

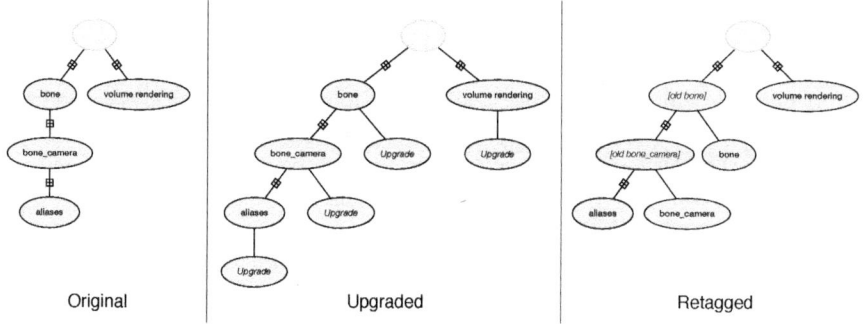

Fig. 5. Workflow Evolution before and after upgrades as well as after retagging the nodes

treated as first-class data in the system, and so the extensive process provenance capabilities of VisTrails can be directly used. For example, upgrade actions can then be used in queries or incorporated into statistical analyses [14,20,21].

5   Related Work

Workflow systems have recently emerged as an attractive alternative for representing and managing complex computational tasks. The goal behind these systems is to provide the utility of the shell script in a more user-friendly, structured manner. Workflow systems incorporate comprehensive metadata which, among other advantages, facilitates programming and distribution of results [15], reproducibility [12], allows better execution monitoring [18], and provides potential efficiency gains [3].

As the auditability and cost of generating results has increased, managing the provenance of data products [22] and computational processes [12] has become very important. Together, these ideas allow users to obtain a fairly comprehensive picture of the programs and data that were used to generate final results. However, these descriptions are, in a sense, static. In general, the processes are assumed to stay the same for the lifetime of the workflow, and, as we have argued before, longevity necessarily introduces changing requirements and interfaces. Our approach serves to detect and manage these changes to underlying implementations while still keeping the attractive features of workflow systems described above.

It is well known that longevity introduces novel challenges for maintainability of software systems, in particular in the presence of complicated dependencies [19]. There have been a number of approaches to problem of managing software upgrades, in particular, in understanding and ensuring safety properties of dynamic updates in, for example, running code or persistent stores [4,10]. In small-scale environments, the solutions tend to involve the description (or prediction) of desired properties to be maintained [16]. For deployments at the scale of entire institutions or large computer clusters, they tend to involve careful scheduling, and staged deployment of upgrades [1,6].

Component-based software has evolved to separate different concerns in order to provide wide-ranging functionality. While usually at a lower level than workflow systems, component objects use well-defined interfaces and are substitutable [24]. For this reason, it is also important to track the component evolution and versioning [23]. The term "dependency hell" was coined to describe problems with compatibility when replacing components with new versions. McCamant and Ernst describe methods to identify such incompatibilities [17] while Stuckenholz proposes "intelligent component swapping" to update multiple components at once [23].

Web services are another kind of component-based architecture. Since the standards do not address the evolution of Web services, developers must rely on design patterns and best practices [5]. Specifically, adding to an interface is possible, but changing or removing from that interface is not. Andrikopoulos et al. formalize the concepts of service evolution [2]. There are a variety of approaches that seek to develop mechanisms to version Web services including using a chain of adapters [13] and hierarchical abstraction [25]. In order to publish such versions, services are distinguished via namespaces or URLs. In contrast to much of the work for component upgrades, our approach seeks to add capability by updating older workflows rather than only maintaining backward compatibility.

In this paper, we focus on the problem of providing a means of describing upgrade paths so that a workflow can be automatically updated, its upgrade history appropriately recorded, and its execution sufficiently similar to the one before the upgrade. Such problems exist even when lower-level upgrades are successfully deployed. In that sense, our mechanisms for coping with upgrades are closer in spirit to mechanisms for automatically updating database queries after relational schemas have changed [7].

6   Conclusion and Future Work

We have proposed a framework for workflow upgrades and described its implementation in the VisTrails system. Our framework handles three types of upgrades—automated, developer-specified, and user-defined, and we have discussed how these can be supported in a systematic fashion. We have also shown how the framework leverages provenance information to accomplish upgrades and produces updated provenance detailing the changes introduced by the upgrades. Our implementation is currently available in nightly releases of VisTrails, and we are planning to incorporate it into the next major release of VisTrails.

One area that we would like to explore further is the interface for involving the user in upgrades. The "replace module" action allows users to specify how an upgrade is accomplished, and we believe a user might drag a new module onto the incompatible module to replace it. At the same time, if the routine specifications do not exactly match, the user should be able to specify the remapping, similar to the method available to developers in their code. We might extend this functionality to allow the user to specify the connections visually.

In addition to capturing the provenance of upgrades and using this information to guide future user-driven, manual upgrades, we believe we might also use this provenance for further analysis. For example, we might be able to examine the actions used in upgrades to mine rules for packages whose developers have not defined upgrade paths. It may also be interesting to try to analyze performance or accuracy changes in workflow execution after upgrades.

Acknowledgments

Our research has been funded by the National Science Foundation (grants IIS-0905385, IIS-0844546, IIS-0746500, ATM-0835821, CNS-0751152, IIS-0713637, OCE-0424602, IIS-0534628, CNS-0514485, IIS-0513692, CNS-0524096), the Department of Energy SciDAC (VACET and SDM centers, and SBIR DE-FG02-85157), and IBM Faculty Awards (2005, 2006, 2007, and 2008).

References

1. Ajmani, S., Liskov, B., Shrira, L.: Scheduling and simulation: how to upgrade distributed systems. In: HOTOS, pp. 8–8 (2003)
2. Andrikopoulos, V., Benbernou, S., Papazoglou, M.P.: Managing the evolution of service specifications. In: Bellahsène, Z., Léonard, M. (eds.) CAiSE 2008. LNCS, vol. 5074, pp. 359–374. Springer, Heidelberg (2008)
3. Bavoil, L., Callahan, S., Crossno, P., Freire, J., Scheidegger, C., Silva, C., Vo, H.: VisTrails: Enabling interactive, multiple-view visualizations. In: Proceedings of IEEE Visualization, pp. 135–142 (2005)
4. Boyapati, C., Liskov, B., Shrira, L., Moh, C.-H., Richman, S.: Lazy modular upgrades in persistent object stores. SIGPLAN Not. 38(11), 403–417 (2003)
5. Brown, K., Ellis, M.: Best practices for Web services versioning. IBM developerWorks (2004),
   http://www.ibm.com/developerworks/webservices/library/ws-version/
6. Crameri, O., Knezevic, N., Kostic, D., Bianchini, R., Zwaenepoel, W.: Staged deployment in mirage, an integrated software upgrade testing and distribution system. SIGOPS Oper. Syst. Rev. 41(6), 221–236 (2007)
7. Curino, C., Moon, H.J., Zaniolo, C.: Automating database schema evolution in information system upgrades. In: HotSWUp, pp. 1–5 (2009)
8. Davidson, S.B., Freire, J.: Provenance and scientific workflows: challenges and opportunities. In: Proceedings of SIGMOD, pp. 1345–1350 (2008)
9. di Cosmo, R.: Report on formal management of software dependencies. Technical report, INRIA,September EDOS Project Deliverable WP2-D2.1 (2005)
10. Dumitraş, T., Narasimhan, P.: Why do upgrades fail and what can we do about it? In: Bacon, J.M., Cooper, B.F. (eds.) Middleware 2009. LNCS, vol. 5896, pp. 1–20. Springer, Heidelberg (2009)
11. Freire, J., Koop, D., Santos, E., Silva, C.T.: Provenance for computational tasks: A survey. Computing in Science and Engineering 10(3), 11–21 (2008)
12. Freire, J., Silva, C.T., Callahan, S.P., Santos, E., Scheidegger, C.E., Vo, H.T.: Managing rapidly-evolving scientific workflows (Invited paper). In: Moreau, L., Foster, I. (eds.) IPAW 2006. LNCS, vol. 4145, pp. 10–18. Springer, Heidelberg (2006)

13. Kaminski, P., Litoiu, M., Müller, H.: A design technique for evolving web services. In: CASCON 2006: Proceedings of the 2006 Conference of the Center for Advanced Studies on Collaborative research, p. 23. ACM, New York (2006)
14. Lins, L., Koop, D., Anderson, E., Callahan, S., Santos, E., Scheidegger, C., Freire, J., Silva, C.: Examining statistics of workflow evolution provenance: a first study. In: Ludäscher, B., Mamoulis, N. (eds.) SSDBM 2008. LNCS, vol. 5069, pp. 573–579. Springer, Heidelberg (2008)
15. Ludascher, B., Altintas, I., Berkley, C., Higgins, D., Jaeger, E., Jones, M., Lee, E.A., Tao, J., Zhao, Y.: Scientific workflow management and the kepler system: Research articles. Concurr. Comput.: Pract. Exper. 18(10), 1039–1065 (2006)
16. McCamant, S., Ernst, M.D.: Predicting problems caused by component upgrades. In: ESEC, pp. 287–296 (2003)
17. McCamant, S., Ernst, M.D.: Early identification of incompatibilities in multi-component upgrades. In: Vetta, A. (ed.) ECOOP 2004. LNCS, vol. 3086, pp. 440–464. Springer, Heidelberg (2004)
18. Microsoft Workflow Foundation, http://msdn2.microsoft.com/en-us/netframework/aa663328.aspx
19. Parnas, D.L.: Software aging. In: Taylor, R.N. (ed.) ICSE-WS 1994 and SE-HCI 1994. LNCS, vol. 896, pp. 279–287. Springer, Heidelberg (1995)
20. Scheidegger, C.E., Vo, H.T., Koop, D., Freire, J., Silva, C.T.: Querying and creating visualizations by analogy. IEEE TVCG 13(6), 1560–1567 (2007)
21. Scheidegger, C.E., Koop, D., Santos, E., Vo, H.T., Callahan, S.P., Freire, J., Silva, C.T.: Tackling the provenance challenge one layer at a time. Concurrency and Computation: Practice and Experience 20(5), 473–483 (2008)
22. Simmhan, Y.L., Plale, B., Gannon, D.: A survey of data provenance in e-science. SIGMOD Rec. 34(3), 31–36 (2005)
23. Stuckenholz, A.: Component evolution and versioning state of the art. SIGSOFT Softw. Eng. Notes 30(1), 7 (2005)
24. Szyperski, C.: Component Software: Beyond Object-Oriented Programming. Addison-Wesley Longman Publishing Co., Inc., Boston (2002)
25. Treiber, M., Juszczyk, L., Schall, D., Dustdar, S.: Programming evolvable web services. In: PESOS 2010: Proceedings of the 2nd International Workshop on Principles of Engineering Service-Oriented Systems, pp. 43–49. ACM, New York (2010)
26. VisTrails, http://www.vistrails.org

Approaches for Exploring and Querying Scientific Workflow Provenance Graphs

Manish Kumar Anand[1], Shawn Bowers[2], Ilkay Altintas[1], and Bertram Ludäscher[1,3]

[1] San Diego Supercomputer Center, University of California, San Diego, USA
[2] Department of Computer Science, Gonzaga University
[3] UC Davis Genome Center, University of California, Davis
mkanand@sdsc.edu, bowers@gonzaga.edu, altintas@sdsc.edu,
ludaesch@ucdavis.edu

Abstract. While many scientific workflow systems track and record data provenance, few tools have been developed that provide convenient and effective ways to access and explore this information. Two important ways for provenance information to be accessed and explored is through browsing (i.e., visualizing and navigating data and process dependencies) and querying (e.g., to select certain portions of provenance graphs or to determine if certain paths exist between items within a graph). We extend our prior work on representing and querying data provenance by showing how these can be effectively and efficiently combined into an interactive provenance browser. The browser allows different views of provenance to be explored and queried, where queries are expressed in a declarative graph-based provenance query language. Query results are expressed as provenance subgraphs, which can be further visualized and navigated through the browser. The browser supports a generic model of provenance that can be used with various workflow computation models, and has a direct translation to the Open Provenance Model. We present the provenance model, the query language, and describe the overall browser architecture and implementation.

1 Introduction

Scientific workflow provenance is commonly represented using data and process *dependency graphs* [1,2] in which dependencies represent causal relationships among data products and/or process invocations. As workflows are executed, many workflow execution environments (e.g., [3,4,5]) store the associated provenance graphs within dedicated *provenance stores* (i.e., databases). This provenance information is of great interest to scientists and other users, e.g., for determining data lineage, result interpretation, and evaluating the quality of workflow results.

While many workflow systems store provenance information, few provide users with tools for effectively and efficiently exploring, accessing, and querying the provenance graphs associated with workflow runs. In this paper, we address problems in exploring and querying provenance information by presenting approaches that combine provenance visualization and navigation with support for incremental query. These approaches have been implemented within a provenance browser application. The browser supports a generic model of provenance that is compatible with a number of existing

D.L. McGuinness, J.R. Michaelis, and L. Moreau (Eds.): IPAW 2010, LNCS 6378, pp. 17–26, 2010.

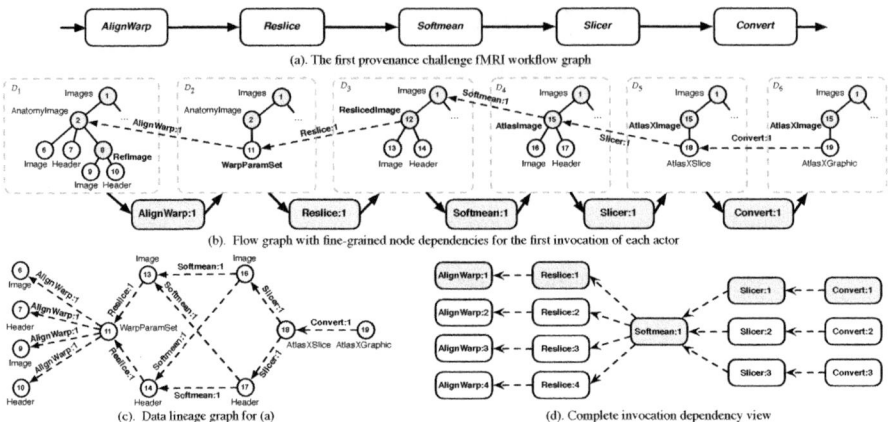

Fig. 1. (a) Workflow for the fMRI image analysis of the first provenance challenge; (b) Trace showing the first invocations of each actor (for a typical run); (c) Implied fine-grain data dependency graph for the data items in (b); and (d) Implied invocation dependency graph for the run, with the first invocations of each actor shown in gray

provenance models (including the Open Provenance Model [1]), and incorporates storage and query optimization that makes browsing and querying over (often large and complex [6]) provenance graphs feasible.

Contributions. This paper describes the different approaches used in implementing the provenance browser (first presented in [7]). In particular, we briefly describe the provenance model and query language (QLP) of the browser and show how these approaches can easily accommodate the Open Provenance Model (OPM). We then present the provenance browser[1] focusing on its architecture, implementation, and optimization techniques. The implementation allows users to easily navigate different aggregated views of underlying provenance graphs and specify new provenance views through incremental queries. Our approach also maintains the user's query history, allowing users to go back to and navigate previous query results.

2   Model of Provenance and Query Language

The Provenance Model. We assume workflow runs follow a standard dataflow-based workflow computation model (e.g., [3,4]). However, our provenance model also supports processes that (1) can execute multiple times in a workflow run (and in parallel), and (2) can recieve and produce data products that are *structured* via labeled, nested collections (e.g., data can be organized into XML structures).

Consider the simple workflow in Fig. 1(a) representing the First Provenance Challenge fMRI workflow [1]. Steps in the workflow are referred to as *actors* that are *invoked*

---

[1] The browser is open-source and can be freely downloaded from
http://www.daks.ucdavis.edu/projects/pb, or from within Kepler as the "provenance-browser" extension module.

over input data supplied by previous steps. This example takes a set of anatomy images representing 3D brain scans and a reference image, and creates a graphical image for each 2D slice. In this example workflow implementation we assume each invocation of an actor receives an XML data structure, performs an update on a portion of that structure, and then sends the updated version of the structure to downstream actors (see Fig. 1(b)).

Fig. 1(b) shows the first invocation of each actor for a typical run of the workflow. The invocation of the AlignWarp actor (*AlignWarp:1*) modifies the first AnatomyImage collection (node 2), and replaces its contents with a WarpParamSet data token (node 11). The invocation of the Reslice actor uses this WarpParamSet to generate a new Image and Header data token (nodes 13 and 14, respectively). Since only a part of an XML data structure D may be modified by an invocation, we also represent explicit data dependencies as part of a run. For example, the dashed arrow from node 11 to node 2 in Fig. 1(b) states that the WarpParamSet was created from the AnatomyImage collection by the first invocilty of AlignWarp. Note that node 11 implicilty depends on each of the descendents of node 2. Each descendent of a collection also implicitly inherits the dependencies of its ancestors, e.g., node 13 depends on node 11 since it is a descendent of node 12. Taken together, Fig. 1(b) denotes a portion of the *trace* for a run of Fig. 1(a), in this case corresponding to the first invocation of each workflow actor.

More formally, we define a *trace* as an acyclic digraph $T = (V,E,\tau,L)$. Each vertex $V = S \cup I$ represents either a data structure $s \in S$ or an actor invocation $i \in I$. Edges $E = E_{in} \cup E_{out}$ are *in-edges* $E_{in} \subseteq S \times I$ or *out-edges* $E_{out} \subseteq I \times S$. Each trace includes a function $\tau : S \to X$ that maps structures $s \in S$ to their corresponding XML trees $\tau(s) \in X$. We assume an underlying space of XML nodes N from which XML trees X are built, and a function $\text{nodes}(x) \subseteq N$ that gives the nodes of a structure $x \in X$. Further, we allow different versions of XML trees $\tau(s) \in X$ to *share* nodes from N. To support fine-grained dependencies we consider ternary node-level *lineage relations* $L \subseteq N \times I \times N$ such that $(n_1,i,n_2) \in L$ implies n_1 was required for the derivation of n_2 by i. We define the relations *in*, *out*, *ddep*, and *idep* using the following Datalog rules.

$$\text{in}(n,i) \text{ :- } E_{in}(s,i),\ n \in \text{nodes}(\tau(s)).$$
$$\text{out}(i,n) \text{ :- } E_{out}(i,s),\ n \in \text{nodes}(\tau(s)).$$
$$\text{ddep}(n_2,n_1) \text{ :- } L(n_1,i,n_2).$$
$$\text{idep}(i_2,i_1) \text{ :- } L(n_1,i_i,n_2), L(n_2,i_2,n_3).$$

The last two relations can be used to construct standard dependency graphs, e.g., see Fig. 1(c) and (d).

Correspondence to the Open Provenance Model (OPM). OPM traces can be represented using the above model (with the major difference being that OPM lacks explicit support for modeling structured data). Within OPM, *artifacts* denote "opaque" data objects (atomic with respect to OPM), *used* edges relate artifacts to the processes they were input to, *wasGeneratedBy* edges relate artifacts to the process they were produced by, *wasDerivedFrom* edges define data dependencies between artifacts, and *wasTriggeredBy* edges denote dependencies between processes. OPM employs the following first-order constraints (i.e., "completion rules") over these edges [1].

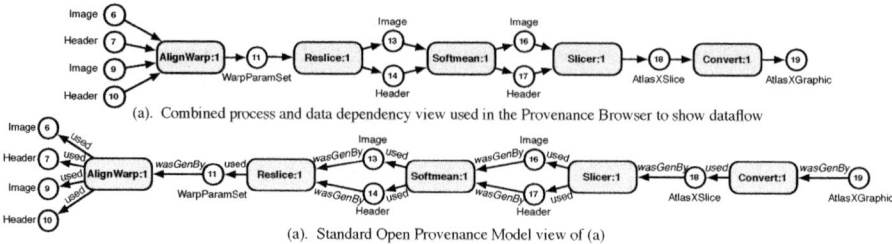

(a). Combined process and data dependency view used in the Provenance Browser to show dataflow

(a). Standard Open Provenance Model view of (a)

Fig. 2. (a) A standard provenance-browser view of a provenance graph; and (b) the same view with corresponding OPM edges

$$\forall a \forall p_1 \forall p_2 (\text{wasGeneratedBy}(a, p_1) \wedge \text{used}(p_2, a) \rightarrow \text{wasTriggeredBy}(p_2, p_1))$$
$$\forall p_1 \forall p_2 (\text{wasTriggeredBy}(p_2, p_1) \rightarrow \exists a (\text{wasGeneratedBy}(a, p_1)) \wedge \text{used}(p_2, a))$$
$$\forall a_1 \forall a_2 (\text{wasDerivedFrom}(a_2, a_1) \rightarrow \exists p (\text{used}(p, a_1) \wedge \text{wasGeneratedBy}(a_2, p)))$$

If OPM artifacts are represented as single-node tree structures, we have the following equivalences: *used* corresponds to the *in* relation; *wasGeneratedBy* corresponds to the *out* relation; *wasDerivedFrom* corresponds to the *ddep* relation; and *wasTriggeredBy* corresponds to the *idep* relation. Given these, it can easily be shown that the OPM completion rules for *wasDerivedFrom* and *wasTriggeredBy* are equivalent to the *ddep* and *idep* rules, respectively. Fig. 2(a) shows a standard provenance view used by the provenance browser that gives the *in* and *out* relations for the first actor invocations of the example in Fig. 1; and Fig. 2(b) shows the same basic view but using the corresponding OPM *used* and *wasTriggeredBy* edges. A similar graph can be constructed for the *ddep* to *wasDerivedBy*, and *idep* to *wasTriggeredBy* correspondences.

The Query Language for Provenance (QLP). QLP queries are expressed against provenance trace graphs, and can include constructs for querying the different dimensions of traces including *lineage relations* among nodes and invocations, *in-out edges* among input and output structures of invocations, and *structural relations* among nodes within and across data structures. The syntax of QLP is similar in spirit to tree and graph-based languages such as XPath and generalized path expressions, such as those used in Lorel [8]. However, QLP queries primarily act as *filters* over lineage relations. That is, given a set of lineage relations, a QLP query selects and returns a subset of the relations.

To illustrate QLP, the lineage queries "*.. 19", "6 .. *", and "#Softmean .. #Convert .. *" return lineage relations denoting sets of paths that: start from any node and end at node 19; start at node 6 and end at any node; and start at invocations of Softmean and pass through invocations of the Convert actor; respectively. See [9] for other QLP constructs and functions.

Applying QLP to OPM Provenance Graphs. QLP queries can be directly evaluated against OPM graphs based on the straightforward mapping described above. QLP queries expressed against OPM graphs of the form "$n_1 .. n_2$" select the set of OPM edges that lie on a *wasDerivedFrom* path starting at artifact n_2 and ending at artifact n_1.

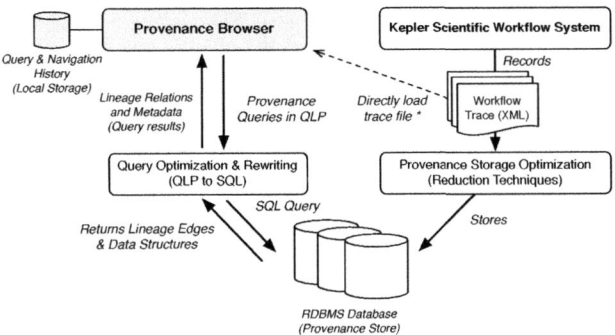

Fig. 3. The basic provenance browser architecture where trace files can be loaded either directly into the browser or through a dedicated provenance store (relational database)

Thus, if n_2 is connected to n_1 either directly or transitively through one or more *wasDerivedFrom* edges, then all edges, processes, and artifacts on this path are returned. QLP queries of the form "$\#p_1 .. \#p_2$" select the set of OPM edges, artifacts, and processes that lie on a *wasTriggeredBy* path from process p_2 to process p_1. Again, if p_2 is connected to p_1 through one or more *wasTriggeredBy* edges, then all edges, processes, and artifacts along the path are returned as a result of the query. For QLP queries of the form "$n .. \#p$" and "$\#p .. n$", we first find the output and input artifacts of process p and then use these artifacts to find *wasDerivedFrom* paths to and from n, respectively. More complicated QLP expressions such as "$n_1 .. \#p_1 .. n_2$" and "$\#p_1 .. n_1 .. n_2 .. \#p_3$" are evaluated based on these simple patterns as described in [10,9].

3   The Provenance Browser

The provenance browser provides an interactive approach for visualizing and querying provenance traces. The basic architecture of the browser is shown in Fig. 3 and two standard views of provenance information are shown using the browser in Fig. 4.

The Provenance Browser Architecture. The provenance browser has been integrated with the Kepler scientific workflow system [3,7] and can also be run as a stand-alone application. Given a trace file, a set of pre-processing steps are applied to the trace prior to storage in a provenance database. The pre-processing steps perform storage reduction techniques (based on factorization) over the data lineage graph of the workflow trace as described in [9]. Using the provenance browser, a user can connect to a provenance store to select traces to view, issue QLP queries against traces, and then display, navigate, and further query these results. As shown in Fig. 3, QLP queries are parsed, optimized, and rewritten to corresponding SQL queries expressed against the provenance database. Optimized and translated SQL queries return sets of lineage edges as query results from which the browser constructs and displays the corresponding lineage graph. Finally, the browser maintains (i.e., caches) query results as well as navigation and query history

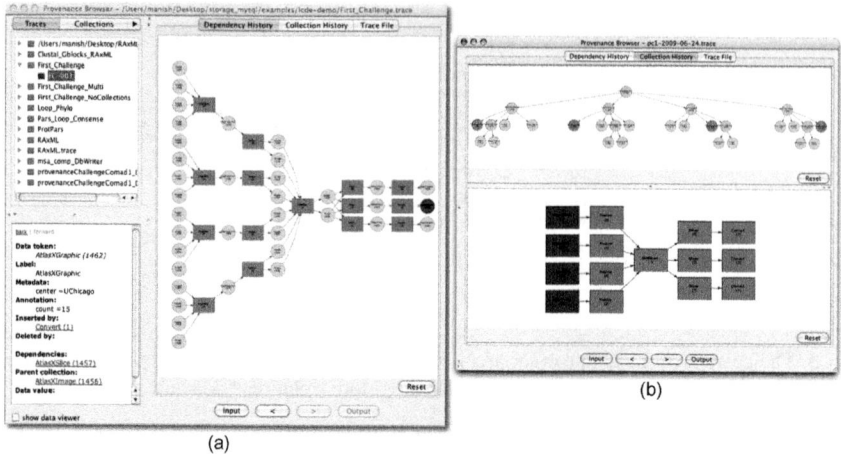

(a)

(b)

Fig. 4. Two basic provenance views supported by the browser: (a) The in-out edge representation over data and invocation dependencies; and (b) the corresponding collection structure and invocation graph after the first set of actor invocations

locally. Local storage, e.g., allows query results to be accessed and viewed efficiently within the browser.

Visualization and Navigation. As shown in Fig. 4(a), the left-side of the provenance browser displays the XML collection structure together with the details of actor invocations. Much like a web browser, this information can be navigated (e.g., to select among different data items and invocations). The browser also displays various provenance views of the execution trace: the *dependency history* view of Fig. 4(a) combines data dependency and process invocation graphs (where data nodes are denoted as circles and invocations as squares); the *collection history* view at the top of Fig. 4(b) shows the data structures input and output by invocations; and the *invocation dependency* view at the bottom of Fig. 4(b) shows process dependencies. Each of these views are synchronized, e.g., selection of a data item in the dependency history view also selects the corresponding item in the collection history view. Within a view, users can also step forward and backward ("VCR-style") through the execution history to display corresponding portions of the XML structures and data dependencies.

Incremental Querying. Fig. 5 shows an example of an incremental query session within the provenance browser. As shown in Fig. 5(c), the provenance browser contains a separate query window for users to issue QLP queries. In this example, we have selected the workflow run "FC-001" (see Fig. 4(a)). In general, users can select one or more traces from a provenance store using the query window. Once selected, the default views of the traces are displayed in the browser. If a workflow is not selected, all traces within the provenance store will be queried (but not initially displayed in the browser). After a query is entered into the query window and executed, the new provenance views that correspond to the query answer are constructed and displayed in the browser. In the

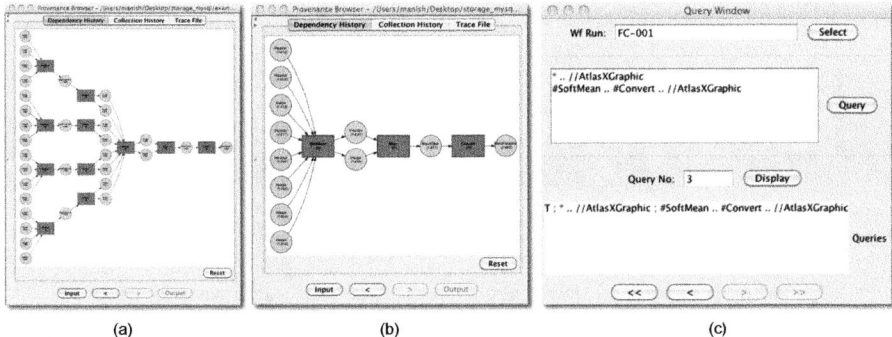

(a)   (b)   (c)

Fig. 5. Incrementally query support in the provenance browser: (a) the result of the first QLP query (expressed over the lineage graph of Fig. 4(a)); (b) the result of the second QLP query expressed over the result of the first query; and (c) the query window

example of Fig. 5, the user first enters the query "* .. //AtlasXGraphic" whose query result is shown in Fig. 5(a). This new view can be explored and navigated in exactly the same way as if the entire trace were displayed. The query result can also be further queried, as shown by the second query in Fig. 5(c) whose result is shown in Fig. 5(b).

Query History. The browser automatically captures the sequence of queries issued by the user (where the initial view is denoted as "T" in the query window). Users can return to a previous query result at any time by selecting the query from the query history or using the forward-backward buttons within the query window. In our example, selecting the first query (denoted query 2, since the initial trace is treated as query 1) would return the view from Fig. 5(b) back to Fig. 5(a). We could then continue browsing, return to the view in Fig. 5(b), move to the original view in Fig. 4(a), or issue a new query to generate a different view. The ability to incrementally query provenance graphs allows users to more easily inspect and explore relevant portions of large provenance graphs (containing, e.g., hundreds or thousands of nodes), which contrasts with more static approaches that simply display entire lineage graphs.

Optimization Techniques. Queries in QLP largely involve evaluation of transitive path queries, expressed in QLP whenever the '..' operator is used. To evaluate queries efficiently, we store both the immediate edges and transitive closure of dependency nodes. Naively materializing transitive closures for each dependency node can have prohibitively large overhead with respect to storage cost. To reduce this storage cost, we employ a "pointer-based" approach that partitions the transitive closure table into smaller tables (based on reduction techniques) where the original transitive closure table can be obtained by joining these smaller tables together [9]. In particular, a naive approach for storing nodes N and their dependencies D is as tuples $P(N,D)$ in which nodes involved in shared dependencies will be stored multiple times. For example, if nodes n_4, n_5, and n_6 each depend on nodes n_1, n_2, and n_3, nine tuples must be stored $P(n_4,n_1), P(n_4,n_2), P(n_4,n_3), P(n_5,n_1), ..., P(n_6,n_3)$, where each node is stored multiple times in P. Instead, we introduce additional levels of indirection through "pointers"

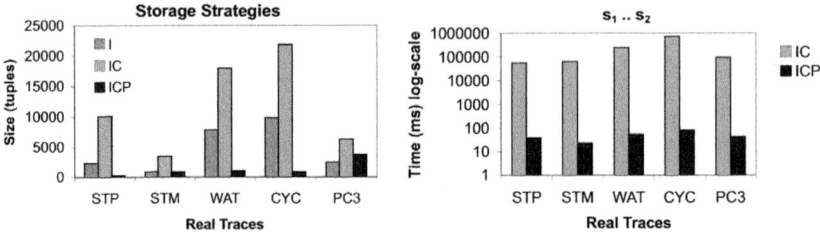

Fig. 6. Example sizes (left) and query time (right) for real provenance traces

(similar to vertical partitioning) for storing reduced sets of dependencies. Thus, we divide $P(N,D)$ into two relations $P_1(N,X)$ and $P_2(X,D)$ where X denotes a pointer to the set of dependencies D of N.[2] For instance, using this approach we store only six tuples $P_1(n_4,\&x)$, $P_1(n_5,\&x)$, $P_1(n_6,\&x)$, $P_2(\&x,n_1)$, $P_2(\&x,n_2)$, and $P_2(\&x,n_3)$ for the above example. Additional levels of indirection are also used to further reduce redundancies within dependency sets based on their common subsets, and similar techniques are used to reduce transitive dependency sets by applying reduction techniques directly to pointers (as described in [11]). We also use a set of optimization techniques [9] to efficiently evaluate the generic lineage path queries of the form $p = N_1 .. N_2 \cdots N_m$, where each N_i can correspond to a set of nodes. It may be the case that not all the nodes in the set N_i share a lineage relationship with all the nodes in the other set. We use techniques to prune each of the sets N_i giving a new pruned set PN_i such that each node $n_i \in PN_i$ shares a dependency relationship with at least one node in all other sets, and vice versa. Each pruned set is computed as $PN_i = (\cap_{j=1}^{j=i-1} N_{F_i}) \cap N_i \cap (\cap_{k=i+1}^{k=m} N_{B_i})$, where N_{F_i} is "forward" lineage nodes for N_i (i.e., $N_i..*$), and N_{B_i} is the "backward" lineage nodes for N_i (i.e., $*..N_i$). We rewrite p to $PN_1 .. PN_2 \cdots PN_m$ and evaluate each simple path $PN_i .. PN_{i+1}$. Each of these simple paths are first evaluated to retrieve the set of nodes N on the lineage path from nodes in PN_i to nodes in PN_{i+1} as $PN_{F_i} \cap PN_{B_i}$. Finally, the set of lineage edges is computed from N.

The left side of Fig. 6 shows the sizes of actual provenance traces generated from metagenomic (STP, STM, and CYC), phylogenetic (WAT), and astronomy (PC3) workflows. As shown, the provenance graphs are relatively large, containing between ~5–20K lineage edges, as shown by the number of tuples when only immediate edges (I) are stored. Even for simple QLP lineage queries, e.g., involving single-step derivation path expressions "$s_1 .. s_2$', standard evaluation techniques result in query execution times that are impractical. For instance, by storing both immediate and transitive dependencies (IC), these simple queries can take upwards of 1000 s (these times are worse if only immediate edges are stored, since recursion is required). As shown in Fig. 6, employing these storage and reduction techniques together with the query optimization approaches reduces query execution time to less than 100 ms, making common (but relatively complex) graph queries practical within the provenance browser.

---

[2] The actual partitioning is slightly more complex than this, but follows the same general idea.

4   Related Work

Many tools have been created (e.g., in Kepler [3] and Taverna [4], among others) that statically display provenance graphs or provide a log of provenance events. Exceptions include VisTrails [5], which provides a browser for displaying workflow edit operations, and the Zoom*UserViews prototype [12], which simplifies provenance graphs by inferring composite invocations. The provenance browser combines visualization with navigation and a declarative, high-level provenance query language (QLP). Standard approaches for querying provenance information (e.g., [13,5]) return sets of nodes (either sets of data items or process invocations) as query results that require additional steps (or queries) to reconstruct causal relations among nodes within a query answer. Instead, QLP returns sets of lineage edges, which enables incremental querying. We've shown here that a subset of our model has a direct mapping to OPM [1]. It also offers a more flexible approach for modeling nested data (e.g., compared to [14]) by not requiring processes to generate entirely new structures, and supporting update semantics.

5   Conclusion

We extend our prior work [15,7] by describing the architecture, implementation, and underlying approaches of the provenance browser. The browser is based on a general model of provenance and a high-level, declarative query language. In addition, we have also shown how OPM aligns with our model of provenance and query language. We would like to extend the provenance browser with the navigation operators [16], so that users visualize, summarize, and query provenance views from this environment.

Acknowledgements. This research was supported in part by NSF grants OCI-0722079, and DBI 0619060, DOE grant DE-FC02-07ER25811, and the Gordon and Betty Moore Foundation award to Calit2 at UCSD for CAMERA.

References

1. Moreau, L., et al.: The open provenance model. Technical Report 14979, ECS, Univ. of Southampton (2007)
2. Davidson, S.B., Boulakia, S.C., Eyal, A., Ludäscher, B., McPhillips, T.M., Bowers, S., Anand, M.K., Freire, J.: Provenance in scientific workflow systems. IEEE Data Eng. Bull. (2007)
3. Ludäscher, B., et al.: Scientific workflow management and the Kepler system. Concurr. Comput.: Pract. Exper. 18, 1039–1065 (2006)
4. Oinn, T., et al.: Taverna: lessons in creating a workflow environment for the life sciences. Concurr. Comput.: Pract. Exper. 18, 1067–1100 (2006)
5. Scheidegger, C., et al.: Tackling the provenance challenge one layer at a time. Comput.: Pract. Exper. 20, 473–483 (2008)
6. Chapman, A., et al.: Efficient provenance storage. In: SIGMOD (2008)
7. Bowers, S., McPhillips, T., Riddle, S., Anand, M., Ludäscher, B.: Kepler/pPOD: Scientific workflow and provenance support for assembling the tree of life. In: Freire, J., Koop, D., Moreau, L. (eds.) IPAW 2008. LNCS, vol. 5272, Springer, Heidelberg (2008)

8. Abiteboul, S., Quass, D., McHugh, J., Widom, J., Wiener, J.L.: The Lorel query language for semistructured data. Intl. J. on Digitial Libraries 1, 68–88 (1997)
9. Anand, M.K., Bowers, S., Ludäscher, B.: Techniques for efficiently querying scientific workflow provenance graphs. In: EDBT (2010)
10. Anand, M.K., Bowers, S., McPhilips, T., Ludäscher, B.: Exploring scientific workflow provenance using hybrid queries over nested data and lineage graphs. In: SSDBM (2009)
11. Anand, M.K., Bowers, S., McPhilips, T., Ludäscher, B.: Efficient provenance storage over nested data collections. In: EDBT (2009)
12. Biton, O., Boulakia, S.C., Davidson, S.B., Hara, C.S.: Querying and managing provenance through user views in scientific workflows. In: ICDE (2008)
13. Holland, D., Braun, U., Maclean, D., Muniswamy-Reddy, K.K., Seltzer, M.: A data model and query language suitable for provenance. In: Moreau, L., Foster, I. (eds.) IPAW 2006. LNCS, vol. 4145, Springer, Heidelberg (2006)
14. Missier, P., Belhajjame, K., Zhao, J., Goble, C.: Data lineage model for taverna workflows with lightweight annotation requirements. In: Freire, J., Koop, D., Moreau, L. (eds.) IPAW 2008. LNCS, vol. 5272, pp. 17–30. Springer, Heidelberg (2008)
15. Anand, M.K., Bowers, S., Ludäscher, B.: Provenance browser: Displaying and querying scientific workflow provenance graphs (Demo) In: ICDE (2010)
16. Anand, M.K., Bowers, S., Ludäscher, B.: A navigation model for exploring scientific workflow provenance graphs. In: WORKS (2009)

Automatic Provenance Collection and Publishing in a Science Data Production Environment—Early Results*

James Frew[1], Greg Janée[2], and Peter Slaughter[2]

[1] Bren School of Environmental Science and Management,
University of California, Santa Barbara
frew@bren.ucsb.edu
[2] Institute for Computational Earth System Science,
University of California, Santa Barbara
{gjanee,peter}@icess.ucsb.edu

Abstract. The Earth System Science Server (ES3) system transparently collects provenance information from executing code. Provenance information (ancestors or descendants) for any process or data granule may then be retrieved from a web service, in both textual and graphical formats. We have installed ES3 in a quasi-production environment, wherein multiple Earth satellite data streams are synthesized into daily grids of global ocean color parameters, and the resulting data granules published online. ES3's non-intrusive nature makes its insertion into such an environment fairly straightforward, but considerations such as collating distributed provenance (from processes spread across computing clusters) and sharing unique identifiers (to link programs and data granules with their separately-maintained provenance) must still be addressed. We present for discussion our preliminary results from assembling such an environment.

1 Introduction

UCSB's Ocean Color Research Group (OCRG)[1] creates and distributes a variety of ocean color data products as candidate NASA Earth science data records (ESDRs). These products range from ocean optical properties and phytoplankton functional groups to phytoplankton growth rates and carbon-based productivity. Many of the products are derived by merging data from multiple satellite sensor systems [7].

All OCRG products have associated quality indices, which comprise both the statistical confidence of individual values, and how the product as a whole relates to previous versions, similar products, and *in situ* validation data. Additionally, OCRG is charged by its cooperative agreement with NASA to track and manage algorithm and data lineage throughout the product generation process, and to

---

* supported by NASA cooperative agreements NNG04GC52A and NNX08AP36A.
[1] http://wiki.icess.ucsb.edu/measures

D.L. McGuinness, J.R. Michaelis, and L. Moreau (Eds.): IPAW 2010, LNCS 6378, pp. 27–33, 2010.
© Springer-Verlag Berlin Heidelberg 2010

implement methods for automatically informing users of updated products or analyses.

ESDRs represent a blurring of the historic distinction between data creators and data providers [2]. Research groups like OCRG are now charged with distributing their data products to the broader research community, as well as developing the science-based algorithms that drive the products' creation.

2 A Non-intrusive Science Data System

OCRG is part of a larger ocean color science community that has its own computational idioms, artifacts, and traditions. While the underlying phenomena are continuous in space and time, the data products are typically generated and exchanged in fixed granularities, based on both natural units (e.g., daily/weekly/monthly aggregations) and historic limitations (e.g., file sizes small enough to transfer expeditiously over slow connections.) Data granules are usually pre-calculated and managed as files or database BLOBs. Granules typically have standard naming conventions that encode significant product semantics (e.g., dates, regions, version numbers) and are distributed in complex formats (e.g., HDF, netCDF) that commingle metadata and multidimensional data.

The ocean color science community has additionally standardized on a specific computational environment (SeaDAS[2]) based on an interpreted array manipulation language (IDL[3]). Data product generation occurs either manually (by invoking specific commands) or quasi-automatically (by batch jobs.) Data publication involves simply moving the product files onto a web server. High-level metadata (e.g., publications describing the algorithms) is available, but supplied separately.

Introducing product and provenance management into such an environment is challenging. We have simplified this problem by adopting a *microservices* approach. Microservices [1, 8] are an architectural pattern, originally developed in the digital curation community, in which a system's functionality is devolved into small, self-contained, interoperable services. While we support a comprehensive array of microservices for data product search, access, and metadata management, we focus here on those associated with identity and provenance management.

3 Identity Management

Persistent identification of datasets, data granules, external metadata, and ancillary resources is critical to maintaining the documentation and reproducibility that are the hallmarks of the scientific method. Strictly speaking, persistence of identifiers over time is an outcome–a result of commitment–but the technical forms of identification can make persistence more or less difficult to achieve.

---

[2] http://oceancolor.gsfc.nasa.gov/seadas

[3] http://www.ittvis.com/idl

For data products that are released in discrete, named versions, such as OCRG products, incorporating versions in identifiers is an additional challenge. Specifically, version-aware identifiers must allow users of a granule to:

- Cite a specific version of a granule;
- Cite the most recent version of a granule, and/or a granule *sans* version; and
- Detect that a version of a granule no longer exists, and be directed to appropriate metadata and from there to a newer version.

We are developing an approach to version-aware identity management that satisfies these requirements and that is built on two technologies: well-known persistent identifier schemes such as Archival Resource Keys (ARKs) [6], and HTTP redirection. A granule identifier in this approach consists of a dataset identifier drawn from a persistent identifier scheme, to handle dataset-level relocation over time, prefixed to a filename that includes a version indicator and other semantics. HTTP redirection rules, in the form of regular expressions, express version defaulting and granule deletion. The net result is an identity management system that requires almost no cooperation from the data providers or data production system.

Our preliminary work on integrating version-related redirections with persistent identifiers has led us to select ARKs as the most appropriate persistent identifier scheme. Unlike Digital Object Identifiers (DOIs)[4], ARKs allow qualifying information (e.g., granule identifiers) to be appended to the dataset identifier and passed along by the identifier resolution system. Unlike Persistent URLs (PURLs)[5], ARKs are self-identifying, and don't require the reservation of a portion of the HTTP URL namespace for their implementation.

4   Provenance Management

The ES3 system [3] collects provenance information from executing code, using a combination of system call tracing, transparent wrapping, and application environment instrumentation (Figure 1.)

For clarity, we will limit the discussion hereafter to ES3's system call tracing ("shell plugin") mode. In this mode, provenance collection entails:

1. The ES3 **collector** process is started on the processing host system. The collector waits for provenance event messages from an instrumented process.
2. A science process is invoked on the processing host system, from an ES3-instrumented command interpreter (usually bash.) The science process may be arbitrarily complex, and is usually a script that invokes several other processes. The science process itself is not modified in any way, and the ES3 command interpreter behaves identically to a standard one; this is why we call ES3 "non-intrusive."

---

[4] http://doi.org
[5] http://purl.org

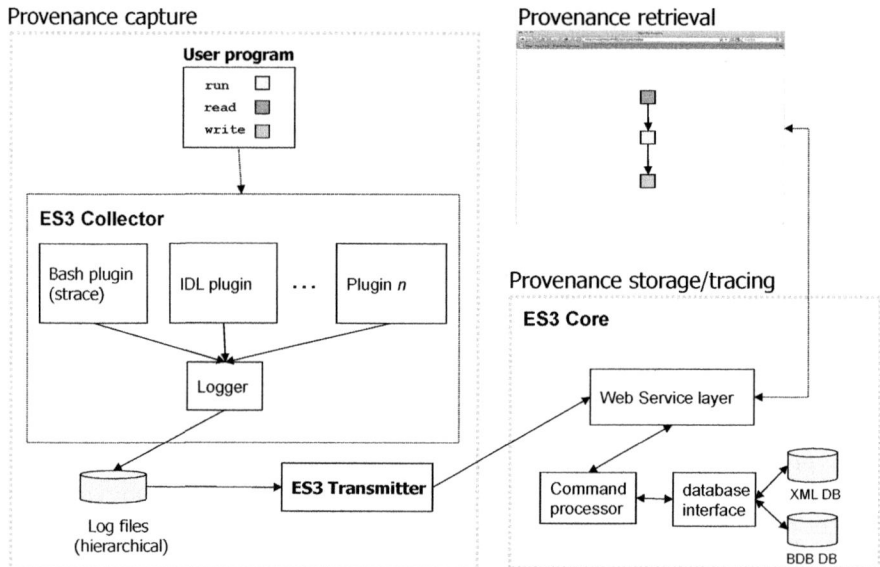

Fig. 1. ES3 architecture

3. The ES3 command interpreter sends traces of all the science process's system interactions to the ES3 collector, which formats them, discards unwanted detail, and saves this "raw provenance" to a log file. Raw provenance is simply a set of tuples of the form
   (*process ID, timestamp, system call, arguments* [, ...])
   where the system calls are limited to "provenance events;" i.e., file access, process creation, or program execution. The collector does some simple editing of the raw provenance (e.g., converts file descriptors to corresponding file names) consistent with near-real-time processing.
4. When the science process exits, the ES3 **transmitter** process is invoked and scans the log file. The transmitter assembles the raw provenance into a provenance graph and submits the graph components to the ES3 database, as follows:

   (a) Provenance graph nodes are created by assigning an automatically generated unique identifier (UUID) to each provenance event.
   (b) Any filesystem object referenced by a provenance graph node and readable by the transmitter is checksummed with a secure hash algorithm (e.g., SHA-1[6]). This checksum is included in the provenance metadata.
   (c) Connected events (e.g., processes writing to and reading from the same file or pipe) are indicated by creating a provenance graph edge between the appropriate UUIDs.

---

[6] http://www.ietf.org/rfc/rfc3174.txt

(d) The provenance graph nodes and edges are formatted as XML messages and sent to the ES3 database.

The ES3 database allows event identifiers to be queried for their associated metadata (date, time, host system parameters, etc.), and of course for their parent and/or child events. The parent/child queries may be recursive, generating forward and/or reverse provenance to any specified depth. Provenance metadata is delivered as serialized graph in XML.

ES3 currently provides post-processors that convert the ES3 native provenance graph format to GraphML[7] or DOT[8], for visualizing in tools such as yEd[9] or Graphviz[10].

Figure 2 shows a portion (immediate ancestors and descendants) of the provenance for a single execution of the OCRG ocean color algorithm, retrieved from ES3 as GraphML and rendered by yEd. Note that ES3 correctly recognizes the nested provenance that results from scripts executing other scripts.

We realize that different kinds of queries or user communities may require alternative provenance renderings [5]. We are therefore exploring connecting the ES3 database to a generic web-based graph browsing system [4].

5   Issues Raised

A meta-issue we address is the need to manage multiple kinds of identifiers–datasets, granules, provenance events–and to make the mappings between them as transparent as possible.

ES3 has been developed in a cluster computing environment, which is a primary reason that it uses a decentralized event identifier scheme (UUIDs.) ES3 transmitters running on multiple hosts can thus submit provenance information to a more centralized (e.g., per-cluster) database without danger of identifier collisions.

Note, however, that the mapping between the provenance *events* recorded by ES3 and the *objects* managed by the rest of the data system is many-to-one: any object may participate in many provenance events. Likewise, the mapping between object identifiers and checksums can be many-to-one, since objects may be updated. The ES3 database therefore supports queries against these mappings (e.g., return an objects's provenance events, given its checksum.)

The identity management service, on the other hand, is concerned with mapping *published* names (persistent identifiers) to the appropriate internal objects. Provenance management enables the partial or complete automation of this mapping by allowing concepts like "product" and "version" to be functionally defined—for example, a particular version of a dataset might defined as all data objects generated by a specific instance (as defined by a checksum) of a particular algorithm (as defined by a filename.)

---

[7] http://graphml.graphdrawing.org
[8] http://www.graphviz.org/doc/info/lang.html
[9] http://www.yworks.com/en/products_yed_about.html
[10] http://www.graphviz.org

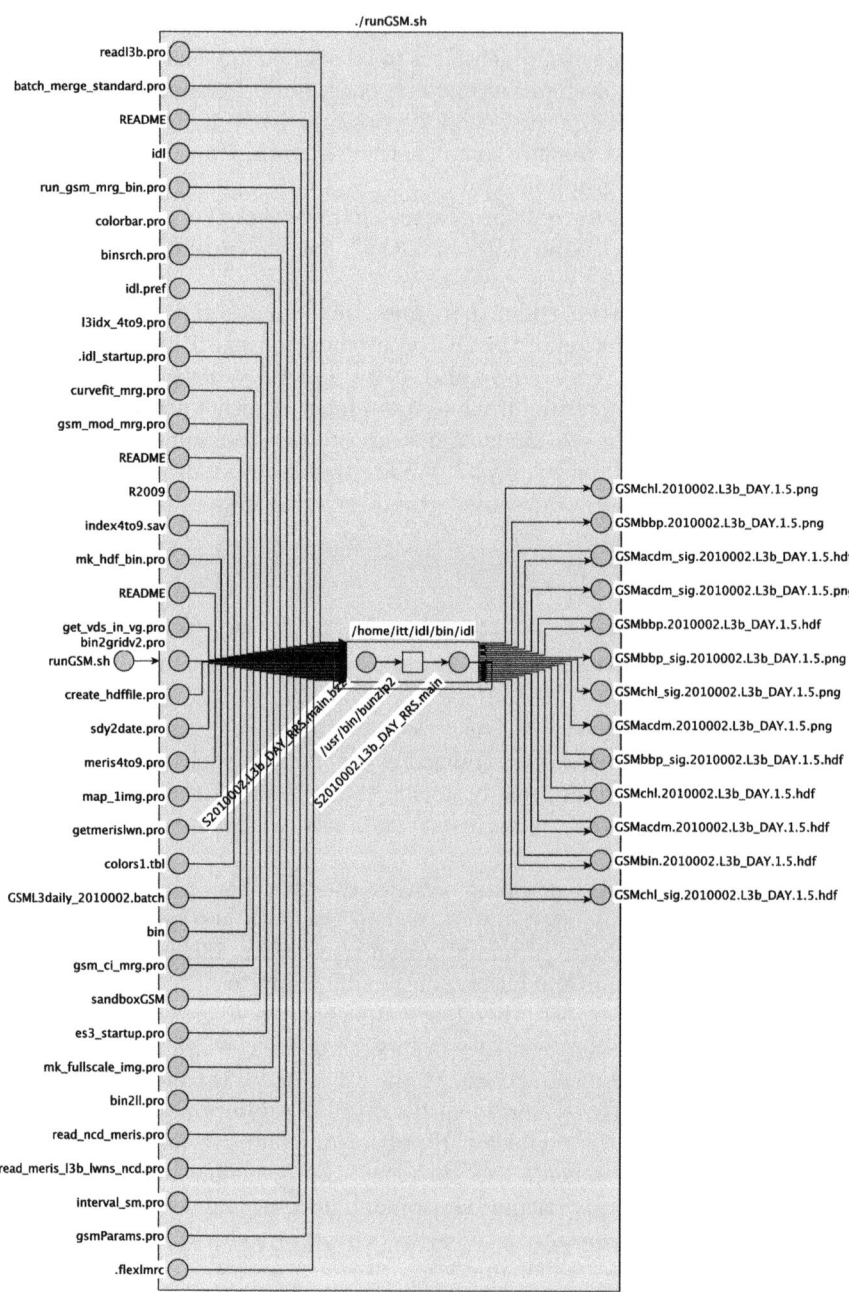

Fig. 2. OCRG ocean color algorithm provenance

We are examining how to best incorporate and advertise published identifiers in metadata, and in the granules themselves.

References

[1] Abrams, S., Kunze, J., Loy, D.: An emergent micro-services approach to digital curation infrastructure. In: Proceedings of the Sixth International Conference on Preservation of Digital Objects, San Francisco, CA (October 2009)

[2] Frew, J., Bose, R.: Lineage retrieval for scientific data processing: A survey. ACM Computing Surveys 37(1), 1–28 (2005)

[3] Frew, J., Metzger, D., Slaughter, P.: Automatic capture and reconstruction of computational provenance. Concurr. Comput.: Pract. Exper. 20(5), 485–496 (2008)

[4] Gretarsson, B., Bostandjiev, S., O'Donovan, J., Hollerer, T.: WiGis: a scalable framework for web-based interactive graph visualizations. In: Eppstein, D., Gansner, E.R. (eds.) Graph Drawing. LNCS, vol. 5849, pp. 119–134. Springer, Heidelberg (2010)

[5] Kunde, M., Bergmeyer, H., Schreiber, A.: Requirements for a provenance visualization component. In: Freire, J., Koop, D., Moreau, L. (eds.) IPAW 2008. LNCS, vol. 5272, pp. 241–252. Springer, Heidelberg (2008)

[6] Kunze, J.A.: Towards electronic persistence using ARK identifiers. In: Masanès, J., Rauber, A., Cobena, G. (eds.) 3rd Workshop on Web Archives, Trondheim, Norway, pp. 4–12 (August 2003)

[7] Maritorena, S., Siegel, D.A.: Consistent merging of satellite ocean color data sets using a bio-optical model. Remote Sensing of Environment 94(4), 429–440 (2005)

[8] Moore, R.: Towards a theory of digital preservation. International Journal of Digital Curation 3(1), 63–75 (2008)

Leveraging the Open Provenance Model as a Multi-tier Model for Global Climate Research

Eric G. Stephan, Todd D. Halter, and Brian D. Ermold

Pacific Northwest National Laboratory
Richland, Wa
{Eric.Stephan,Todd.Halter,Brian.Ermold}@pnl.gov

Abstract. Global climate researchers rely upon many forms of sensor data and analytical methods to help profile subtle changes in climate conditions. The U.S. Department of Energy's Atmospheric Radiation Measurement (ARM) program provides researchers with a collection of curated Value Added Products (VAPs) resulting from continuous sensor data streams, data fusion, and modeling. We are leveraging the Open Provenance Model as a foundational construct that serves the needs of both the VAP producers and consumers. We are organizing the provenance in different tiers of granularity to model VAP lineage, causality at the component level within a VAP, and the causality for each time step as samples are being assembled within the VAP. This paper shares our implementation strategy and how the ARM operations staff and the climate research community can greatly benefit from this approach to more effectively assess and quantify VAP provenance.

Keywords: Provenance, Climate.

1 Introduction

In this paper we present how the Atmospheric Radiation Measurement (ARM) program is relying upon the Open Provenance Model [1] and its overlapping accounts feature to track provenance for data processing at different granularity levels.

The Pacific Northwest National Laboratory (PNNL) has been an integral part of the Department of Energy (DOE) ARM [2] program's infrastructure team since its inception in 1998. The ARM Data Management Facility manages data flow for over 300 sensors located around the world, ingests the data into an ARM standard format, performs quality control on the data through the ARM Data Quality Office, performs reprocessing on the data through the ARM Reprocessing Center, and transfers the resulting data sets to the ARM Archive. In addition, the facility is responsible for the development and deployment of Value Added Products (VAPs) [2] that provide derived data products through complicated processing pipelines. VAPs fuse information from sensors, models, algorithms, and other VAPs to derive information of interest that is either impractical or impossible to measure directly. The information of interest includes (but is not limited to) cloud microphysics, aerosol properties, atmospheric state, and radiometric properties. VAPs can also be used to improve the quality of existing sensor data, and when multiple sensors are producing the same

D.L. McGuinness, J.R. Michaelis, and L. Moreau (Eds.): IPAW 2010, LNCS 6378, pp. 34–41, 2010.

type of data a "best estimate" VAP will identify the highest quality data. This experience has given us significant familiarity with a variety of climate data sets, as well as production-level experience handling streaming data, long-term data sets, and data reprocessing. ARM data is stored in a NetCDF file format that provide a structure that supports the storage of the data sets annotated with metadata. A significant need from the users is to directly disseminate provenance into the ARM NetCDF results, providing transparency to the user and greatly adding value to the analysis without requiring significant changes to the large body of existing analysis workflow. From an operational standpoint, it is foreseen that the number of sensors and ARM data products will increase significantly, dwarfing today's complexity of algorithm interdependency. We envision provenance as an overarching data-driven standard advancing many of the day-to-day tasks relating to data processing and reprocessing, error detection and troubleshooting in analytical methods. This is in contrast today where there is no standardization and all tasks are managed from scripts, legacy codes, and developer defined log files.

For the past twenty years most questions could be answered either through web reports or by relying on knowledgeable operations staff to determine the source of any problem by examining log and configuration files and performing database queries. However, with the deployment of new instruments, an order of magnitude increase in data throughput, and new advanced data products, a need for formalized methodologies was identified to automate analysis of the data products to efficiently continue to maintain strict quality assurance and quality control measures. In addition to this, data consumers began wanting a clearer understanding of the sources (instrument, data ingest processes, and higher order climate algorithms) relied upon for data, the confidence scores associated with the data, and other relevant information for each sample point.

In our early assessment of provenance needs using the Open Provenance Model (OPM) XML schemata, provenance exceeded sample datum by a storage space ratio of 1:23,000. In the past, we were accustomed to thinking of causality being considerably smaller than the resulting data, and that one causality graph consisting of hundreds of artifacts, processes, and relationships could represent the entire workflow history [3][4]. Because of diverse provenance-related questions being asked at different granularities, we also needed a flexible model that could be dissected in a variety of ways to support a number of analytical mash-ups. Based on all these factors a multi-scale conceptual model resulted [5].

2 Relevant Research

From a modeling perspective the provenance community has explored multi-tier approaches in the past. A visual analytic tool [6] developed for provenance exploration relied upon a multi-tier model approach for depicting multiple levels of provenance granularity. OPM uses accounts to depict overlapping provenance models, refinements, and hierarchies.

To describe the organization and structure of provenance for VAP-run instances the mathematical construct hedge is borrowed from the tree automaton community. A hedge is defined as a tree with an ordered sequence of unranked subtrees[7][8].

While we expect there to be mathematical or statistical properties of trees (and by extension hedges) that can be leveraged to derive additional provenance information or insights into either usual or anomalous states of the data analysis workflow, it is still too early to determine what can be leveraged until we can perform a deep dive into the provenance actually being generated by the VAP runs. This is needed before mathematical tools can be applied to augment the analysis.

3   Multi-tier Provenance Model

ARM provenance is being used as a means to more uniformly describe a complete history of VAP sample generation, VAP runs, and VAP interdependency. The rationale behind using a multi-tier model as opposed to a monolithic model is that each tier (or component) has a unique purpose, different characteristics, and distinct levels of granularity. The term multi-tier could be thought of as multi-part, with each tier being a separate component representation, but sharing overlapping parts. The model is broken into three distinct levels of granularity (Table 1) that are interconnected. To help visualize the model in its entirety we think of the three tiers as a landscaped park with directed paths running from hedge to hedge, and branches ordered along the hedge trunk.

Table 1. Granularity and purpose for each provenance tier

Granularity	Purpose	Tier	Account
High	Sample	Branch	
Middle	Run	Hedge	
Low	Interdependency	Path	

Branch Tier: As each VAP sample is processed the execution history will also be captured. This means that for a VAP that provides temperature measurements at a one second interval over a twelve month period, 500,000 samples will result along with a separate execution history (branch) for each data point occupying approximately 15GB of uncompressed storage (1 GB compressed). Because each sample is produced autonomously an ordered set of acyclic spanning trees are formed that can be analyzed to find missing samples, periodic anomalies in the workflow, or sporadic exceptions that may occur.

The Branch tier will rely on the following components in OPM: accounts, entities, and relationships. Each branch will be identified by its own account using an identifier that pertains to a corresponding sample time step. Because the time step interval is consistent, time will be inferred by sample order within the hedge tier. Each branch account will share with its parent hedge account a common process that initiates the sample analysis process as shown in Figure 1.

Processes will include references to sample analysis algorithms, workflow control logic, and data processing. Artifacts will include references to informational messages collected during processing along with warnings, errors, fatal messages, QC codes, and sample origin. These entities rely on the following statements to depict relationships and on directionality to depict the execution history: Artifact Used By Process, Process Triggered By Process, Artifact Generated By Process. The definition of artifacts will be extended to include the Dublin Core Element Set [9].

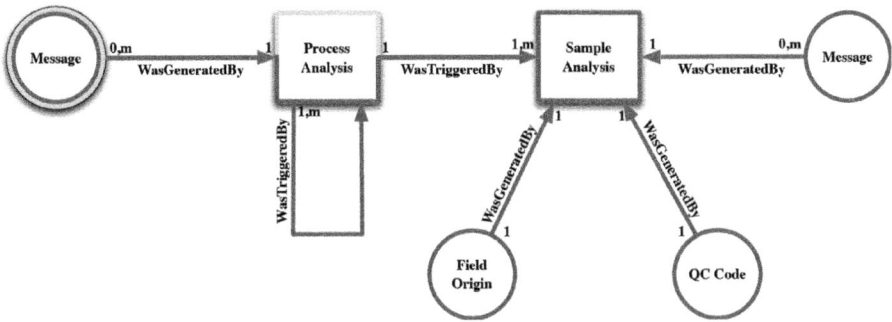

Fig. 1. Branch Tier

Hedge Tier: All sample points within a VAP rely upon the same overall workflow control logic and configuration parameters to process all samples. From a workflow perspective the VAP is a simple workflow that prepares data for analysis, performs analysis through a huge control loop that iterates over each sample, and then performs post-processing by storing the VAP in a NetCDF file. From a provenance perspective this forms an overarching graph of the VAP workflow history. Each VAP has only one hedge tier and one account that will be uniquely identified with a corresponding VAP identifier. As shown in Figure 2, the middle tier in the hedge account overlaps with each branch account (each iteration through the control loop), but leaves the detail of the sample analysis to the branch tier to separately provide these details. The hedge tier also interfaces with the Path Tier that will be described in the next section.

The Agent entity describes the person or control that initiated the VAP run. Artifact entities correspond to VAP parameter settings along with VAP or sensor data streams to build the product. The definition of artifacts will be extended to include the Dublin Core Element Set along with emerging standards from the Climate and Forecast Working Group.

Process entities include workflow controller logic, and data pre and post processing along with Dublin Core metadata describing the software identity and version number. These entities rely upon relationships and directionality to form the following statements: Process Controlled By Agent, Artifact Used by Process, Process Triggered by Process (branch), and Artifact Generated by Process.

Path Tier: Understanding lineage is extremely important because most of the VAPs are a composite of sensor streams disseminated from existing VAPs. Understanding this interdependence is vital to ARM operations staff that periodically must invalidate VAPs due to discoveries of error conditions. This creates a cascading effect, impacting VAPs reliant upon erroneous data. To track these conditions only one Account is used to track lineage. The Path account overlaps with each Hedge account. The VAP

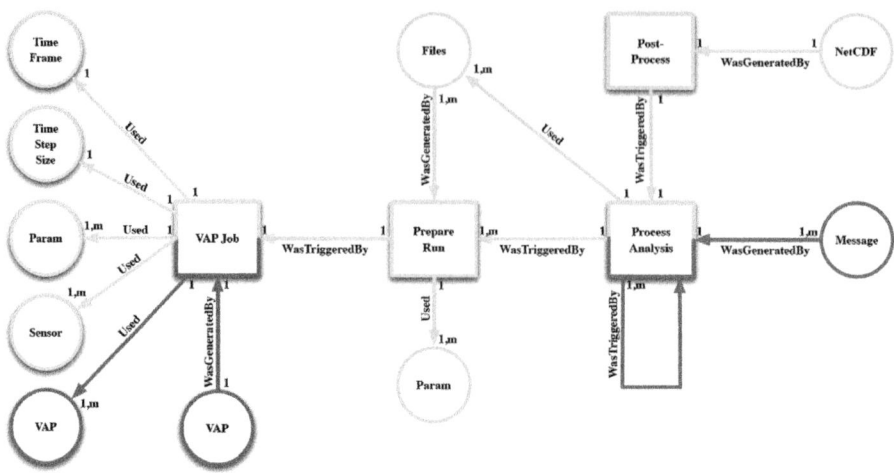

Fig. 2. Hedge Tier

Artifacts and the main VAP processes are shared between the Path and Hedge Tiers. The OPM entities included at this tier are: Artifacts, Processes, and Agents. Agents are considered a production batch process; otherwise the developer initiates a VAP run. The Process tracked is the overall VAP script used, and the Artifacts are the sensor streams and VAPs relied upon to create the VAP. These entities rely upon relationships and directionality to form the following statements: Process controlled by Agent, Artifact Generated by Process, and Artifact Used by Process.

4 Discussion

In this section we describe how provenance is automated, and how producers and consumers will use the model. Relying on the provenance model gives us the opportunity to automate and streamline many of the quality-related processes.

Automating Provenance: The data producers are responsible for the full life cycle of VAPs, algorithms used within the VAP, managing the interdependencies between the VAP runs, and maintaining the latest products. Our current plan is to apply a provenance listener that ties into the ARM error handler and message logging system. This is currently deployed in the ARM environment and has already been abstracted to track events from a developer's perspective.

For any given VAP run, provenance will be generated in the following top-down context: path, hedge, and branch. The script or workflow generating the VAP will be responsible for attaching any referential information and the associated event history along with any relevant event history.

Once the provenance is captured, it will be managed by maintaining synchronization between the different provenance tiers in the store. Provenance will be stored persistently as separate storage blocks. The path tier block provides references to the hedge block; the hedge tier will in turn provides references to each branch block. Because of the foreseen storage bloat issues we are remaining flexible on our storage technical solution to determine the best overall approach and depending on the producer/consumer needs how long the raw provenance will be retained. Some alternatives under consideration are: distributed file stores with provenance formatted as XML or RDF N3 format, and relying upon the Open Source Array Database being developed by SciDB [10] which is expected to be released in 2010.

Analytical Methods – At least three automated analytical methods are now available that were either not previously available or easily attainable without provenance: automated quantitative analysis, interference, and discovery. We foresee many other types of analysis obtainable in the future. Quantitative analysis is extremely important at the sample level. Erroneous conditions typically are not self evident when looking at a single branch, rather, anomalies may occur due to a faulty instrument reading at a particular time of the day. Only by comparing multiple branches side by side are the conditions apparent. Squarified treemap [11] display tree structures as flattened nested boxes and arrange similar looking boxes together. In our tests we relied on VAPs that collected cloud cover data. Through the squarified treemap we were able to visualize conditions corresponding to clear skies where no samples were collected and processed. By rendering branches into summary level views over selected time periods (day, hour minute) of distinct entity (artifacts or processes) counts in a relational database schemata we were able to detect times when provenance branches contained atypical number of nodes this we were not only able to detect and rendered branches. OPM provides transitive closure is relied upon to determine is workflows successfully completed, and we explored uses of discovery either by providing a web-based search engine based on selected indexed provenance and by using a tree structure visualization tool Prefuse [12] to browse selected portions of the path, hedge, and branch tiers.

In addition to the flexibility offered to analytical methods is also scalability by means of being able to discretely dissect provenance horizontally along one tier, or vertically between one or more tiers by selecting accounts based on VAP interdependency, VAPs themselves, or specific branches representing time slices of different VAPs. The branches represent a wealth of knowledge needed for comparative analysis. It may become quite common to detect various anomalies from different branch time slices to differentiate between sensor mechanical problems and natural phenomena. In this example to thoroughly conduct this analysis the time branches for the last ten years over a given month might be necessary to confirm the origin of a sensor's behavior. Because each branch is a non overlapping acyclic graph, groups of branches can be analyzed one group at a time or potentially distributed and analyzed over multiple compute nodes to increase efficiency.

Uses – It was important to tie the analytical methods and provenance to practical examples to demonstrate how provenance might be used by scientists and operations. We split out a special category, developers, which are part of operations and who have a special need for provenance related to debugging activities [5].

From the consumer perspective the scientist's primary motivation in examining historical evidence has more to do with establishing confidence in their VAP of interest. In most cases we anticipate their interest at the hedge and branch tier of a given VAP run. At the hedge level the input deck used, the specific algorithms (including version) relied upon, along with the time span time step intervals used in the VAP run are fundamental to helping the researcher establish the context of how the VAP was created.

From our preliminary research we found that while the data producers are generally interested in the resulting graph representation of the branch, the scientists prefer a flattened view derived from each branch. This view currently consists of at least two fields: field origin and quality control codes. Each will correspond to a sample datum within the NetCDF file. This will provide scientists with a detailed knowledge of how the product was assembled at an incremental level and will allow them to understand possible reasons for trends or anomalies themselves.

While we do not have implementation details at this time we are determining how best to disseminate this knowledge to the user community. Simply showing the raw OPM data does not seem effective for end users. Our current plan is to disseminate provenance as part of the VAP as an encoded bit pack describing instruments used, parameters used, and quality/confidence level based on the provenance results. This encoded information may result from the branch tier for sample level data, or may be associated from the hedge tier associated with an overall VAP run. The key is that provenance for a given VAP instance will reside within the archive and the provenance encoding or will be distributed in the NetCDF file for each sample.

5 Conclusion

The Open Provenance Model has provided ARM a strong foundation for supporting overlapping provenance models that represent different processing refinements during the creation of the VAP. While we have identified some initial ways to exploit the provenance information there are many more to explore. We also believe that with the abundance of provenance, workflow query, and analysis, that exposing the hedges will make it far easier for future applications to transform, query, and analyze VAP results.

Acknowledgments. This research is supported by the Laboratory Directed Research and Development Program at the Pacific Northwest National Laboratory operated by Battelle for the U.S. Department of Energy under contract DE-AC05-76Rl0 1839.

We also acknowledge the collaborative efforts of U.S. Department of Energy as part of the Atmospheric Radiation Measurement Program.

References

1. Moreau, L., Clifford, B., Freire, J., Gil, Y., Groth, P., Futrelle, J., Miles, S., Myers, J., Simmhan, Y.L., Stephan, E.G.: The Open Provenance Model Core Specification, v1.1 (2010)
2. Atmospheric Radiation Measurement Climate Research Facility. ARM Annual Report. Technical report available from U.S. Department of Energy as DOE/SC-ARM-0706
3. Gibson, T.D., Stephan, E.G.: Application of Provenance for Automated and Research Driven Workflows. In: Tara at Second International Provenance and Anotation Workshop, June 17, Salt Lake City, UT (2008)
4. Gibson, T.D., Schuchardt, K.L., Stephan, E.G.: Application of Named Graphs Towards Custom Provenance Views. In: 1st Workshop on the Theory and Practice of Provenance (TaPP 2009), USENIX, Berkeley, CA (2009)

5. Stephan, E.G., Halter, T.D., Gibson, T.D., Beagley, N., Schuchardt, K.L.: A Multi-Tier Provenance Model for Global Climate Research. In: International Conference on Network-Based Information Systems (NBIS 2009), Indianapolis, Indiana, August 19-21, pp. 481–486. IEEE, Piscataway (2009), doi:10.1109/NBiS.2009.16
6. David, G., Michelle, Z.: Characterizing Users' Visual Analytic Activity for Insight Provenance (2008)
7. Comon, H., Dauchet, M., et al.: Tree automata techniques and applications (1997), `http://www.grappa.univ-lille3.fr/` [11] 10
8. Courcelle, B.: On recognizable sets and tree automata. In: Nivat, M., Ait-Kaci, H. (eds.) Resolution of Equations in Alegebraic Structures,
9. Dublin Core metadata semantics: An analysis of the perspectives of information professionals Park and Childress. Journal of Information Science (2009); 0165551509337871v16
10. Stonebraker, M., Becla, J., Dewitt, D., Lim, K., Maier, D., Ratzesberger, O., Zdonik, S.: Requirements for Science Data Bases and SciDB. In: Conference on Innovative Data Systems Research, CIDR (2009)
11. Bruls, D.M., Huizing, C., van Wijk, J.J.: Squarified Treemaps. In: de Leeuw, W., van Liere, R. (eds.) Data Visualization 2000, Proceedings of the joint Eurographics and IEEE TCVG Symposium on Visualization, pp. 33–42 (2000)
12. Heer, J., Card, S.K., Landay, J.A.: Prefuse: A Toolkit for Interactive Information Visualization. In: CHI 2005, Portland, OR, April 2-7 (2005)

Understanding Collaborative Studies through Interoperable Workflow Provenance

Ilkay Altintas[1,2], Manish Kumar Anand[1], Daniel Crawl[1], Shawn Bowers[3],
Adam Belloum[2], Paolo Missier[4], Bertram Ludäscher[5], Carole A. Goble[4],
and Peter M.A. Sloot[2]

[1] San Diego Supercomputer Center, University of California, San Diego, USA
`{altintas,mkanand,crawl}@sdsc.edu`
[2] Computational Science, University of Amsterdam, The Netherlands
`{A.S.Z.Belloum,p.m.a.sloot}@uva.nl`
[3] Department of Computer Science, Gonzaga University
`bowers@gonzaga.edu`
[4] School of Computer Science, University of Manchester, Manchester, UK
`{pmissier,carole.goble}@cs.man.ac.uk`
[5] UC Davis Genome Center, University of California, Davis
`ludaesch@ucdavis.edu`

Abstract. The provenance of a data product contains information about how the product was derived, and is crucial for enabling scientists to easily understand, reproduce, and verify scientific results. Currently, most provenance models are designed to capture the provenance related to a single run, and mostly executed by a single user. However, a scientific discovery is often the result of methodical execution of many scientific workflows with many datasets produced at different times by one or more users. Further, to promote and facilitate exchange of information between multiple workflow systems supporting provenance, the Open Provenance Model (OPM) has been proposed by the scientific workflow community. In this paper, we describe a new query model that captures implicit user collaborations. We show how this model maps to OPM and helps to answer collaborative queries, e.g., identifying combined workflows and contributions of users collaborating on a project based on the records of previous workflow executions. We also adopt and extend the high-level Query Language for Provenance (QLP) with additional constructs, and show how these extensions allow non-expert users to express collaborative provenance queries against this model easily and concisely. Furthermore, we adopt the Provenance Challenge 3 (PC3) workflows as a collaborative and interoperable usecase scenario, where different stages of the workflow are executed in three different workflow environments - Kepler, Taverna, and WSVLAM. Through this usecase, we demonstrate how we can establish and understand collaborative studies through interoperable workflow provenance.

1   Introduction

As scientific knowledge grows and the number of studies that require access to knowledge from multiple scientific disciplines increase, the complexity of scientific problems

D.L. McGuinness, J.R. Michaelis, and L. Moreau (Eds.): IPAW 2010, LNCS 6378, pp. 42–58, 2010.
© Springer-Verlag Berlin Heidelberg 2010

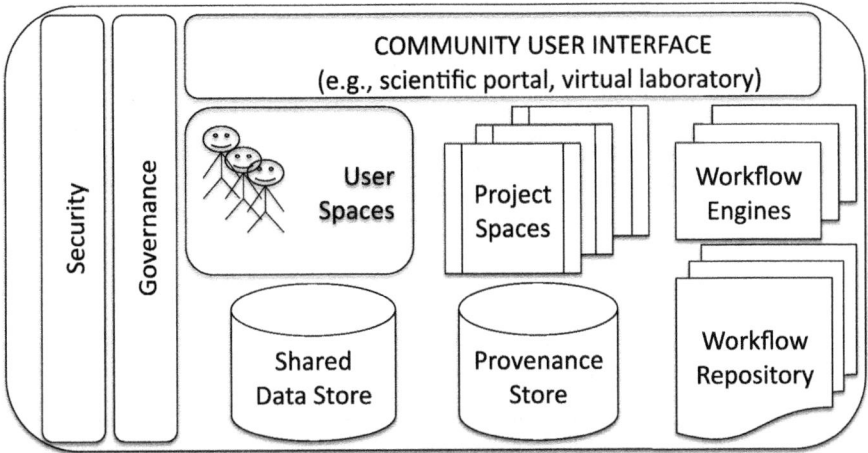

Fig. 1. Component architecture of a typical scientific research infrastructure (external data, service and computational infrastructure not shown)

amplifies. To cope with this complexity, scientists use computational methods that are evolving almost daily. However, the basic scientific method remains the same while being continuously transformed from manual to automated with the advances in computer science and technology. This gradual shift from manual process execution to automation of repeatable patterns resulted in the creation of scientific workflow systems.

Scientific workflow management systems [1,2,3,4] are critical to the way a modern scientist conducts studies today by making technological advances more approachable through integrative interfaces and abstractions for underlying computational and data resources. Scientific workflow systems allow scientists to develop formal, customizable, reusable and extensible definitions for all or part of a scientific process and execute them efficiently. In addition, using scientific workflows to perform computational experiments on data unleashes the possibility to maintain its provenance [5]. Typically designed iteratively by a user and ran multiple times by one or more users, the provenance of a scientific workflow provides a rich source for conducting similar future scientific studies [6]. However, this is still only a partial solution to the modern scientific process that relies on multi-disciplinary collaborative teams working on different parts of scientific studies. Currently, provenance support in workflow systems are mostly designed to capture the information related to a single workflow run by a user. On the other hand, the collaborative process often involves design and execution of multiple workflows [7] where different members of a team conceptualize their contribution as workflows and make it available through a common infrastructure. A scientific discovery is the result of methodical execution of many of these workflows with many datasets at different times by one or more users.

Community portals [8], virtual laboratories [9], and Web2.0-based social networking and sharing environments [10] are popular platforms to establish a common infrastructure where community members can contribute to data, workflows and projects through

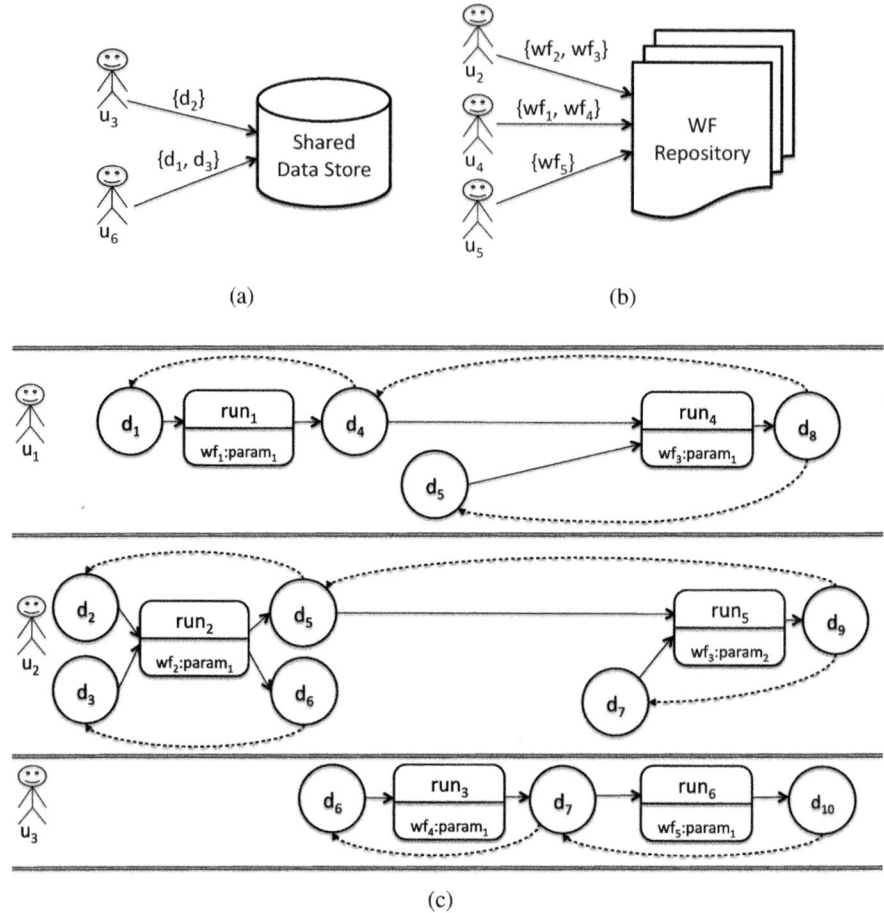

Fig. 2. Different observables of shared data, workflows and their runs in a typical scientific research project: (a) data ($\{d_1, d_2, d_3\}$) published by users in $\{u_1, u_6\}$; (b) ready to run workflows ($\{wf_1 .. wf_5\}$) published by users in $\{u_2, u_4, u_5\}$; (c) flow graph for published workflow runs (customized through their parameters) and related data ($\{d_1 .. d_{10}\}$) in user spaces ($\{u_1, u_2, u_3\}$), separated by horizontal dashed lines

their user spaces under generic governance rules. Workflows could be executed multiple times by one or more scientists, potentially from an end-user interface that combines several workflows. In addition, the executed workflows use data from external data resources and the scientific outputs are saved in data repositories, optionally along with intermediate results and the process provenance. A typical set of components for such an infrastructure is illustrated in Fig. 1.

The discussion in this paper lies in the heart of these sharing and execution practices in e-science projects where the overall execution of a set of workflows can result in an overarching model of the scientific process leading to data artifacts. All the observables

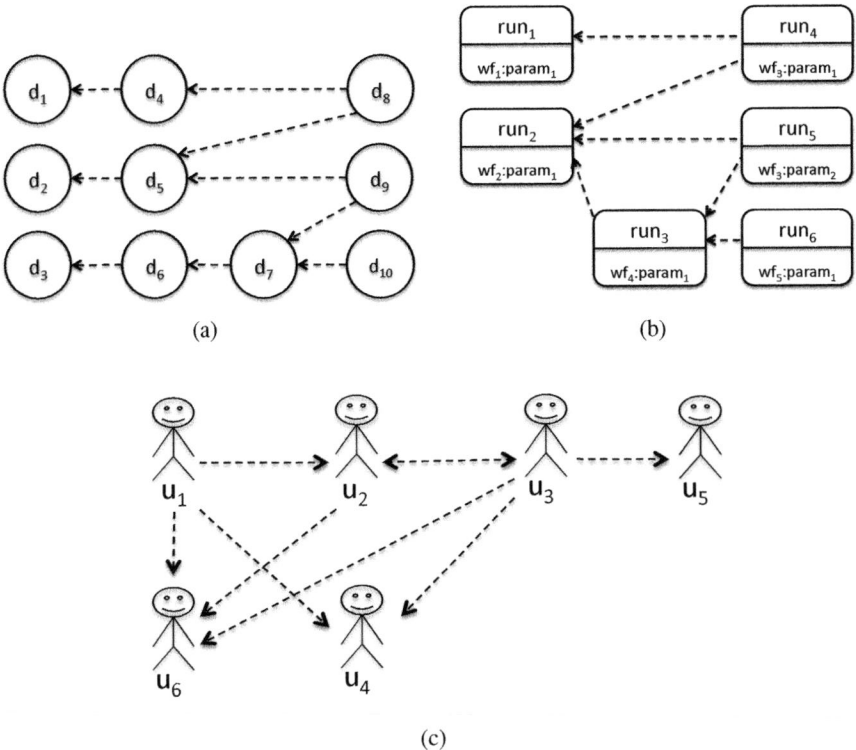

Fig. 3. Different views generated by modeling and analysis of runs in a typical scientific research project: (a) data dependency view; (b) run dependency view; (c) overall non-transitive directed implicit user ($\{u_1 .. u_6\}$) collaboration view

in such a project within a three- dimensional space of users, workflows and data are illustrated in Fig. 2. The history of workflow runs in different user spaces $\{u_1, u_2, u_3\}$ depicted in Fig. 2(c) shows the usage of published data in Fig. 2(a) and workflows in Fig. 2(b). Users who performed the workflow runs or used published data start an "implicit collaboration". In Fig. 2(c), a run node identifies the provenance of a previous workflow run and the fine-grained data dependencies are shown by dashed links between data nodes. One can identify the flow of workflow executions leading to a data artifact that is published as a "scientific discovery" by chaining together the runs performed by users. This chaining happens through data artifacts consumed and produced by workflow runs, e.g., in Fig. 2(c), d_5 produced by run_2 of u_2 is consumed by run_4 performed by u_1, creating a link between run_2 and run_4.

A goal of this approach is to extend the current single-workflow and single-user targeted provenance approach to a number of workflow runs within a controlled environment such as a website community portal for sharing data and workflows. In this paper, we assume that the data store is publicly shared between users. Using this extended information, one can generate views of data dependencies, related workflow executions and user collaborations, as seen in Fig. 3(a), Fig. 3(b) and Fig. 3(c) respectively. In addition, it becomes possible to answer queries for potential acknowledgements of a scientific result and the correction trail of a faulty data item. Another important goal is to propose and demonstrate an architecture that facilitates the interoperability of different workflow systems through provenance of workflow runs and related data. We assume the model of provenance is shared between different workflow systems and provides a global repository of data artifact identifiers, i.e., an artifact produced by one workflow system and consumed by another can be uniquely identified. The design of this repository is not in the scope of this paper. This new approach puts user actions and collaborations in the center of the conducted research independent of computational technologies used to generate results.

Contributions. We investigate the implicit user collaborations in a QLP-based [11] query model that maps to OPM [12] using observables in an e-science infrastructure (Fig. 2) and for generating views on top of them (Fig. 3). This approach links OPM graphs for workflow runs that have an input or output data dependency and helps to answer queries such as identifying data connections between workflow runs and contributions of users collaborating on a project based on the records of past executions. We adopt and extend a high-level query language for provenance, QLP, to express complex collaborative provenance queries. We also establish a mapping between QLP and OPM. Furthermore, through the PC3 (http://twiki.ipaw.info/bin/view/Challenge/) usecase scenario, we demonstrate the feasibility of how our approach will lead to development of systems that increase *interoperability* and *reusability* of workflow results by integrating provenance coming out of *different* workflow systems and, in turn, enhancing efficiency in modern collaborative research.

Outline. The organization of this paper is as follows. In Section 2, we introduce the concept of collaborative views and queries over interoperable provenance data. Section 3 explains QLP and the extensions we build on top of QLP that map to OPM constructs along with the QLP expressions of queries defined in Section 2. A feasibility study for the explained techniques is provided in Section 4, based on PC3 workflows. We review background work in Section 5 and conclude in Section 6.

2   Building Collaborative Views

The lifecycle of scientific workflows—which includes the design, execution, sharing, and management of data and provenance products—depends not only on the workflow itself, but also the overall scientific research infrastructure and scientific collaborations within which scientists use these workflows. In this section, we introduce the concept of collaborative views based on the provenance of workflows and user actions within a scientific infrastructure (see Fig. 2). We also present example queries that are enabled by our provenance model, including those that allow scientists to determine implicit collaborative relationships. The basic relations we use to develop collaborative views are shown in Fig. 4. We first describe these relations, and then show how they enable the construction of both standard and collaborative provenance views.

The relation Run(r,w) states that r is a run (i.e., execution) of a workflow w (shown using rounded boxes in Fig. 4). We assume every run is of exactly one workflow. Each run

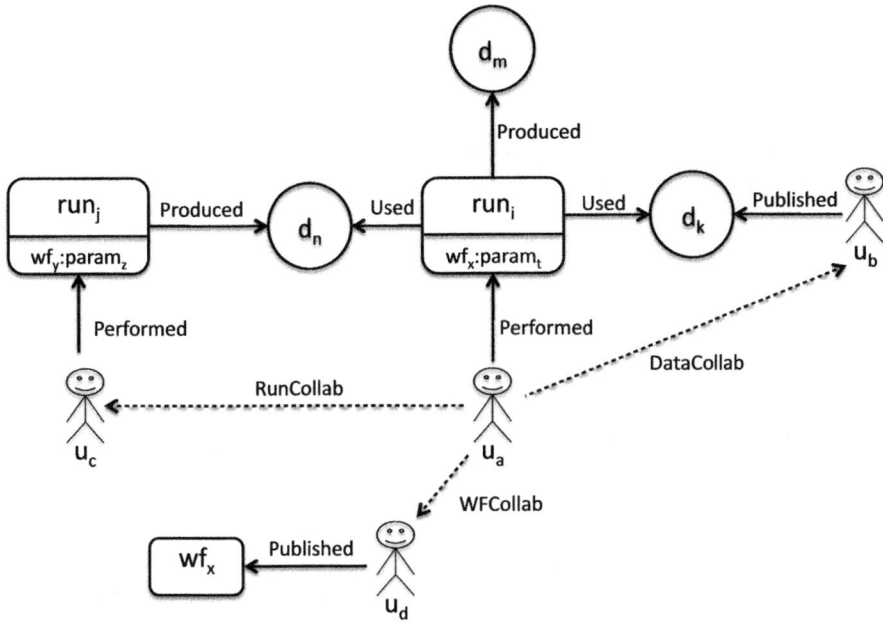

Fig. 4. The main entities and edges of the collaborative provenance model

r can take zero or more data artifacts d_{in} as input according to the relation $\mathsf{Input}(r, d_{in})$, which states that d_{in} was input to r. Each run r can also have zero or more data artifacts d_{out} as outputs according to the relation $\mathsf{Output}(r, d_{out})$, which states that d_{out} was an output of r. A data artifact can be an output of at most one run, but can be used as an input to zero or more runs.

Although not shown directly in Fig. 4, we assume a relation $\mathsf{DerivedFrom}(d_{out}, r, d_{in})$ for capturing causal dependencies between input and output data items of a run r. Given a fact $\mathsf{DerivedFrom}(d_{out}, r, d_{in})$, we say that d_{out} was derived from r using d_{in}. Each derivation also implies that d_{in} was an input to r, i.e., $\mathsf{Input}(r, d_{in})$, and d_{out} was an output of r, i.e., $\mathsf{Output}(r, d_{out})$. This constraint is captured in first-order logic (FO) as

$$\forall d_{in}, r, d_{out} \ (\mathsf{DerivedFrom}(d_{out}, r, d_{in}) \rightarrow \mathsf{Input}(r, d_{in}) \wedge \mathsf{Output}(r, d_{out})).$$

We define the relation $\mathsf{DDep}(d_{out}, d_{in})$ as the set of all immediate data dependencies given by $\mathsf{DerivedFrom}$, where d_{out} is said to depend on d_{in}. We can easily compute DDep using the following Datalog rule.

$$\mathsf{DDep}(d_{out}, d_{in}) \ :\text{-} \ \mathsf{DerivedFrom}(d_{out}, r, d_{in}).$$

We write DDep^* to denote the transitive closure of the DDep relation.

The Used and Produced relations (as shown in Fig. 4) are variants of Input and Output that additionally imply a derivation relationship. These relations are defined as views over Input and Output using the following Datalog rules.

$$\text{Used}(r, d_{in}) \; :- \; \text{DerivedFrom}(d_{out}, r, d_{in}).$$
$$\text{Produced}(r, d_{out}) \; :- \; \text{DerivedFrom}(d_{out}, r, d_{in}).$$

The first rule states that a data artifact d_{in} was used by a run r if d_{in} derived an output d_{out} of r. The second rule states that a data artifact d_{out} was produced by a run r if it was derived by an input d_{in} of r. Note that these relations do not explicitly link the inputs and outputs of a derivation, which is only done through the DerivedFrom relation.

We define the relation $\text{RDep}(r_2, r_1)$ as the set of all immediate run dependencies, where r_2 is said to depend on r_1. The RDep relation is defined as the following view in Datalog.

$$\text{RDep}(r_2, r_1) \; :- \; \text{Output}(r_1, d_1), \text{Used}(r_2, d_1).$$

Specifically, a run dependency is established between a run r_2 and r_1 whenever the output of r_1 is used by r_2 to derive a data artifact.

We assume the relation $\text{Published}(u, w)$ records the case when a user u published a workflow w to the workflow repository; and similarly, $\text{Published}(u, d)$ records the case when u published a data artifact d to the shared data store (see Fig. 2). A user u may also perform, i.e., execute and then publish, a workflow run r, which is captured by the relation $\text{Performed}(u, r)$. When a user performs a run, we assume all outputs of the run are published to the data store, which is captured by the following FO constraint.

$$\forall u, r, d \; (\text{Performed}(u, r) \land \text{Output}(r, d) \rightarrow \text{Published}(u, d)).$$

As shown in Fig. 4, we consider three variants of collaboration, which we define as views using the following Datalog rules.

$$\text{WFCollab}(u_2, u_1) \; :- \; \text{Published}(u_1, w), \text{Run}(r, w), \text{Performed}(u_2, r).$$
$$\text{DataCollab}(u_2, u_1) \; :- \; \text{Published}(u_1, d_1), \text{Used}(r, d_1), \text{Performed}(u_2, r).$$
$$\text{RunCollab}(u_2, u_1) \; :- \; \text{Performed}(u_1, r_1), \text{Output}(r_1, d_1), \text{Used}(r_2, d_1),$$
$$\text{Performed}(u_2, r_2).$$

The first rule states that a *workflow collaboration* (WFCollab) is established between two users whenever the second user executes a workflow that is publishes by the first user. The second rule states that a *data collaboration* (DataCollab) is established between two users whenever a data artifact published by the first user was used as an input by a run that is performed by the second user. The third rule states that a *run collaboration* (RunCollab) is established between two users whenever a run performed by the second user uses the output of a run by the first user.

A collaboration dependency $\text{CDep}(u_2, u_1)$ between two users is established whenever they participate in one of the three collaborations defined above (where u_2 depends on u_1). The CDep relation is easily defined in Datalog as follows.

$$\text{CDep}(u_2, u_1) \; :- \; \text{WFCollab}(u_2, u_1).$$
$$\text{CDep}(u_2, u_1) \; :- \; \text{DataCollab}(u_2, u_1).$$
$$\text{CDep}(u_2, u_1) \; :- \; \text{RunCollab}(u_2, u_1).$$

Table 1. Example queries across workflow executions and collaborations

Q1	Which data artifacts were used explicilty or implicitly to generate data artifact d?
Q2	Which runs were used in the generation of a data artifact d?
Q3	If data artifact d is detected to be faulty, which runs were affected by d?
Q4	Which users depended on data artifact d?
Q5	Which user collaborations were involved in the derivation of artifact d_2 from artifact d_1?
Q6	Who are the potential acknowledgements for a publication of a data artifact d?

Each of the views shown in Fig. 3 can be reconstructed from the provenance model described here. The relations DDep and RDep defined above can be used to construct the standard data and run dependency graphs shown in Fig. 3(a) and 3(b), respectively. More importantly, using the CDep relation, we can also construct user collaboration views (i.e., the collaboration dependency graph) as in Fig. 3(c). With these three dependency graphs, it becomes possible to answer both standard provenance queries as well as queries that involve user collaborations. In the following section we extend the model presented here (with respect to the three dependency graphs) to addtionally support lineage-based path queries. Our approach provides a simple mechanism for filtering dependency graphs to answer provenance queries such as those in Table 1.

3 Expressing Collaborative Queries

We use QLP (the *Query Language for Provenance*) [11] for expressing lineage queries, and in particular, to filter the dependency graphs described in Section 2. In general, answering standard provenance questions (including those of Table 1) requires the generation of recursive queries over lineage graphs. Such queries are often complex to express and expensive to evaluate [12,13,14,15]. QLP provides a simple, declarative, path-based language (similar, e.g., to XPath) for expressing such queries, and optimization techniques have been developed that make answering QLP queries over large provenance repositories feasible [16]. QLP queries work over sets of lineage edges, e.g., represented by the DerivedFrom relation. A QLP path query p can be viewed as a filter that selects matching paths within the lineage graph induced by the underlying edges. The result of a QLP query is the set of edges along matching paths of the induced graph. Thus, QLP is a closed language that returns a subset of a given set of lineage edges. Closed languages such as QLP have a number of benefits including the ability to construct views, "incremental" querying, and visualization [17,18].

QLP queries are expressed and evaluated against a selected provenance view, which can be a single workflow run, the entire repository of runs, or the provenance view resulting from a previous query. In the collaborative provenance query scenario, users can use QLP expressions to filter the various dependency views of Fig. 3. Below we present the basic constructs of QLP and show how QLP can be used to filter dependency graphs (and subsequently answer the queries of Table 1; see Table 2).

In the scenario illustrated by Fig. 2, the lineage information is recorded at a "coarse-grain" level, where only the lineage relationships between inputs and outputs of a run

Lineage-preserving path queries (examples)	
$*$ .. e_n	Lineage graph that resulted in nodes in e_n.
e_n .. $*$	Lineage graph for nodes derived from nodes in e_n
e_{n_1} .. e_{n_2}	Lineage graph for paths from nodes in e_{n_1} to nodes in e_{n_2}
e_{n_1} .. r_i .. e_{n_2}	Lineage graph for paths from nodes in e_{n_1} to e_{n_2} passing through run r_i
Functions over lineage path queries	
exists(p)	True if the selected view contains a path defined by path query p
runs(p)	The runs of the lineage graph returned by path query p
workflows(p)	The workflows of the lineage graph returned by path query p
artifacts(p)	The data nodes of the lineage graph returned by path query p
inputs(p)	The source nodes of the lineage graph returned by path query p
outputs(p)	The sink nodes of the lineage graph returned by path query p
Views over lineage path queries	
DATA-DEP(p)	Data dependencies (Fig. 3(a)) of the lineage graph selected by path query p
RUN-DEP(p)	Run dependencies (Fig. 3(b)) of the lineage graph selected by path query p
COLLAB-DEP(p)	Collaborations (Fig. 3(c)) of the lineage graph selected by path query p

Fig. 5. Basic QLP constructs and functions, where e_n is a node expression comprised of either a data artifact identifier, a run identifier, a data artifact type (denoting the set of artifacts having that type), or a workflow (denoting the set of runs of the workflow). We use p to denote a QLP path query, and r_i to denote a run.

are stored. In the following, we restrict the underlying lineage model of QLP to be over workflow runs, as opposed to the standard use of QLP that supports queries over indidvidual processes within runs (thus modeling lineage at a "fine-grain" level).

Table 5 introduces some of the basic constructs and functions of QLP, together with the extensions described here, including the DATA-DEP, RUN-DEP, and COLLAB-DEP functions. As a simple example of a QLP path query, the expression "$*$ .. d_7" returns lineage edges denoting paths starting from any node in the lineage graph and ending at node d_7. Similarly, the query "d_2 .. $*$" returns lineage edges denoting paths starting at node d_2 and ending at any node in the lineage graph. Both "ends" of a path can be fixed in QLP, e.g., the query "d_5 .. d_9" returns all edges on paths in the lineage graph that start at d_5 and end at d_9. QLP queries can restrict paths to include intermediate objects, e.g., the query "$\#r_2$ .. d_6 .. $\#r_5$ .. $*$" returns the set of lineage edges denoting paths that start at run r_2, go through artifact d_6 followed by (via one or more lineage edges) run r_5, and end at any node.

3.1 Filtering Dependency Views Using QLP

The DATA-DEP, RUN-DEP, and COLLAB-DEP functions construct data, run, and collaboration dependency graphs, respectively, that result from evaluating a QLP query over the current provenance view. Thus, these functions, unlike the DDep, RDep, and CDep relations defined in Section 2, create views purely out of lineage relations.

Filtering Data Dependency Views. We write $v(p)$ to denote the set of lineage edges of the form $\langle d_2, r, d_1 \rangle \in L$ returned after evaluating a QLP path query p over a set of lineage edges L [16]. We directly use this evaluation to define the DATA-DEP function as follows.

$$\text{DATA-DEP}(p) := \{\langle d_2, d_1\rangle \mid \exists r : \langle d_2, r, d_1\rangle \in v(p)\}$$

As shown in Table 2, we can use the DATA-DEP function to answer Q1 of Table 1, which returns the subset of the data-dependency graph that ends at artifact d. Note that the DATA-DEP function computes a subset of the DDep relation restricted to lineage edges.

Filtering Run Dependency Views. Similarly, to construct a filtered run-dependency graph, we again use the evaluation function as follows.

$$\text{RUN-DEP}(p) := \{\langle r_2, r_1\rangle \mid \exists d_1, d_2, d_3 : \langle d_3, r_2, d_2\rangle \in v(p) \wedge \langle d_2, r_1, d_1\rangle \in v(p)\}$$

Note that each output of a run within a lineage graph returned by a QLP query is required to be dependent on some input (since only derivation edges are considered). Thus, the run dependencies returned by the RUN-DEP function have the additional constraint that each output is dependent on some input (within the query result) of the run. This can be viewed as restricting the RDep relation to only selecting from Produced edges instead of Output edges. We can use the RUN-DEP function to answer Q2 and Q3 of Table 1, as shown in Table 2.

Filtering User Collaboration Views. Let DATA-DEP$^*(p)$ be the set of edges of the transitive closure of the edges returned by DATA-DEP(p). We define the COLLAB-DEP function as:

$$\text{COLLAB-DEP}(p) := \text{C-DEP}_{WF}(p) \cup \text{C-DEP}_{DATA}(p) \cup \text{C-DEP}_{RUN}(p),$$

where the functions C-DEP$_{WF}$, C-DEP$_{DATA}$, and C-DEP$_{RUN}$ are defined as follows.

$$\text{C-DEP}_{WF}(p) := \{\langle u_2, u_1\rangle \mid \exists r, w : \text{Run}(r, w) \wedge \text{Published}(u_1, w) \wedge \\ \text{Performed}(u_2, r)\}$$

$$\text{C-DEP}_{Data}(p) := \{\langle u_2, u_1\rangle \mid \exists d_1, d_2, r : \text{Published}(u_1, d_1) \wedge \text{Performed}(u_2, r) \wedge \\ \langle d_2, r, d_1\rangle \in v(p)\}$$

$$\text{C-DEP}_{Run}(p) := \{\langle u_2, u_1\rangle \mid \exists d_0, d_1, d_2, r_1, r_2 : \text{Performed}(u_1, r_1) \wedge \\ \langle d_1, r_1, d_0\rangle \in v(p) \wedge \langle d_2, r_2, d_1\rangle \in v(p) \wedge \text{Performed}(u_2, r_2)\}$$

The COLLAB-DEP function can be used to answer queries Q4-Q6 of Table 1, as shown in Table 2.

3.2   Relation between the Collaborative Model and OPM

The Open Provenance Model (OPM) [12] has emerged from the e-science community, and has evolved as a standard representation to facilitate the exchange of information between multiple provenance systems. OPM is based on a model and set of inference rules for directed acyclic provenance graphs, which represent casual dependencies between data products and processes. OPM defines three primary entities (nodes): (1)

Table 2. Example queries expressed using the dependency functions defined for QLP

Q1	DATA-DEP(* .. d)
Q2	RUN-DEP(* .. d)
Q3	RUN-DEP(d .. *)
Q4	COLLAB-DEP(d .. *)
Q5	COLLAB-DEP(d_1 .. d_2)
Q6	COLLAB-DEP(* .. d)

Artifacts: immutable piece of data; (2) *Processes*: actions or series of actions performed on or caused by artifacts; and (3) *Agents*: entities that enable, facilitate, control, or affect execution of processes. OPM also defines five primary types of causal dependencies (edges) that comprise provenance graphs: (1) *used*: a process used artifact(s); (2) *wasGeneratedBy*: an artifact was generated by a process; (3) *wasTriggeredBy*: a process was triggered by another process(es); (4) *wasDerivedFrom*: an artifact was derived from another artifact(s); and (5) *wasControlledBy*: a process was controlled by an agent.

The collaborative model, e.g., as in Fig. 4, roughly contains the same entities and five causal dependencies of OPM. A lineage (i.e., DerivedFrom) relation is of the form $\langle d_{out}, r, d_{in} \rangle$ for data nodes (artifacts in OPM) d_{in} and d_{out} and run (or processes in OPM) r. For example, in Fig. 3(b) $\langle d_4, r_1, d_1 \rangle$ is a lineage relation stating that artifact d_1 was *used* by the run r_1 to produce artifact d_4 (i.e., artifact d_4 *wasDerivedFrom* artifact d_1), and artifact d_4 *wasGeneratedBy* workflow run r_1. Adjacent lineage relations, e.g., $\langle d_7, r_3, d_4 \rangle$ and $\langle d_4, r_1, d_1 \rangle$ state that run r_3 *wasTriggeredBy* run r_1. Similarly, users in the collaborative model can be viewed as a form of agents in OPM, where Performed edges are similar to *wasControlledBy* edges in OPM. To the best of our knowledge, OPM does not provide support for recording when users publish data and workflows, which is essential in the collaborative model proposed here for creating the various types of user collaborations described in Section 2.

4   Conceptual Interoperability Scenario

To further illustrate our approach, we describe (i) an interoperability scenario, derived from the Third Provenance Challenge (PC3), (ii) some prototypical collaborative queries, and (iii) an architecture for its implementation. A similar example based on the First Provenance Challenge is currently being implemented in the context of a DataONE[1] student project.

Usecase. The workflows selected for PC3 are part of an image-processing pipeline in the Pan-STARRS[2] project. A next generation panoramic telescope surveys the sky looking for asteroids or comets that may impact the Earth. The telescope may generate several TBs of data nightly, which must be reduced and stored into an object data management framework that is publicly accessible by astronomers. Based on this usecase,

---

[1] http://dataone.org
[2] http://pan-starrs.ifa.hawaii.edu

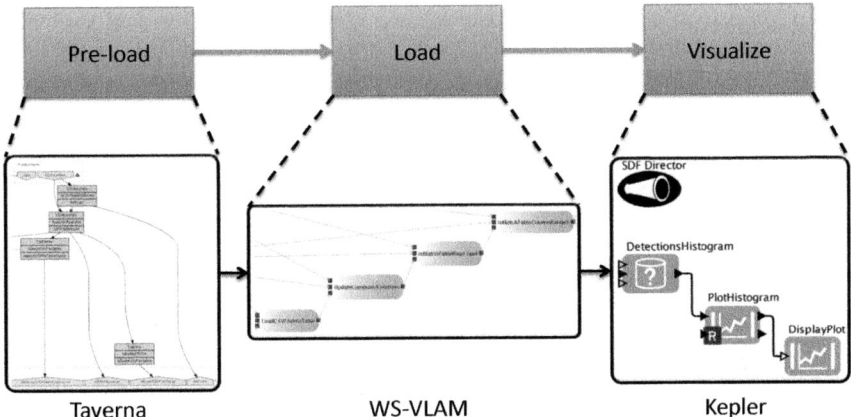

Fig. 6. Conceptual process for the Provenance Challenge 3

the main PC3 workflow ingests CSV files containing readings from the telescope into an SQL database and the plotting workflow creates histograms of the ingested data.

To build a collaborative workflow environment, we assume that we executed the fragments of these PC3 workflows in three different workflow systems as shown in Fig. 6. In this scenario, Taverna [19] performs the initialization and pre-loading checks, WS-VLAM [20] loads the CSV files into the database and updates the column counts, and Kepler [21] creates the histograms. We chose this division of the PC3 workflows to evenly and logically divide the tasks among the workflow engines.

An example history of observables and actions within this usecase is shown in Table 3. In this scenario, all three workflow engines use the same MySQL database when executing their subset of the PC3 workflows. In the pre-load tasks, Taverna verifies the contents of the input CSV files and creates the tables in the database. Next, WS-VLAM reads the contents of the CSV files into these tables, and verifies the row counts and data values. Finally, Kepler produces histograms from these data. For example, the second row refers to run_1 performed by u_2 using $wf_{preload}$ published by u_1. In run_1, u_2 used $d_{J062941}$ as an input and the run produced $d_{J062941-1}$ as its output.

Collaborative PC3 Queries. The following are example queries on Table 3 expressed using the QLP functions defined in Section 3.

Q1. What data contributed to $d_{histogram}$?
 DATA-DEP(* .. $d_{histogram}$)

Q2. If $d_{J062942-2}$ is determined to be faulty, what other data products may be faulty based on $d_{J062942-2}$?
 DATA-DEP($d_{J062942-2}$ .. *)

Q3. What runs contributed to the generation of $d_{J062941-2}$?
 RUN-DEP(* .. $d_{J062941-2}$)

Q4. Which users contributed workflows that produced $d_{histogram}$?
 COLLAB-DEP(* .. $d_{histogram}$)

Table 3. The publish and run observables in interoperable PC3 scenario. The contents of the table shall be read as follows: e.g., the second row refers to run_1 performed by u_2 using $wf_{preload}$ published by u_1. In run_1, u_2 used $d_{J062941}$ as an input and the run produced $d_{J062941-1}$ as its output.

u_1	Published			$wf_{Preload}$				
u_2	Performed	run_1	Used	$wf_{Preload}$	Used	$d_{J062941}$	Produced	$d_{J062941-1}$
u_3	Performed	run_2	Used	$wf_{Preload}$	Used	$d_{J062942}$	Produced	$d_{J062942-2}$
u_4	Published			wf_{Load}				
u_5	Published			$wf_{Visualize}$				
u_2	Performed	run_3	Used	wf_{Load}	Used	$d_{J062941-1}$	Produced	$d_{J062941-2}$
u_3	Performed	run_4	Used	$wf_{Visualize}$	Used	$d_{J062941-2}$	Produced	$d_{histogram}$
u_3	Published			$d_{histogram}$				

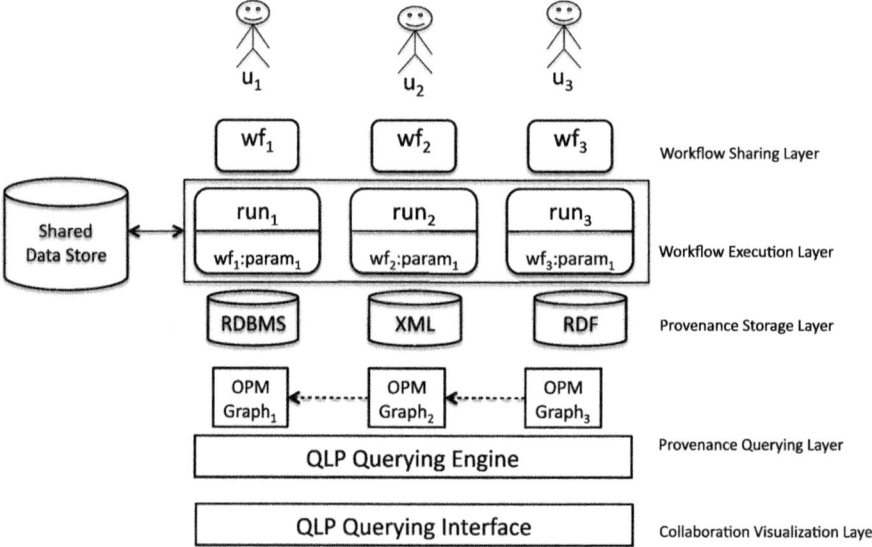

Fig. 7. Architecture for answering collaborative queries

QLP-based Interoperable Query Framework. Fig. 7 shows the design of an end-to-end framework that can be plugged into any scientific infrastructure with the ability to publish data and workflows, to execute workflows using different workflow engines, to collect workflow provenance and to express and evaluate QLP queries. In this architecture, workflows use a shared data space with common data identifiers. To generate data dependency views, using the QLP mapping to OPM, the QLP Querying Engine transforms users QLP queries into OPM queries. In addition, the same querying engine routes the mapped queries to distinct provenance stores using the developed SQL (RDBMS), XQuery (XML) and SPARQL (RDF) interfaces.

5 Related Work

The ideas presented in this paper depend on previous work in scientific workflow provenance and collaborative scientific platforms. Below we present the related work.

Provenance in Scientific Workflows. Scientific workflow systems are being used in many scientific domains, and many approaches have been proposed recently for representing and storing workflow provenance [5,6]. However, most of the existing provenance approaches store provenance for a single runs, and do not capture or maintain associations across runs [22,23,24,25]. The framework described in [7] records associations between multiple related workflow runs. Vistrails provides a spreadsheet where users can compare the results of multiple workflows, or multiple workflow runs[26]. However, our work is based on capturing associations not only across workflow runs, but also across users, where users play an active role of publishing data, or publishing workflows, or executing workflow runs. Our work captures these associations and establishes user collaboration views based on provenance.

Querying Provenance. Approaches for querying provenance are largely based on physical data representations [14], e.g., relational, XML, or RDF schemas, where users express provenance queries through corresponding query languages, i.e., SQL, XQuery, or SPARQL. Provenance queries often require computing transitive closures over dependency relations, and expressing such queries using standard approaches is typically done using recursion or stored procedures [15,16,27]. Expressing such queries is both cumbersome and error-prone, and requires considerable user expertise. High-level languages such as QLP provide a separation between the logical provenance model and its underlying physical representation, which allows for the use of different representation schemes and additional optimization techniques. Also, QLP is closed under lineage relations, where answers to lineage queries are sets of lineage dependencies (edges) forming provenance subgraphs, i.e., provenance preserving.

Collaborative Applications in E-Science. Since collaborative research studies require substantial infrastructure, we often see infrastructure projects that facilitate conducting a number of these multi- disciplinary scientific studies for a particular domain, e.g., Virolab [28], VL-e [9] and CAMERA [8]. In the VL-e project, the WFBus focuses on the execution of workflows developed in various workflow management systems. Collaborative views through provenance covers both the execution and provenance aspects of an aggregate workflow. In the context of the CAMERA project, workflow-related scientific products and their provenance are stored in data repositories that are accessible through the project portal, allowing for collaborative views and queries over these runs. In the ViroLab virtual laboratory, scientific applications are executed as scripts and their provenance is recorded by collecting events emitted by the GridSpace engine that executes the experiment scripts. Collaborative views over the provenance of these executing scripts can be captured by explicit reuse of results from previous experiments. An interesting opportunity arises from the support for Scientific Research Objects [29] by myExperiment [10]. Applications such as portal environments can deploy the content of SROs in new ways and collaborative views over them.

6 Conclusion

In this paper, we introduced the concept of collaborative views and queries over interoperable provenance data in a collaborative scientific research. We adopted and extended a high-level query language for provenance, QLP, to express complex collaborative provenance queries. We also established a mapping between QLP and OPM. Finally, we showed the feasibility of our approach on collaborative queries through PC3-inspired usecase workflows and described our planned architecture for its future implementation. The contributions of this paper tie together users actions with multiple workflow executions that create a chain of custody for data generated by collaborations.

This is the right time to introduce such provenance models and query languages as collaborative research projects are ever growing and Web2.0-oriented scientific sharing environments, e.g., myExperiment, are being introduced to allow for sharing and execution of workflows in different workflow system by groups of users. Thanks to Provenance Challenge efforts, OPM is starting to be adopted by workflow systems participating in the challenge pushing OPM as a standard for provenance data.

Future Work. In the future, we plan to publish an implementation of the QLP based collaborative query engine based on the PC3 workflow using workflows in Kepler, Taverna and WSVLAM. We are currently conducting a larger bioinformatics usecase from the CAMERA project where users share data, workflows and runs through shared stores. We also intend to work on aspects of restricted user spaces and optimization of collaborative query evaluation.

Acknowledgements. The authors would like to thank for their collaboration to the Vi-roLab consortium and the Kepler team. This research was supported by the Dutch Bsik project VL-e: Virtual Laboratory for e-Science and the European ViroLab grant INFSO-IST-027446, NSF SDCI Award OCI-0722079 for Kepler/CORE, DOE grant DE-FC02-01ER25486 for SciDAC/SDM, NSF CEO:P Award No. DBI 0619060 for REAP, NSF IIS-0630033 for pPOD and Gordon and Betty Moore Foundation award to Calit2 at UCSD for CAMERA.

References

1. Ludäscher, B., Goble, C. (eds.) Special section on scientific workflows. ACM SIGMOD Record 34(3) (2005)
2. Taylor, I.J., Deelman, E., Gannon, D.B., Shields, M. (eds.) Workflows for e-Science. Springer, Heidelberg (2007)
3. Gil, Y., Deelman, E., Ellisman, M., Fahringer, T., Fox, G., Gannon, D., Goble, C., Livny, M., Moreau, L., Myers, J.: Examining the challenges of scientific workflows. IEEE Computer 40(12), 24–32 (2007)
4. Deelman, E., Gannon, D., Shields, M., Taylor, I.: Workflows and e-science: An overview of workflow system features and capabilities. Future Generation Computer Systems 25, 528–540 (2009)
5. Simmhan, Y.L., Plale, B., Gannon, D.: A survey of data provenance in e-science. SIGMOD Record 34, 31–36 (2005)
6. Freire, J., Koop, D., Santos, E., Silva, C.T.: Provenance for computational tasks: A survey. Computing in Science and Engineering 10, 11–21 (2008)

7. Bowers, S., McPhillips, T., Wu, M.W., Ludäscher, B.: Project Histories: Managing Data Provenance Across Collection-Oriented Scientific Workflow Runs. In: Cohen-Boulakia, S., Tannen, V. (eds.) DILS 2007. LNCS (LNBI), vol. 4544, pp. 122–138. Springer, Heidelberg (2007)

8. Altintas, I., Lin, A.W., Chen, J., Churas, C., Gujral, M., Sun, S., Li, W., Manansala, R., Sedova, M., Grethe, J.S., Ellisman, M.: Camera 2.0: A data-centric metagenomics community infrastructure driven by scientific workflows. In: Proceeding of The IEEE 2010 Fourth International Workshop on Scientific Workflows, Miami, Florida (2010)

9. Zhao, Z., Booms, S., Belloum, A., de Laat, C., Hertzberger, B.: Vle-wfbus: A scientific workflow bus for multi e-science domains. In: International Conference on e-Science and Grid Computing (2006)

10. Roure, D.D., Goble, C., Stevens, R.: Designing the myexperiment virtual research environment for the social sharing of workflows. In: E-SCIENCE 2007: Proceedings of the Third IEEE International Conference on e-Science and Grid Computing, Washington, DC, USA, pp. 603–610. IEEE Computer Society Press, Los Alamitos (2007)

11. Anand, M.K., Bowers, S., Mcphillips, T., Ludäscher, B.: Exploring scientific workflow provenance using hybrid queries over nested data and lineage graphs. In: SSDBM 2009: Proceedings of the 21st International Conference on SSDM, pp. 237–254. Springer, Heidelberg (2009)

12. Moreau, L., Freire, J., Futrelle, J., McGrath, R.E., Myers, J., Paulson, P.: The Open Provenance Model: An Overview. In: Freire, J., Koop, D., Moreau, L. (eds.) IPAW 2008. LNCS, vol. 5272, pp. 323–326. Springer, Heidelberg (2008)

13. Anand, M.K., Bowers, S., Ludäscher, B.: A navigation model for exploring scientific workflow provenance graphs. In: WORKS 2009: Proceedings of the 4th Workshop on Workflows in Support of Large-Scale Science, pp. 1–10. ACM, New York (2009)

14. Cohen, S., Cohen-Boulakia, S., Davidson, S.B.: Towards a model of provenance and user views in scientific workflows. In: Leser, U., Naumann, F., Eckman, B. (eds.) DILS 2006. LNCS (LNBI), vol. 4075, pp. 264–279. Springer, Heidelberg (2006)

15. Heinis, T., Alonso, G.: Efficient lineage tracking for scientific workflows. In: SIGMOD 2008: Proceedings of the 2008 ACM SIGMOD International Conference on Management of Data, pp. 1007–1018. ACM P, New York (2008)

16. Anand, M.K., Bowers, S., Ludäscher, B.: Techniques for efficiently querying scientific workflow provenance graphs. In: EDBT 2010: Proceedings of the 13th International Conference on Extending Database Technology, pp. 287–298. ACM, New York (2010)

17. Anand, M.K., Bowers, S., Altintas, I., Ludäscher, B.: Approaches for exploring and querying scientific workflow provenance graphs. In: IPAW (2010)

18. Anand, M.K., Bowers, S., Ludäscher, B.: Provenance browser: Displaying and querying scientific workflow provenance graphs (Demo). In: 26th IEEE International Conference on Data Engineering (2010)

19. Turi, D., Missier, P., Goble, C., De Roure, D., Oinn, T.: Taverna workflows: Syntax and semantics. In: International Conference on e-Science and Grid Computing, pp. 441–448 (2007)

20. Korkhov, V., Vasyunin, D., Wibisono, A., Guevara-Masis, V., Belloum, A., de Laat, C., Adriaans, P., Hertzberger, L.: Ws-vlam: towards a scalable workflow system on the grid. In: WORKS 2007: Proceedings of the 2nd workshop on Workflows in Support of Large-scale Science, pp. 63–68. ACM, New York (2007)

21. Ludäscher, B., Altintas, I., Berkley, C., Higgins, D., Jaeger-Frank, E., Jones, M., Lee, E., Tao, J., Zhao, Y.: Scientific workflow management and the Kepler system. Concurrency and Computation: Practice and Experience. Special Issue on Scientific Workflows (2005)

22. Altintas, I., Barney, O., Jaeger-Frank, E.: Provenance collection support in the kepler scientific workflow system. In: Moreau, L., Foster, I. (eds.) IPAW 2006. LNCS, vol. 4145, pp. 118–132. Springer, Heidelberg (2006)

23. Davidson, S.B., Boulakia, S.C., Eyal, A., Ludäscher, B., McPhillips, T.M., Bowers, S., Anand, M.K., Freire, J.: Provenance in scientific workflow systems. IEEE Data Eng. Bull. 30, 44–50 (2007)
24. Bowers, S., Mcphillips, T., Riddle, S., Anand, M.K., Ludäscher, B.: Kepler/ppod: Scientific workflow and provenance support for assembling the tree of life. In: Freire, J., Koop, D., Moreau, L. (eds.) IPAW 2008. LNCS, vol. 5272, pp. 70–77. Springer, Heidelberg (2008)
25. Zhao, J., Goble, C., Stevens, R., Turi, D.: Mining taverna's semantic web of provenance. Concurrency and Computation: Practice and Experience, Special Issue on The First Provenance Challenge 20, 463–472 (2007)
26. Scheidegger, C.E., Vo, H.T., Koop, D., Freire, J., Silva, C.T.: Querying and re-using workflows with vstrails. In: SIGMOD 2008: Proceedings of the 2008 ACM SIGMOD International Conference on Management of Data, pp. 1251–1254. ACM, New York (2008)
27. Anand, M.K., Bowers, S., McPhillips, T., Ludäscher, B.: Efficient provenance storage over nested data collections. In: EDBT 2009: Proceedings of the 12th International Conference on Extending Database Technology, pp. 958–969. ACM, New York (2009)
28. Malawski, M., Bartynski, T., Bubak, M.: Invocation of operations from script-based grid applications. Future Generation Computer Systems 26, 138–146 (2010)
29. De Roure, D., Goble, C.: Research objects for data intensive research. In: E-Science (2009)

Provenance of Software Development Processes

Heinrich Wendel, Markus Kunde, and Andreas Schreiber

Simulation and Software Technology
German Aerospace Center (DLR)
51147 Cologne, Germany
{Heinrich.Wendel,Markus.Kunde,Andreas.Schreiber}@dlr.de
http://www.dlr.de/sc

Abstract. "Why does the build fail currently?" - This and similar questions arise on a daily basis in software development processes (SDP). There is no easy way to answer these questions, the required information is stored throughout different tools, the version control and continuous integration systems in this example. The tools mainly live in isolated worlds and no direct connection between their data exists. This paper proposes a solution to such problems, based on provenance technologies. After outlining the complexity of a SDP, the questions arising on a daily basis are categorized. Finally an approach to make the SDP provenance-aware is proposed based on PRiME, the Open Provenance Model and a SOA architecture using Neo4j to store the data, Gremlin to query it and REST webservices as connection to the tools.

1 Introduction

Research in provenance focuses on a variety of topics, ranging from suitable models to useable libraries and informative visualizations. Those technologies have been tested on real world use cases, mainly scientific workflows from areas like engineering, medicine and bioinformatics. Moreau provides a very detailed overview over the research performed in this area [1]. This paper focuses on a new field of application, namely software development processes (SDP).

Some effort has been invested to record the execution of programs, e.g., by recording all Java method calls [2]. Traceability deals with the links between requirements, design artifacts, tests and code in both directions [3]. Application Lifecycle Management Systems (ALM) provide integrated tool suites to manage artifacts and their relationships in an SDP [4]. Recording the interaction of tools has been handled in the Taverna project, related to scientific workflows [5]. Automatic reasoning on collected information, stored using semantic web technologies, can be done using the Proof Markup Language [6].

In contrast to those approaches the paper focuses on recording the interactions between developers and a distributed tool suite in an SDP and the resulting artifacts. Stored in a graph databases provenance questions can be executed using a graph query language.

Chapter 2 describes a typical SDP and the tools used in it, showing the need of the proposed solution. Chapter 3 gives a categorization of questions

D.L. McGuinness, J.R. Michaelis, and L. Moreau (Eds.): IPAW 2010, LNCS 6378, pp. 59–63, 2010.
© Springer-Verlag Berlin Heidelberg 2010

occuring during the process. Those questions have to be answerable through the information collected by the provenance system outlined in chapter 4. Finally a summary and evaluation of the approach is given in chapter 5.

2   Software Development Processes

Due to the complexity of today's software a large number of development process models evolved. Although those processes not necessarily force the usage of certain tools, the development can be simplified and sped up by their usage. A typical tool suite at DLR consists of an integrated development environment, a version control system, an issue tracker, a continuous integration framework and a documentation management system.

A lot of interaction occurs between developers, the tools they use during the development process and automatically between different tools. Examples of those interactions are: i) discussion about a feature request; ii) entering or changing requirements in an issue tracking system; iii) automatic code style checks during a check-in.

Information about those processes is, if available at all, distributed over the different tools used. Version control systems feature a history of all files and their editors, issue tracking systems a list of all comments for an issue. Still, the missing link between these different tools makes it either impossible to draw conclusions from this information or is at least very time-consuming, especially when the immense amount of available data is considered.

3   Questions

A lot of questions arise during such complex processes. Based on an internal survey at DLR they have been categorized into one or more of the following groups:

Error Detection: During day to day development it often happens that builds or unit tests suddenly fail. In such cases it is important to identify the source of the error. In many cases this might be the responsible developer, who should be contacted first, because he has the most knowledge to fix the problem. Sometimes it might also be the failure of a tool, e.g., ocurring after an upgrade.

Quality Assurance: Customers are always interested in a product with maximal quality, therefore quality assurance has always been a very important topic, not only in the domain of software engineering. The number of unit tests or code coverage percentages give important hints on where the quality of the product is very good or still deficient.

Process Validation: Following a defined process is another way of performing quality assurance. By following norms like ISO 9001 the quality of the final product is not assured, but the quality of the process that led to the product. This is especially important in the area of medical software, where a process validation is required.

Monitoring: Often problems do not become visible until a closer look at the project. Automatic monitoring and notifications can help to identify those problems, e.g., to see if an issue takes longer to implement than expected.

Statistical Analysis: Statistics help to interpret and draw conclusions out of collected data. They can be used by managers, e.g., to decide if the project is in time, needs more resources or if developers can be put into another project. Developers are interested in statistics to see how they perform or compare to others.

Process Optimization: Another use of monitoring, error detection and statistics is the optimization of the process itself. E.g., a lot of commits related to one issue might show that the issues should be split more fine-grained next time. A build tool that fails in a lot of cases because of segmentation faults might be replaced by a new one.

Developer Rating: There is no widely accepted method to rate the productivity of developers; and it might not be a popular topic. Still the collected data can give some hints in order to decide which developer to assign to a specific problem. It might show that some developers are better in writing unit tests and some in documentation and helps to improve the process.

Informational: Sometimes data has to be collected for informational purposes, e.g., when creating a release announcement it shall contain a list of all bugs fixed.

4   A Provenance-Aware Software Development Process

In order to answer such questions the SDP has to be made provenance-aware using PRiME [7]. Originally PRiME was created for applications, not for processes or the later developed Open Provenance Model (OPM), therefore a few adaptions are needed to apply it to SDPs. First, the breakdown into individual application components, has to be changed to a breakdown into individual subprocesses. Second, instead of using interaction graphs, OPM graphs are used to picture the interactions between the actors. Using this methodology an OPM meta-model for the individual SDP can be created.

Based on the Neo4j graph database, which has successfully been used to store provenance information [8], a service oriented architecture to record information using this meta model can be implemented. Served by a web server, individual interfaces are exposed via REST to allow the insertion of new data. The services are secured using HTTP basic authentication. Afterwards each tool has to be extended to call the appropiate REST interface when new actions are performed. Usually the core of the tool must not be changed, because they provide some kind of hook mechanism which allow the execution of actions on specific events.

Finally a second interface is provided, allowing to query the recorded data using the graph programming language Gremlin [9]. The questions, previously stated in a human-readable format and analyzed by its starting item and scope using PRiME, can be translated into Gremlin queries. The queries can be executed using a provenance console served by a webserver.

5   Evaluation and Conclusions

The proposed approach has been implemented and evaluated using the SDP of the distributed simulation framework Remote Computing Environment [10] at DLR. The adapted metholodogy and selected technolgies could be successfully used and offers the possibility to answer questions from all categorizes summarized in chapter 3. The integration into the distributed tool suite was possible and showed a reasonable performance.

Some minor issues in the detailed modelling process regarding index structures and best practices for using Neo4j remain. Furthermore it is questionable if OPM is really needed for modelling or any arbitrary graph would suffice. OPM produces some overhead and could still be used as data exchange format.

Although it was possible to answer all given questions using the Turing-complete language Gremlin it is not intuitive to use. More work can be spend on visual query technologies. The Eclipse plug-in Neoclipse already offers graph navigation mechanisms. Combined with a meta-model definition, currently under development for Neo4j, a way to graphically specify queries could be developed.

Medical software must be developed following certain process models, the provenance model could be used to verify the compliance to the process. Even if the process itself is valid the tools might fail and prevent the process from working, which could also be detected. Moreover it might be possible to extend the approach to development processes in general, not focusing on software, but, e.g. system design or other engineering domains.

References

1. Moreau, L.: The foundations for provenance on the web. Technical report, University of Southampton (2009)
2. Miles, S.: Automatically adapting source code to document provenance. In: Proceedings of the 3rd International Provenance and Annotation Workshop, Springer, Heidelberg (2010)
3. Kannenberg, A., Saiedian, D.H.: Why software requirements traceability remains a challenge. CrossTalk The Journal of Defense Software Engineering (2009)
4. Schwaber, C.: The changing face of application life-cycle management. Technical report, Forrester (2006)
5. Zhao, J., Goble, C., Stevens, R., Turi, D.: Mining taverna's semantic web of provenance. Concurrency and Computation: Practice and Experience 20(5), 463–472 (2008)
6. da Silva, P.P., McGuinness, D.L., Fikes, R.: A proof markup language for semantic web services. Inf. Syst. 31(4), 381–395 (2006)

7. Munroe, S., Miles, S., Moreau, L., Vázquez-Salceda, J.: Prime: a software engineering methodology for developing provenance-aware applications. In: SEM 2006: Proceedings of the 6th International Workshop on Software Engineering and Middleware, pp. 39–46. ACM, New York (2010)
8. Tylissanakis, G., Cotronis, Y.: Data provenance and reproducibility in grid based scientific workflows. In: GPC 2009: Proceedings of the 2009 Workshops at the Grid and Pervasive Computing Conference, pp. 42–49. IEEE Computer Society, Los Alamitos (2009)
9. Gremlin - a graph-based programming language,
   http://wiki.github.com/tinkerpop/gremlin/
10. Remote component environment, http://www.rcenvironment.de/

Provenance-Awareness in R

Chris A. Silles and Andrew R. Runnalls

School of Computing
University of Kent
Canterbury, UK
{C.A.Silles,A.R.Runnalls}@kent.ac.uk

Abstract. It is generally acknowledged that when, in 1988, John Chambers and Richard Becker incorporated the $S\ AUDIT$ facility into their S statistical programming language and environment, they created one of the first provenance-aware applications. Since then, S has been spiritually succeeded by the open-source R project; however, R has no such facility for tracking provenance. This paper looks at how provenance-awareness is being introduced to $CXXR$ (http://www.cs.kent.ac.uk/projects/cxxr), a variant of the R interpreter designed to allow creation of experimental R versions. We explore the issues surrounding recording, representing, and interrogating provenance information in a command-line driven interactive environment that utilises a lazy functional programming language. We also characterise provenance information in this domain and evaluate the impact of adding facilities for provenance tracking.

1 Introduction

The use of computer systems for recording information has proliferated in recent years; however, facilities for recording *how* this data has come to be in its present state have only recently started to catch up due to research in the field of provenance-aware computing. This discipline has developed quickly over the last decade and is now reaching maturity with the Open Provenance Model for the representation and exchange of provenance information [1].

In this paper we look at how facilities for recording and examining provenance have been introduced to the interactive statistical environment and programming language, CXXR, which is based on the popular R project [2]. Recording process documentation for the purpose of reproducible computing in R has previously been researched in *Sweave* [3], a system based on concepts of literate programming [4].

Making applications provenance-aware is not in itself a new concept [5]; however, CXXR presents some novel challenges, primarily to the way in which provenance is represented conceptually, but also to the way in which provenance needs to be presented to the user, and how particular features of the language require modelling in order to capture complete provenance.

The structure of this paper is as follows. Section 2 provides an introduction to the software and describes the approach to handling provenance therein. We then, in Section 3, detail the implementation steps we have taken. We conclude with a summary of findings and what we are looking forward to in Section 4.

D.L. McGuinness, J.R. Michaelis, and L. Moreau (Eds.): IPAW 2010, LNCS 6378, pp. 64–72, 2010.

2   CXXR

2.1   History

CXXR is a variant of *R*, which is an open-source implementation of *S*.

S. S is a language and interactive environment for statistical computing, graphics, and exploratory data analysis [6]. It was developed during the mid-1970s at Bell Laboratories by John Chambers and Richard Becker. S emerged from Bell Labs at around the same time as the C programming language, and this is reflected in both its syntax and name. Despite this, it uses the semantics of a functional programming language, including employment of lazy evaluation.

S AUDIT. 'New S' was released in 1988 sporting a new feature entitled *S AUDIT* [7]. While a user operated a session within S, a record was maintained of each top-level expression evaluated; as well as objects read from and written to during the course of evaluation.

The accompanying S AUDIT program was able to process this record and allow the user to interrogate it. S AUDIT was able to perform a number of queries on the audit record, such as displaying the full sequence of statements; those statements responsible for reading from, or writing to, a specific object; or simply providing a list of all objects in the session.

A more intriguing feature of S AUDIT was its ability to create an *audit plot*, which was a directed-acyclic graph with statements as nodes arranged on the circumference of a circle (anti-clockwise in order of creation), and edges each representing an object written by one statement, later being read by another. Audit plots enabled users to visualise how objects were being used over their lifetime.

New S, therefore, became one of the first *provenance-aware* software applications, and even featured visualisation of provenance: features that were at the time innovative, and still remain novel today.

R and CXXR. While S as an application continues life as a commercial product called S+ retailed by TIBCO [8], the language, library and environment have been reimplemented as part of the open-source R project [2]. The R distribution comprises an interpreter and a number of packages for common functionality, which have been written in a mixture of C, Fortran, and R itself. It is maintained by a nineteen-strong team of core developers, and enjoys a large and active userbase working in areas as diverse as retail strategy, genetics, education, pharmacology, proteomics, and data and text mining.

CXXR is a project to reengineer the fundamental components of the R interpreter from C into C++, while fully preserving functionality of the standard R distribution [9]. The primary objective of CXXR is to enable experimental versions of the R interpreter to be created, allowing new functionality to be easily introduced.

Listing 1. Example R commands

```
> 1+2
[1] 3
> three <- 1+2
> square <- function(x) { x*x }
> nine <- square(three)
> nine
[1] 9
```

2.2 How R Works

Data Types. R has many data types, the most important of which is the *vector*. Vectors are homogeneous arrays of data, and may be composed of elements of types including integers, booleans, strings, and real and complex numbers. Vectors are ubiquitous in R. Even a single value (e.g. 3.14) is treated as a vector having only one element.

Example. Listing 1 shows the evaluation of some commands in R. The > character is the prompt, at which the user enters commands. The first statement performs a simple addition, and R prints the result. The square brackets indicate that the result is a vector, and the number signifies the index of the element at the beginning of the line. The second and third statements show assignment of a vector and a function to objects respectively.

Objects. When the user performs an assignment, a *binding* is created between a *symbol* object and a *value* object. The space in which bindings are stored is known as an *environment*. Environments are used, among other things, to define scope. The two environments with which we are concerned here are the *global* and *base* environments. The workspace the user operates in is the *global* environment, and the standard library functions reside in the *base* environment. In the second statement of Listing 1, a binding is created in the global environment between the symbol `three`, and an integer vector containing the single element '3', as illustrated by Figure 1.

Garbage Collection. R — and CXXR likewise — is *garbage collected*, so objects that can no longer be accessed by the user because they have either been manually deleted or bindings to them have been reassigned to reference other objects, will at some point be destroyed by the garbage collector, which then releases unused memory.

2.3 Making CXXR Provenance-Aware

The principal objective of this work is to enable CXXR to identify the following information of any given object: -

1. The *process* that led to it – the sequence of commands executed;
2. Its *ancestors* – which other objects it depends on;
3. Its *descendants* – which other objects depend on it.

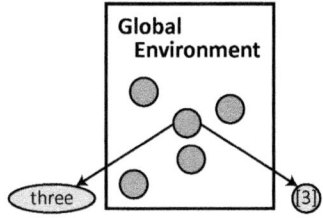

Fig. 1. Bindings exist within environments and connect symbols to values. In this case, the symbol 'three' with a singleton integer vector '3'.

2.4   What Provenance?

The use of the word 'object' in R is unfortunately ambiguous. As mentioned above, what is commonly referred to as an 'object' in R is really a binding in an environment between a symbol and an object representing a value. The R language is *dynamically typed*, which means a variable (i.e. 'object') has no intrinsic type, and simply takes on the type of the object assigned to it. When referring to 'object x', what is often intended is *the value of a binding referred to by symbol* x *in a particular environment*. So what exact provenance are we interested in?

A binding allows an object to exist in an environment and be utilised in expressions, but it also gives an object meaning.

Consider the following R code:

```
> x <- 1:5
> y <- x
```

The first expression creates an integer vector composed of the values 1 to 5, and establishes a binding between the symbol x and the newly created vector. The second expression assigns x to y; or speaking more strictly, it binds y to a copy of x's vector. It's a trivial example, but understanding what happens in a case like this is critical to understanding how provenance is defined in this context.

The object referred to by x — in the strict sense, meaning the integer vector 1,2,3,4,5 — has not changed. All that has happened to it is that a clone of it has been created. To understand where x and y have come from, we need to know what has been bound to them in a particular environment.

Therefore, in order for provenance information to have meaning, it needs to be associated not with an *object*, but with a *binding*.

3   Implementation

The fundamental addition to CXXR required for recording provenance is the introduction of read and write *monitors*, which are attached to environments and get triggered when a binding in that environment is either read from or is created or overwritten.

3.1 Storing

Three C++ containers have been introduced to store various aspects of provenance information.

The `Provenance` class is central to storing provenance for a binding. It is composed of the *timestamp* of when the binding was created; the top-level *expression* that was being evaluated; the *symbol* that is bound; and references to the *parentage* and *children* of the binding.

Binding B1 is a **parent** of binding B2 (and conversely B2 is a **child** of B1) if binding B1 was read in the course of evaluating the top-level expression that gave rise to binding B2. Parentage is represented by the `Parentage` class, which inherits from the C++ Standard Template Library (STL) `std::vector` class, and stores pointers to `Provenance` objects.

A `ProvSet` of provenance objects is used to store references to `Provenance` objects. This collection is an `std::set`, and its members are ordered by time of creation. It is used primarily for storing references to children.

The class collaboration diagram for the relationship between new classes and existing CXXR classes is shown in Figure 2.

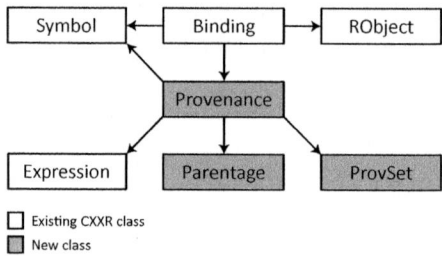

Fig. 2. Class collaboration diagram

3.2 Recording

The mechanism responsible for reading commands from the standard input, evaluating them, and printing the result is known as the Read-Evaluate-Print-Loop (REPL). Provenance for each REPL iteration is recorded according to the following algorithm: -

- Begin with the following empty collections:
  - *Seen* set: Provenance of bindings either read from or written to;
  - *Parentage* list: Provenance of bindings read from (in sequence).
- On read of binding to symbol x:
  - If x is not in the *Seen* set, add it to *Parentage* and *Seen*.
- On write of binding to symbol y:
  - Create a new *Provenance* object comprising:
    * A reference to the current top-level expression;
    * A reference to symbol y;

* A reference to the current *Parentage*;
* The current timestamp;
* An empty set of children;
- Register the new Provenance object as a child of each of its parents, as recorded by the current Parentage list;
- Associate this *Provenance* object with the *Binding* of y;
- Add y to *Seen*.

3.3   Retrieval

In order for the user to be able to interrogate provenance information a couple of new R commands have been introduced. The `provenance(x)` function returns a list detailing the provenance of the current binding of x: the date and time of its creation, the expression immediately responsible for its current state, its symbol, and a list of both its parent and child Provenances.

The `pedigree(x)` function describes the full sequence of commands executed that led to the current binding of x. A full ancestry is collated by recursively looking at each Provenance's parentage starting from x; ordering all ancestors by time of binding creation; and printing their respective expressions, which are by definition relevant and their order chronological.

Listing 2 shows the result of these functions applied to one of the bindings resulting from evaluating the expressions shown in Listing 1. Firstly, the call to the `provenance` function shows information about `nine`, most interestingly that it has two parents: `square`, a function; and `three`, an integer vector of a single element. Secondly, the sequence of commands resulting in the current state of binding `nine` is detailed by the `pedigree()` function.

3.4   Issues

Loops. Although their use is not generally encouraged, loops are present in R. Consider the following loop to compute the sum of integers 1 to 5 and store this in object x:

```
> x <- 0            # Initialise x to zero
> for (n in 1:5)    # n = {1..5}
+   x <- x + n      # Increment x by n
```

There are two top-level expressions being evaluated here: The first initialises x, and the second (split across two lines, as indicated by the continuation prompt beginning with +) is a loop in which n iteratively takes the values from 1 to 5 and gets added to x. During each iteration of the loop, bindings x and n are both read and written.

Our initial implementation did not model this behaviour correctly because for each iteration of the loop, Provenances of bindings to x and n were added multiple times to the current parentage.

A more natural representation of this is, when a binding is read, to only add the associated Provenance to the current Parentage if it has not previously been

Listing 2. Example of provenance inspection functions

```
> provenance(nine)
$command
nine <- square(three)

$symbol
nine

$timestamp
[1] "03/15/2010 03:34:27 PM.241776"

$parents
[1] "square" "three"

$children
NULL

> pedigree(nine)
three <- 1 + 2
square <- function(x) x*x
nine <- square(three)
```

written to or read from during the current top-level expression evaluation. This is the purpose of the *seen* set. In the case of the above loop, this strategy records only one parent for each x and n: the initial binding of x created by the first expression. This is illustrated by Listing 3.

Promises. The R language is capable of *lazy evaluation* of expressions, meaning they are not evaluated unless and until their value is required. The mechanism at the heart of lazy evaluation in R is a *promise*, which comprises an expression to be evaluated, and an environment in which the expression is to be evaluated. As in other programming languages, lazy evaluation prevents expressions from being evaluated unnecessarily in function bodies. R also installs the standard library functions into the base environment as promises that only load the full function definition when it is required. This practice is referred to as *lazy loading*.

When a promise is *forced*, that is to say its expression gets evaluated, its original binding may be succeeded by a new one. According to the algorithm outlined above, this would then get placed in the *seen* set and thus be excluded from appearing in the current parentage. This meant that during the first invocation of a lazily-loaded function, it could not appear as a parent to any object written. Subsequent invocations worked as desired because no additional binding creation precluded attribution of parentage. We handle this by not including in the *seen* set any binding created as a result of forcing a promise.

Source. R's source(input) function reads expressions from file input and evaluates each line in turn. This needs to be handled as a special case as these evaluations fall outside of the main Read-Evaluate-Print-Loop (REPL) mechanism.

Listing 3. Example illustrating how our refined implemention handles loops

```
> x<-0
> for (n in 1:5) x<-x+n
> provenance(x)
$command
for (n in 1:5) x <- x + n

$symbol
x

$timestamp
[1] "11/06/2009 11:39:11.230680"

$parents
[1] "x"
```

For the purposes of provenance collection, we view source as a *white box*, so that objects written are directly attributed to the precise statement within the file that resulted in their creation. This is opposed to a *black box* approach, which would simply describe a resulting object as having been created by a call to *source* with a particular input.

This more precisely describes the sequence of commands responsible for the current state of data, but not how that sequence came to be evaluated, since no record of the input file usage is made.

4   Conclusion

This work demonstrates how it is possible to introduce facilities for provenance awareness into an interactive, command-line driven statistical environment. CXXR has provided a number of challenges, the most novel of which are the necessity of attaching provenance to bindings rather than objects; facilities for lazy loading; and evaluating expressions from a file as opposed to the command line.

4.1   Further Work

Looking forward, one of our priorities is to enable *cross-session provenance tracking*. That is to say, when the user terminates a session, the objects are serialised along with relevant provenance information so the user is then able to restore a session with not only the object data, but also the pedigree of that data. This will require modifying the serialisation formats of CXXR, and draws into question how best the provenance information collected can be mapped to the Open Provenance Model [1].

CXXR is currently only aware of provenance in the global and base environments. Other environments, such as local environments in user defined functions, and those associated with attached data frames, will eventually have their provenances tracked. This will present new challenges, in particular the user interface will need to provide an effective method of allowing the user to inspect provenance in different environments, and displaying the information in an intuitive way.

References

1. Moreau, L., Clifford, B., Freire, J., Gil, Y., Groth, P., Futrelle, J., Kwasnikowska, N., Miles, S., Missier, P., Myers, J., Simmhan, Y., Stephan, E., den Bussche, J.V.: The open provenance model — core specification (v1.1). Future Generation Computer Systems (December 2009)
2. The R Foundation: The R Project for Statistical Computing, http://www.r-project.org
3. Gentleman, R.: Reproducible research: A bioinformatics case study. Statistical Applications in Genetics and Molecular Biology 4(1), Article 2 (2005)
4. Knuth, D.E.: Literate programming. Comput. J. 27(2), 97–111 (1984)
5. Callahan, S.P., Freire, J., Scheidegger, C.E., Silva, C.T., Vo, H.T.: Towards provenance-enabling paraview, pp. 120–127 (2008)
6. Becker, R.A.: A brief history of S. Computational Statistics – Papers Collected on the Occasion of the 25th Conference on Statistical Computing at Schlosz Reisensburg, pp. 81–110 (1994)
7. Becker, R.A., Chambers, J.M.: Auditing of Data Analyses. SIAM Journal on Scientific and Statistical Computing 8, 747–760 (1988)
8. TIBCO Software Inc: Spotfire S+, http://spotfire.tibco.com
9. Runnalls, A.R.: CXXR project, http://www.cs.kent.ac.uk/projects/cxxr

SAF: A Provenance-Tracking Framework for Interoperable Semantic Applications

Evan W. Patton, Dominic Difranzo, and Deborah L. McGuinness

Rensselaer Polytechnic Institute,
110 8th StreetTroy, NY, USA, 12180
{pattoe,difrad,dlm}@cs.rpi.edu

Abstract. This paper describes the foundations of a framework for constructing interoperable semantic applications that support recording of provenance information. The framework uses a client-server infrastructure to control the encoding of application. Provenance records for application components, settings, and data sources are stored as part of the final application file using the Open Provenance Model (OPM) [1]. The application can render events such as setting changes to users so that they can identify when collaborators make changes to the application. We demonstrate how the system can be used to collaborate on a project, identify errors in data sources, and extrapolate insights to other data sets by making changes to the application. Lastly, we outline some key issues related to using asymmetric key encryption for tracking changes in semantic content and how we address them (or not) within this framework.

Keywords: provenance, semantic framework, semantic collaboration.

1   Introduction

As open linked data continues to proliferate on the World Wide Web, better methods of building applications will need to be established to cover the wide range of issues that rise from maintaining and interacting with this complex network of data. Tracking provenance, both of the underlying data sources and the application processes and configurations, will be critical to maintaining integrity of information and knowledge exchange between individuals, and is a key issue that needs to be solved as part of the growth of the Semantic Web. This paper describes the foundations of an application programming framework that provides a possible solution to maintaining application process and configuration integrity when applications are shared across multiple users.

Since collaboration of data, processes, and users is one of the primary drivers for provenance on the Semantic Web, the Semantic Application Framework (SAF) was designed for building applications that pass data between themselves and track when users make changes to individual settings, resulting in changing application behavior.

Use case. A user should be able to instantiate one or more semantically enabled applications within the application workspace, link those applications together to form a workflow, and import one or more datasets to explore using the composite application the user generated.

D.L. McGuinness, J.R. Michaelis, and L. Moreau (Eds.): IPAW 2010, LNCS 6378, pp. 73–77, 2010.
© Springer-Verlag Berlin Heidelberg 2010

Our approach aims to encode provenance data and the application structure and settings using RDF+XML. , The exported file is signed using asymmetric encryption so that other users can verify the integrity of the application when the receive it. Additional modifications by third-party users must be tracked in order to identify when individuals change the behavior of the application.

2 Related Work

The Semantic Application Framework is aimed to bring workflow-style construction to web-based compositions of data and applications. Rather than thinking of applications as segmented processes completely independent of one another, the SAF treats them as individual components that can be linked together by end users, making data and processes of one application available to another, much like existing scientific workflow systems such as Kepler [2]. Unlike Kepler, SAF-based applications work entirely within the Resource Description Framework, so that any applications that understand a common vocabulary can manipulate and annotate the same data.

One of the goals of this work is to wrap existing web applications with SAF so that users can make use of semantics in existing Web 2.0 tools and record provenance of themselves and others interacting with existing data. Similar advances have been made using plugin models, such as the VisTrails system [3], that provides a socket-based method for applications to record events, replay events, and provide a visual representation of the provenance trace to the user. This has been tested in two environments: radiology [3] and 3D modeling [4]. In both scenarios, a plugin for an existing software tool provides records of user interaction by tracking the undo stack and reporting changes to the VisTrails server. Users can then backtrack by simply choosing a point in the generated revision history tree.

3 Demonstration

We will walk through an example of how the Semantic Application Framework allows different users to collaborate and build dynamic web applications together. In this example Alice and Bob, two students in a 20th century history class, want to build a small web application to visualize the major battles in World War II. Alice starts off wanting to visualize the timeline of battles in the European theatre for World War II, so she creates a SPARQL endpoint application instance, a timeline application instance, and links them together. She then identifies a third party SPARQL endpoint where the World War II information is located for the SPARQL app. She can then visualize the data in the timeline app. She selects a particular time frame, saves the application, and emails it to Bob.

Bob likes the timeline but wants to see more information regarding the progress of the Allies through Europe. He believes a map displaying the location of the battles would help show this. He augments his copy of Alice's original application by creating a second SPARQL application to query for location information and a map application instance to plot the points. He combines the output of the timeline application with his copy of the SPARQL application as input for the map application. By changing the timeline's frame, he can now see how the battle points move through the map over time. He saves the application and sends it back to Alice.

Using the provenance data that SAF collects, Alice can observe the changes in the application Bob made and track what datasets, applications, and users have been added since he emailed it. Alice thinks the modifications Bob made results in a powerful visualization of the European theatre, and wants to use the same system to investigate the Pacific theatre. She updates the SPARQL applications to point to the appropriate endpoints and uses the visualization to identify some key conflicts. She then saves the application and sends it to Bob.

Bob opens the file, and can observe the changes Alice has made to the application. He notices that some of the map locations for the battles don't match up, and that the marker for the Battle of Midway seems to be too far east as compared to his textbook. He decides the data source Alice included for map locations may not be trustworthy, and identifies alternative data source to replace it.

4 Implementation

4.1 Architecture and Security Model

The Semantic Application Framework (SAF) uses a client-server architecture combined with X509 certificates over the secure socket layer (SSL) to enforce provenance tracking. These certificates are used for signing the application so that other users can use the server to verify the authenticity of an application description and the provenance associated with that application.

When an application is exported, the server generates an RDF file that describes the application, the provenance of the application, and a pointer to the server that generated the application. This file is then signed using the server's private key, and the signature is included as a triple. Any other SAF-capable server can reverse this process to verify that a third party has not tampered with the RDF file.

4.2 Client-Side Implementation

The client-side portion of SAF is written in JavaScript, and provides a number of high-level classes that provide necessary fundamentals for engineering provenance-tracking applications. Data sources are loaded into the application by way of the RDF parser used by Tabulator [5]. Applications derive from these classes, and use a provided set of function calls to establish mechanisms for both user-application interaction and application-application interaction. Lastly, the implementation is responsible for providing tools for the user to identify changes to the application, which it does by rendering a trace on the right-hand side of the browser window.

Application-application interaction. For applications to interact with one another, they must establish input and output bindings. A binding is a point where RDF data is supplied to or generated by the application. The user can then link applications together by identifying what bindings should be linked together. When data appears on an output binding, all of the applications with input bindings bound to it are sent a notification for them to respond to the presence of this new data.

User-application interaction. Applications must instantiate an instance of a SA-FUserInterface object or derivative that encapsulates an HTML div element where the application can render its interface. The interface renders settings, although the mode of those settings may change from application to application. In the sample application discussed above, for example, the timeline encodes a start date-time and an end date-time through the selection boxes that the user can drag. When a user makes a change to a setting, the application should call the setSettingValue function to register the change for provenance tracking.

5   Summary

In this paper, a framework for the foundation of provenance-supporting semantic applications was discussed with respect to students collaborating on a research project for a class. Such methods, however, can be generalized to any source of semantic data on the World Wide Web. We will present a demonstration using our implementation that shows how applications built within a shared framework can allow users to build collaborative applications and keep attribute and track changes to applications by users.

6   Future Work

There are many elements to this Semantic Application Framework that need to be further developed. The use of asymmetric encryption raises the issue syntactic versus semantic equivalence. The signing mechanism only works if the files are not modified in any way. However, viewing a file then saving it could result in content reordering while maintaining exact semantics. Algorithms must be made more robust to this.

Additionally, SAF does not take advantage of OPM metadata tied to existing data sources. When a user imports a data source, the software does not utilize any existing provenance information stored in that data source. Therefore, it can be difficult to detect when a change to the data source may have occurred that could change the application behavior. Future versions will have to take care to identify OPM information, or follow rdf:seeAlso to look for metadata resources to better capture all of the available provenance information. We will also investigate using another provenance Interlingua – PML – for more completely encoding inferences.

Lastly, the current implementation works on a single client communicating with a single server. One of the planned extensions to the software involves the composition of applications running on separate servers through the use of WSDL [6] interfaces using OWL-S [7] or similar service markup languages.

References

1. Moreau, L., Clifford, B., Freire, J., Gil, Y., Groth, P., Futrelle, J., Kwasnikowska, N., Miles, S., Missier, P., Myers, J., Simmhan, Y., Stephan, E., Van den Bussche, J.: The Open Provenance Model Core Specification (v1.1),
   http://eprints.ecs.soton.ac.uk/18332/1/opm.pdf

2. Altintas, I., Berkley, C., Jaeger, E., Jones, M., Ludascher, B., Mock, S.: Kepler: an extensible system for design and execution of scientific workflows. In: Scientific and Statistical Database Management (2004)
3. Freire, J., Silva, C.T., Callahan, S.P., Santos, E., Scheidegger, C.E., Vo, H.T.: Managing Rapidly-Evolving Scientific Workflows. In: Moreau, L., Foster, I. (eds.) IPAW 2006. LNCS, vol. 4145, Springer, Heidelberg (2006)
4. Callahan, S.P., Freire, J., Scheidegger, C.E., Silva, C.T., Vo, H.T.: A Process-Driven Approach to Provenance-Enabling Existing Applications.
5. Berners-Lee, T., Chen, Y., Chilton, L., Connolly, D., Dhanaraj, R., Hollenbach, J., Lerer, A., Sheets, D.: Tabulator: Exploring and Analyzing linked data on the Semantic Web. In: Proceedings of the 3rd International Semantic Web User Interaction Workshop
6. Christensen, E., Cubera, F., Meredith, G., Weerawarana, S.: Web Services Description Language (WSDL) 1.1., http://www.w3.org/TR/wsdl
7. Martin, D., Paolucci, M., McIlraith, S., Burstein, M., McDermott, D., McGuinness, D.L., Parsia, B., Payne, T., Sabou, M., Solanki, M., Srinivasan, N., Sycara, K.: Bringing Semantics to Web Services: The OWL-S Approach. In: Cardoso, J., Sheth, A.P. (eds.) SWSWPC 2004. LNCS, vol. 3387, Springer, Heidelberg (2005)

Publishing and Consuming Provenance Metadata on the Web of Linked Data

Olaf Hartig[1] and Jun Zhao[2]

[1] Humboldt-Universität zu Berlin
hartig@informatik.hu-berlin.de
[2] University of Oxford
jun.zhao@zoo.ox.ac.uk

Abstract. The World Wide Web evolves into a Web of Data, a huge, globally distributed dataspace that contains a rich body of machine-processable information from a virtually unbound set of providers covering a wide range of topics. However, due to the openness of the Web little is known about who created the data and how. The fact that a large amount of the data on the Web is derived by replication, query processing, modification, or merging raises concerns of information quality. Poor quality data may propagate quickly and contaminate the Web of Data. Provenance information about who created and published the data and how, provides the means for quality assessment. This paper takes a first step towards creating a quality-aware Web of Data: we present approaches to integrate provenance information into the Web of Data and we illustrate how this information can be consumed. In particular, we introduce a vocabulary to describe provenance of Web data as metadata and we discuss possibilities to make such provenance metadata accessible as part of the Web of Data. Furthermore, we describe how this metadata can be queried and consumed to identify outdated information.

1   Introduction

During recent years an increasing number of data providers adopted a set of best practices for publishing and connecting structured data on the Web, leading to the creation of a globally distributed dataspace – the Web of Data [1]. While this dataspace holds an enormous potential, using data from the Web poses questions of information quality and trustworthiness. These questions can be addressed by methods that use provenance information about the data. We present approaches how such provenance information can be made available in the Web of Data.

1.1   The Web of Data

The best practices that enable the creation of the Web of Data are basically four principles that became known as the *Linked Data principles* [2]. These principles require to identify entities with HTTP URIs that can be resolved over the Web into data that describes the identified entity. This data is represented

D.L. McGuinness, J.R. Michaelis, and L. Moreau (Eds.): IPAW 2010, LNCS 6378, pp. 78–90, 2010.
© Springer-Verlag Berlin Heidelberg 2010

using the Resource Description Framework (RDF). RDF is a generic data model that represents data using triples of the form (subject, predicate, object). Each element of such an RDF triple can be a URI or a local identifier for unnamed entities; objects can also be a literal. A set of RDF triples is called an RDF graph. The predicate in an RDF triple specifies how subject and object of the triple are related. These relationships as well as classes of entities are defined in vocabularies. Since vocabulary definitions can be represented as RDF data, vocabularies can also be published as Linked Data; the terms introduced in vocabularies just have to be identified with dereferencable HTTP URIs, enabling a Linked Data aware application to retrieve and utilize the definition of terms used in the currently processed data. Furthermore, the Linked Data principles require that the provided RDF graphs should include RDF links pointing to RDF data from other data sources on the Web. An RDF link is an RDF triple where the subject is a URI in the namespace of one data source and the object is a URI in the namespace of another source. By connecting data from different sources via RDF links a single, globally distributed dataspace emerges.

We call RDF graphs that can be retrieved by resolving URI references *Linked Data object*. Usually, Linked Data objects are part of a *linked dataset* which is a larger RDF graph that contains data about multiple entities. Typical approaches to create a linked dataset are Linked Data interfaces over native RDF stores and wrappers over relational databases or over Web APIs. Some wrappers materialize the created linked dataset, others convert the data on the fly.

1.2   The Need for Provenance Metadata in the Web of Data

The rapid growth and the wide adoption of the Web of Data is driven by the openness of the Web. The same linked dataset can be replicated and hosted at different locations on the Web, under the same or different URI namespaces. Different copies of linked datasets can be created using the same source data. Datasets can be connected by different sets of RDF links, created using different tools or methods and maintained by different publishers. The openness of the Web means that once the data and links are made available on the Web, these different copies of statements about the same set of entities –which might be in conflict and of varied quality– become completely interconnected and intertwined. Finding data about a specific entity may result in multiple URIs identifying this entity and linking to Linked Data objects from different sources. Which of these links should be followed? Which of the Linked Data objects provides more trustworthy or more up-to-date information about the entity? To answer these questions we need not only data about the entity but also information about how the data became available. Hence, we require information about the provenance of Linked Data.

We identify two main sources for obtaining provenance information about data: information recorded by the application that performs the provenance-based evaluation of the data and provenance-related metadata published by the providers of the data. Only a small amount of provenance can be recorded by applications itself if these applications process data consumed from the Web.

Hence, to obtain more complete knowledge these applications rely on provenance metadata from third parties such as the data providers. However, in a recent study [3] we discovered a general lack of provenance-related metadata about data on the Web. Reasons are the lack of suitable vocabularies to describe Web data provenance and a lack of tools to generate and provide provenance metadata.

1.3   Contributions and Structure

To overcome the problem of missing provenance metadata about Linked Data we present approaches to publish such metadata; and we discuss how this metadata can be retrieved and used in applications. To allow for a successful consumption of provenance metadata we conceive it as an absolute necessity that this metadata becomes an integral part of the Web of Data. This is only possible if the publication of this metadata adheres to the same principles that are used for the data itself. Therefore, we present a vocabulary that allows providers of Linked Data to describe the provenance of their data with RDF. Furthermore, we discuss how these RDF based provenance descriptions can be published as Linked Data on the Web. To reduce the required effort for this publication we extended several Linked Data publishing tools, enabling them to automatically provide provenance metadata. The main goal of consuming this provenance metadata is to assess quality and trustworthiness of data retrieved from the Web. Hence, we also discuss how this metadata can be retrieved and we demonstrate its use in an example scenario, identifying outdated information in the Web of Data.

This paper is organized as follows: Section 2 introduces our Provenance Vocabulary; in Section 3 we describe options to publish provenance metadata and we present our provenance extensions to Linked Data publishing tools. Section 4 discusses consuming provenance metadata and describes our experiment of using this metadata to compare the timeliness of data. Section 5 reviews related work and we conclude in Section 6.

2   Describing Provenance of Linked Data

Our aim is to enable Linked Data providers to offer provenance-related metadata in the form of Linked Data. Providing provenance information as Linked Data requires vocabularies that can be used to describe the different aspects of provenance. In this section we introduce our Provenance Vocabulary[1] and illustrate its use by a running example. Furthermore, we describe the design principles applied to the development of the vocabulary.

2.1   Overview of the Provenance Vocabulary

The Provenance Vocabulary is defined as an OWL ontology[2] and it is partitioned into a core ontology and supplementary modules. To avoid making the core

---

[1] http://purl.org/net/provenance/

[2] The introduction in this paper refers to revision 0.5 of the Provenance Vocabulary as is available at http://purl.org/net/provenance/ns-20100710

ontology too complex the modules provide less frequently used concepts and a broad range of specializations of the core concepts. At present we provide three supplementary modules: Types, Files and Integrity Verification.

The development of our vocabulary is motivated by the need to describe the main aspects of provenance of data consumed from the Web. In [3] we identify two main dimensions of provenance that are typical in this context: data creation and data access. Some, more general concepts, such as actors, processes, and artifacts, are relevant in both these dimensions. Consequently, the Provenance Vocabulary consists of three parts: general terms, terms for data creation, and terms for data access.

The **general terms** include classes for the general types of provenance elements: `Actor`, `Execution` and `Artifact`. `Actor` has sub-classes `HumanActor` and `NonHumanActor`; `Artifact` has sub-classes `DataItem` and `File`. Furthermore, the general terms include properties that relate individuals of the general classes with each other (cf. Figure 1, central section): an `Artifact` was `yieldedBy` an `Execution` which may have used further `employedArtifacts`. An `Execution` was `performedAt` a specific time; it was `performedBy` an `Actor`, and it might have had other `involvedActors`. A `NonHumanActor` was `operatedBy` a `HumanActor` and it may have `deployedSoftware`. An `Artifact` might have been `serializedBy` a `File`; a `DataItem` might have been `containedBy` another `DataItem`; and a `DataItem` might have been `precededBy` a former version of this item. Notice, some of these properties are abstract (`yieldedBy`, `involvedActor`, and `employedArtifact`) which means they are not intended to be used to describe instance data but to provide an abstract base for other properties.

With these general terms we can describe the main provenance elements of a running example using RDF data[3]:

```
<> a prv:DataItem ;
    foaf:primaryTopic <http://example.org/gene/0030840> ;
    foaf:topic <> .
<http://example.org /flybase> a void:Dataset ;
                              void:exampleResource <http://example.org/gene/0030840> .
<http://example.org/triplify> a prv:Actor, prv:NonHumanActor ;
                              prv:operatedBy <http://example.org/orga> ;
                              prv:deployedSoftware _:b1 .
_:b1 rdf:type doap:Version ;
     doap:revision "0.5" .
_:b2 rdf:type doap:Project ;
     doap:release _:b1 ;
     doap:homepage <http://triplify.org> .
<http://example.org/orga> a foaf:Organization , prv:Actor, prv:HumanActor .
```

This data describes: a data item which primarily represents data about a gene identified by the URI `http://example.org/gene/0030840`; a linked dataset, identified by `http://example.org/flybase`; and an instance of the Triplify service [4], a Linked Data publishing tool. This instance, identified by the URI `http://example.org/triplify`, is operated by organization `http://example.`

---

[3] We use RDF Turtle notation (http://www.w3.org/TeamSubmission/turtle/); URI namespace prefixes used are: `rdfs` for `http://www.w3.org/2000/01/rdf-schema#`, `prv` for `http://purl.org/net/provenance/ns#`, `prvTypes` for `http://purl.org/net/provenance/types#`, `doap` for `http://usefulinc.com/ns/doap#`, and `void` for `http://rdfs.org/ns/void#`

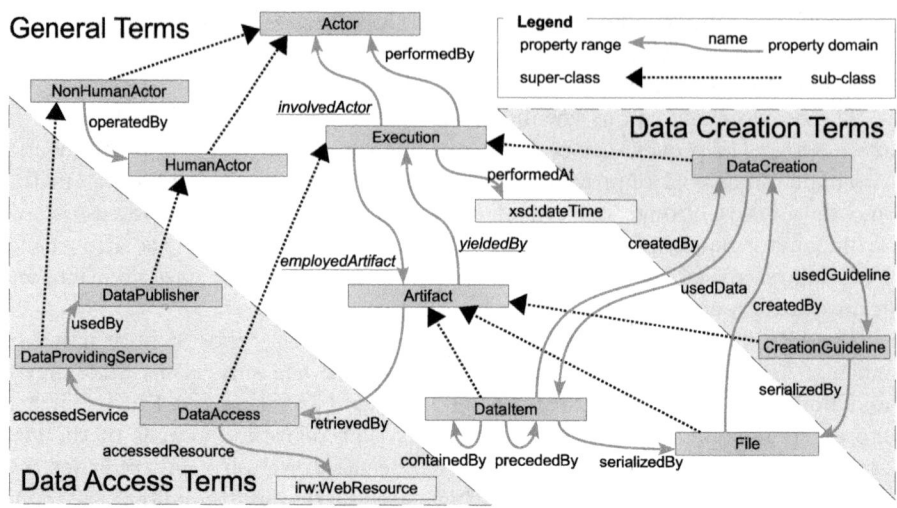

Fig. 1. Classes and properties defined by the Provenance Vocabulary core ontology

org/orga. In our running example, the linked dataset is a Linked Data version of FlyBase, the central genetic database for *Drosophila* research. Triplify publishes this dataset by creating Linked Data objects on the fly, using results of queries to the JDBC endpoint of the relational FlyBase database. The data item in the description represents such a Linked Data.

The terms in the **data creation** dimension (cf. Figure 1, upper-right section) describe how a DataItem has been createdBy a DataCreation. The property usedData refers to source data used during a DataCreation; usedGuideline refers to guidelines such as transformation rules or mapping definitions that were used to guide a DataCreation. Using the data creation terms, the creation in our running example could be described as follows:

```
<http://example.org/triplify> a prvTypes:DataCreatingService .
<> prv:createdBy [
        a prv:DataCreation ;
        prv:performedAt "2010-03-01T12:38:42+00:00"^^xsd:dateTime ;
        prv:performedBy <http://example.org/triplify> ;
        prv:usedData _:x ;
        prv:usedGuideline _:y ] .
_:x a prv:DataItem ;
    foaf:homepage <http://flybase.org/> ;
    prv:createdBy [ a prv:DataCreation ;
                 prv:performedAt "2010-02-19T00:00:00+00:00"^^xsd:dateTime ] .
_:y a prv:CreationGuideline , prvTypes:TriplifyConfiguration ;
    prv:createdBy [ a prv:DataCreation ;
                 prv:performedBy <http://example.org/orga> ] .
```

The example data item was created by a DataCreation execution performed by the Triplify service on Mar.1, 2010. The creation was based on unnamed source data from the Feb.19, 2010 release of the FlyBase database; the creation was guided by an unnamed Triplify configuration created by the organization who operates the Triplify service.

The **data access** dimension (cf. Figure 1, lower-left section) focuses on retrieving data items from the Web. Using the data access terms in provenance descriptions is, in particular, recommended to provide information about the retrieval of source data items and of creation guidelines. The Provenance Vocabulary allows to describe how a `DataItem` has been `retrievedBy` the execution of a `DataAccess`. The retrieved `DataItem` is a Web representation of the `accessedResource`. The `accessedService` is a `DataProvidingService` which was `usedBy` the `DataPublisher`; furthermore each `DataProvidingService` is usually `operatedBy` a `HumanActor`. In our running example, the Triplify service retrieved the FlyBase relational data that was used to create the example Linked Data object from the FlyBase JDBC endpoint:

```
_:x prv:retrievedBy [
           a prv:DataAccess ;
           prv:accessedService [ a prv:DataProvidingService , prvTypes:JDBCService ;
                              foaf:homepage <http://flybase.org/> ] ;
           prv:performedAt "2010-03-01T12:38:42+00:00"^^xsd:dateTime ;
           prv:performedBy <http://example.org/triplify> ] ] .
```

Notice, since the Linked Data object was created on the fly, the execution time of the data access described is equal to the creation time of the object.

To allow for a wide range of applications the vocabulary does not prescribe a specific granularity by which provenance information has to be described. Hence, the classes in the core ontology are quite general. For instance, a `DataItem` could a single RDF triple or it could be a specific RDF graph that represents a Linked Data object as in the example. More specific specializations of the general classes are provided with the types module. However, while our vocabulary, including its modules, provides a basic framework to describe the provenance of data from the Web it does not aim to support the description of every aspect and detail of provenance. In particular, to provide a detailed description of a specific data creation we propose to use more specialized vocabularies and associate these descriptions with the corresponding `DataCreation` entity. In the documentation for our vocabulary we propose some examples of how other vocabularies can be used together with the Provenance Vocabulary.

2.2   Design Principles of the Provenance Vocabulary

We develop the Provenance Vocabulary with understandability and usability in mind. For this reason we apply a consistent scheme for property names, using the simple past form of a verb followed by a class name or the preposition *by*. Furthermore, we omit inverse properties to avoid interoperability problems in Linked Data consuming systems that do not apply OWL-DL based reasoning in many cases.

Some of the properties in our vocabulary are shortcuts, allowing for a more convenient use. For instance, many data creations are based on the creation of a file that serializes the created data item. Since it is more convenient to describe these file-based data creations implicitly by referring to the creation of the file instead of the data item itself, our vocabulary provides additional terms for these file-based descriptions. Hence, it is also possible that a `File` has been `createdBy` a `DataCreation`; this implies the `DataItem` that was `serializedBy` the File was also created by the same DataCreation. The vocabulary definition includes rules to enable reasoners to infer such kind of implications. Similarily, the properties usedGuidelineFile and usedDataFile introduced in the Files module are alternatives to usedGuideline and usedData, respectively.

Another good practice for Linked Data vocabularies is the interlinking of related terms between vocabulary definitions. Such "schema-level links" improve the degree to which published data is self-describing. The Provenance Vocabulary adheres to this practice. For instance, the Actor class is defined to be equivalent to the Agent class in the FOAF vocabulary. This relationship enables a FOAF-aware application to infer actors in a provenance description are FOAF agents and to deal with them accordingly, e.g., in visualizations.

3 Publishing Provenance Descriptions about Linked Data

To achieve the goal of integrating provenance of Linked Data into the Web of Data it is not only necessary to provide a vocabulary but also to actually make the provenance descriptions available to Linked Data based applications. Therefore, we provide recommendation for publishing provenance-related metadata as Linked Data in this section. These recommendations should be understood as a proposal while best practices still have to emerge.

The primary location of metadata about a linked dataset is its voiD description, that is, an RDF document on the Web which describes the dataset based on the Vocabulary of Interlinked Datasets (voiD) [5]. A voiD description should comprise general provenance information for the described dataset. In addition to general provenance information about a linked dataset we suggest to provide more detailed information with each access to the dataset. There are basically three options to provide access to a linked dataset on the Web: Linked Data objects, RDF dumps, and SPARQL endpoints. While these options do not exclude each other they require the application of different provenance publication approaches as we discuss in the remainder of this section.

3.1   Adding Provenance to Linked Data Objects

The Linked Data object that can be retrieved by resolving the HTTP URI for an entity is an RDF graph that –according to the Linked Data principles– contains data about the entity identified by the URI. We propose that these Linked Data objects additionally contain provenance-related metadata (i.e. additional RDF triples) about themselves and about the contained RDF triples. Provenance of specific RDF triples could be described using RDF reification. The provenance of the whole Linked Data object should be expressed as illustrated by our running example: the provenance metadata presented in Section 2.1) describes a representation of a Linked Data object. To accelerate the adoption of the practice to augment Linked Data objects with (provenance) metadata we extended several, widely used Linked Data publishing tools as we describe in Section 3.4.

If possible, the provided provenance description should also comprise detailed provenance information about source data and creation guidelines that have been used during the creation of the Linked Data object. Furthermore, the provenance description should cover the linked dataset of the Linked Data object. However, instead of augmenting the object itself with provenance metadata about its dataset we propose to link to a voiD description using an HTTP URI that identifies the dataset (as illustrated in the running example).

3.2   Adding Provenance to RDF Dumps

A linked dataset can be provided as an RDF dump, that is, an RDF document which contains the whole linked dataset. Usually, an RDF dump represents a linked dataset as a single RDF graph. We propose to augment this graph with provenance metadata about itself, similar to the practice proposed in the previous section for Linked Data objects. However, in this case the added provenance metadata describes the provenance of the whole dataset and, thus, is likely to be similar to the information provided with a voiD description for the dataset. In addition to this information the metadata should also describe the provenance of the RDF dump itself.

It is also possible to serialize a linked dataset as a collection of Named Graphs [6], i.e. RDF graphs named with a URI. In this case each of these graphs could contain provenance metadata about itself. Alternatively, the collection of Named Graphs could contain an additional Named Graph that describes the provenance of the other graphs.

3.3   Providing Provenance Information at SPARQL Endpoints

A third possibility to provide access to a linked dataset is via a SPARQL endpoint, i.e., a query service that executes SPARQL queries over the dataset. SPARQL is the query language for RDF data. We propose to make provenance metadata a part of the dataset published via such a SPARQL endpoint so that queries can ask for provenance information. Furthermore, a provenance-enhanced SPARQL query engine could also add provenance metadata automatically to query results. SPARQL defines four different query result forms: select, construct, describe, and ask. The result of construct and describe queries is an RDF graph. Similar to the practice proposed for Linked Data objects, a provenance-enhanced SPARQL query engine could add provenance metadata to these result graphs. The result of a select query is a set of variable bindings that can be represented as a table; ask queries result in a boolean value. To exchange these types of results over the Web, SPARQL endpoints usually serialize the results using a standard XML format or a JSON format. It requires future work to define a possibility how these serializations can be extended with provenance descriptions.

3.4   Metadata Extensions that Simplify the Publication

A large-scale augmentation of the Web of Data with provenance metadata can only be achieved when the effort for creation and for publication is kept to a minimum. For this reason, we extended several tools that are widely used for publishing Linked Data on the Web, including Triplify, Pubby[4] and D2R server[5], with a metadata component [7]. These new components automatically generate and serve provenance metadata with Linked Data objects as proposed in Section 3.1. Due to our extensions data publishers can easily enrich their data with provenance metadata by simply configuring a few parameters, such as the name and the URI identifying the publisher or the URI of the dataset. Hence, with data providers upgrading their Linked Data servers to the latest release of these tools we can expect a significant increase in the amount of provenance information added to the Web of Data.

4   Consuming Provenance from the Web of Data

Consuming provenance information from the Web of Data includes retrieving provenance metadata from the Web and making use of it. In this section, we present approaches to query for provenance metadata and we demonstrate its use in an example scenario, identifying outdated information in the Web of Data.

4.1   Querying for Provenance Metadata

A simple approach to query for provenance requires that provenance metadata is accessible through the SPARQL endpoints for linked datasets as we propose in Section 3.3. This practice enables applications to issue queries as in the following example:

Example 1. SPARQL query (prefix declarations omitted) that asks for the creation time of the source data used to create a linked dataset.

```
SELECT ?creation_time WHERE {
  <http://example.org/dataset> prv:createdBy [ prv:usedData ?source_data ] .
  ?source_data prv:createdBy [ prv:performedAt ?creation_time ] }
```

If the provenance metadata is provided as a part of Linked Data objects (cf. Section 3.1) and the metadata is properly interlinked (i.e. it includes links to voiD descriptions etc.) then provenance can be queried using the link traversal based query execution paradigm [8] as implemented in SQUIN[6]. This query approach evaluates SPARQL queries as in Example 2 over a dataset that is continuously augmented with Linked Data objects from the Web. These objects are discovered by following RDF links that correspond to partial query results.

Example 2. SPARQL query asking for the creation time of the source data used to create a Linked Data object about a specific gene.

```
SELECT ?creation_time WHERE {
  ?data foaf:primaryTopic <http://example.org/gene/0030840> .
      prv:createdBy [ prv:usedData ?source_data ] .
  ?source_data prv:createdBy [ prv:performedAt ?creation_time ] }
```

In the remainder of this section we present an example scenario in which we retrieve provenance information using SQUIN to execute queries as in Example 2.

---

[4] http://www4.wiwiss.fu-berlin.de/pubby/
[5] http://www4.wiwiss.fu-berlin.de/bizer/d2r-server/
[6] http://squin.org

4.2   The Example Scenario

Our experiment scenario is based on two databases that provide complementary knowledge for *Drosophila* genetic research: FlyBase and another relational database, FlyTED, which is a specialized gene expression image repository for *Drosophila* testis. Using these databases we create three linked datasets and publish their provenance information using our Provenance Vocabulary and voiD.

Our first dataset, D_{FB}, is created by transforming a subset of FlyBase on-the-fly using Triplify as in our running example. The other two datasets, D_{FT1} and D_{FT2}, are created by transforming two different snapshots of FlyTED into RDF and publishing these RDF dumps as Linked Data using Pubby.

While the provenance of Linked Data objects about genes from D_{FB} corresponds to our running example, Figure 2 illustrates the provenance of a Linked Data object gd_j about a gene from D_{FT1} or D_{FT2}. Each gd_j is created by a Pubby instance that accesses the SPARQL endpoint for the corresponding FlyTED linked dataset; this endpoint executes queries over the RDF dump created by transforming the corresponding FlyTED database snapshot.

Our metadata extensions to Triplify and Pubby (cf. Section 3.4) provide provenance metadata for all the Linked Data objects from the three datasets. Additionally, we, manually, create voiD descriptions with provenance metadata for these datasets and publish these descriptions as Linked Data on the Web.

For biologists interested in a more complete knowledge about genes it is useful to connect FlyBase and FlyTED. We may create `owl:sameAs` links between genes from D_{FB} and those in D_{FT1} and D_{FT2}. However, without additional context information a search for FlyTED gene entities that are `owl:sameAs` to a FlyBase gene will return all matching FlyTED genes no matter when their data was created. Some of these data mappings might no longer be correct because gene names are changed regularly in biological databases, whenever additional knowledge about genes and their functions becomes available. The goal of our scenario is to identify those genes from D_{FB} that are mapped to multiple genes from D_{FTn} and to analyze whether some of the mappings point to outdated information.

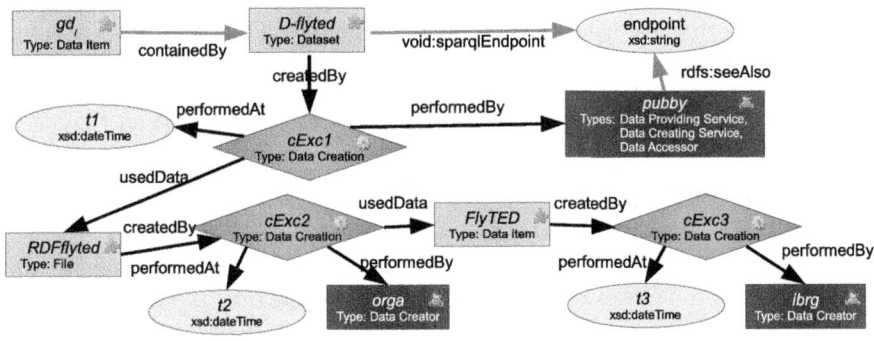

Fig. 2. Illustration of the creation process of a FlyTED gene data object

4.3   Comparing the Timeliness

Each FlyTED gd_i is part of the linked dataset D_{FT1} or D_{FT2}. Since the creation of these Linked Data objects is performed by the Pubby instance accessing the SPARQL endpoints, the timeliness of these objects depends on the freshness of the data used for creating the endpoint, i.e., the RDF dumps. The timeliness of these dumps depends on the timeliness of the original FlyTED database snapshots. In order to identify which gene data is more outdated we need to compare their timeliness. Because all gd_i are generated on the fly by Pubby, they all have the same creation time. Hence, we need to compare the creation time of their source data, the FlyTED database snapshots.

A SPARQL query similar to the query in Example 2 can be used to retrieve this information. For example, the two FlyTED gene entities $CG12993$ and p-cup both have an `owl:sameAs` relationship to the same gene in FlyBase. Using link traversal based query execution we search for the creation time of the source data used to create data about these genes. The query result shows that the creation time of the source data about $CG12993$ is earlier than p-cup because the Linked Data object $gd_{CG12993}$ about $CG12993$ is derived from a gene record from an older version of FlyTED and therefore it is less fresh than $gd_{\text{p-cup}}$ for p-cup. Based on these results, we conclude that $gd_{CG12993}$ is more outdated than $gd_{\text{p-cup}}$. In fact, the gene name CG12993 is no longer used by the community and is now replaced by p-cup. The Linked Data object $gd_{CG12993}$ might contain outdated and misleading information about this p-cup gene. Linked Data users should choose the more up-to-date gene URI if they would like to access more accurate knowledge.

Based on an analysis of all the gene entities from D_{FT1} and D_{FT2} we found that 9 different FlyBase genes are mapped to more than one FlyTED genes. For each of these FlyBase genes we compared the timeliness of the data about the FlyTED genes mapped to the FlyBase gene. This comparison revealed that all these FlyBase genes are linked to at least one outdated FlyTED gene URI, all of which have been replaced in the more up-to-date FlyTED linked dataset.

This small experiment is just one example which shows how crucial it is to assess the timeliness of Linked Data objects. Without this contextual information, users of Linked Data face the danger of using poor quality data that might contain wrong information without even being aware of it. Our experiment is a very first step of demonstrating the importance of integrating provenance in the Web of Data and the importance of provenance metadata for reducing potential errors in Linked Data applications and, thus, enhancing the trust in Linked Data.

5   Related Work

Representing and analyzing provenance is a topic of research since many years [9]. While many approaches exist for representing provenance of data creation [10,11], none of these explicitly addresses the characteristics of data access, e.g., the retrieval of data from the Web. Although this type of provenance is not always required in self-contained systems such as a DBMS or a workflow management system, it needs be captured for the Web of Linked Data. The Provenance Vocabulary presented in this paper allows to describe both aspects, data creation and data access.

Many related work on provenance for the Web have emerged in the context of Semantic Web research. Harth et al. [12] propose a "social dimension to associate provenance with the originator (typically a person) of a given piece of information". Our Provenance Vocabulary encourages to represent human actors and their relation to data items.

Ding et al. [13] understand the provenance of RDF data as the RDF graphs of which parts of an analyzed RDF graph has been derived from. The authors argue that tracking complete RDF graphs is too coarse-grained and that a representation on the level of single RDF statements is unsuitable, too. Hence, Ding et al. introduce RDF molecules as the finest sub-graphs to decompose an RDF graph. Our vocabulary models data items on an abstract level. They can represent data of any level of granularity: RDF graphs, statements, or RDF molecules.

Da Silva et al. use the term knowledge provenance to refer to information about the origin of knowledge and about the reasoning processes used to produce answers [14]. In [15] the authors present the Proof Markup Language to describe justifications for results of an answering engine or a reasoner. These justifications may describe the execution of a specific type of data creation process modeled by our Provenance Vocabulary.

Moreau et al. propose the Open Provenance Model (OPM) which aims to provide a community-compliant, general-purpose provenance model [16]. OPM contains many concepts similar to the general terms in our vocabulary. However, in contrast to the domain-independent approach of OPM our vocabulary explicity addresses the provenance of Linked Data published on the Web. Hence, our vocabulary can be defined as an OPM profile, created for the Web of Data application domain. Such an alignment with OPM will help us to ground our vocabulary with a community data model and, thus, is part of our future work.

Similarily to OPM, Sahoo et al. propose Provenir [17], an upper-level provenance ontology that defines abstract classes and properties which can be refined for a specific domain. An alignment of the Provenance Vocabulary with Provenir is also part of our future work.

6 Conclusion

This paper presents a Provenance Vocabulary that assists providers of Linked Data to describe the provenance of their data using RDF. We explain how this vocabulary can be used to describe data items of different granularity and we propose approaches how metadata with such provenance descriptions can become an integral part of the Web of Data. Furthermore, we discuss how such provenance metadata can be consumed in order to support an example scenario of identifying outdated information from the Web of Data. An alignment with other existing provenance models and vocabularies is part of our future work. We will also continue our investigation of using provenance to support the evaluation of information quality.

References

1. Bizer, C., Heath, T., Berners-Lee, T.: Linked Data - The Story So Far. In: Int. Journal on Semantic Web and Information Systems. Special Issue on Linked Data (2009)
2. Berners-Lee, T.: Design issues: Linked data, http://www.w3.org/DesignIssues/LinkedData.html (retrieved March 19 2010)
3. Hartig, O.: Provenance Information in the Web of Data. In: Proceedings of the Linked Data on the Web Workshop (LDOW) at WWW (2009)
4. Auer, S., Dietzold, S., Lehmann, J., Hellmann, S., Aumueller, D.: Triplify: Lightweight linked data publication from relational databases. In: Proceedings of the 18th International Conference on World Wide Web, WWW (2009)
5. Alexander, K., Cyganiak, R., Hausenblas, M., Zhao, J.: Describing linked datasets. In: Proceedings of the Linked Data on the Web Workshop (LDOW) at WWW (2009)
6. Carroll, J.J., Bizer, C., Hayes, P., Stickler, P.: Named graphs, provenance and trust. In: Proceedings of the 14th International World Wide Web Conference, WWW (2005)
7. Hartig, O., Zhao, J., Mühleisen, H.: Automatic integration of metadata into the web of linked data. In: Proceedings of the Demo Session at the 2nd Workshop on Trust and Privacy on the Social and Semantic Web (SPOT) at ESWC (2010)
8. Hartig, O., Bizer, C., Freytag, J.C.: Executing SPARQL queries over the web of linked data. In: Bernstein, A., Karger, D.R., Heath, T., Feigenbaum, L., Maynard, D., Motta, E., Thirunarayan, K. (eds.) ISWC 2009. LNCS, vol. 5823, Springer, Heidelberg (2009)
9. Bose, R., Frew, J.: Lineage retrieval for scientific data processing: A survey. ACM Computing Surveys 37(1) (2005)
10. Simmhan, Y., Plale, B., Gannon, D.: A Survey of Data Provenance in e-Science. SIGMOD Record 34(3) (2005)
11. Tan, W.C.: Provenance in Databases: Past, Current, and Future. IEEE Data Engineering Bulletin 30(4) (2007)
12. Harth, A., Polleres, A., Decker, S.: Towards a Social Provenance Model for the Web. In: Proceedings of the Workshop on Principles of Provenance (2007)
13. Ding, L., Finin, T., Peng, Y., da Silva, P.P., McGuinness, D.L.: Tracking RDF Graph Provenance using RDF Molecules. Technical Report TR-CS-05-06, UMBC (2005)
14. da Silva, P.P., McGuinness, D.L., McCool, R.: Knowledge Provenance Infrastructure. Data Engineering Bulletin 26(4) (2003)
15. da Silva, P.P., McGuinness, D.L., Fikes, R.: A Proof Markup Language for Semantic Web Services. Information Systems 31(4-5) (2006)
16. Moreau, L., Clifford, B., Freire, J., Futrelle, J., Gil, Y., Groth, P., Kwasnikowska, N., Miles, S., Missier, P., Myers, J., Plale, B., Simmhan, Y., Stephan, E., den Bussche, J.V.: The open provenance model core specification (v1.1). In: Future Generation Computer Systems (in Press 2010) (accepted Manuscript)
17. Sahoo, S., Thomas, C., Sheth, A., York, W., Tartir, S.: Knowledge modeling and its application in life sciences: a tale of two ontologies. In: Proceedings of the 15th International Conference on World Wide Web, WWW (2006)

POMELo: A PML Online Editor

Alvaro Graves

Tetherless World Constellation
Department of Cognitive Sciences
Rensselaer Polytechnic Institute
Troy, NY 12180
gravea3@rpi.edu

Abstract. This paper introduces POMELo, a simple, web-based PML (Proof Markup Language) editor. The objective of POMELo is to allow users to create, edit, validate and export provenance information in the form of PML documents. This application was developed with provenance novices in mind, making it usable in various settings, from educational to scientific. Since this is a web-based application, users do not need to install or run any software aside from a normal web browser, which simplifies its adoption and makes it more attractive for inexperienced users.

Keywords: PML, Web Application, Graphical Editor, Validation.

1 Introduction

There is an increasing acknowledgement of the importance of provenance information in different areas, from Semantic Web and eScience[15] to Ancient Art market[11]. Currently, there are powerful tools[4][12] that allow experts to edit and manage complex graphs describing provenance information. However, we see a need for simpler tools that can be used for educational purposes as well as being used by experts. Furthermore, most of the currently available applications related to provenance require installation of special software and libraries, making it difficult for novice users to create, visualize, edit and export provenance data.

In the past few years, application development for the web has become widespread. Nowadays, it is possible to write documents, read emails and edit spreadsheets using web applications. Web applications have multiple benefits: On one hand, the Web provides an open, interoperable platform where users can access resources from different locations. Moreover, these "web apps" usually do not require the user to install third party software, simplifying their adoption. These factors inspired the development of POMELo: A simple application that allow users to view and edit provenance information without the need for writing PML directly or installing software.

The rest of this paper is organized as follows: Section 2 provides a brief description of PML; Section 3 presents the related work; Section 4 discusses available

D.L. McGuinness, J.R. Michaelis, and L. Moreau (Eds.): IPAW 2010, LNCS 6378, pp. 91–97, 2010.

features in POMELo; Section 5 gives examples of situations where POMELo can be useful; Section 6 describe future work and potential extension for POMELo; Finally, Section 7 shows the conclusions.

2   Proof Markup Language (PML)

The Proof Markup Language[13] is an interlingua designed for sharing explanations and representing provenance knowledge over the Web. PML was designed modularly through three different ontologies.

2.1   PML-P: Provenance

The first component in PML is the provenance ontology, which aims to provide a set of primitives to represent provenance information. Thus it is possible to use PML-P for describing pieces of information, as well as their sources, languages, and formats in which they are expressed.

2.2   PML-J: Justification

The justification component provides primitives for explaining the steps taken in a process to draw a conclusion. PML-J allows users to express inference steps, assumptions, assertions, as well as sets of rules and engines used to obtain a specific conclusion.

2.3   PML-T: Trust

The Trust ontology allows users to indicate their trust in other users as well as their beliefs in assertions. This information can be expressed using numerical values (usually between 0 and 1). Is important to note that the method or algorithm for establishing a specific value is left to the user.

3   Related Work

Over the years, several initiatives have appeared to visualize and deal with provenance information. The Inference Web Browser (IWBrowser)[3] is a web-based tool for visualizing PML documents. This tool allows users to visualize PML proofs and show the results in english or in a graphical tree structure. *Provenance Explorer*[1] is another tool focused on visualizing provenance information expressed in OWL[14] (using an extension of ABC ontology[10]) and SWRL[8] and supports inference using Algernon[2] as an inference engine. *VisTrails* was developed by Freire et al.[7] and allows users to keep track of provenance information from workflows as well as data, and visualize it graphically. *VisTrails* was developed with scientists as the target audience and provides a rich infrastructure, including a workflow creator, a repository and a programming API. *Probe-It!*[4] is a Java-based application for visualizing PML documents obtained from inference engines. Users can see the justification behind a certain conclusion in a graphical way as well as explore data through different views (results, justification, provenance).

4   Features of POMELo

POMELo was based on "RDF Editor"[9] and the ARC2 library[16] for parsing RDF/XML. Implementation of POMELo was done using PHP, Javascript, AJAX and JQuery. A screenshot of POMELo can be seen in Figure 2. We now describe the most important features available in POMELo.

Graphical Visualization: One of the main features in POMELo is the use of graphical visualization to manage PML: Each entity is shown as a rectangle (green for resources and blank nodes, blue for literals) while the predicates are described as labeled edges. These nodes and edges can be rearranged for better display. Finally, hovering the mouse over a resource, it is possible to obtain its type (when available). An example can be seen in Figure 1.

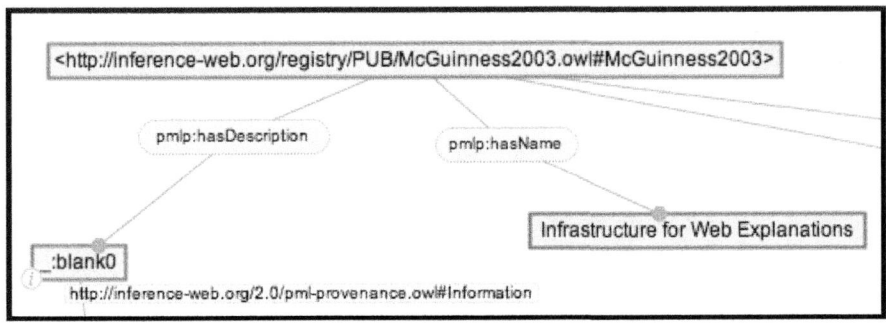

Fig. 1. Graphical representation of PML

Editing: Users can edit and curate provenance data. They can add Information Sources, Agents, Inference steps and other entities from PML based on four menus available on the left panel (one for each component of PML plus Literals). They can include them as resources or blank nodes. It is also possible to link different resources using predicates available from PML-P (PML's provenance ontology), PML-J (justification ontology) and PML-T (trust ontology).

Import and Export: POMELo allow users to import PML documents in the RDF/XML format. Users need to provide the URL where the PML document is located and POMELo will retrieve, parse and display it graphically. In the same way, it is possible to export the current PML model into RDF/XML.

Validation: POMELo can also validate PML graphs against the Inference Web PML Validation Service[5]. This service allows users to verify if their PML document is valid by making 10 evaluations, from loading of the data to issues related to typing of the resources. The validations may return warnings, errors or fatal errors. In turn, the user can make modifications to their model and perform follow-up validation. In this way, users can create valid PML documents using an integrated platform.

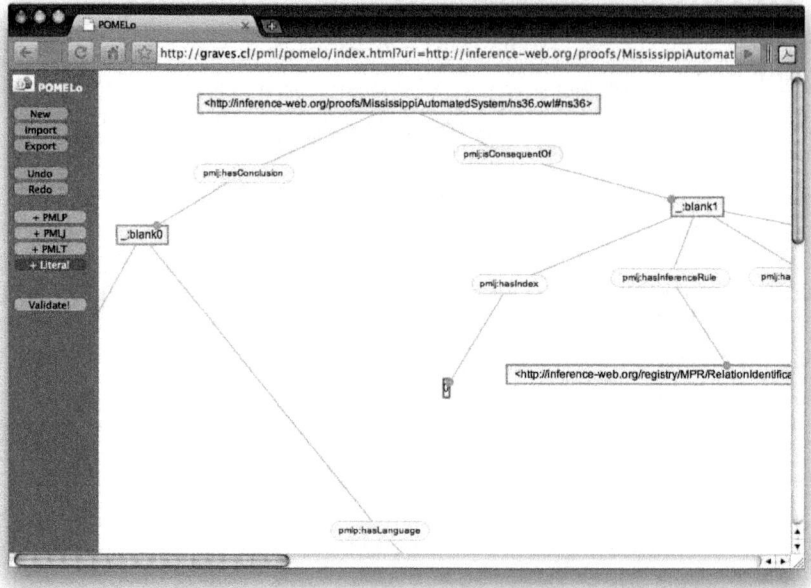

Fig. 2. Example of a PML document loaded into POMELo

5   Examples of Use

POMELo can be used for several purposes: First, it can help with curating small portions of a bigger provenance model, where a user may not be interested in the whole model but only a small part. He may load that portion into POMELo, study it, make edits and finally export it again.

It is also possible to use POMELo for educational purposes. People interested in studying provenance and in particular PML may not want to install additional software. To use POMELo, only a web browser and Internet connection is required.

5.1   Example 1: Visualizing PML

Professor A is giving a lecture on using provenance (in particular on how to express provenance information using PML). For that purpose, Professor A prepared several examples as documents in RDF/XML format available on the Web. In turn, students can use POMELo to visualize these documents.

5.2   Example 2: Editing and Validating PML

A scientist B receives a URI from scientist C containing provenance information about an experiment in PML. B opens the document using POMELo for visualizing it. After a few minutes studying it, she decides to add more information to the PML graph (for example, adding a new antecedent to justify the default value in a sensor). In order to confirm that she has not made any mistake editing the provenance information, B validates the current PML graph using the "Validate!" button. POMELo indicates that the PML information is valid, but also report a warning because of not using a more specific type for the Information node. Figure 3 shows an example of a successful validation in POMELo. Finally she exports her work in RDF/XML format.

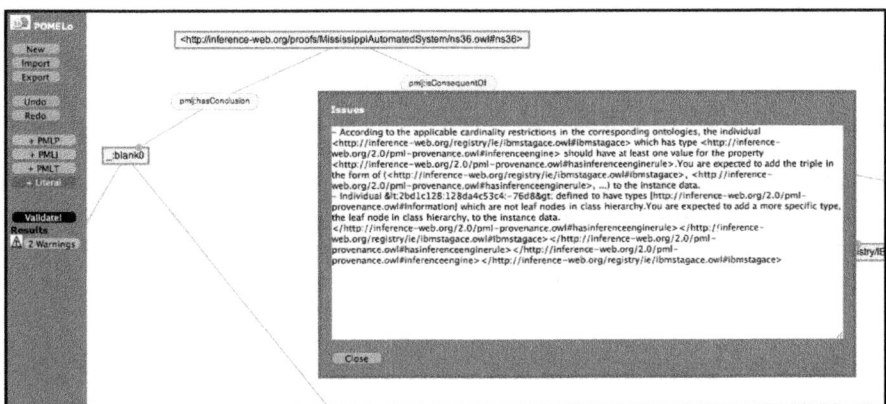

Fig. 3. POMELo validates a PML document using the PML validation service. The dialog box indicates warnings related to this document.

6   Future Work

There are several improvements that can be made to POMELo: First, the default layout was developed based on the assumption that trees will be the most likely structure found in PML documents (i.e., a documents describes the provenance of one thing). While this is useful, we have found certain situations where PML documents refers to several entities, making the tree layout inappropriate. To solve this, we are already working in integrating graphviz[6] as a "layout manager" that can coordinate how POMELo should render the nodes depending on the graph structure of the PML document. Another interesting feature would be to cluster specific parts of the PML document and visualize them as one node. Due the nature of PML, the use of blank nodes and other different levels intermediate types of nodes may overload the screen (e.g., when describing a list of authors). Thus, it would be desirable to allow users to group several recurrent sub-structures in a PML document into one node, alleviating from an overload of nodes on the screen.

Another direction we have considered is to allow users to collaboratively visualize and edit a PML document: This could make easier for students to understand provenance and in particular to use PML. Also, the ability for exporting in different formats and publishing documents from POMELo, would add value from the educational perspective as well as from the professional point of view. Finally, the possibility of uploading PML documents directly from POMELo to a central repository would make the whole process of creating, editing and publishing provenance information more fluid and easy for users.

7   Conclusions

In this paper, we presented POMELo, a web application that allows users to work with provenance information using PML. The aim of this application is to allow users to visualize, modify and export provenance information in PML. One of the goals of POMELo is to serve as a tool that can be adopted by expert as well as novice users. Since it is based on the Web, POMELo does not need special libraries, but only a web browser and an Internet connection. We show the functionalities of POMELo, including its integration with PML Validator that allow users to create, verify and correct their model in a simple, unified interface. A demo of POMELo can be seen at `http://graves.cl/pml/pomelo`.

Acknowledgement

Thanks to James Michaelis for helping in the revision of this paper.

References

1. Cheung, K., Hunter, J.: Provenance Explorer–Customized Provenance Views Using Semantic Inferencing. In: Cruz, I., Decker, S., Allemang, D., Preist, C., Schwabe, D., Mika, P., Uschold, M., Aroyo, L.M. (eds.) ISWC 2006. LNCS, vol. 4273, pp. 215–227. Springer, Heidelberg (2006)
2. Crawford, J.M., Kuipers, B.J.: Algernona tractable system for knowledge-representation. ACM SIGART Bulletin 2(3), 44 (1991)
3. Da Silva, P., Sutcliffe, G., Chang, C., Ding, L., Del Rio, N., McGuinness, D.: Presenting TSTP proofs with inference web tools. In: CEUR Workshop Proceedings, Citeseer, vol. 373, pp. 81–93.
4. Del Rio, N., da Silva, P.: Probe-it! visualization support for provenance. In: Bebis, G., Boyle, R., Parvin, B., Koracin, D., Paragios, N., Tanveer, S.-M., Ju, T., Liu, Z., Coquillart, S., Cruz-Neira, C., Müller, T., Malzbender, T. (eds.) ISVC 2007, Part II. LNCS, vol. 4842, pp. 732–741. Springer, Heidelberg (2007)
5. Ding, L., Tao, J., McGuinness, D.: An initial investigation on evaluating semantic web instance data (2008)
6. Ellson, J., Gansner, E., Koutsofios, L., North, S., Woodhull, G.: Graphviz, open source graph drawing tools. In: Graph Drawing, pp. 594–597. Springer, Heidelberg (2001)
7. Freire, J., Silva, C., Callahan, S., Santos, E., Scheidegger, C., Vo, H.: Managing rapidly-evolving scientific workflows. In: Provenance and Annotation of Data, pp. 10–18

8. Horrocks, I., Patel-Schneider, P., Boley, H., Tabet, S., Grosof, B., Dean, M.: SWRL: A semantic web rule language combining OWL and RuleML. W3C Member submission 21 (2004)

9. Krsulovic, E.: Rdf editor (2009), http://code.google.com/p/tesis-e/

10. Lagoze, C., Hunter, J.: The ABC ontology and model. Journal of Digital Information 2(2), 77 (2001)

11. Levine, J.: et al. The importance of provenance documentation in the market for ancient art and artifacts: The future of the market depend on documenting the past. DePaul J. Art Tech. & Intell. Prop. L. 19, 219–421 (2009)

12. McGuinness, D., da Silva, P., Chang, C.: IWBase: Provenance metadata infrastructure for explaining and trusting answers from the web. Technical report, Citeseer

13. McGuinness, D., Ding, L., da Silva, P., Chang, C.: PML 2: A modular explanation interlingua. In: Proceedings of AAAI, vol. 7 (2007)

14. McGuinness, D., Van Harmelen, F., et al.: OWL web ontology language overview. W3C recommendation, February10 (2004)

15. Miles, S., Groth, P., Deelman, E., Vahi, K., Mehta, G., Moreau, L.: Provenance: The bridge between experiments and data. Computing in Science and Engineering 10(3), 38 (2008)

16. Nowack, B.: Arc, rdf classes for php (2006), http://arc.semsol.org/

Capturing Provenance in the Wild

M. David Allen, Adriane Chapman, Barbara Blaustein, and Len Seligman

The MITRE Corporation
{dmallen,achapman,bblaustein,seligman}@mitre.org

Abstract. All current provenance systems are "closed world" systems; provenance is collected within the confines of a well understood, pre-planned system. However, when users compose services from heterogeneous systems and organizations to form a new application, it is impossible to track the provenance in the new system using currently available work. In this work, we describe the ability to compose multiple provenance-unaware services in an "open world" system and still collect provenance information about their execution. Our approach is implemented using the PLUS provenance system and the open source MULE Enterprise Service Bus. Our evaluations show that this approach is scalable and has minimal overhead.

Keywords: provenance, capture, distributed systems.

1 The Challenge of "Open World" Provenance Capture

Provenance, or the history of information, has garnered interest in government, commercial and scientific circles. However, provenance systems will only become ubiquitous when it can be easily captured in the heterogeneous, distributed environments typical of most real-world enterprises.

In contrast to this need, current provenance capture techniques assume a closed world – a contained environment about which the provenance system has considerable knowledge and control. In application-embedded provenance, capture is limited to the data and processes within a particular application [4, 5, 7]. Workflow-based systems, such as [2, 8, 12], can only capture provenance for events that occur within that workflow system. More generic provenance management systems [3, 6, 13] provide a provenance reporting interface; however, because provenance is not a central feature of most applications, the incentives do not exist for them to report provenance. Operating system based systems [11] only capture provenance within a particular machine and, as a result, fail to support distributed interactions across heterogeneous environments. Also, OS-based provenance is usually at too low a semantic level to help users understand the business processes that have acted upon their data. Even the most "unplanned" provenance capture system today, for user-created mashups [7], assumes the applications used in the mash-up are provenance aware and report metadata in a particular format.

All these approaches assume a single system controlled by a central provenance collecting entity. Among our U.S. government customers though, it is common for data to flow across organizational boundaries and for each autonomous stakeholder to use and transform data with their own applications. Therefore, provenance capture

D.L. McGuinness, J.R. Michaelis, and L. Moreau (Eds.): IPAW 2010, LNCS 6378, pp. 98–101, 2010.

must cross system and organizational boundaries. While these systems often expose some interface, their implementation technology is often unknown.

We advocate for a solution that does not require system-invasive strategies and also does not restrict the user's choice of applications. To be useful in an "open world", the solution must capture provenance 1) across multiple systems with no assumption of control over those systems, 2) from legacy systems that are not provenance aware, and 3) at the level of application interaction, not at the level of protocol interaction or foundational technology stack (i.e. OS, filesystem).

2   Provenance Capture at Distributed System Coordination Points

Among MITRE's customers, there are often *points of coordination* in the interactions among distributed, heterogeneous systems. Popular examples include enterprise service buses, business process execution engines, and proxy servers. These coordination points present a previously untapped opportunity to log provenance that spans systems and organizations without requiring application modification.

To explore the feasibility of capture at distributed system coordination points, we created a provenance capture module using an enterprise service bus (ESB) which addresses the requirements described above. An ESB is a tool for integrating multiple applications with different messaging specifications, and for specifying the way in which they interact with one another (the implicit workflow). The popular open source ESB MULE [10] provides built-in support for automatic message routing and translation between different technologies such as Java Messaging Service (JMS), SOAP, etc., greatly simplifying communication among services in a distributed, heterogeneous environment. An ESB is a perfect point for provenance capture in the wild: it is a point of coordination among multiple distributed systems.

By tying capture into a service such as MULE, it is possible to capture provenance of implicit workflows—as opposed to pre-planned explicit workflows—across disparate, autonomous systems. We implemented our approach in the MULE Capture Agent (MCA), which uses the provenance reporting API of PLUS [3], a provenance manager with a model similar to OPM [9]. MCA also uses MULE's "Envelope Interceptor" interface, which allows inspection of the ESB's state both immediately before and after a service is executed. When MCA encounters a new object, it records the object in the provenance store and "tags" the object with a unique identifier. This identifier is carried as the message flows throughout the system, permitting previously unconnected single-step provenance to be linked into meaningful provenance DAGs.

MULE and other ESBs provide a large amount of metadata relevant to service invocations (e.g., a given request came from Firefox or the time of the response was 09:07:23). MCA can access this metadata and report it to PLUS whenever it is anticipated that future provenance queries might require it. In addition to message metadata, some applications that leverage provenance may also require excerpts from the underlying message payload. For example, latitude and longitude may need to be extracted if future provenance queries might include location predicates ("show me the derivation of all today's situation reports within 20km of Port-au-Prince"). In such cases, the ability to peek at the message payload is required. MCA uses several techniques to introspect into messages, including *reflection*, a java ability to examine the runtime behavior of applications in the VM. Whether the information comes from message metadata or is extracted from the message payload, PLUS manages it using its extensible facility for attaching attribute-value pairs to provenance nodes.

3 Evaluation

We tested[1] MCA on two different workflows: LoanBroker is a standard MULE test scenario, and CoTLooper is a scenario that uses Cursor on Target (CoT) [1] messages. CoTLooper is a simple test that provides an example of operational messages containing real and necessary metadata such as latitude, longitude, entity identifiers, and other information used by several tracking and sensor-fusion systems.

Figure 1 shows the average time required to capture one node using the MULE capture mechanism. For this experiment, we used LoanBroker, and ran through 1000 loan requests. Each loan request requires checking with a credit bureau and requesting candidate loan quotes from 3 different banks. We measured the time to invoke the provenance capture function and log the information. While there is a high startup cost because of connection pooling, since MULE is typically used for high-volume and long-running distributed systems, the *more accurate capture times are found to the right of the graph*, where the number of interactions dwarfs the number of connections. In a system where several hundred messages are sent per second, the average per-transaction cost of provenance capture is very low.

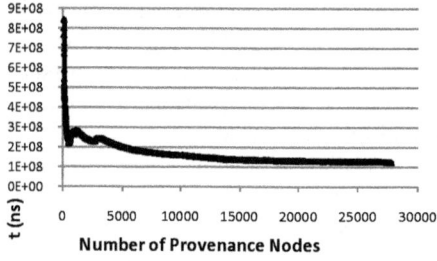
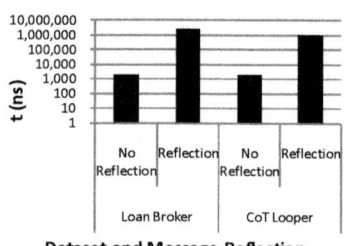

Fig. 1. The average time to log provenance within MULE over time

Fig. 2. Message Reflection effect on Message Capture Time

Figure 2 shows the time for collecting information about the message to place in the provenance store, and uses the Loan Broker and CoTLooper workflows, giving a sampling of four different message types, three from Loan Broker and one from CoTLooper. Additionally, while CoTLooper is a toy workflow, the messages it passes utilizes real production APIs for Cursor on Target version 2 messages, serialized in XML. There is a significant impact for utilizing message reflection compared to no reflection[2]. The time to reflect within a message depends on how the class being

---

[1] All experiments were performed on a Linux 2.6.18 (CentOS 5.3) Quad-core box with 1.6Ghz processors and 4GB RAM, running MULE v2.1.2 and PLUS. All data is measured in nano-seconds, through the use of Java 1.6's System.nanoTime().

[2] Reflection in this case refers to calling a method dynamically at run-time, when the provenance capture mechanism was not compiled against the code defining that method.

reflected into is implemented; a simple "getter" method, such as getLatitude() from CoT Messages, which returns a stored value will be very fast. By contrast, a method which needs to parse a file will be much slower. The provenance capture mechanism cannot make any guarantee about how long it takes to invoke these methods, but it can provide infrastructure for doing so, and minimize the infrastructure cost.

4 Conclusions

In this work, we take the first step towards providing an automatic and simple mechanism for capturing provenance in open world systems. By enabling the MULE ESB with provenance collecting abilities, any application that is built to use MULE is automatically provenance enabled without underlying application modification or user knowledge. The approach captures previously implicit workflows, logging exactly what happened rather than what was expected to happen. In addition, no modifications to the capture mechanism are needed as applications evolve over time.

We see this work as an initial step toward multi-organizational provenance capture. Additional provenance collectors would be required, of course, since not all distributed, heterogeneous services use an ESB. We envision a variety of capture agents, each tailored to a different type of coordination point.

References

[1] Cursor on Target, http://cot.mitre.org/
[2] Altintas, I., Barney, O., Jaeger-Frank, E.: Provenance Collection Support in the Kepler Scientific Workflow System. In: Moreau, L., Foster, I. (eds.) IPAW 2006. LNCS, vol. 4145, pp. 118–132. Springer, Heidelberg (2006)
[3] Blaustein, B.T., Seligman, L., Morse, M., Allen, M.D., Rosenthal, A.: PLUS: Synthesizing privacy, lineage, uncertainty and security. In: ICDE Workshops, pp. 242–245 (2008)
[4] Buneman, P., Chapman, A., Cheney, J.: Provenance Management in Curated Databases. In: ACM SIGMOD, pp. 539–550 (2006)
[5] Frew, J., Metzger, D., Slaughter, P.: Automatic capture and reconstruction of computational provenance. Concurr. Comput.: Pract. Exper. 20, 485–496 (2008)
[6] Groth, P., Miles, S., Moreau, L.: PReServ: Provenance Recording for Services. UK OST e-Science second AHM (2005)
[7] Groth, P.T., Miles, S., Moreau, L.: A model of process documentation to determine provenance in mash-ups. ACM Trans. Internet Tech. 9 (2009)
[8] Missier, P., Belhajjame, K., Zhao, J., Goble, C.: Data lineage model for Taverna workflows with lightweight anotation requirements. In: Freire, J., Koop, D., Moreau, L. (eds.) IPAW 2008. LNCS, vol. 5272, pp. 17–30. Springer, Heidelberg (2008)
[9] Moreau, L., Ludäscher, B., et al.: Special Issue: The First Provenance Challenge. Concurrency and Computation: Practice and Experience 20, 409–418 (2008)
[10] Mulesoft.org, MULE 2.x (2009),
http://www.mulesoft.org/display/MULE2INTRO/Home
[11] Muniswamy-Reddy, K.-K., Holland, D.A., Braun, U., Seltzer, M.I.: Provenance-Aware Storage Systems. In: USENIX, pp. 43–56 (2006)
[12] Scheidegger, C.E., Vo, H.T., Koop, D., Freire, J., Silva, C.: Querying and Re-Using Workflows with VisTrails. In: SIGMOD (2008)
[13] Simmhan, Y., Plale, B., Gannon, D.: Karma2: Provenance Management for Data Driven Workflows. Journal of Web Services Research 5 (2008)

Automatically Adapting Source Code to Document Provenance

Simon Miles

Department of Informatics, King's College London, UK

Abstract. Being able to ask questions about the provenance of some data requires documentation on each influence on that data's existence and content. Much software exists, and is being developed, for which there is no provenance-awareness, i.e. at best, the data it outputs can be connected to its inputs, but with no record of intermediate processing. Further, where some record of processing does exist, e.g. as logs, it is not in a form easily connected with that of other processes. We would like to enable compiled software to record useful documentation without requiring prior manual adaptation. In this paper, we present an approach to adapting source code from its original form without manual manipulation, to record information on data provenance during execution.

1 Introduction

Many systems have been developed where the processing performed is documented during execution. The documentation allows us to answer questions about the processes which led to a data item being produced, i.e. its *provenance*. The documentation commonly contains copies of intermediate data items, otherwise discarded by the completion of a process, and causal dependencies between data items. In some cases, recording is performed *automatically* and *transparently*, as a side-effect of the execution, without either the author or user of a process being involved in what is recorded or how.

Such automatic, transparent recording has been built into workflow systems [1], and operating environments in which user actions are performed, e.g. the Provenance-Aware Storage System [2] or ES3 [3]. In the former, transparent recording means documenting the connection between data on them being inputs and outputs to the same workflow step. In the latter, OS (or higher) events are intercepted to document how an executed process reads and writes files.

Whether processes are enacted as pre-scripted workflows or ad-hoc user actions, the component steps are compiled from some *source code* and the intermediate data created within compiled components or the details of how outputs depend on inputs may be as important as intermediate data or dependencies at the workflow/OS level. In some cases, we want a record of what occurred during the execution of compiled code. To some extent, this can be provided by logging, but here there is no interoperability with the wider execution setting: we wish to know not only the list of events occurring between the executable's

D.L. McGuinness, J.R. Michaelis, and L. Moreau (Eds.): IPAW 2010, LNCS 6378, pp. 102–110, 2010.

initiation and termination, but also that the executable's inputs were themselves provided as part of a larger, distributed workflow. Such interoperability is a goal of the Open Provenance Model (OPM) [4], which documents processes as causal graphs allowing independently produced graphs to be combined.

Braun et al. [5] considered issues inherent in achieving automatic collection of provenance data. One consideration is that the *granularity* of provenance information a user is interested in is generally coarser/higher-level than an automatic collection mechanism records. It is important that some parts of an execution could and, sometimes can only, remain relatively *opaque*, described in coarse-grained terms. Another, related, consideration is that, for storage and privacy reasons, it may be undesirable to automatically record all that could be. A way to resolve this is to allow, but not require, *configuration* of what will be recorded, thus retaining transparency as far as it does not have a negative effect.

In more theoretical work, Souilah et al. [6] provided a formalism for languages expressible as asynchronous π-calculus, whereby the provenance of values exchanged across channels (and of the channels themselves) would be maintained throughout execution. In this work, the values are automatically augmented with their provenance as metadata, and thus propagated through the system. Processes can make decisions (accepting a value or not) by filtering on static patterns within the provenance data, which is expressed as a list of communication events. Buneman et al. [7] examined how the semantics of database query and update languages implied the provenance of data within the databases, and so could automatically be augmented with actions to record how the data was transformed. The provenance was expressed as the propagation of colours, denoting data remaining the same in value or in kind, as the database was transformed. In both the latter papers, a correctness property of the provenance, with regards to what actually occurred in the system, was articulated and proven.

In this paper, we describe a preliminary approach, *SourceSource*, whereby source code is automatically adapted to document its processing during execution. While we argue the approach is generally applicable to procedural languages, our preliminary work is applied to a case study Java program. To enable configuration by the developer, where desired, the code retains its original form as far as possible in the adapted form, with recording statements inserted in the same language. Configuration is aided by treating the code as a set of components, some amenable to adaptation and some not (opaque), and allowing the developer to decide if a component should not be adapted to record its execution except at a coarse-grained level (merely connecting component inputs to outputs). The documentation is recorded as an OPM causal graph, allowing the program's execution to be connected with the preceding processes producing the program's inputs and succeeding processes consuming its outputs.

2   Overview and Case Study

Following OPM, the *provenance* of some data is the *processes* and *artifacts* which ultimately cause it to exist, and causal relations between them. An artifact is a constant data item and a process is the execution of some procedure, taking artifacts as input (*used* relation) and producing artifacts as output (*wasGeneratedBy* relation). An artifact may be generated by one process then later used by another, indirectly connecting the two processes. A set of OPM artifacts, processes and relations between them forms an *OPM graph*. An OPM graph may document the provenance of multiple artifacts, and we say that the graph is a set of *process documentation* from which the provenance of individual artifacts can be extracted by querying. Finally, each artifact, process and relation can be annotated with multiple *annotations*, each having a type and value.

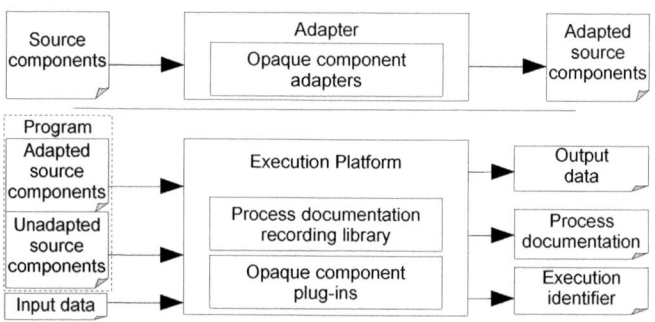

Fig. 1. Adaptation of source code (top) and then its execution (bottom) (top)

Fig. 1 (top) depicts SourceSource architecture. The *adapter* component takes source code and produces an adapted version. A program comprises one or more *source components* for which the code is adaptable, e.g. class files in Java, plus one or more *opaque components* for which code is not available, e.g. databases, third-party libraries. The user can choose which components are adapted. The adapted version is augmented to interleave execution with calls to a recording library to document execution, making use of *opaque component adapters* triggered for statements where an opaque component is used. When the code is executed (bottom of figure) on its standard platform, the execution of the adapted components is automatically documented. For an opaque component, the relevant plug-in is invoked to document the execution (as far as is possible) and connect it to the source execution which called the component. The recording library outputs process documentation and an identifier for the execution.

We take as our case study the workflow used in the third Provenance Challenge[1], an analysis of astronomy data from the Pan-STARRS project [8], implemented in Java. The aim of our approach is to automatically adapt code so that OPM documentation of its execution is recorded, without prior modification of the code to suit our approach. Therefore, a key fact about the case

---

[1] http://twiki.ipaw.info/bin/view/Challenge/

study is that it was developed *independently* from our work, with no knowledge that the SourceSource approach would be applied. In the provenance challenge, queries were performed over the process documentation to demonstrate its efficacy. For example, one query, inspired by program slicing [9], asked 'Which operation executions were strictly necessary for the Image table to contain a particular (non-computed) value?'. We refer readers to the challenge website for more details.

3   Process Documentation

We first describe the process documentation produced in our approach, then in Section 4 explain how SourceSource adapts code to record this. SourceSource primarily documents statements being executed (processes in OPM) and variables having particular values (OPM artifacts). A variable may take on multiple values during execution, so the recording library holds a mapping from each variable name to the artifact denoting its *most recent* value. When a variable has a new value, this is recorded as a new artifact by the adapted code and the *most recent* mapping is updated. When a variable is used in a statement, the most recent artifact for that variable is found, and connected by a causal (used) relation to the process representing the statement's execution. For example, in Fig. 2 (top), the first statement assigns a value to a variable `FileEntry`, then the second depends on that value, and this dependency holds even if there were other statements between the two shown.

```
for (LoadAppLogic.CSVFileEntry FileEntry : ReadCSVReadyFileOutput) {
   boolean IsExistsCSVFileOutput = LoadAppLogic.IsExistsCSVFile (FileEntry);


LoadWorkflow_main_Statement5
for (LoadAppLogic.CSVFileEntry FileEntry : ReadCSVReadyFileOutput) {
   LoadWorkflow_main_Declaration6
   boolean IsExistsCSVFileOutput = LoadAppLogic.IsExistsCSVFile (FileEntry);


for (LoadAppLogic.CSVFileEntry FileEntry : ReadCSVReadyFileOutput) {
   Recorder.process ("LoadWorkflow_main_Statement5");
   Recorder.variable ("LoadWorkflow_main_FileEntry", "LoadWorkflow_main_Statement5", FileEntry);
   Recorder.pass ("IsExistsCSVFile", 0, "LoadWorkflow_main_FileEntry");
   Recorder.push ();
   boolean IsExistsCSVFileOutput = LoadAppLogic.IsExistsCSVFile (FileEntry);
   Recorder.pop ();
   Recorder.process ("LoadWorkflow_main_Declaration6");
   Recorder.variable ("LoadWorkflow_main_IsExistsCSVFileOutput", "LoadWorkflow_main_Declaration6",
                       IsExistsCSVFileOutput);
   Recorder.generated ("LoadWorkflow_main_IsExistsCSVFileOutput", "Assigned Value In",
                       "LoadWorkflow_main_Declaration6");
   Recorder.used ("LoadWorkflow_main_Declaration6", "LoadWorkflow_main_FileEntry",
                  "Used In Expression");
```

Fig. 2. A snippet of code from the case study unadapted (top), with naming annotations (middle), and after adaptation (bottom)

3.1   Identifiers and Querying

Regardless of query language, a user querying for the provenance of data, maybe long after the process which produced it took place, will only have certain information available. Such a user cannot be expected to have available identifiers which are not part of the source code, input data, or outputs of adaptation or execution, and just because an identifier is somewhere in the process documentation we cannot assume the user knows what it identifies.

We can decompose a provenance query into: identifying the start item of which to find the provenance; expressing what in the potentially large set of documentation connected to the start item is relevant for the query; and how the relevant documentation is post-processed to answer the query. All stages require identifiers (for input, output and intermediate data) to be known. We take the following approach to identification in SourceSource (see Chapman and Jagadish on the general problems of identifying intermediate data [10]).

- An execution of a statement is identified by: the statement's scope identifiers (e.g. package and method names in Java), a unique *statement identifier* generated by SourceSource, and the count of which *iteration* of this statement this execution denotes (how many times the statement has been executed).
- A variable value is identified by: the statement execution where the value is assigned/used, the variable's scope and its name.
- Each program execution is identified by a generated *execution identifier*.

The identifiers above are annotated to the relevant artifacts/processes in the OPM graph. The execution identifier is also the filename of the serialised graph, allowing a user to connect the execution with its documentation. In combination, the above ensure there is a unique way to identify each documented artifact/process across executions, and identifiers can be known to querying users through being connected to the artifact/process either in the original source code, the adapted source code, or the execution output.

In the case study, each Java statement is given a name scoped by its class, e.g. `LoadWorkflow_main_Statement5` (in class LoadWorkflow, in method main, the 5th statement). These can be used to query for the provenance of the iterations of executing the statements. A tool is provided to see what names statements are given to aid those building queries. A snippet of the output this tool produces is shown in Figure 2 (middle), where each statement is preceded by its identifier. The opaque plug-ins must identify processes and artifacts appropriately for their components. For the case study database plug-in, described below, each database entry is given an identifier comprised of the table name and the primary key fields of the entry, e.g. `table=P2DETECTION, objID=113191992826421637`.

3.2   Granularity and Procedure Calls

The provenance of a data item can be expressed in different ways, suitable for different purposes. In particular, a description of its provenance can be expressed at a coarser or finer *granularity* of detail. OPM allows for multiple granularities of documentation to be demarcated by *account* identifiers. At a coarse granularity, the execution of a procedure call can be described as a black-box process which produces outputs given inputs, implying a possible causal connection between the outputs and inputs. At a fine granularity, the execution of a procedure call can be described as the caller's arguments being used as inputs to a succession of processes which comprise the procedure executed, ultimately resulting in outputs returned to the caller. SourceSource always records the coarse-grained account for a procedure call in an adapted procedure, and will record the fine-grained account where the called procedure is also adapted. The two accounts are connnected, by the identifiers of the call inputs and outputs being common to both accounts, and by an OPM refinement relationship.

Each procedure's execution is documented as a separate OPM sub-graph, with the final graph produced from the program's execution being the union of those sub-graphs. In Figure 3, we illustrate a snippet of the OPM graph produced by executing the adapted case study source, corresponding to the part shown in Figure 2. There are three accounts: one for the execution of the main method (FineGrained1), one for the invocation of the IsExistsCSVFile method (CoarseGrained2), and one for the execution of that method (FineGrained2).

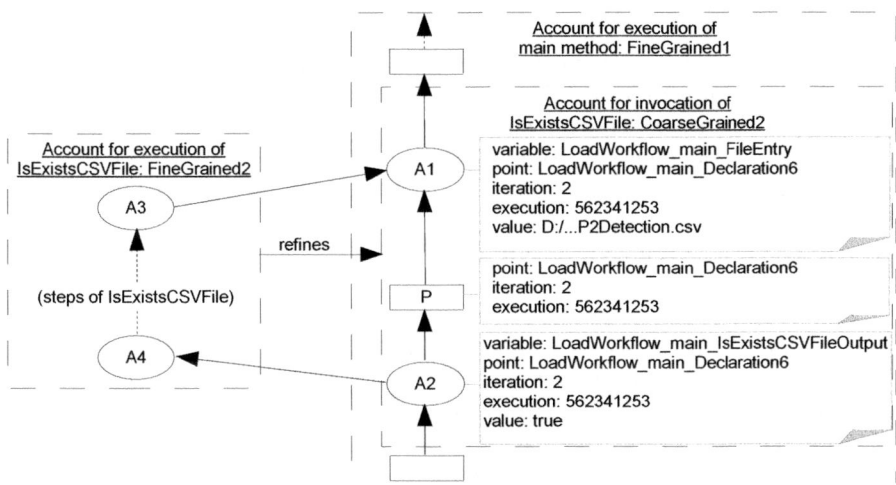

Fig. 3. Fragment of OPM graph produced in case study (ovals denote artifacts, solid rectangles denote processes, relations are arrows pointing from effect to cause, and key-value lists are annotations, dashed rectangles demarcate accounts)

In account CoarseGrained2 we see an artifact A1 for the FileEntry variable passed as argument to the invocation process, P, and A2 for the value assigned to variable IsExistsCSVFileOutput. In account FineGrained2, the same values are assigned to variables local to method IsExistsCSVFile, and are different artifacts derived from (and identical in value to) A1 and A2. Each artifact and process is annotated with its identifier (Section 3.1), plus variable values for artifacts. If the developer chose not to adapt the source component containing IsExistsCSVFile, the left-hand part of the graph would be excluded, without disconnecting the graph on the right-hand side.

4   Adaptation

Adaptation consists of three stages: *explicate* to transform code to enable addition of recording statements; *identify* to determine unique (within a single execution) identifiers for every occurrence which will be documented as an artifact or process; and *augment* to insert recording statements interleaved with execution. To perform adaptations in all three stages, we use TXL [11], a tool to transform source code from one form to another. A TXL rule takes a subtree of a given form, and transforms it into another subtree following the same grammar.

4.1   Explicate and Identify Stages

The first stage of adaptation is to, as minimally as possible, add structure to the code to enable recording steps to be inserted. In Java, this means that the body of if and similar control statements are represented as blocks (if (C) then {X}) rather than single statements (if (C) then X).

As discussed above, to be able to query the process documentation after recording, the entities to be referred to must be identifiable. This has two implications: *(i)* entities which have no natural identifier in the source code must be given one, *(ii)* the identifier to use on recording should be determined for each entity prior to augmenting with recording statements using those identifiers. In the first case, the primary entities in question are the statements, as they do not by default have a name by which they can be referred by a querier.

The first phase of the *identify* stage is to go through and annotate each statement with a name unique within its method, e.g. Statement5. TXL allows *attributes* to be inserted into the parse tree which will not be apparent in the transformed output, but can be used by other rules, and so the names are prepended to statements as such. In the second phase, we use attributes to provide global identifiers to code entities (variables, methods, statements). We ensure names are unique across the execution by constructing them from their scopes, e.g. a method's local variable is named by the package name, class name, method name, and variable name. As described in Section 3.1, we provide a tool to enable the identifiers of each source code line to be seen. A snippet of the output is shown in Fig. 2 (middle).

4.2   Augment Stage

In the *augment* stage, for each occurrence of a process/artifact, and for each causal relation between them, a recording statement is inserted into the code. Processes could include method calls, expression evaluations, or variable assignments. Currently, we augment at the statement level. In Fig. 2 top and bottom, we show a snippet of the case study code before and after augmentation. There is a loop across the elements of a collection, whose body's first line is the assignment of the result of a method call to a new variable (new each time round the loop). In augmenting that code snippet, our TXL scripts insert the following recording statements (other operations on the recording API document receipt of parameters, return of values from methods etc.)

1. Each loop iteration expression is a process, so a statement is inserted at the start of the loop body to document this process, named ...`_Statement5` in the *identify* stage. On execution, this recording statement will insert a process node into the OPM graph.
2. We document the state of the loop variable, ...`_FileEntry`, which will insert an artifact into the OPM graph with the variable's new value, and put the value the *most recent* mapping in memory.
3. The next statement in the original source includes a method call, so we need to keep track of the arguments passed to connect them with the parameters inside the called method. We store this as a tuple: the method being called, the index of the argument and the most recent value of the variable passed.
4. Each method invocation is documented in a separate account. The `push` method continues any subsequent recording in a new account, pushing the current one onto a stack. When the invocation completes, `pop` returns to the original account being used and creates a refinement relationship between the call (in a new coarse-grained account) and the invoked method accounts.
5. A process node is recorded for the assignment statement, and a generated artifact for the newly assigned variable.
6. We record relations, `used` and `generated`, documenting the artifacts (variable values) were used and generated by the assignment statement.

In many cases, source code which could be adapted using SourceSource will make calls to libraries, databases or other components for which the SourceSource approach cannot apply. Where this occurs, the call to the component in the source code can be adapted to invoke a *plug-in* which handles recording process documentation for components of that type (before and/or after the call, as appropriate). For the case study, we developed and used one plug-in, very much tailored to the case study, for the database holding the experiment results.

5   Conclusions

Where distributed processes include a compiled tool which does not record any documentation about its processing, the provenance of those processes' results will be more limited, will exclude some potentially relevant intermediate data items, and may be disconnected (it may not be apparent where the tool's outputs depend on its inputs). Making a tool provenance-aware manually can be expensive, so we would rather that the tool could, without manual modification, automatically recorded documentation during execution. The solution we present in this paper is to automatically adapt the tool's source code to record documentation in OPM. The approach is particularly applicable where the tool's developer should have control over the recording, e.g. to manage volume, to protect privacy, to remove irrelevant details. By inserting recording statements into the code in the same language, we require nothing of the developer but make it easier for them to configure recording afterwards.

The work described here is preliminary, so while everything achieved in Source-Source can be applied to any Java program, only those code features essential for completing the case study have been tested. While the principles of only minimally changing the code structure and using the same source language are adhered to, there are undoubtably improvements possible in how recording statements are inserted, e.g. to ensure low overhead costs. Checking and improving performance overhead requires a larger case study: both the original and adapted case study code execute trivially quickly.

References

1. Barga, R., Digiampietri, L.A.: Automatic generation of workflow execution provenance. In: Moreau, L., Foster, I. (eds.) IPAW 2006. LNCS, vol. 4145, pp. 1–9. Springer, Heidelberg (2006)
2. Muniswamy-Reddy, K.-K., Holland, D., Braun, U., Seltzer, M.: Provenance-aware storage systems. In: Proceedings of the 2006 USENIX Annual Technical Conference, Boston, MA (June 2006)
3. Frew, J., Slaughter, P.: ES3: A Demonstration of Transparent Provenance for Scientific Computation. In: Freire, J., Koop, D., Moreau, L. (eds.) IPAW 2008. LNCS, vol. 5272, pp. 200–207. Springer, Heidelberg (2008)
4. Moreau, L., Clifford, B., Freire, J., Gil, Y., Groth, P., Futrelle, J., Kwasnikowska, N., Miles, S., Missier, P., Myers, J., Simmhan, Y., Stephan, E., den Bussche, J.V.: The open provenance model core specification (v1.1). Future Generation Computer Systems (to appear, 2010)
5. Braun, U., Garfinkel, S., Holland, D.A., Muniswamy-Reddy, K.K., Seltzer, M.I.: Issues in automatic provenance collection. In: Moreau, L., Foster, I. (eds.) IPAW 2006. LNCS, vol. 4145, pp. 171–183. Springer, Heidelberg (2006)
6. Souilah, I., Francalanza, A., Sassone, V.: A formal model of provenance in distributed systems. In: TAPP 2009: First workshop on on Theory and practice of provenance, USENIX Association, Berkeley, CA, USA, pp. 1–11 (2009)
7. Buneman, P., Cheney, J., Vansummeren, S.: On the expressiveness of implicit provenance in query and update languages. ACM Trans. Database Syst. 33(4), 1–47 (2008)
8. PS1 Consortium: Pan-STARRS, http://ps1sc.org/ (last accessed March 2010)
9. Weiser, M.: Program slicing. In: Proceedings of the 5th International Conference on Software Engineering (ICSE 1981), pp. 439–449 (1981)
10. Chapman, A., Jagadish, H.V.: Provenance and the price of identity. In: Freire, J., Koop, D., Moreau, L. (eds.) IPAW 2008. LNCS, vol. 5272, pp. 106–119. Springer, Heidelberg (2008)
11. Cordy, J.: The TXL Source Transformation Language. Science of Computer Programming 61(3), 190–210 (2006)

Using Data Provenance to Measure Information Assurance Attributes

Abha Moitra[1], Bruce Barnett[1], Andrew Crapo[1], and Stephen J. Dill[2]

[1] General Electric Global Research, 1 Research Circle, Niskayuna, NY 12309
{moitraa,BarnettBr,Andrew.Crapo}@ge.com
[2] Lockheed Martin IS&GS,
321 Ballenger Center Drive, MS 125/1F10, Frederick, MD
Stephen.J.Dill@lmco.com

Abstract. Data Provenance is multi-dimensional metadata that specifies Information Assurance attributes like Confidentiality, Authenticity, Integrity, Non-Repudiation etc. It may also include ownership, processing details and other attributes. Further, each Information Assurance attribute may itself have sub-components like objective and subjective values or application security versus transport security. Traditionally, the Information Assurance attributes have been specified probabilistically as a belief value (or corresponding disbelief value) in that Information Assurance attribute. In this paper we introduce a framework based on Subjective Logic that incorporates uncertainty by representing values as a triple of <belief, disbelief, uncertainty>. This framework also allows us to work with conflicting Information Assurance attribute values that may arise from multiple views of an object. We also introduce a formal semantic model for specifying and reasoning over Information assurance properties in a workflow. Data Provenance information can grow substantially as the amount of information kept for each object increases as well as the complexity of a workflow increases. In such situations, it may be necessary to summarize the Data Provenance information. Further, the summarization may depend on the Information Assurance attributes as well as the type of analysis used for Data Provenance. We show how such summarization can be done and how it can be used to generate trust value in the data. We also discuss how the Information Assurance values can be visualized.

Keywords: data provenance, information assurance, subjective logic, semantic model, uncertainty framework, Figure of Merit, trust, confidence.

1 Introduction

Our primary interest is in calculating the assurance in data. Components used to calculate this are the Information Assurance (IA) communication attributes, which include attributes of confidentiality, integrity, authenticity, non-repudiation, and availability. Factors that impact this include opinions of the data sources and of the certificate authorities used during the authentication process. These values are based on the observer's viewpoint, loyalties, and knowledge, and are therefore highly subjective.

D.L. McGuinness, J.R. Michaelis, and L. Moreau (Eds.): IPAW 2010, LNCS 6378, pp. 111–119, 2010.

For simplicity we will not address these factors in this paper. Instead, we will focus on the information assurance attributes of the communication itself, related to the communication channel and process. If all parties agree on the relative strength of cryptographic algorithms at a certain point in time, then this forms the basis for an objective and consistent measurement of information assurance values across multiple parties regarding a set of messages.

In this paper we describe a model of information flow based on simple and complex messages (messages with attachments) about which objective information assurance attribute values are collected. This model includes the capability to rollup data provenance information over a complex message and/or over a multi-step information flow. We call these aggregations a *Figures of Merit* or *FoM*.

Given objective information assurance attribute values for a message or a figure of merit, our next goal is to summarize these in a simple visual icon that allows those who must act on information quickly to understand how confidential, authentic, and unmodified the data is, therefore allowing them to make more educated choices when dealing with the data.

2 Previous Work

In our previous work [1], we developed a generalized and flexible framework that was independent of any implementation, yet allowed a series of data provenance records to be captured, and analyzed. We summarize the framework below.

Each time a message is moved between agents, systems or processes, a single Data Provenance (DP) record is created. This record might be stored or sent along in parallel with the message. During the analysis, all of the records related to a single message are assumed to be available. Each DP record has two parts: one from the sender and one from the receiver.

Each part has an invariant and a variant section. The variant section may contain routing information to forward the message to the final destination, and may change during the routine process. The invariant part remains unchanged, allowing cryptographic hashes of this section to be consistent. The sender's invariant section may include the following components:

- Identity of the Author of the message
- Message ID
- Timestamp
- Message contents and type
- References to other message IDs, e.g., attachments
- Destination
- Security label or classification
- Outgoing Information Assurance values

It also includes the hash value (and name of hash algorithm) of the message contents. The sender (or someone acting as a proxy) may optionally sign the DP record, or attach a hash encrypted with a private key of the record, as assurance the DP record has not been modified.

The receiver appends his own values to the record, adding

- Identity of the Receiver of the message
- Timestamp
- Incoming Information Assurance values
- Hash of the message body as seen by the receiver

The receiver may append a signature or an encrypted hash based on both the sender and receiver's records. One important characteristic of this approach is that third parties can validate the DP record at a later date.

There are several possible variations of the format. The timestamp may be part of the message ID. Some systems may split the message body from the record, and retrieve it by message ID when validating the record. Also, the message may be encrypted and the receiver may not have the key, as it may be forwarding the encrypted message to a third party. The receiver can create a record that they received an encrypted message, and provide a signed hash as proof. DP records can also have multiple signatures from multiple parties, if desired. This is useful in multiple trust domains. It is also possible that some of these fields may be blank, as the sender may not have any encryption capabilities.

Using this foundation, we build a system that implements this framework. We then developed a mechanism to calculate the information assurance attributes based on the DP records that are available.

3 Subjective Logic

We needed a flexible mechanism to calculate confidence that also allowed us to deal with uncertainty. We used Jøsang's Subjective Logic [2], which uses three values b, d, and u, where:

b = belief, or the belief that the proposition is true
d = disbelief, or the belief the proposition is false
u = uncertainty, or the amount of uncommitted belief
These components satisfy $b + d + u = 1$, and $b, d, u \in [0,1]$

4 Implementation Details

In order to make our prototype implementation more transparent to both our team members and to our sponsor, we chose to capture our models of information flow and of the data provenance at each point along the flow in a semantic model rather than in a traditional programming language. Our target representation was the Web Ontology Language (OWL) with a rules layer to capture domain inferences not implied by the formal models. We used a controlled English representation called the Semantic Application Design Language (SADL) as the authoring environment [6]. SADL is a language that maps directly and unambiguously into OWL and Jena Rules or SWRL. An Eclipse-based SADL-IDE supports the authoring, testing, and version control of the models.

Information flow in our prototype is represented as instances of Message passed between instances of Agent. Snapshots of the data provenance state of the Message are captured as instances of DPInfo. When an Agent sends a Message, a SenderD-PInfo (subclass of DPInfo) captures relevant data provenance information. When an Agent receives a Message, a ReceiverDPInfo (also a sub class of DPInfo) captures the data provenance state at receipt. There is an association between these two DPInfo instances and the process of moving a Message from a sending Agent to a receiving Agent is called a Hop. A series of Hops is called a Flow.

The definitions of DPInfo, SenderDPInfo, and ReceiverDPInfo are shown in Figure 1 in SADL syntax. Note that common attributes include measures of Integrity, Confidentiality, and Authenticity expressed as Subjective Logic values.

```
SLValue is a top-level class,
    described by belief with values of type float,
    described by disbelief with values of type float,
    described by uncertainty with values of type float,
    described by apriori with values of type float.

SenderDPInfo is a type of DPInfo.
ReceiverDPInfo is a type of DPInfo,
    described by boundaryCrossed with a single value of type boolean,
    described by senderInfo with values of type SenderDPInfo.

DPInfo is a type of DPMeasure,
    described by timestamp with values of type date,
    described by owner with values of type Agent,
    described by message with values of type Message,
    described by context with a single value of type Domain,
    described by hashOfUnencryptedContent with values of type data,
    described by hashOfEncryptedContent with values of type data,
    described by hashAlgorithm with values of type string,
    described by signed with values of type boolean,
    described by signatureAlgorithm with values of type SignatureAlgorithm,
    described by signatureVerified with values of type boolean,
    described by messageEncrypted with values of type boolean,
    described by encryptionAlgorithm with values of type EncryptionAlgorithm,
    described by hashesOfContentMatch with values of type boolean,
    described by dpSignatureAlgorithm with values of type SignatureAlgorithm,
    described by authenticity with values of type SLValue,
    described by confidentiality with values of type SLValue,
    described by integrity with values of type SLValue,
    described by transport_secure with values of type SLValue,
    described by transport_confidential with values of type SLValue,
    described by boundaryCrossingInCompliance
      with a single value of type boolean.
```

Fig. 1. Definition of DPInfo in SADL

Messages can be complex, meaning that a Message can include Attachments (subclass of Message), which can in turn have Attachments, etc. For a given Hop, the top-level Message, which is not an Attachment at that point in the Flow, is referred to as the root container. It is desirable to roll up information across the parts of a complex message to obtain a single composite representation of the data provenance state of the whole Message. We call such a composite view a Figure Of Merit. Note that while a Figure Of Merit is a simplifying aggregation, which can more easily be perceived by a human observer, the DPInfo instances used in the rollup will normally be available so that drilldown into details is possible if desired. Note that we were measuring attributes of the transmission of the information, and did not measure attributes related to the contents of the messages. We considered the contents to be opaque. We also did not address contents editing, annotations, etc.

While SADL provides a useful way of authoring and testing models, it does not currently provide an easy mechanism for creating visualizations of scenarios and graphical representations of the Subjective Logic values of instances of DPInfo and FigureOfMerit. To do the latter, we implemented an Excel client user-interface with the desired graphical representations. We put together a representative scenario to demonstrate the flexibility and usefulness of our approach. From the scenario and from the user supplied input values, a situation-specific instance data model in the form of an OWL n-triple file is automatically created by the client. This model is passed to a Jena reasoner which reasons over both the logic of the formal model, e.g., transitive closure over class hierarchy, and over the domain rules to create an inferred model. The client then passes a SPARQL query to the reasoner to retrieve the desired information from the inferred model. It uses this information to populate the iconic graphical representations of the DP attributes of simple Messages and the Figure Of Merit rollups of complex Messages.

5 Analyzing the Records

We first assigned values to the various cryptographic algorithms. Generally, the stronger a cryptographic function is, the stronger the belief that it provides protection. The weaker a cryptographic function is, the greater the uncertainty whether someone has defeated the algorithm. For instance, any message that is signed with Message Digest 5 (MD5) is given a low belief and high uncertainty because of the recent demonstrations of MD5's defeatability [3]. If we had knowledge that the account was compromised, then we would assign a high value to disbelief of the message's attribute, and the belief and uncertainty values would decrease in response.

Knowledge of the individual information assurance attributes enables better decisions that can adapt to different situations. For instance, if a warfighter was told to investigate evidence that a terrorist was seen entering a building, knowledge of the source of information could affect their reaction to unexpected events. If the source of information was not over a confidential channel, then the warfighter's arrival may be anticipated. If the message has low integrity, then the information could have been distorted and may have to be verified. If the information was not strongly authenticated, then the information may come from an unreliable source. Because of this, we decided to calculate each of IA attributes individually, rather than use a single value to indicate trust. We then created a visual summary of the IA values, to assist in the decision process.

5.1 Integrity

To verify the integrity, first the hash is verified to correspond to the message body. In addition, when the message enters the system, the hash can be compared with the most recent hash. The resulting value is based on the strength of the weakest hash algorithm used.

If the hash values differ when traveling through a person or device, it would indicate a man-in-the-middle attempt. If, for a single hop, the incoming and outgoing hash values differ, then the entity forwarding the message modified it. If the hash differs in a single record, then a substitution occurred during the transmission process.

5.2 Authenticity

If the creator of the message signs the initial DP record, authenticity can be based on the algorithmic strength used to sign the record. We should further adjust these values based on the strength of the algorithms used by the certificate authorities. As others have done this [4], we focused on the core attributes, which could be further adjusted based on more subjective opinions (which Subjective Logic can provide).

If the message enters the system unsigned, one of the parties forwarding the message can sign the message. This entity can become a proxy for the sender's ID. Belief of authenticity then becomes subjective based on confidence in the proxy.

5.3 Confidentiality

There is no easy way, using just the DP records, to determine if some person ordevice has revealed information using other communication channels. However, we can lower the confidence value every time some entity received a message that they could read. Essentially, the more that know a secret, the less confidence there is in the confidentiality.

We can also base the calculation on the encryption properties of each transmission. If any single transmission is sent unencrypted, the belief in the confidentiality of the message drops to zero, and the uncertainty approaches one.

If the sender and receiver's belief in the confidentiality differ, then this may indicate a system problem. For instance, if a sender believes a message is confidential, but the receiver believes the message has no security, this may indicate an implementation flaw.

5.4 Non-repudiation

Non-repudiation is provided for when the sender signs the DP record, which includes the signature of the message author.

5.5 Availability

There is no way to calculate the availability of the information, based on just the DP records. This requires knowledge of system characteristics and past history. Given synchronized timestamps, and knowledge of the frequency and expected latency of the messages, is it possible to detect attacks that delay or prevent messages from being received.

6 Summarizing Information with an Icon

When summarizing a complex message with multiple components, there are two different issues to be resolved. The first is the analysis of a simple message from beginning to end. We described how we addressed this in the previous section.

The second issue is summarizing a message containing multiple messages, photos, etc. There are several different consensus functions one can use with Subjective Logic [4]. We considered them, but these make the most sense when dealing with the truthfulness of the content of messages. Since we are only addressing the communication channel, and we ignore the semantic meaning of the messages, we chose a minimum function that summarized a message based the lowest valued attribute of the sub-components.

For the visualization, we use a simple 3-column icon that shows Confidentiality, Integrity, and Authenticity, with green, red, and gray values representing belief, disbelief, and uncertainty respectively. An example is shown in Figure 3, which uses the colors from top to bottom of green, red, and grey.

Fig. 2. Icon of Information Assurance Attributes

This example icon shows somewhat high belief in confidentiality, less belief in the integrity, and for illustrative purposes, disagreement on the authenticity of a message as both green and red is shown. Our implementation did not capture any conflict, as it was measuring objective information gathered during the distribution process.

7 Sample Visualization

In a sample demonstration, we have 6 messages from five sensors being referenced and included by two analysts, who in turn forwarded their information to a third analyst. The final report consists of 6 images, and the output from the first two analysts. In this workflow, none of the messages are modified. The workflow is shown in Figure 4.

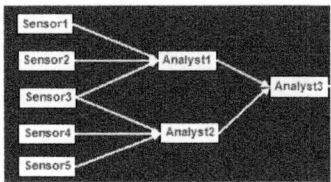

Fig. 3. Sample Workflow

The GUI is built on top of Microsoft Excel, which also generated the icon. The algorithms used for each of the Information Assurance attributes for each of the sensors, and the reports from the analysts, are selectable. Authenticity is determined by the strength of the algorithm the creator uses to sign the message. The integrity is determined by the strength of the algorithm to sign the Dpinfo record. The confidentiality of the message is determined by the strength of the algorithm used to encrypt the message. In addition, we can introduce security failures in the demonstration, such as invalid signatures, and incorrect hash values. After generating a set of messages corresponding to the conditions of the scenario, the resulting Figure of Merit (FoM) is shown for each of the messages in Figure 5. We assume that each person and device sends information in the most secure way. Because of this, on each outgoing message each of the senders assigned high confidence in their information, and the icons are all green. The receiver may downgrade the trust if stronger encryption algorithms are possible. If any of the cryptographic verifications fail, belief becomes zero, and disbelief is increased, showing red in the FoM icon.

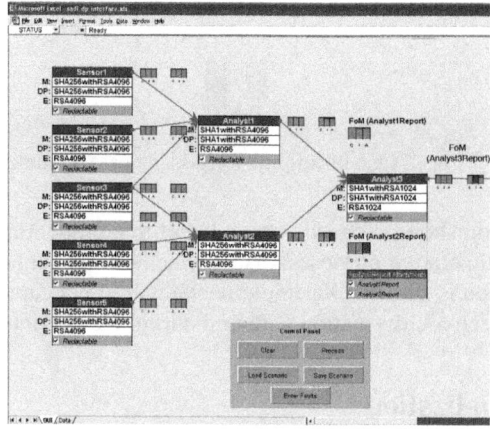

Fig. 4. Sample Results

In Figure 5, we show a sample workflow with 2 failures introduced: Analyst 2's report had an invalid signature (the authentication column is red), and Analyst 3's report indicates a hash mismatch (the integrity column is red), perhaps indicating a man-in-the-middle attack. Note how the icons allowed someone to quickly spot any potential problems. Also note how the authenticity of Analyst 3's report has some uncertainty (some grey on the top of the authentication column), as the signature used the weaker RSA1024 instead of RSA4096.

8   Conclusion

We believe that the framework described in this paper is suitable for capturing, summarizing, and analyzing objective evidence about the information assurance attributes of a message at various points in its life cycle, from creation to final destination. We believe that measuring the information assurance attributes of the infrastructure is an essential component in measuring the overall trust in a more complex system. We also believe the approach to be suitable for including more subjective information such as opinions and knowledge of outside conditions. Subjective logic provides a well-founded mechanism to resolve conflict and to rollup summary values. The iconic summary is a suitable mechanism to visually display the information assurance attributes of messages and figures of merit, and allows one to quickly identify weaknesses in the communication infrastructure.

Acknowledgements. This paper was prepared by GE Global Research as an account of work sponsored by Lockheed Martin Corporation. Information contained in this paper is the property of Lockheed Martin Corporation. Neither GE nor Lockheed Martin Corporation, nor any person acting on behalf of either; (a). Makes any warranty or representation, expressed or implied, with respect to the use of any information contained in this paper, or that the use of any information, apparatus, method, or process disclosed in this paper may not infringe privately owned rights; or (b). Assume any liabilities with respect to the use of, or for damages resulting from the use of, any information, apparatus, method, or process disclosed in-this paper."

References

1. Moitra, A., Barnett, B., Crapo, A., Dill, S.: Data Provenance Architecture to Support Information Assurance in a Multi-Level Secure Environment. In: MILCOM 2009, Boston (2009)
2. Jøsang, A.: Artificial Reasoning with Subjective Logic. In: Proceedings of the Second Australian Workshop on Commonsense Reasoning, Perth (1997)
3. Sotirov, A., Stevens, M., Appelbaum, J., Lenstra, A., Molnar, D., Osvik, D.A., de Weger, B. (2008-12-30).: MD5 considered harmful today,
   http://www.win.tue.nl/hashclash/rogue-ca/ (retrieved December 30, 2008) Announced at the 25th Chaos Communication Congress
4. Jøsang, A.: An Algebra for Assessing Trust in Certification Chains. In: Proceedings of the Network and Distributed Systems Security Symposium, NDSS 1999 (1999)
5. Josang, A.: The Consensus Operator for Combining Beliefs. Artificial Intelligence Journal 141(1-2), 157–170 (2002),
   http://persons.unik.no/josang/papers/Jos2002-AIJ.pdf
6. Crapo, A.: Semantic Application Design Language,
   http://sadl.sourceforge.net/

Explorations into the Provenance of High Throughput Biomedical Experiments

James P. McCusker and Deborah L. McGuinness

Tetherless World Constellation
Department of Computer Science
Rensselaer Polytechnic Institute
110 8th Street Troy, NY 12180, USA
{mccusj,dlm}@cs.rpi.edu
http://tw.rpi.edu

Abstract. The field of translational biomedical informatics seeks to integrate knowledge from basic science, directed research into diseases, and clinical insights into a form that can be used to discover effective treatments of diseases. We demonstrate methods and tools to generate RDF representations of a commonly used experimental description format, MAGE-TAB, mappings of MAGE documents to two general-purpose provenance representations, OPM (Open Provenance Model) and PML (Proof Markup Language). We show through a use case simulation that the data represented in MAGE documents can be completely represented in OPM and PML through use of round trip analysis of certain examples. The success in mapping MAGE documents into general-purpose provenance models shows that promise in the implementation of the translational research provenance vision.

1 Introduction

Translational biomedical research focuses on translating findings in basic science into advances in treatment and diagnosis of diseases for patients in the clinic, and has become a major research priority in the last five years. [1,2] Translational research requires the coordination and collaboration of a number of different disciplines, including basic science, clinical research, and increasingly, biomedical informatics. [3] As the scale and complexity of biomedical experiments has increased, so has the role of biomedical informatics. It plays an active role in the design, execution, and analysis of most biomedical research. The translational research pipeline, often thought of as a cycle of knowledge from the experimental "bench" to the clinical "bedside" and back, requires the management of many different kinds of data and artifacts by specialists in their disciplines. This includes information about the collection, management, and disposition of human, animal, and xenographic biomaterials, collection and management of participants in clinical research and trials, management of patient histories and charts, data from lab results, diagnostic imaging at the radiological and histopathological scales, as well as experiments using high-throughput technologies such as

D.L. McGuinness, J.R. Michaelis, and L. Moreau (Eds.): IPAW 2010, LNCS 6378, pp. 120–128, 2010.
© Springer-Verlag Berlin Heidelberg 2010

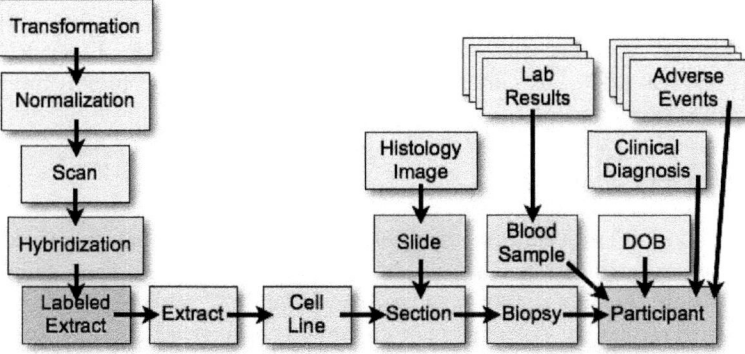

Fig. 1. Some common experimental and clinical artifacts that are created or used in the process of translational biomedical research. This example is common of translational cancer research.

microarray assays and high throughput sequencing. Common derivations and artifacts from the translational research pipeline are shown in Figure 1 on page 121.

1.1   The Translational Research Provenance Vision

The vision is relatively simple: It should be possible for a research scientist, clinician, patient or legal guardian to be able to query, assess, and collate the knowledge needed to make decisions about research and patient care. In order to be able to do this, the information that is used to make these decisions must have at hand the provenance of those materials, so as to be able to judge the relevance and veracity of the information they need. For this to happen, there must be a consistent model of provenance that can be used regardless of the origin, domain, or format of the information at hand.

By accomplishing this, we make it possible to gain a complete picture of how experiments were conducted, if they are comparable, and how well confounding variables have been controlled for. In the longer term, it also offers an opportunity to build experiments based on previous work, by understanding what kinds of methods have been used on certain kinds of problems, and to find new avenues of research. Provenance also makes electronic health records much more portable, as it becomes possible for clinicians to assess if lab work performed at other institutions is comparable with work done at their own. For patients, access to a consistent model of the provenance of their medical state means being able to take control of their own health, and to understand the reasoning behind clinical treatments and advice.

The World Wide Web Consortium (W3C) has chartered a incubator group for provenance representations[1] and has developed a number of biomedical use

---

[1] http://www.w3.org/2005/Incubator/prov

cases. Many of these use cases describe specific steps along the path to realizing this translational research provenance vision. Additionally, existing automated computational workflow systems, such as Wings/Pegasus [4], Taverna/myGrid [5], and VisTrails [6], have started to converge towards a common interchange language for provenance.

1.2   High Throughput Experiments and Provenance

Scientists look to provenance information, such as experimental workflow, to learn about experiments and results in their field. Critical to their understanding is: (1) how the experiment was performed, and (2) what needs to be known to be able to repeat it. As such, it is vital that systems that support the sciences provide a framework for incorporating provenance information at every step of the research chain. This is especially true for high throughput assays such as microarrays. Each microarray can measure hundreds of thousands to more than a million nuclear material hybridizations. Because of the scale of measurement, an experimental design must overcome a potentially high False Discovery Rate (FDR) [7] through use of many biological replicates for each experimental condition. Additionally, the context that is provided by richly encoded provenance can be used to automate certain aspects of scientific research.

In bioinformatics and computational biology, the problem of provenance has been an issue for some time. Goble [8] identifies a number of provenance-related issues in re-use and propagation of database information. The rapid growth and evolution of experimental techniques has makes it ever more difficult for scientists to evaluate the soundness and validity of the data at hand. This growth has resulted in the establishment of a standard for describing microarray-based experiments. The MIAME (Minimal Information About a Microarray Experiment) and MAGE (MicroArray and Gene Expression) standards [9] established metadata requirements for microarray experiments in informal (MIAME) and formal (MAGE) terms. MAGE currently has a number of representations, including MAGE-ML (MAGE Markup Language) and MAGE-TAB (MAGE TABle). These standards, combined with data sharing requirements from most funding institutions such as the National Institutes of Health in public databases such as the National Center for Biotechnology Information's (NCBI) GEO (Gene Expression Omnibus) [10] and the European Bioinformatics Institute's (EBI) ArrayExpress [11], along with those databases' adoption of the MAGE and MIAME standards, have resulted in thousands of microarray experiments stored in a consistent standardized format.

However, this format is designed specifically for microarray experiments. New assay types, such as tissue microarrays [12], high-throughput sequencing, and other low or medium throughput experiments require a more generalized data model. Additionally, information about findings is absent from MAGE and MIAME, as is the detailed information about the biospecimens that were used in the experiment gathered and managed by the biospecimen bank. This is all valuable information that can benefit from a common data model, if one were available. Integration with other data sources in the translational pipeline, such as biospecimen management tools, Laboratory Information Management Systems (LIMS), and computational workflow automation tools through the use of a common model of provenance can provide a complete picture of the provenance of experiments. A first step in this process is to convert experimental data into a common provenance representation. We accomplish this by implementing a simulation the following use case:

MAGE Data Sharing Use Case: Two databases, A and B, are repositories for microarray experiments that conform to the MAGE standard. B would like to load some experiments from A, which publishes a web service that describes its experiments using a general purpose provenance model. B should be able to re-create the information about the experiments it retrieves from A without loss.

Implementing this use case using a general purpose provenance model would demonstrate that it is possible to transform MAGE-compliant experimental metadata into that provenance model without losing any information. We create implementation simulations of this use case using the Open Provenance Model (OPM) [13] and Proof Markup Language (PML) [14]. Through these implementations, we show that it is possible to represent microarray experimental metadata fully and without loss in two common general purpose provenance models, and with the continuing adoption of general purpose provenance models by computational workflow systems, establishes the first link in the chain of provenance for the translational research provenance vision.

2   Related Work

There is a significant amount of related work to this topic. We highlight three areas, which the following subsections each discuss. The first area is work related to the MAGE object model. MAGE is a standard used to describe microarray experiments in a consistent manner. The second area is work related to analysis of data format compatibility using round trip analysis. We use this type of analysis to determine the suitability of representing MAGE-based experiment metadata in general purpose provenance models. The third area is work related to general purpose provenance models, specifically OPM. OPM has been used as a common representation for provenance interchange at two provenance challenges [15,16].

2.1   MAGE

The MAGE object model and related representations has been in wide use for a considerable period [9] in bioinformatics. Currently, the most commonly used MAGE format is MAGE-TAB [17], a delimited text-based format encompassing a number of file formats, of which we use information from the Investigation Design Format (IDF), which contains global information about an experiment, including submitters, publications, protocols, experimental factors, etc.; Sample and Data Relationship Format (SDRF), which describes the experimental workflow and how samples and other data and physical artifacts relate to each other.

2.2   Round Trip Analysis

Round-Trip analysis of data representations, especially meta-models, have been a gold standard for validating the expressivity of those models. Farquhar *et al.* [20] uses a similar method validate conversion from various ontology languages into a common format. Antkiewicz *et al.* [21] discusses round-trip engineering, or using round-trip analysis to show that Framework-Specific Modeling Languages (FSMLs) can be shown to reliably represent Domain-Specific Modeling Languages (DSMLs) in the Java Eclipse platform.

2.3   General Purpose Provenance Models

A commonly used provenance interlinguas is the Open Provenance Model. OPM has its roots in the workflow world, where it has evolved as a proposed common interchange language for computational workflow management and execution tools, and was used as a standard interchange for the second and third Provenance Challenges. A number of scientific workflow applications have participated in these challenges, which involved the generation of OPM graphs by each team for query by the other team members. Because of this, Taverna [22] and Pegasus/Wings [4] now support the export of provenance information in OPM. This support makes it very attractive as a first link between disciplines within the translational pipeline, as bioinformaticians often use computational workflow automation tools for research.

3   Methods

We simulate the MAGE data sharing use case in a semantic web environment using the MGED Ontology [23] as a foundation for the representation of MAGE documents in RDF. The overall process flow is seen in Figure 2 on page 125. We start by converting MAGE-TAB documents into RDF using MAGETAB2MAGERDF[2] and feed the resulting RDF into an OPM processor that infers the relevant OPM structure from the original RDF. A separate engine extracts the statements relating to OPM so that the resulting document is a pure instance of provenance data in OPM. A second processor attempts to reverse the initial step, taking the provenance data and generating the original MAGE RDF document. Finally, a comparison processor takes the difference between the original MAGE RDF and the regenerated MAGE RDF and outputs the statements that are missing in the regenerated document. The process of converting MAGE-TAB to RDF and the mapping from MAGE-RDF to OPM is discussed in depth in McCusker and McGuinness [24].

3.1   Evaluation

To evaluate our mappings, we perform an extraction of OPM-specific information from the resulting output RDF graphs and reverse the mapping process discussed

---

[2] http://magetab2rdf.googlecode.com

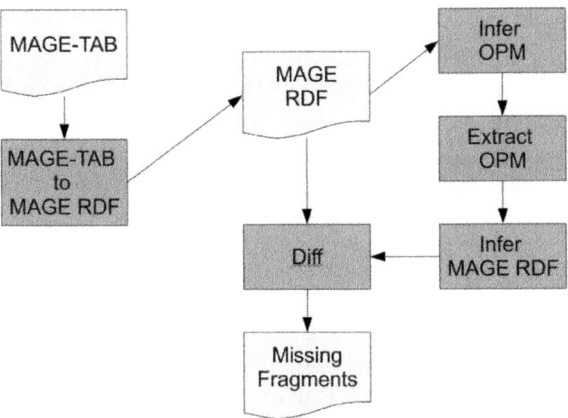

Fig. 2. The round trip analysis process. A MAGE-TAB file is converted to RDF and is fed into a processor that infers OPM from the original MAGE RDF. The OPM is extracted, ensuring only information represented in the provenance model remains. A processor then re-creates the original RDF to the best of its abilities from OPM. The resulting RDF is compared to the original to find missing statements.

above. We then compare the graphs to determine what statements are missing from the reconstructed graph as compared to the original.

We extract data relevant to a particular ontology in order to ensure that only data relating to that ontology or its imports remains. Only statements that use properties from the ontology import closure and individuals with a rdf:type of a class in the ontology import closure are extracted, everything else is filtered out. We perform the data extraction using three Jena models: (1) a base comparison model with only the ontology import closure, (2) an input model with the ontology import closure and the input graph to extract from, and (3) an output model with starts with the ontology import closure. The algorithm then iterates over all the classes and properties in the base comparison model and copies all statements relating to those classes and properties.

For the conversions back to MAGE from OPM, we reverse the rules discussed in McCusker and McGuinness [24]. These rules are described in opm2mage.rules[3]. The same generic inferencing processor, using the Jena API and rules engine, is used to run the conversion of OPM back into MAGE.

We use the Jena API to compare the reconstructed MAGE RDF graph with the original by creating a Jena models for the original and reconstructed graphs, and take difference of the original graph against the reconstructed graph. This results in a model that contains all statements that are in the original graph that are not in the reconstructed graph.

---

[3] https://scm.escience.rpi.edu/svn/public/mageprovenance/rules/opm2mage.rules

4 Results

For the mapping of MAGE to OPM, we performed a round-trip analysis on the ArrayExpress experiment E-MEXP-986[4], a small-scale but well-annotated exemplar experiment on *Arabidopsis thaliana*. We report that on conversion of the experiment to OPM and back to MAGE, there are no missing statements from the reconstructed RDF graph.

5 Discussion

A successful mapping of one of the most widely-used experimental description formats to a general purpose provenance model suggests two things: (1) descriptions of high-throughput experiments can be successfully represented using a general purpose model, and (2) OPM is sufficiently mature as a model of provenance to support real-world descriptions of experimental workflows in the biological sciences. Given this successful mapping, it is now possible to support a wide range of biomedical experiments within existing provenance models without a need for domain-specific extensions. It also means that the vision of consistent provenance representations across the translational research pipeline is possible, and points to interesting future work in representing biospecimen history and clinical information using general-purpose provenance models.

5.1 Future Work

We are currently working on scaling the declarative mapping for OPM and developing a procedural mapping for Proof Markup Language, another provenance representation [14]. The MAGE object model represents a small part of the derivational history of biospecimens that are used in these experiments. Future work of providing biospecimen history and analysis, as well as patient clinical history in a provenance model, we look to realize the translational research provenance vision laid out in this paper. More generally, each part of the translational research pipeline represents future work that is needed to realize the translational research provenance vision. Finally, research is needed in visualization and search of large graphs of provenance before generalized provenance models can be used effectively. Biomedical informaticians already use graph-based tools such as Cytoscape to visualize large molecular interaction graphs, but clinicians and patients will probably require a different perspective.

6 Conclusion

We proposed a vision of provenance for translational biomedical research that supports the integration of clinical and research artifacts across the translational research pipeline, provided an overview into the translational research pipeline,

---

[4] http://www.ebi.ac.uk/microarray-as/ae/files/E-MEXP-986

and showed how high throughput experiments provide a critical role in current biomedical research. We also demonstrated mappings of MAGE descriptions of experiments onto a general purpose models of provenance, OPM, and showed that the mappings are faithful and complete using an analysis of the round trip mapping of exemplar data. We also provided a framework for analyzing conversions of data from one RDF model to another. We discussed the advantages and pitfalls of declarative and procedural mappings. Finally, we gave a window into future work in implementing the translational research provenance vision.

References

1. Zerhouni, E.A.: Translational and clinical science–time for a new vision. New England Journal of Medicine 353(15), 1621 (2005)
2. Zerhouni, E.A.: US biomedical research: basic, translational, and clinical sciences. Jama 294(11), 1352 (2005)
3. Payne, P.R.O., Johnson, S.B., Starren, J.B., Tilson, H.H., Dowdy, D.: Breaking the translational barriers: the value of integrating biomedical informatics and translational research. Journal of Investigative Medicine 53(4), 192 (2005)
4. Kim, J., Deelman, E., Gil, Y., Mehta, G., Ratnakar, V.: Provenance trails in the Wings/Pegasus system. Concurrency and Computation: Practice and Experience 20(5), 587–597 (2008)
5. Zhao, J., Goble, C., Stevens, R., Turi, D.: Mining taverna's semantic web of provenance. Concurrency and Computation: Practice and Experience 20(5), 463–472 (2008)
6. Scheidegger, C., Koop, D., Santos, E., Vo, H., Callahan, S., Freire, J., Silva, C.: Tackling the provenance challenge one layer at a time. Concurrency And Computation 20(5), 473 (2008)
7. Benjamini, Y., Hochberg, Y.: Controlling the false discovery rate: a practical and powerful approach to multiple testing. Journal of the Royal Statistical Society. Series B (Methodological), 289–300 (1995)
8. Goble, C.: Position statement: Musings on provenance, workflow and (Semantic web) annotations for bioinformatics. In: Workshop on Data Derivation and Provenance, Chicago (2002)
9. Brazma, A., Hingamp, P., Quackenbush, J., Sherlock, G., Spellman, P., Stoeckert, C., Aach, J., Ansorge, W., Ball, C., Causton, H., et al.: Minimum information about a microarray experiment (MIAME)-toward standards for microarray data. Nature genetics 29(4), 365–372 (2001)
10. Barrett, T., Troup, D.B., Wilhite, S.E., Ledoux, P., Rudnev, D., Evangelista, C., Kim, I.F., Soboleva, A., Tomashevsky, M., Marshall, K.A., Phillippy, K.H., Sherman, P.M., Muertter, R.N., Edgar, R.: NCBI GEO: archive for high-throughput functional genomic data. Nucl. Acids Res. 37(suppl. 1), D885–D890 (2009)
11. Parkinson, H., Kapushesky, M., Kolesnikov, N., Rustici, G., Shojatalab, M., Abeygunawardena, N., Berube, H., Dylag, M., Emam, I., Farne, A., et al.: ArrayExpress update–from an archive of functional genomics experiments to the atlas of gene expression. In: Nucleic Acids Research (2008)
12. Berman, J., Edgerton, M., Friedman, B.: The tissue microarray data exchange specification: A community-based, open source tool for sharing tissue microarray data. BMC Medical Informatics and Decision Making 3(1), 5 (2003)

13. Moreau, L., Miles, S., Missier, P., Simmhan, Y., Futrelle, J., Myers, J., Stephan, E., Kwasnikowska, N., den Bussche, J.V., Freire, J., et al.: The open provenance model (v1. 1) (2009)
14. McGuinness, D., Ding, L., Pinheiro da Silva, P., Chang, C.: Pml 2: A modular explanation interlingua. In: Proceedings of AAAI, vol. 7 (2007)
15. Davidson, S.B., Freire, J.: Provenance and scientific workflows: challenges and opportunities. In: Proceedings of the 2008 ACM SIGMOD International Conference on Management of Data, pp. 1345–1350 (2008)
16. Moreau, L., Kwasnikowska, N., Van den Bussche, J.: The Foundations of the Open Provenance Model (2009)
17. Rayner, T., Rocca-Serra, P., Spellman, P., Causton, H., Farne, A., Holloway, E., Irizarry, R., Liu, J., Maier, D., Miller, M., Petersen, K., Quackenbush, J., Sherlock, G., Stoeckert, C., White, J., Whetzel, P., Wymore, F., Parkinson, H., Sarkans, U., Ball, C., Brazma, A.: A simple spreadsheet-based, MIAME-supportive format for microarray data: MAGE-TAB. BMC Bioinformatics 7(1), 489 (2006)
18. Bian, X., Klemm, J., Basu, A., Hadfield, J., Srinivasa, R., Parnell, T., Miller, S., Mason, W., Kokotov, D., Duncan, M., et al.: Data submission and curation for caArray, a standard based microarray data repository system (2009)
19. Stokes, T., Torrance, J., Li, H., Wang, M.: ArrayWiki: an enabling technology for sharing public microarray data repositories and meta-analyses. BMC bioinformatics 9(Suppl 6), S18 (2008)
20. Farquhar, A., Fikes, R., Rice, J.: The ontolingua server: A tool for collaborative ontology construction. International Journal of Human-Computers Studies 46(6), 707–727 (1997)
21. Antkiewicz, M., Czarnecki, K.: Framework-specific modeling languages with round-trip engineering. In: Wang, J., Whittle, J., Harel, D., Reggio, G. (eds.) MoDELS 2006. LNCS, vol. 4199, p. 692. Springer, Heidelberg (2006)
22. Missier, P., Belhajjame, K., Zhao, J., Goble, C.: Data lineage model for Taverna workflows with lightweight annotation requirements. In: Freire, J., Koop, D., Moreau, L. (eds.) IPAW 2008. LNCS, vol. 5272, pp. 17–30. Springer, Heidelberg (2008)
23. Whetzel, P., Parkinson, H., Causton, H., Fan, L., Fostel, J., Fragoso, G., Game, L., Heiskanen, M., Morrison, N., Rocca-Serra, P., et al.: The MGED Ontology: a resource for semantics-based description of microarray experiments. Bioinformatics 22(7), 866 (2006)
24. McCusker, J.P., McGuinness, D.L.: Representing high throughput biomedical experiments using the open provenance model. Technical report, Technical Report TW-2010-14, Tetherless World Constellation, Rensselaer Polytechnic Institute, USA (2010)
25. Shannon, P., Markiel, A., Ozier, O., Baliga, N., Wang, J., Ramage, D., Amin, N., Schwikowski, B., Ideker, T.: Cytoscape: a software environment for integrated models of biomolecular interaction networks. Genome research 13(11), 2498 (2003)

Janus: From Workflows to Semantic Provenance and Linked Open Data

Paolo Missier[1], Satya S. Sahoo[3,*], Jun Zhao[2,**],
Carole Goble[1], and Amit Sheth[3]

[1] School of Computer Science, University of Manchester, UK
{pmissier,carole}@cs.man.ac.uk
[2] Department of Zoology, University of Oxford, UK
jun.zhao@zoo.ox.ac.uk
[3] The Kno.e.sis Center, Wright State University, Dayton, OH, USA
{sahoo.2,amit.sheth}@wright.edu

Abstract. Data provenance graphs are form of metadata that can be used to establish a variety of properties of data products that undergo sequences of transformations, typically specified as workflows. Their usefulness for answering user provenance queries is limited, however, unless the graphs are enhanced with domain-specific annotations. In this paper we propose a model and architecture for semantic, domain-aware provenance, and demonstrate its usefulness in answering typical user queries. Furthermore, we discuss the additional benefits and the technical implications of publishing provenance graphs as a form of Linked Data. A prototype implementation of the model is available for data produced by the Taverna workflow system.

1 Introduction

Experimental science increasingly relies upon computational techniques and large-scale data management to achieve its goals. As with any experimental method, either manual or automated, an important step of the scientific process is the validation of its results. In the case of automated, high-throughput data generation and transformation pipelines, implemented for example as workflows, the complexity of the processes and the volumes of data call for validation procedures to be automated, too. One of the prominent approaches involves the analysis of detailed traces of the data transformations that are recorded during the execution of the data pipeline. These traces are a form of metadata, relative to the data involved in the process, known as data provenance. The growing realisation of the importance of this type of metadata for experimental science has in recent years spurred a wealth of research in provenance acquisition and analysis [17,1,5,7].

Provenance metadata is structured as a causal graph amongst data elements as they undergo several transformations through some composition of processes.

---

* This work was partly funded by NIH RO1 Grant# 1R01HL087795-01A1.
** This work was partly funded by EPSRC Grant# EP/G049327/1.

D.L. McGuinness, J.R. Michaelis, and L. Moreau (Eds.): IPAW 2010, LNCS 6378, pp. 129–141, 2010.

The two main strains of research in this area concentrate on (i) provenance modelling, with the goal of supporting the users' data validation tasks; and (ii) data architectures for provenance management. The work presented in this paper falls in the former of these two categories. Most of the provenance models proposed so far, including those just cited, have been focusing on describing the causal relationships amongst data products, without specific concern for the semantic characterisation of those products. We refer to these graphs as *domain-agnostic*, as they do not include any reference to domain-specific terms. In contrast, we propose a new semantic model of provenance, embodied by *domain-aware* graphs, designed to support data derivation questions that are formulated by user-scientists using domain-specific terminology. Fig. 1 clarifies the distinction between the two types of graphs[1]. The main differences between Fig. 1(a) and Fig. 1(b) are the additional semantic annotations shown in the latter. In this limited example, these are of the form V `instance-of` C or V `has-source` C', where V is a value, and C, C' are terms in some domain vocabulary, for biology concepts and biological database resources, respectively. We expect that, regardless of the specific formalism chosen to specify these annotations, domain-aware graphs be useful to answer a broader class of user questions than their domain-agnostic counterparts (namely those questions that rely upon domain terms).

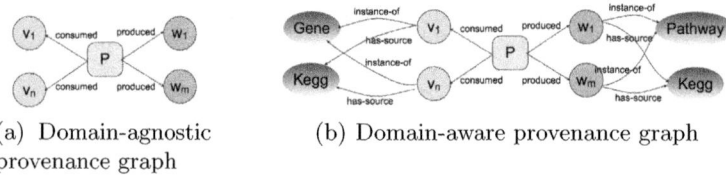

(a) Domain-agnostic provenance graph   (b) Domain-aware provenance graph

Fig. 1. Adding simple annotations to provenance graphs

Taking this idea further, we also note that grounding a provenance model in the Semantic Web framework presents additionally opportunities for supporting an even broader class of user questions. In particular, we explore the idea of making semantic provenance graphs a part of the broad Web of Data, an increasingly rich source of interconnected data that is uniformly represented according to the principles and conventions of Linked Open Data (LOD) [4]. In practice, we show how mapping data elements in the graph to equivalent data that is published elsewhere in the Web of Data, makes it possible for queries to retrieve properties of data, which are not explicitly represented in the provenance graph or its annotations, but are instead associated with their equivalent external representations.

---

[1] We use an abstract notation that is close to the one adopted in the Open Provenance Model http://www.openprovenance.org, where data values (the circles) are either produced or consumed by processes (the squares).

1.1 Paper Scope and Contributions

The idea of semantic provenance was first proposed in [15], but few concrete examples exist to date of its realisation beyond, for example, [6]. In this paper we take a concrete step towards the implementation of a semantic provenance model, code-named *Janus*, cast specifically in the context of provenance for data processed by Life Sciences workflows. We describe a practical implementation of *Janus*[2] , which is grounded in the Taverna workflow model [10] and (domain-agnostic) provenance model [12], and demonstrate its technical feasibility as well as its benefits to users in terms of enhanced query answering capabilities. The paper offers the following specific contributions. Firstly, we set *Janus* in the Semantic Web framework, where we define its model as an extension of the *Provenir* upper ontology for workflow-based data provenance [16]. In this setting, *Janus* consists of a domain-agnostic part, which models essentially the same entities as the existing Taverna provenance model, and a domain-aware part, obtained by extending the ontology to include properties and classes like those shown earlier in Fig 1(b). Secondly, we describe the prototype implementation of an extension to the current Taverna provenance architecture, which produces semantic, RDF-based provenance graphs for workflow runs, that conform to the *Janus* ontology.

Thirdly, we show how the RDF provenance graph can be domain-enhanced by associating semantic types from a variety of public ontologies to some of its elements. We also discuss how existing semantic annotations on the workflow and its composing services, when available, can be automatically propagated to the provenance graph. We then show how, in this setting, we can answer a class of user queries that predicate on the domain annotations. Finally, we show on a practical example how the provenance graph can "blend in" as part of the Web of Data, and exemplify our approach by mapping data identifiers in the graph to those in the Bio2RDF project [2], resulting in extended semantic provenance queries.

1.2 Related Work

While provenance data model is a well studied topic [17], the challenge of associating domain semantics to it has received relatively little attention. The Open Provenance Model (OPM) [13] provides the annotation framework to support the need for adding extra information to provenance entities. However, this framework is not defined in the current OPM OWL ontology[3]. Previous work by Cao et al. [6] and Zhao et al. [18] experimented with providing semantic annotations to provenance logs by post-processing, but without a clear data model for accommodating domain-semantics. Such a data model is essential for building a domain-aware provenance collection architecture that could scale beyond case studies. In this paper, we extend the Provenir ontology to create the domain-aware Janus provenance model to address the challenge.

---

[2] *Janus* is publicly available at: http://purl.org/net/taverna/janus#
[3] http://openprovenance.org/model/opm.owl

Query frameworks and user-facing visualizations to support a user-oriented view of provenance can be found in the work by Biton et al. [3] and Howe et al. [9]. Provenance queries that present information in a more meaningful way to the domain scientists have been implemented by Cao et al. [6] and McGuinness et al. [11]. This work takes it further by connecting domain-enhanced provenance graphs created locally with the global Web of Data in order to expand the possible semantic provenance queries.

2   A Concrete Example

Our running example consists of a bioinformatics workflow designed to find all known relationships between a specific region in the mouse genome, known as a QTL (Quantitative Trait Loci), and the metabolic pathways involving genes that are present in that region. A schematic representation of the workflow is given in Fig. 2(a).[4] The workflow starts by retrieving all the genes known to the Ensembl public database for a given input region, using the Biomart service. It then retrieves all metabolic pathways from the KEGG pathways database, such that at least one of those genes are involved.[5] Note that the schematic representation does not include the many adapter scripts that are required in reality to accomplish this composite task.

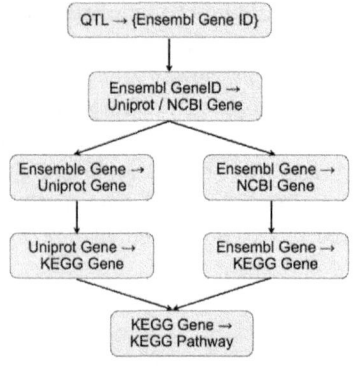

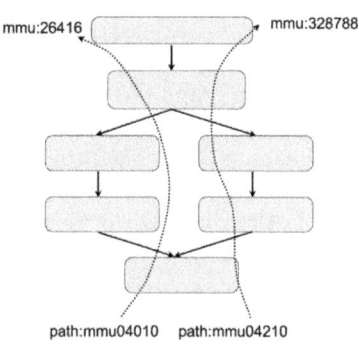

(a) Schematic representation of a Taverna workflow

(b) Schematic representation of a provenance graph for a workflow run

Fig. 2.

A scientist may want to ask a number of high-level questions regarding the relationship between the outputs and some of the inputs of a workflow execution ("run"). Amongst these, we are going to consider the following two, which can be expressed in terms of queries on a provenance graph:

---

[4] The actual workflow, too large to be reproduced here, can be found on the myExperiment Web site: http://www.myexperiment.org/workflows/931

[5] Ensembl: www.ensembl.org,
Biomart: www.biomart.org/,
KEGG: www.genome.jp/kegg/pathway.html

1. for each *Kegg pathway* observed in the workflow output (or for a specific one), find all *genes* that are within the input *QTL* and are involved in that pathway;
2. amongst all *genes* that are known to *perform a certain biological function*, list those that are involved in a certain *pathway*.

The terms in italics refer to concepts in the bioinformatics domain, similar to those in Fig. 1(b). Intuitively, one can answer (1) for a particular run, by traversing a domain-aware provenance graph for that run, like the one sketched in Fig. 2(b). An output value o for the workflow depends on some input or intermediate value i, if and only if there is a path from i to o in the graph. Thus, (1) can be reduced to a query that finds all pairs (i, o) such that o is of type *pathway*, i is of type *gene*, and there is a path from i to o. In Sec. 3.3 we show how our proposed semantic provenance framework supports this query.

The graph, however, is not sufficient to answer question (2), which refers to the *biological function* of a gene, a concept that is not included in the semantic annotations. Our approach in this case is based upon the idea that the genes that appear in the graph may also be published elsewhere in the broad Web of Data, where the missing annotations can potentially be found. When this is the case, one can formulate a hybrid query that (i) retrieves the biological functions of all the *genes* that appear in the graph, using a Linked Data query, and (ii) for those genes that satisfy the condition, find all paths to the corresponding *pathways* in the graph[6]. We elaborate on this strategy and on its limitations in Sec. 4, showing in particular how that the gene IDs in the graph can be mapped to Bio2RDF genes.

3   The *Janus* Semantic Provenance Infrastructure

The examples from the previous section highlight the need for incorporating domain semantics as part of the provenance model, to bridge the gap between the domain-agnostic provenance produced during workflow execution, and the users' domain-oriented view of provenance. An expressive provenance model with well-defined formal semantics not only enables complex domain-specific information to be modeled, but also facilitates provenance interoperability and supports reasoning over large sets of provenance information. As mentioned in the introduction, formally *Janus* is an extension of *Provenir*, an upper-level reference OWL DL ontology for provenance modeling designed to be extended to represent provenance in multiple domains. In turn, Provenir extends concepts from the well-known Basic Formal Ontology (BFO)[7] to define a set of provenance terms, including the three fundamental concepts of *data*, *process*, and *agent*. Provenir also defines a set of 11 *named relationships* amongst classes, including partonomy relations, temporal information, precedence, and causal relationships, providing

---

[6] Note however, that there is no guarantee that the gene will be found in the Web of Data, or that the condition on its external annotations can be evaluated there.
[7] http://ontology.buffalo.edu/bfo/

a foundation for the semantic modelling of provenance. As an upper-level reference model for provenance, Provenir ensures a common modeling approach, conceptual clarity of provenance terms, and use of design patterns for consistent provenance modeling.

3.1   Modeling Domain-Agnostic Provenance in *Janus*

The Taverna provenance model defined in [12] includes both a static and a dynamic portion. The static portion describes the graph structure of a workflow specification (processors, processor ports, and data dependencies as links between ports), such as the one in our running example of Fig. 2(a). The dynamic portion accounts for multiple invocations of a processor that occur during workflow execution, as well as for the binding of actual values to the processors ports. In the first step of the design, we model the existing Taverna provenance model as an OWL ontology. As illustrated in Fig. 3, the classes in the static portion (janus:workflow_spec, janus:processor_spec, and class janus:port) extend corresponding *Provenir* classes and are associated through appropriate properties, for example janus:processor_spec provenir:has_parameter janus:port. Note that data links in the workflow are modelled using the link_from property from port onto itself. Individuals in these classes include the workflow itself (gene_pathway_workflow), its processors (eg. genes_in_qtl), and the processors' ports (eg. qtl_end_position, chromosome_name). In turn, these individuals may be related to one or more run-time counterparts in the dynamic portion of the ontology through object property has_execution:

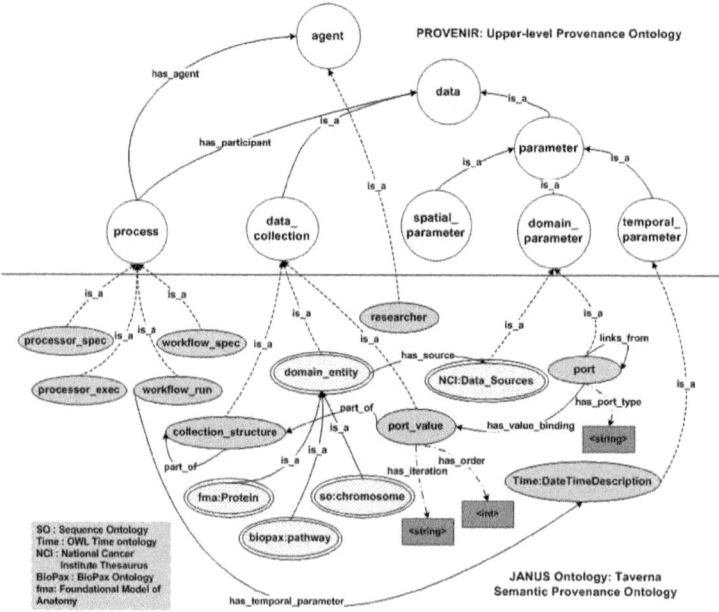

Fig. 3. Domain-aware *Janus* as an extension of *Provenir*

$dom(\texttt{has\_execution}) = \texttt{workflow\_spec or processor\_spec}$

$range(\texttt{has\_execution}) = \texttt{workflow\_exec or processor\_exec}$

and `has_value_binding`:

$dom(\texttt{has\_value\_binding}) = \texttt{port}, \quad range(\texttt{has\_value\_binding}) = \texttt{port\_value}$

3.2   Modeling Semantic Provenance in *Janus*

We now describe the *Janus* extension to include domain-specific terms. A variety of scientific communities are creating ontologies to model domain knowledge, for example the National Center for Biomedical Ontologies (NCBO)[8] currently lists 166 publicly available ontologies in the Life Sciences domain. To model semantic provenance in *Janus*, we re-use the classes defined in four public ontologies listed at NCBO, namely the BioPAX, National Cancer Institute Thesaurus, Foundational Model of Anatomy (FMA), and the Sequence ontologies, while the fifth ontology, OWL Time[9] is available from the W3C. This reuse strategy facilitates the interoperability of *Janus*-conformant provenance graphs with large public datasets. For example, these graph can be easily linked to the KEGG, Reactome, and BioCyc databases, which currently make their biological pathway datasets available as BioPAX-conformant RDF datasets.

These extensions are used to annotate both workflow processors and their ports. For example, the three input ports for our example workflow: `chromosome_name`, `start_position` and `end_position`, are annotated with concepts `so:chromosome` and `so:base_pair`, respectively, where the so prefix denotes the NCBO-listed Sequence Ontology. Similarly, ports that denote proteins and pathways are annotated using terms `fma:protein` and `biopax:pathway`, from the FMA and the BioPax ontology, respectively. In general, semantic types are associated to ports in an extensible way through the generic `has_value_type` property, according to the following pattern:

$dom(\texttt{has\_value\_type}) = \texttt{port}, \quad range(\texttt{has\_value\_type}) = \texttt{domain\_entity}$

`BioPax:pathway  owl:subClassOf  domain_entity`

`FMA:protein  owl:subClassOf  domain_entity`

For each workflow run, the Taverna provenance component produces domain-agnostic provenance in the form of an RDF graph that conforms to the *Janus* ontology just described, i.e., it contains RDF statements of the form N `rdf:type` C, where N is a node in the provenance graph and C is some *Janus* concept. The semantic annotation of these graphs assumes that the workflow specification is itself semantically annotated, and it involves automatically propagating those annotations, first to the static portion of the provenance graph, and then to the dynamic portion. Statically annotating the workflows

---

[8] http://www.bioontology.org/

[9] http://www.w3.org/TR/owl-time

prior to their execution is a realistic proposition. While this may involve a manual curation process, typical workflows never include more than a handful of services, and furthermore, in the long run one can assume that these annotations will be available through a registry that describes the services that compose the workflow (Taverna workflows essentially specify Web service compositions). The BioCatalogue registry for Life Science services[10], for example, is set out to provide semantic annotations for hundreds of services, and these annotations carry over to the workflows where the services are invoked.

The propagation of workflow annotations to the provenance graph is fairly straightforward. Firstly, consider a static workflow element, say port $X =$ chromosome_name, annotated with concept $C =$ so:chromosome in the workflow (using any available formalism). In the provenance graph this is expressed using the pattern:

X rdf:type Port, $C = \{c\}$, X has_value_type c

for example:

chromosome_name rdf:type Port, so:chromosome = {singleton_chromosome}

chromosome_name has_value_type singleton_chromosome

Secondly, the annotations on a port carry over to each of the values that are bound to that port[11], using a collection of inference rules like the following:

$$\frac{X \text{ rdf:type Port} \quad C = \{c\} \quad X \text{ has\_value\_type } c \quad X \text{ has\_value } v \quad v \text{ rdf:type PortValue}}{v \text{ rdf:type } C}$$

This rule asserts the value v as an individual of the *Janus* class C. The set of rules accounts for various annotations, for example the following rule:

$$\frac{X \text{ rdf:type Port} \quad X \text{ has\_source } S \quad X \text{ has\_value } v \quad v \text{ rdf:type PortValue}}{v \text{ has\_source } S}$$

annotates v with the data source of the port (for instance, the KEGG database).

As a proof of concept, the *Janus* ontology currently models the semantic provenance terms that are adequate for representing the domain semantics of our example workflow, using less than 30 classes and properties with a DL expressivity of $ALCH(D)$. Many of the classes, for example to model collection data structures, have not been described as they are less relevant to our discussion in this paper. In the future, we plan to extend *Janus* with the domain terms used to annotate the default set of services in the Taverna release version.

3.3   Provenance Query Infrastructure for *Janus*

We now describe the *Janus* query infrastructure that has been implemented to support the example provenance queries discussed in Sec. 2. The query

---

[10] http://www.biocatalogue.org

[11] This assumes that the ports are strongly typed, i.e., that all values bound to the port have the same type as the port.

infrastructure is implemented using the open source Jena ARQ tool[12], and supports provenance queries expressed in the SPARQL query language [14]. We composed the SPARQL query pattern corresponding to the example query (1) from Sec. 2: "Find all the QTL genes that are involved in KEGG pathways". The SPARQL query pattern first identifies port values that are individuals of class `biopax:pathway` and are linked to values "KEGG", which are themselves individuals of class `NCI:Data_Sources`, through property `has_source`. In the next step, the query pattern traverses the property `has_value_binding` between a `port` and a `port_value`, followed by traversal of the property `links_from` between individuals of class `port`, until it reaches individuals of class `so:base_pair` that represent the result QTL genes (the second provenance query proposed in Sec. 2: "Find pathways that contain genes with specific functions," is discussed in the next section).

Provenance queries typically involve a recursive traversal of the graph to compute a transitive closure, namely over the `links_from` property. We had two options for implementing the transitive closure function, namely a function that is tightly coupled to the RDF data store implementation, or a generic module that can be used with any RDF data store. We chose a generic implementation using the SPARQL ASK function, which allows the provenance query infrastructure to be used over multiple RDF stores. The SPARQL ASK function allows "application to test whether or not a query pattern has a solution," [14] without returning a result set or graph. The transitive closure functions starts with the port instance linked to the input value and then recursively expands the SPARQL query expression using the ASK function until a *false* value is returned. The SPARQL ASK function, in contrast to the SELECT and CONSTRUCT functions, does not bind the results of the query to variables in the query pattern, and is therefore a low-overhead function for computing transitive closures.

4   Taverna Provenance and Linked Data

So far we have shown how the domain-aware extensions to *Janus* enable answering domain-specific semantic provenance queries. In this section we describe how we can, in addition, also use these semantic annotations to link *Janus*-compliant provenance graphs to the open Web of Data in order to expand the range of supported domain provenance queries.

4.1   Publishing Taverna Provenance as Linked Data

Because *Janus* provenance is already available as RDF graphs, we only need to make these graphs Linked data-compliant and accessible on the Web. This means that 1) each Janus entity URI should be derefenceable, and 2) wherever possible, the data URIs under the *Janus* namespace should be mapped to other linked data URIs on the Web. We use existing Linked Data publication tools, namely Pubby[13], to implement the first step. In order to connect *Janus* graphs with

---

[12] http://jena.sourceforge.net/ARQ/
[13] http://www4.wiwiss.fu-berlin.de/pubby/

LOD we create `rdfs:seeAlso` links between *Janus* data URIs and Bio2RDF [2] data URIs. We use Bio2RDF data URIs because Bio2RDF is one of the earliest linked datasets and it is regarded as a nucleus of the Life Science datasets. Using the semantic annotations associated with *Janus* provenance, we define a set of rules for the identity mapping. Given a *Janus* data item d_i with value $value(d_i)$, its mapping Bio2RDF URI $URI(d_i)$ is determined by the type of d_i and the data source where d_i comes from, according to the following rules:

- IF isType(d_i) == Gene AND isSource(d_i) == Entrez THEN
  - URI(d_i) = http://bio2rdf.org/geneid: + value(d_i)
- IF isType(d_i) == Gene AND isSource(d_i) == UniProt THEN
  - URI(d_i) = http://bio2rdf.org/uniprot: + value(d_i)
- IF isType(d_i) == Gene AND isSource(d_i) == KEGG THEN
  - URI(d_i) = http://bio2rdf.org/kegg: + value(d_i)
- IF isType(d_i) == Pathway AND isSource(d_i) == KEGG THEN
  - URI(d_i) = http://bio2rdf.org/path: + value(d_i)

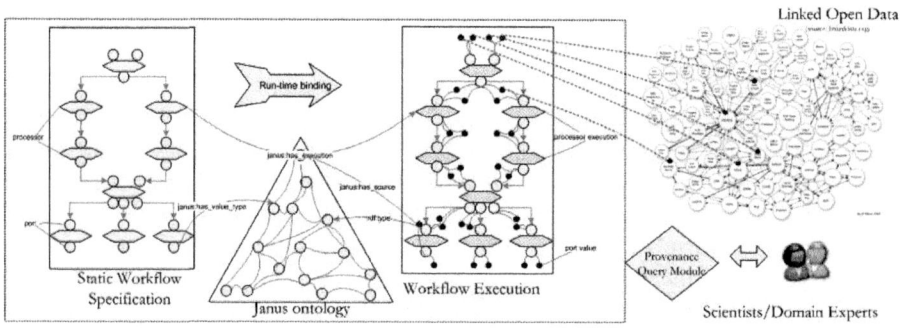

Fig. 4. Semantic provenance for Taverna in the Linked Data context

4.2   Consuming Taverna Provenance as Linked Data

As mentioned, creating Janus Linked Data provenance that is connected to Bio2RDF makes the provenance graphs an integral part of the Web of Life Science data (see Figure 4). This opens the provenance graph to queries that run on the Web of Data. Furthermore, provenance graphs that are created during different workflow runs are now indirectly, and automatically connected through their common external data URIs, thus supporting queries that span across multiple runs.

To demonstrate this, we show how we can support a semantic provenance query that requires access to both *Janus* and the various Bio2RDF repositories, by executing a single SPARQL query against SQUIN [8], a Linked Data query engine. Instead of having to write separate SPARQL queries against each individual data source, SQUIN allows us to treat the whole Web of Data as one single data space. It is a query engine that applies the "follow your nose" principle of Linked Data: it traverses the whole Web of Data to retrieve all relevant data

sources for a query by taking the URIs in the query and those in the intermediate results, following links of these URIs to other data sources, and applying
the querying graph pattern to the intermediate result space in order to obtain
relevant results.

Our example query below searches for the functions of those proteins encoded
by the Entrez genes that were generated by the executions of the example workflow in Figure 2(b). The domain knowledge about the genes is drawn from two
Bio2RDF data repositories and the knowledge about which Taverna data products are Entrez genes comes of the domain-enhanced *Janus* provenance. This
simple SPARQL query needs access to at least three linked datasets. SQUIN
query engine allows us to write one single query against these multiple data
sources. The result will return the biological process related to the data products from any workflow runs that are Entrez genes. We can then use semantic
provenance queries similar to the one presented in Sec. 3.3 to search for KEGG
pathways that contain these genes.

```
PREFIX uniprot: <http://purl.uniprot.org/core/>
PREFIX ex: <http://purl.org/net/taverna/janus/>
PREFIX : <http://purl.org/net/taverna/janus#>
SELECT distinct ?entrezgene ?function
WHERE {
ex:dataproudct1 rdf:type <http://purl.org/obo/owl/sequence#gene> .
ex:dataproudct1 :has_source :entrez_gene .
ex:dataproudct1 rdfs:seeAlso ?entrezgene .
?entrezgene <http://bio2rdf.org/bio2rdf_resource:xPath> ?protein .
?protein  uniprot:classifiedWith ?function.
}
```

This example shows that drawing on the domain knowledge from the Linked
Data cloud enables us to extend the kind of domain-level provenance queries
that we can implement that are more meaningful to the scientists. Finding specific KEGG pathways that are related to genes of interesting functions will help
scientists quickly identify potential pathways from hundreds of experiment results. The above example query could enable scientists to quickly identify the
presence of pathways that consistently exist in different experimentations, including those that were conducted by the scientists themselves.

5   Conclusions and Further Work

We have presented a semantic provenance model for workflow data, called *Janus*,
and a prototype implementation for the Taverna workflow system and provenance model. The implementation demonstrates the benefits of collecting semantic provenance, by showing exemplars semantic provenance queries that can
now be answered by the system.

The main objection that is often raised in connection with semantic annotations, is the annotation cost. We have noted, in Sec. 3, that the annotation
effort is actually limited to the workflow specification, and indeed, possibly just
to the services used in the workflow, when those are annotated once and for all

as part of the service registry curation process. In turn, this observation provides additional motivation for the development of registries like Biocatalogue.

Our investigation into the idea of publishing provenance graphs as Linked Data is still preliminary and requires additional insight. For instance, the simple rules used to link *Janus* provenance with the Web of Data do not consider the possibility that the workflow and Bio2RDF refer to different copies of the same database. Also, some of the mapping Bio2RDF URIs might not exist at all or are actually linked to mismatching data entities, and the precision of the mapping between *Janus* and Bio2RDF data URIs needs to be evaluated. Finally, we plan to conduct a user assessment as a way to establish the perceived value of semantic provenance from the users' perspective.

References

1. Barga, R.S., Digiampietri, L.A.: Automatic capture and efficient storage of e-Science experiment provenance. Concurrency and Computation: Practice and Experience 20, 419–429 (2008)
2. Belleau, F., Nolin, M.A., Tourigny, N., Rigault, P., Morissette, J.: Bio2RDF: Towards a Mashup to Build Bioinformatics Knowledge Systems. Journal of Biomedical Informatics 41, 706–716 (2008)
3. Biton, O., Cohen Boulakia, S., Davidson, S.B.: Zoom*UserViews: Querying Relevant Provenance in Workflow Systems. In: VLDB, pp. 1366–1369 (2007)
4. Bizer, C., Heath, T., Berners-Lee, T.: Linked Data - The Story So Far. Int. Journal on Semantic Web and Information Systems, Special Issue on Linked Data (2009) (in press)
5. Bowers, S., McPhillips, T.M., Ludäscher, B.: Provenance in collection-oriented scientific workflows. Concurrency and Computation: Practice and Experience 20, 519–529 (2008)
6. Cao, B., Plale, B., Subramanian, G., Missier, P., Goble, C., Simmhan, Y.: Semantically Annotated Provenance in the Life Science Grid. In: Freire, J., Missier, P., Sahoo, S.S. (eds.) 1st International Workshop on the Role of Semantic Web in Provenance Management. CEUR Proceedings (2009)
7. Davidson, S.B., Freire, J.: Provenance and scientific workflows: challenges and opportunities. In: SIGMOD Conference, pp. 1345–1350 (2008)
8. Hartig, O., Bizer, C., Freytag, J.C.: Executing SPARQL queries over the web of linked data. In: Bernstein, A., Karger, D.R., Heath, T., Feigenbaum, L., Maynard, D., Motta, E., Thirunarayan, K. (eds.) ISWC 2009. LNCS, vol. 5823, pp. 293–309. Springer, Heidelberg (2009)
9. Howe, B., Lawson, P., Bellinger, R., Anderson, E., Santos, E., Freire, J., Scheidegger, C., Baptista, A., Silva, C.: End-to-end escience: Integrating workflow, query, visualization, and provenance at an ocean observatory. In: Procs Fourth IEEE International Conference on eScience, pp. 127–134 (2008)
10. Hull, D., Wolstencroft, K., Stevens, R., Goble, C., Pocock, M.R., Li, P., Oinn, T.: Taverna: a tool for building and running workflows of services. Nucleic acids research 34, 729–732 (2006)
11. McGuinness, D.L., Fox, P., Pinheiro da Silva, P., Zednik, S., Del Rio, N., Ding, L., West, P., Chang, C.: Annotating and embedding provenance in science data repositories to enable next generation science applications. In: American Geophysical

Union, Fall Meeting (AGU 2008), Eos Trans. AGU, Fall Meet. Suppl., Abstract IN11C-1052, vol. 89(53) (2008)

12. Missier, P., Paton, N.W., Belhajjame, K.: Fine-grained and efficient lineage querying of collection-based workflow provenance. In: Procs. of EDBT, Lausanne, Switzerland (2010)
13. Moreau, L.: The Open Provenance Model v 1.1 (2009)
14. Prud'ommeaux, E., Seaborne, A.: SPARQL Query Language for RDF. W3C Recommendation (2008)
15. Sahoo, S.S., Sheth, A., Henson, C.: Semantic provenance for eScience: Managing the deluge of scientific data. IEEE Internet Computing 12, 46–54 (2008)
16. Sahoo, S.S., Sheth, A.: Provenir ontology: Towards a Framework for eScience Provenance Management (2009)
17. Simmhan, Y., Plale, B., Gannon, D.: A survey of data provenance in e-science. SIGMOD Record 34, 31–36 (2005)
18. Zhao, J., Wroe, C., Goble, C., Stevens, R., Quan, D., Greenwood, M.: Using Semantic Web Technologies for Representing e-Science Provenance. In: McIlraith, S.A., Plexousakis, D., van Harmelen, F. (eds.) ISWC 2004. LNCS, vol. 3298, pp. 92–106. Springer, Heidelberg (2004)

Provenance-Aware Faceted Search in Drupal

Zhenning Shangguan, Jinguang Zheng, and Deborah L. McGuinness

Tetherless World Constellation,
Computer Science Department, Rensselaer Polytechnic Institute,
110 8th Street, Troy, NY 12180, U.S.A.
{shangz,zhengj3,dlm}@cs.rpi.edu

Abstract. As the web content is increasingly generated in more diverse situations, provenance is becoming more and more critical. While a variety of approaches have been investigated for capturing and making use of provenance metadata, arguably no single best-practice approach has emerged. In this paper, we investigate an approach that leverages one of the most popular content management systems – Drupal. More specifically, we study how provenance metadata can be captured and later published as structured data on the Web using Drupal. We also demonstrate how provenance metadata can be used to facilitate faceted search in Drupal.

Keywords: Provenance, Faceted Search, PML, Drupal.

1 Introduction

Information on the Web is increasingly generated using a wide variety of diverse sources. It is also pointed out in [1] that capturing provenance both within and across systems, and publishing that provenance provides potential for many benefits, such as tracing audit trails of data, reproducing scientific experimental results, finding useful information, evaluating data quality, establishing information accountability, etc.

Although there have been numerous previous research efforts aimed at representing and tracking provenance in both closed and open systems, even at different levels of granularity, many of the approaches have limitations and inflexibilities that result from decisions made from targeting a specific system, application, or scenario. Moreover, historically provenance research has often focused on capturing provenance metadata; currently there is an increasing interest in studying how provenance can be used in different ways.

With the goal of exploring the issues mentioned above, this short paper describes some of our ongoing efforts related to provenance using a Drupal-based solution. Our proposed demonstration will highlight two areas:

- Representing and publishing provenance metadata. We are exploring the configurability and extensibility of Drupal. Our approach is to create a provenance-aware Drupal-based platform for web applications.
- Providing provenance-aware faceted search. We are designing and implementing a Drupal-based faceted search that can search over metadata and use provenance to help inform search results and help filter results. We will demonstrate

D.L. McGuinness, J.R. Michaelis, and L. Moreau (Eds.): IPAW 2010, LNCS 6378, pp. 142–147, 2010.

how provenance-aware search can be more efficient, and provide insight into ranking and presentation options. We also will expose how provenance facets, such as temporal facets related to the creation and modification time of some Drupal content, are being used in our search functionality.

The rest of the paper is organized as follows. Section 2 highlights the related work. Section 3 demonstrates our initial effort to capture, encode, and publish provenance information as structured RDF. Section 4 describes how to make use of these provenance metadata to facilitate faceted search. Finally, we conclude the paper and outline some future work in section 5.

2   Related Work

Four areas of work are considered related to the topic of our paper.

There is a diverse literature on systems and applications that are capable of capturing provenance metadata, for example, Taverna [2], VisTrails [3], REDUX [4], Pegasus [5], Karma [6]. While they successfully demonstrate different approaches of capturing provenance, they can be viewed as having an application-dependent nature and thus they can be less flexible and less extensible when applications differ greatly from those that these approaches were designed to satisfy. Our work differs from these approaches in that we are investigating mechanisms to capture and publish provenance using Drupal, which has the potential to serve as the foundation of an application-independent solution.

Another spectrum of related research is the generic provenance models and vocabularies, most notably the Open Provenance Model (OPM) [1], Provenance Markup Language (PML) [7], and the Provenance Vocabulary [8]. While providing different vocabularies for representing provenance, there are certain conceptual overlaps between them. For example, both OPM and Provenance Vocabulary have similar basic concepts, i.e., Agents (OPM) and Actors (Provenance Vocabulary) denoting people, Processes (OPM) and Executions (Provenance Vocabulary) representing executions of actions or processes, and Artifacts (both OPM and Provenance Vocabulary) representing the entity produced or manipulated. Currently, we are using PML to encode the provenance metadata. However, supporting provenance representations using different domain-independent provenance vocabularies is planned as one of our future work areas.

Faceted search for exploration has been widely studied over the past years. Numerous research efforts [9] [10] [11] have demonstrated benefits including usability and flexibility of faceted browsers when interacting with structured data (e.g., relational databases, XML, RDF). In this paper, we are making use of the generated provenance metadata to facilitate faceted search and help locate the desired information.

Drupal, one of the most popular CMS systems, has been widely deployed. Recently, there is an emerging effort from both the Semantic Web community and the Drupal development community to enable Drupal to publish semantic metadata (e.g., RDF, RDFa) [12]. Our implementation makes use of some of the Drupal modules introduced in [12] to create provenance related node fields. We are also developing Drupal module of our own to publish provenance metadata encoded in PML.

3   Capturing and Publishing Provenance in Drupal

The information that Drupal[1] organizes and manages is called *content*. Usually, a piece of content in Drupal corresponds to a single *node* (in the form of a *page*) that has a title, an optional body text description, and perhaps several additional *fields*. Every node also belongs to a particular *content type*, such as Person, Blog and etc. The site administrator uses the Content Construction Kit (CCK)[2] to create a node by specifying its content type (e.g., Person), title (e.g., name of the person), body text (e.g., short bio of the person), and fields (e.g., first name, last name, email of the person). Furthermore, the RDF CCK[3] module extends the functionality of CCK to enable the definition of mappings between: 1) a specific content type (e.g., Person) and an RDF class (e.g., foaf:Person), and 2) a node field (e.g., field_firstname) and an RDF property (e.g., foaf:givenName).

Currently, our initial implementation of the Drupal provenance module is capable of capturing provenance at two levels of granularity.

- Node-level: This level focuses on the provenance metadata associated with a node in Drupal, such as who created the node, when the node was first created, and when the node was last modified.
- Content-level: This level keeps track of the provenance metadata associated with all the revisions of a node in Drupal, such as who modified the body text of the node and changed the values of the fields, when these modifications and changes happened, as well as the texts/values after every revision.

The benefit of having both the node-level and content-level provenance is that the former captures the basic provenance metadata about the node while the latter keeps track of the detailed edit history information.

The implementation of capturing node-level provenance is straightforward: we can use CCK and RDF CCK to define several provenance related fields and map them to the RDF properties from our chosen provenance vocabulary. Currently, we define two fields for every node in Drupal and map them to *pmlp:hasCreationDateTime* and *pmlp:hasModificationDateTime*, representing when the node was first created and last modified respectively.

In contrast to capturing node-level provenance, keeping track of the content-level provenance is not natively supported in Drupal. Thus we develop our own provenance module[4], making use of various Drupal core hook function and core API.

Besides capturing provenance metadata, our module is also capable of publishing these metadata as RDF on the Web. To access both the node-level and the content-level provenance metadata, users can follow the URL pattern *http://your_domain_name/drupal-dir/node/node-id/pml* for every node in a standard Drupal installation

---

[1] We are using Drupal version 6.16 and PHP 5.2 at the time of this writing. Unless explicitly stated, this holds for all the discussions throughout this paper.

[2] Content Construction Kit (CCK) module: http://drupal.org/project/cck.

[3] RDF CCK module: http://drupal.org/project/rdfcck.

[4] The source code for our provenance module can be found at http://tw2.tw.rpi.edu/drupal-dev/provenance.zip.

without clean URLs[5] turned on. Currently we are only using PML to represent the provenance metadata, with support for OPM and Provenance Vocabulary in progress. Figure 1 shows the exported provenance metadata for a node in our experimental Drupal installation.

Fig. 1. Exported Provenance Metadata for a Drupal node

4 Provenance-Aware Faceted Search in Drupal

Being able to capture both the node-level and content-level provenance immediately brings about a lot of benefits, especially for provenance-ware search in Drupal. Currently our provenance-aware faceted search is implemented using the Exhibit module[6] of Drupal. More specifically, we leverage the functionality of it to build the faceted search interface, with some facets generated from the node-level provenance metadata, such as *pmlp:hasCreationDateTime* and *pmlp:hasModificationDateTime*. Our initial implementation is demonstrated in Figure 2, with the "Creation Time" facet generated from the *pmlp:hasCreationDateTime* node field.

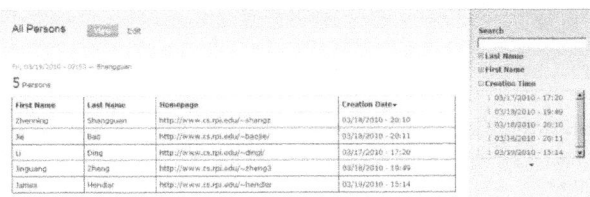

Fig. 2. Initial implementation of provenance-aware faceted search

5 Conclusion and Future Work

In this paper we described some of our ongoing effort to capture and publish provenance metadata in Drupal. With the help of various Drupal modules, such as CCK and

---

[5] Drupal clean URLs: http://drupal.org/getting-started/clean-urls. The provenance metadata can also be accessed via a similar URL pattern by appending "/pml" to the end of a node URL.

[6] Exhibit Drupal module: http://drupal.org/project/exhibit.

RDF CCK, node-level provenance can be captured by defining node fields and establishing mappings between them and RDF properties in the chosen provenance model, which is PML in our case. We also developed a provenance module in order to capture content-level provenance, which can be used to trace the revision history of nodes in a deployed Drupal website. Finally, our initial effort to facilitate faceted search with the help of the captured provenance metadata is also presented. We plan to provide a demonstration of our provenance-aware faceted search in one (or more) of our eScience applications at IPAW.

We identify two general directions for future work. First, our current implementation supports provenance encodings using only PML, without giving the user the ability to choose which provenance model to use. We plan to further enable the user to specify their desired provenance model when exporting the provenance metadata. Second, at present only the node-level provenance is exploited in the faceted search. However, content-level provenance might also contain useful properties to generate facets, such as revision time, date, and the user who made that revision. Moreover, content-level provenance can also be used to generate the edit history of the contents managed by Drupal. Therefore, another important aspect of our future work is to take advantage of the content-level provenance to further improve faceted search and generate edit history information of the nodes (pages) in Drupal. We also plan to leverage provenance data to help filter search results when result sets are large.

References

1. Moreau, L.: The Foundations for Provenance on the Web. J. Foundations and Trends in Web Science (2009)
2. Zhao, J., Goble, C.A., Stevens, R., Turi, D.: Mining Taverna's semantic web of provenance. Concurrency and Computation: Practice and Experience 20(5), 463–472 (2008)
3. Freire, J., Silva, C.T., Callahan, S.P., Santos, E., Scheidegger, C.E., Vo, H.T.: Managing rapidly-evolving scientific workflows. In: Moreau, L., Foster, I. (eds.) IPAW 2006. LNCS, vol. 4145, pp. 10–18. Springer, Heidelberg (2006)
4. Barga, R.S., Digiampietri, L.A.: Automatic capture and efficient storage of e-science experiment provenance. Concurrency and Computation: Practice and Experience 20(5), 419–429 (2008)
5. Kim, J., Deelman, E., Gil, Y., Mehta, G., Ratnakar, V.: Provenance trails in the wings/pegasus system. Concurrency and Computation: Practice and Experience 20(5), 587–597 (2008)
6. Simmhan, Y.L., Plale, B., Gannon, D.: Karma2: Provenance management for data-driven workflows. Int. J. Web Service Res. 5(2), 1–22 (2008)
7. McGuinness, D.L., Ding, L., Pinheiro da Silva, P., Chang, C.: PML2: A modular explanation Interlingua. In: ExaCt (2007)
8. Hartig, O., Zhao, J.: Using Web Data Provenance for Quality Assessment. In: Proceedings of the 1st Int. Workshop on the Role of Semantic Web in Provenance Management (SWPM) at ISWC, Washington, DC, USA (2009)
9. Hildebrand, M., van Ossenbruggen, J., Hardman, L.: /facet: A Browser for Heterogeneous Semantic Web Repositories. In: Cruz, I., Decker, S., Allemang, D., Preist, C., Schwabe, D., Mika, P., Uschold, M., Aroyo, L.M. (eds.) ISWC 2006. LNCS, vol. 4273, pp. 272–285. Springer, Heidelberg (2006)

10. Oren, E., Delbru, R., Decker, S.: Extending Faceted Navigation for RDF Data. In: Cruz, I., Decker, S., Allemang, D., Preist, C., Schwabe, D., Mika, P., Uschold, M., Aroyo, L.M. (eds.) ISWC 2006. LNCS, vol. 4273, pp. 559–572. Springer, Heidelberg (2006)
11. Schraefel, M.C., Karam, M., Zhao, S.: mSpace: interaction design for user-determined, adaptable domain exploration in hypermedia. In: AH 2003: Workshop on Adaptive Hypermedia and Adaptive Web Based Systems, pp.21–235 (2003)
12. Corlosquet, S., Delbru, R., Clark, T., Polleres, A., Decker, S.: Produce and Consume Linked Data with Drupal. In: Bernstein, A., Karger, D.R., Heath, T., Feigenbaum, L., Maynard, D., Motta, E., Thirunarayan, K. (eds.) ISWC 2009. LNCS, vol. 5823, pp. 763–778. Springer, Heidelberg (2009)

Securing Provenance-Based Audits

Rocío Aldeco-Pérez and Luc Moreau

School of Electronics and Computer Science, University of Southampton,
Southampton SO17 1BJ, UK
{raap06r,l.moreau}@ecs.soton.ac.uk

Abstract. Given the significant increase of on-line services that require personal information from users, the risk that such information is misused has become an important concern. In such a context, information accountability is desirable since it allows users (and society in general) to decide, by means of audits, whether information is used appropriately. To ensure information accountability, information flow should be made transparent. It has been argued that data provenance can be used as the mechanism to underpin such a transparency. Under these conditions, an audit's quality depends on the quality of the captured provenance information. Thereby, the *integrity of provenance information* emerges as a decisive issue in the quality of a provenance-based audit. The aim of this paper is to secure provenance-based audits by the inclusion of cryptographic elements in the communication between the involved entities as well as in the provenance representation. This paper also presents a formalisation and an automatic verification of a set of security properties that increase the level of trust in provenance-based audit results.

1   Introduction

In recent years, an increasing number of on-line services have appeared on the Web, e.g. social networks, governmental sites, on-line selling sites. Most of them offer personalised services that require private personal information from their users. By disclosing personal information, users get access to a wide range of new functionalities, such as recommendations or customisation. But at the same time, they face the risk that their information is misused.

Within this context, it is desirable to allow users to verify whether their information was misused or not. In order to achieve this, information usage should be made transparent so it can be determined later whether the use of such information is appropriate [1]. In other words, the transparency of information usage enables information accountability, a property according to which users can inspect such information usage through a process we refer to as audit.

Weitzner *et al.* have recognised that provenance, which consists of causal dependencies between data and events explaining what contributed to a result in a specific state [2], can be used as a mechanism to achieve information accountability [1]. Thus, if provenance of data is available, processing becomes transparent since the provenance of data can be audited to decide whether information was used in a proper way.

D.L. McGuinness, J.R. Michaelis, and L. Moreau (Eds.): IPAW 2010, LNCS 6378, pp. 148–164, 2010.
© Springer-Verlag Berlin Heidelberg 2010

In order to support such a vision, systems should be made *provenance-aware* [3] by describing all the steps and data derivations involved in their execution, in the form of *process documentation* [4]. Information related to the use of a specific piece of data can be obtained from process documentation by means of a provenance query [5], resulting in a provenance graph, which can be analysed to decide whether information was used appropriately [6].

Against this background, the *integrity of the captured process documentation and the provenance graph derived from it* becomes a vital issue in guaranteeing the quality of a provenance-based audit. Therefore, we address this problem by developing a framework that secures the communication between the entities that are part of a provenance-aware system as well as the provenance query result representation. Specifically, we secure the process documentation created by entities and the result of provenance queries by including cryptographic elements in both.

The contributions of this paper are: *(i)* A secure provenance-aware communication protocol that addresses the integrity of the information exchanged between entities, *(ii)* A specially designed provenance graph that allows us to check the integrity of its content and, *(iii)* An automatic verification of the integrity of a Secure Provenance-based Auditing Architecture, which increases the level of trust in the audit results generated by it. The remainder of this paper is structured as follows. In Section 2, an overview of the provenance model this work relies upon is presented. In Section 3, to address the integrity property in the communication between entities, the secure communication formalisation, which is related to the Provenance-based Auditing Architecture [6], is presented. In Section 4, to address the integrity property in a provenance graph, we presented the Secured Provenance Graph and an algorithm that checks its integrity. In Section 5, the formal verification of the integrity property of one protocol related to the Provenance-based Auditing Architecture is presented and explained. Finally, Section 6 discusses some related work and Section 7 offers some concluding remarks.

2   Provenance Model Overview

In this section, we present a brief overview of the provenance model and concepts that we use in this paper [7]. We assume that applications capture extra information describing what occurred during their execution. Such extra information is referred to as *process documentation*, which is recorded in a storage component called *Provenance Store*, and queried to obtain the provenance of some data. Process documentation consists of a set of *assertions*, created by the applications' components. These assertions contain a description of the data exchanged by such components and *relationships* expressing causal dependencies between them. A *provenance graph*, which is a view of past execution in which its nodes are data and its edges are labelled with causal relationships' names [8], can be obtained by querying the Provenance Store. If a provenance graph is later analysed during an audit, it is possible to answer questions regarding past executions of applications. One important assumption of this model is that all participants are not malicious and send provenance information faithfully [3].

The information flow of an auditable provenance-aware system consists of four stages. *(1) Recording* of process documentation in which components make assertions related to the actions they perform and record them in a Provenance Store. *(2) Storage* of process documentation in which assertions are persistently stored in a Provenance Store. *(3) Querying* of process documentation in which process documentation is queried to obtain a provenance graph. *(4) Analysis* of a provenance graph to answer questions regarding the execution of the entities within the system the result of which is an audit report. Requirements such as processing of data is compatible with the purpose for which it was captured and only information to be processed was captured can be checked in the analysis stage. These requirements are not presented in this paper, however, initial work related to that analysis can be found in [6]. In order to guarantee a correct audit report, it is necessary to ensure during all these stages the integrity of the information in which such an analysis is based.

To do that, we create two mechanisms that guarantee the integrity of assertions. One is used in the recording and storage stages, whereas the other is used in the querying and analysis stages. The reason for having two separated mechanisms is to maintain the independence between the creation of distributed assertions and the querying of them in a centralised repository.

In Section 3, we discuss the mechanism used to secure the recording and storage stages. In Section 4, we explain the mechanism used to secure the querying and analysis stages.

3   Securing the Recording and Storage Stage

In this section, we discuss how the assertions created by the entities of a provenance-aware system can be secured. The assertions that are recorded during the recording stage are created from the information exchanged between the participating entities, i.e. during their communication. If this information is maliciously altered then, the quality of the audit can be compromised.

In order to address this problem, we need to secure the messages exchanged between entities and also the assertions that they are sending to the Provenance Store. To achieve that, we add some cryptographic components to both messages and assertions.

To exemplify this process, we formalise a secure communication protocol between the entities that are part of a provenance-based auditing system, specifically we secure the Provenance-based Auditing Architecture presented in [6]. This formalisation process relies on UML sequence diagrams that model a security protocol enabling the involved entities to apply security functions to the transferred data and, thus, protect it. To this end, we use the UML extension UMLsec, which offers a cryptographic notation for secure systems development [9].

In this formalisation, we assume that entities establish communication by using the TLS (Transport Layer Security) protocol [10], which allows them to verify each others' identities and create a session key used to encrypt/decrypt exchanged messages. We also assume that entities' public and private keys are created and interchanged.

The sequence diagram presented in Section 3.2 models four basic security characteristics: *confidentiality, authentication, non-repudiation* and *integrity*. Data integrity is the state that exists when computerized data is the same as that in the source documents and has not been exposed to accidental or malicious alteration or destruction [11]. If data integrity is not supported by auditable systems, the quality of an audit report will be affected. Due to the the importance of this property, we only focus on the verification of it; the remaining characteristics can be verified using a similar technique.

3.1   Provenance-Based Auditing Architecture

The Provenance-based Auditing Architecture, which is presented in [6] and briefly explained in this section, is depicted in Figure 1. This architecture uses provenance to audit the correct use of private information to later make accountable the involved entities for any information misuse. The architecture is inspired by the roles introduced in the Data Protection Act [12], which places restrictions on how organisations can use personal information that they request from individuals. It contains the actors Data Controller (DC), who is the individual or organisation that decides the purpose for which, and the manner in which, personal information is to be processed; the Data Subject (DS), who is an individual whose information is held by DC, and the Data Processor, who is an individual or organisation that processes personal information on behalf of DC. In order to make this architecture provenance-aware the Provenance Store (PS) component is introduced. This component represents a provenance repository in which provenance information is maintained. Finally, to be able to perform audits, the Auditor actor is introduced. This actor represents an internal or external entity that assesses the use of Data Subject's private information.

Communication's architecture can be structured in three protocols. The *Data Request protocol* represents a request for personal information issued by a Data Controller to a Data Subject. The *Task Request protocol* represents a request for delegating a task issued by a Data Controller to a Data Processor. The *Query Request protocol* represents the querying of the assertions stored in the Provenance Store issued by an Auditor to a Provenance Store. The Data Request and the Task Request protocols model the recording and storage stage. The Query Request protocol models the querying and analysis stage. As Data Request and Task Request are similar protocols [6], we focus on the Data Request protocol in the next section. The query request protocol is introduced in Section 4.

3.2   Data Request Protocol Formalisation

This section presents and explains the Data Request sequence diagram, which is used in the formalisation of the Data Request protocol.

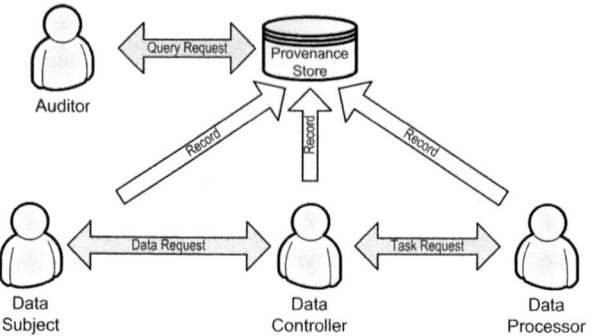

Fig. 1. Provenance-based Auditing Architecture

Data Request Protocol. The Data Request protocol represents the process in which the Data Controller establishes communication with the Data Subject to request personal information. The process is the following: DC requests some personal information from DS for a given purpose that indicates the way in which this personal information can be used, DS authenticates the identity of DC and after a successful authentication, DS responds with the requested information. Finally, when DC receives such information, DC acknowledges it reception. At the same time, both actors (DS and DC) record in the Provenance Store the assertions related to such a process.

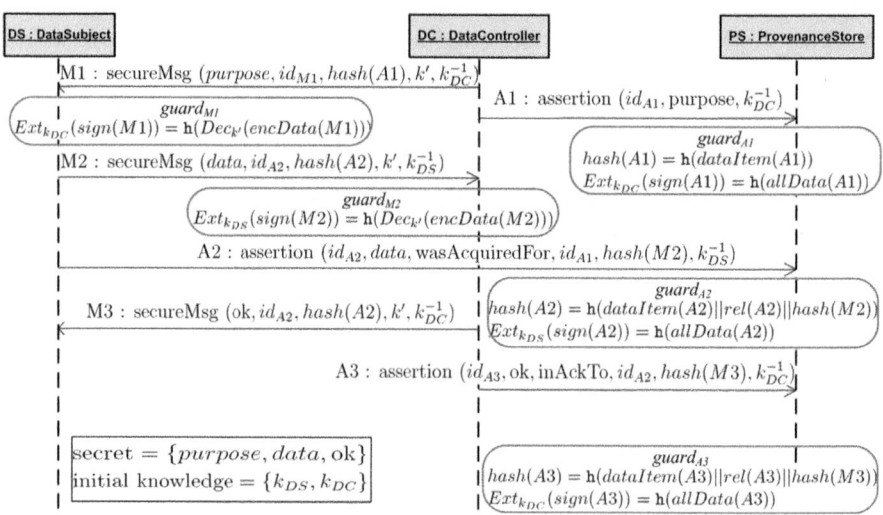

Fig. 2. Data Request UMLsec Sequence Diagram

Messages. In the Data Request sequence diagram, which is displayed in Figure 2, the messages interchanged between DS and DC are marked with Mi. These messages use the notation showed in Table 1, Equation (1). To provide confidentiality, non-repudiation and integrity, these messages are symmetrically encrypted and signed. These messages also contain a unique identifier id_i and a hash-value h_i related to their corresponding assertions, which are used to create the relationship and the hash-value of the next assertions.

To make this communication protocol provenance-aware, the entities should record assertions related to the messages they send. Then, the sender of a message generates an assertion related to it indicating the relationship with the previous message. In the sequence diagram, the messages marked with Ai are assertions recorded by actors in the Provenance Store. These messages use the notation showed in Table 1, Equation (2) and (3), in which id_i is a unique assertion identifier of the cause and id_{i-1} of the effect of an optional relationships rel in the Provenance Store. These identifiers are created locally by the entities. d is the data contained in the message to which this assertion is related to. To provide integrity of the information asserted by entities, a hash-value h is introduced. This hash-value is created by the sender to protect the content of the assertion and its relationship with the previous message. For that reason, this hash-value includes the hash-value of the previous assertion, which is identified by the corresponding id. To provide non-repudiation, assertions also contain a signature, which is computed by the sender. If an assertion related to the first message of a protocol is created, this assertion does not contain a relationship and a hash-value then, the Equation (2) is used.

Cryptographic Elements. In this protocol, a hash-value h is computed by a hash function h, and represented as $h = \mathbf{h}(d)$. The concatenation operation is represented by $\|$. For the signature, the public and private keys of an actor A are represented by k_A and k_A^{-1} respectively. The signature s is computed by $s = Sign_{k_A^{-1}}(h)$ and the verification of s by $Ext_{k_A}(s) = h$. In this digital signature scheme, a hash-value of data is signed, so after verifying the signature the hash-value should be verified too. The encryption of a piece of data d is computed by $x = \{d\}_{k'}$ and the decryption by $Dec_{k'}(x) = d$, where k' is a symmetric key. This symmetric key is created during the execution of the TLS protocol and it is used to encrypt the information that is considered private. During the TLS execution the entities also check their identities. Due to space restriction, messages related to the TLS protocol are not presented. However, TLS formalisation can be found in [9].

Guards. When this protocol is executed, the guards, which are shown in the sequence diagram of Figure 2 in rounded rectangles and are identified by the names $guard_{Mi}$ and $guard_{Ai}$, are used to verify the content of message Mi and assertion Ai, respectively. The Data Request protocol proceeds by exchanging six messages between DS, DC and PS. Message M1 contains purpose, which is symmetrically encrypted using the session key and signed using the private key of DC. With this message DC requests personal information from DS indicating the purpose from which this information is captured. When M1 is received, it is later verified and decrypted, as guard$_{M1}$ shows. In response, DS sends the encrypted personal data requested (data) in message M2, which is also signed by DS. When DC receives M2, the signature is verified and the data is decrypted, as guard$_{M2}$ shows. Then, DC sends an acknowledgement to the reception of the data to DS in M3, which is also verified and decrypted (even its corresponding guard is not presented to avoid cluttering the diagram).

Table 1. Auxiliar Functions

$$secureMsg(d, id_i, h_i, k', k_A^{-1}) = \left\langle \{id_i||d||h_i\}_{k'}, sign_{k_A^{-1}}(\mathbf{h}(d||id_i||h_i)) \right\rangle \tag{1}$$

If $Mi = secureMsg(d, id_i, h_i, k', k_A^{-1})$ then

$encData(Mi) = \{id_i||d||h_i\}_{k'}, sign(Mi) = sign_{k_A^{-1}}(\mathbf{h}(d||id_i||h_i)), hash(Mi) = h_i$

$$assertion(id_i, d, k_A^{-1}) = \left\langle id_i, d, \mathbf{h}(d), sign_{k_A^{-1}}(\mathbf{h}(id_i||d)) \right\rangle \tag{2}$$

If $Ai = assertion(id_i, d, k_A^{-1})$ then

$cause(Ai) = id_i, dataItem(Ai) = d, hash(Ai) = \mathbf{h}(d),$

$sign(Ai) = sign_{k_A^{-1}}(\mathbf{h}(id_i||d)), allData(Ai) = id_i||d$

$$assertion(id_i, d, rel, id_{i-1}, h_i, k_A^{-1}) = \tag{3}$$

$\left\langle id_i, d, rel, id_{i-1}, \mathbf{h}(d||rel||h_i), sign_{k_A^{-1}}(\mathbf{h}(id_i||d||rel||id_{i-1}||h_i)) \right\rangle$

If $Ai = assertion(id_i, d, rel, id_{i-1}, h_i, k_A^{-1})$ then

$cause(Ai) = id_i, dataItem(Ai) = d, rel(Ai) = rel,$

$effect(Ai) = id_{i-1}, hash(Ai) = \mathbf{h}(d||rel||h_i),$

$sign(Ai) = sign_{k_A^{-1}}(\mathbf{h}(id_i||d||rel||id_{i-1}||h_i)), allData(Ai) = id_i||d||rel||id_{i-1}||h_i$

Turning to assertions, A1 creates an assertion related to the first message of the process, then, it does not create a relationship. When A1 is received by PS the hash-value and the signature contained in it are checked, as guard$_{A1}$ shows. A2 creates a relationship indicating that data contained in M2 *was Acquired For* the purpose contained in M1. Again, when this assertion is received by the PS, its hash-value and signature are checked according to guard$_{A2}$. Finally, A3 records a relationship indicating that M3 was sent in acknowledgement to (*in Ack To*) M2. Similarly, this assertion is checked according to guard$_{A3}$. If any of the guards related to the assertions does not check, it means that the integrity of the asserted information was compromised. Then, the protocol terminates in a failed state and the appropriated measures should be carried out. After each guard is successfully checked, the corresponding assertion is stored in the Provenance Store.

3.3   Storage Stage

After a successful execution of the protocol, the assertions are stored in the Provenance Store; we are then able to check the integrity of its complete content by checking each of the hash-values and signatures of the assertions. That guarantees that the assertions were not modified during their exchange or during their storage. This checking can be used to frequently inspect the integrity of the stored information and take the necessary measures if a problem is found. This mechanism also prevents internal attacks, such as attacks from the Provenance Store administrator that can maliciously modify the stored assertions, as the assertions' hash-values were created by the architecture entities.

Another important issue is the maliciously insertion of assertions. This can occur in three different ways: insert a malicious message in the communication that creates a malicious assertion, an entity creates a malicious assertion to record it in the Provenance Store, or a malicious assertion is inserted directly to the Provenance Store. To prevent the first one, we rely on nounce numbers included in the interchanged messages as part of the TLS protocol [10]. This technique prevents the insertion of malicious messages, and consequently, the creation of assertions related to them. To prevent the second one, we assume that all the entities creating assertions are properly authenticated, so we can trust in the assertions created by them. In the last one, we assume that the Provenance Store is properly protected and just entities with the right credentials can record assertions.

So far, we have secured the assertions created by the entities of our architecture. However, as our architecture can contain various entities that interchange information at different times, new relationships can be created continuously. For example, suppose that an entity A produced a result r that is later reused by an entity B. When A produced r, it was not aware that r would be reused by another entity. Therefore, A did not create any relationship related to that reusing process. When B reuses r, it creates a relationship indicating the way in which r is reused by B. If we obtain the complete provenance graph of r, we will get two relationships: one created by A, indicating how r was produced, and one by B, indicating how r was reused. During the querying process, both relationships are linked by the Provenance Store to the item r. However, as such a link is created at the querying stage, the mechanism explained in Section 3 does not secure it. For that reason, we create a different mechanism to protect the integrity of provenance graphs. This mechanism is presented in the next section.

4   Securing the Querying and Analysis Stage

At this point, we can guarantee that the assertions generated by entities and stored in the Provenance Store have not been maliciously altered during the recording and storage stages. Then, they can be queried to obtain provenance graphs containing the provenance of some data. To maintain the integrity of these provenance graphs during the querying stage, the Provenance Store includes new cryptographic components in them. To achieve that, we have developed a *Secured Provenance Graph*, which defines a data structure that is included in each node of a provenance graph and is later used to verify its integrity. By including this structure, we are protecting the provenance graphs from any malicious alteration performed by an attacker, including the auditors. In the next section, the Secured Provenance Graph is presented and explained.

4.1 Secured Provenance Graph

Let us consider a set of node identifiers Id, a set of references to data D, a set of hash-values H, and a set of relationships' names R. A *Secured Provenance Graph* $G = (V, E, Node, Edge)$ is a directed acyclic graph, where $V = Id$, $E \subseteq Id \times Id$, $Node : Id \rightarrow D \times H$ and edges are labelled using the function $Edge : E \rightarrow R$.

Let us consider a secured provenance graph G. Each node contains a reference to a piece of data and a hash-value. Then, given an $id \in V$, we obtain its corresponding data by the accessor $data_G(id)$ and its corresponding hash-value by the accessor $hash_G(id)$. We also obtain the list of ancestors' identifiers by the accessor $ancestor_G(id)$, which is lexicographically ordered. The hash-value contained in each node is calculated according to Equation (4).

$$compHash_G(id) = \mathbf{h} \left(data_G(id) \underset{id_i \in ancestor_G(id)}{\Big|\Big|} edge(id, id_i) \| hash_G(id_i) \right) (4)$$

Equation (4) creates a hash-value that is used to verify not only the integrity of the data and the relationships related to id but also the integrity of the past of such data. This is achieved by including the hash-values of the id's ancestor, which creates an unforgeable reference to the id's past. The complete Provenance Secured Graph is protected by the signature of the Provenance Store, so it is not possible for another entity to reproduce or alter it without being noticed. Then, after the graph is created, we compute the signature $S = Sign_{k_{PS}^{-1}}(G)$, which is attached to the corresponding provenance graph.

Figure 3 presents an example of a Secured Provenance Graph, in which nodes are represented by circles containing references to data d_i, the directed edges are labelled with relationships r_i and the hash-values associated with each node are represented as h_i. Note that the Provenance Store does not always have access to the data that is part of a provenance graph, for that reason the nodes contain references to data. This way, we also avoid any problems related to the privacy of this information. Here, we assume that the data itself is protected by access control techniques implemented in the corresponding data repository.

It is important to note that the order of the relationships and the hash-values in each node is a very important issue. In graphs, the outgoing edges of a node are not ordered. However, if we want to create and later verify the hash-values contained in such a node, it is necessary to preserve certain order in the checking process. For example, the hash-value of node d_3, which is presented in Figure 3, can be created in two different ways. If we take r_5 in first place, we obtain the hash-value $h_3 = \mathbf{h}(d_3 r_5 h_6 r_6 h_7)$. But, if we take r_6 in first place, its hash-value is $h_3 = \mathbf{h}(d_3 r_6 h_7 r_5 h_6)$. Both hash-values represent the same node

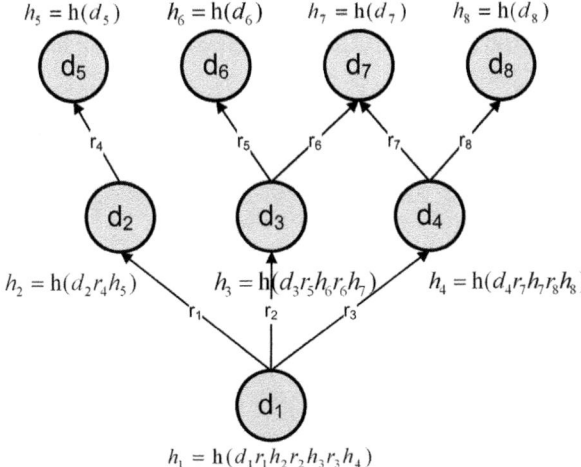

Fig. 3. Secured Graph Example

in the provenance graph. Nevertheless, if we do not know the order in which the hash-value was created, its checking will be incorrect as $h(d_3 r_5 h_6 r_6 h_7)$ is different from $h(d_3 r_6 h_7 r_5 h_6)$. In our case, the list of ancestors' identifiers is lexicographically ordered according to the relationship's names. Then, the correct hash-value is $h_3 = h(d_3 r_5 h_6 r_6 h_7)$. Note that a provenance graph can contain nodes with no relationships. This does not mean that such nodes do not have a "past". Instead, however, it means that the provenance graph does not contain the past of such nodes because it is not relevant for the analysis stage. If for some reason, a problem is found in these nodes without explicit past, the auditor can request to the Provenance Store a provenance graph showing its past. Later, this new provenance graph can be checked.

4.2 Secured Provenance Graph Integrity Checking

After a provenance graph is received by an auditor, its integrity needs to be checked. In that way, we can detect any malicious alteration made to it by any attacker or by the auditor. Hence, in this section, we present the algorithm used to verify the integrity of a Provenance Secured Graph.

In order to check the integrity of a Secured Provenance Graph, the procedure INTEGRITYCHECK is introduced in Algorithm 1. Initially, the signature associated with such a graph is verified using the public key of the Provenance Store, k_{PS}. This signature is used to check that the content of the complete graph was not altered. If the signature cannot be verified, there is no reason to continue with the rest of the process, then the algorithm returns 0.

If the signature checks, then the algorithm verifies the hash-value of each node in the graph. This is achieved by visiting each graph's node to create a new hash-value by calling the *compHash$_G$* function, which is presented in Equation (4).

Algorithm 1. Secured Provenance Graph Integrity Checking

1: **procedure** INTEGRITYCHECK(G :Secured Provenance Graph, k_{PS} : $publicKey$)
2:     id : node identifier $\in V$
3:     **if** $Ext_{k_{PS}}(Sign_{k_{PS}^{-1}}(G)) \neq \text{h}(G)$ **then**
4:         **return** 0   ▷ signature does not check
5:     **end if**
6:     **for** all $id \in G$ **do**
7:         **if** $hash_G(id) \neq (compHash_G(id))$ **then**
8:             **return** -1   ▷ integrity is compromised in id
9:         **end if**
10:     **end for**
11:     **return** 1   ▷ Success
12: **end procedure**

This new hash-value depends on the ancestors' hash, which in turn depends on the hash-values of its ancestors. Later, the new hash-value is compared against the hash-value contained in the node. If they are not the same, the integrity of this node has been compromised, and the algorithm returns -1. If after visiting all the nodes no problem is found, the nodes' integrity is intact, and the algorithm returns 1.

If the integrity of any of the provenance graph nodes has been compromised, it will be indicated which one was altered using the corresponding id. Then, the auditor can access the information related to such id stored in the Provenance Store to check if it was altered since the recording stage. If none of them were altered, then an audit process is allowed to begin. In this way, we can guarantee that the results derived from the analysis of a secured provenance graph are based on information that has not been maliciously altered.

In our scheme deletion of provenance information is not allowed as, to be able to perform a successful audit, we need all the assertions that our model records. Moreover, if one or more assertions are deleted, the presented algorithm finds an integrity problem, as the hash-values will not check, and not a problem of deletion of assertions. To avoid that, provenance repositories should implement appropriate access control techniques. In certain scenarios, deletion is used to enforce privacy of the information avoiding the identification of a specific individual through personal data. To support that, instead of deletion we use anonymisation. This is a technique that uses references to data in provenance information instead of real data [13]. These references, which are references to data stored in a database, are solved by accessing such a database. In that way, we only have access to the anonymised data if we have the right permissions and credentials.

5   Securing Provenance Based-Audits

In this section, we explain how we check the model of the Provenance-based Auditing Architecture presented in Section 3.1. The architecture model consist of three sequence diagrams (Data Request, Task Request and Query Request, which represents the processes presented in Section 4), which need to be verified separately. For space restrictions, we only present the verification of the integrity property in the Data Request sequence diagram presented in Section 3.

To verify that the integrity property is held by the data exchanged in our sequence diagram, we use UMLsec to create attacks against the modelled protocol using an adversary model. The adversary model we use here represents a network attacker that can eavesdrop, modify or insert messages on the communication channel with malicious intentions, and shows that these attacks fail. This adversary model relies on an extended Dolev-Yao adversary model [14], in which an adversary can read messages sent over the communication channel to include them in its knowledge set to later use them to derive new knowledge. If the adversary breaks the integrity of the sent messages, then it can modify the messages without being detected.

The adversary object contains three types of predefined values: secret, initial knowledge and guard. The values associated with secret describe the types of data that should be protected from the attacker, in this case they should hold the integrity property to ensure the integrity of the data. The values associated with initial knowledge denote the information known by the attacker beforehand, whereas, $guard_n$ represents the operations to be performed by the receiver of message n before such a message is received.

Returning to the diagram presented in Section 3, the items purpose, data and OK are part of the secret type indicating that they need to be protected during the execution of the process. The initial knowledge set contains the public keys of the actors in the diagram (k_{DC} and k_{DS}).

In the Data Request sequence diagram, we model the messages exchanged between entities and the assertions recorded by them in the Provenance Store. The integrity of the messages is verified by using a digital signatures scheme (hash) whereas the integrity of assertions is checked by using the included hash-value and its corresponding checking, which is represented by the guards in the diagram.

To verify that the integrity property is maintained during the execution of the protocol modelled in the Data Request sequence diagram, we use the model checker Viki [15]. Viki is a software that receives as input a UML sequence diagram and its adversary model to return the possible attacks that can be performed by the given attacker in the modelled protocol. Viki obtains the security requirements from the UMLsec elements and the predefined values used in sequence diagrams [15]. Then, these requirements are formalised in First-Order Logic and analysed with automatic theorem provers (e-SETHEO [16] and SPASS [17]) to find a flaw. If a flaw is found, a Prolog engine can be used to generate the attack trace of such flaw and solve it. Each modelled sequence diagram and its corresponding adversary model are executed at the same time to verify if the defined security properties are held during the whole execution [18]. As in this context, an attack means that a property is not held [18], we define an integrity attack as follows.

Definition 1 (Successful Integrity Attack). *A sequence of protocol transitions that lead to a piece of data to be modified without being noticed.*

Then, the integrity property that Viki checks is the following.

Lemma 1 (Integrity Property). *For the Data Request protocol, no successful integrity attack is possible.*

The verification of this lemma relies on the collision resistant nature of the used cryptographic hash function guaranteeing that an adversary cannot alter the integrity of a piece of data (messages or assertions) without having a visible effect in the output. Neither an adversary can insert an entirely new piece of data without being detected. Then, under the assumption that we use a collision resistant hash function, we can guarantee the integrity property in the modelled protocol. After performing the verification using Viki, the outcome is that the modelled protocol holds the Integrity Property. Therefore, we can guarantee that the assertions generated by this protocol hold the Integrity Property and can be used for creating query results.

For each protocol of the Provenance Based-Auditing Architecture four lemmas have been derived, which cover the confidentiality, integrity, non-repudiation and authentication properties. Considering that we model three protocols in our architecture, then we derived a total of 12 lemmas. Due to the lack of space, these lemmas are not shown. However, we present the following theorem, which covers the complete architecture.

Theorem 1 (Secure Provenance Based-Auditing Architecture). *A Provenance Based-Auditing Architecture is secure if for the protocols Data Request, Task Request and Query Request, the Integrity, Confidentiality, Non-Repudiation and Authentication properties are held.*

The verification of this theorem relies on the proofs of each of the property lemmas derived from each of the protocols of the architecture. If each of the properties is held by all of the protocols in our architecture, then the theorem holds.

Since Theorem 1 holds for our architecture, we can conclude that the architecture is secure and, therefore, the audits performed on it are secure too. Then, the results derived from these secure audits are based on correct information. This theorem was verified by using Viki, which concluded that the modelled architecture is secure.

6   Related Work

Recently, researchers have realised that provenance should be preserved in its original form while is created, transported, recorded and queried. This way, we are able to trust in all result derived from its analysis. For that reason, some researchers [19,20,21,22,23,24] have focused on presenting and solving the problem of securing provenance information.

Tan *et al.* [19] expose and discuss the problem of security provenance in a SOA-based Provenance System. Here, to ensure accountability, liability and integrity of assertions, they make use of digital signatures providing non-repudiati- on and ensuring that assertions are not changed intentionally or accidentally. Contrary to our work, they discuss basic security issues within provenance system and mention some solutions but they do not explain how these solutions can be implemented in practice. Moreover, this work mostly relies on access control techniques implemented in the provenance repository.

Hasan *et al.* [20] present the problem of securing provenance as an issue that had not been explored but is essential when provenance is used in law, digital forensic, regulatory compliance and authorships context. They identify integrity, availability and confidentiality as the main properties that a provenance-aware system should handle to provide trustworthy provenance. They also base their analysis in a different provenance model in which provenance is represented by linear chains. Even the secure provenance problem is introduced and discussed, a practical approach to implement it is not presented. In another work by Hasan *et al.*, they present a secure provenance scheme for linear chain provenance representation [24]. Such model support confidentiality and integrity of provenance information. Their scheme is similar to our approach in the sense that they also include extra cryptographic information to the provenance information to ensure the mentioned properties. The main difference between their work and ours is that we protect the complete information flow of a provenance-aware system. We also are able to protect a non-linear provenance representation (i.e. provenance graphs as in OPM).

Braun *et al.* also discuss the securing provenance problem [21]. In this case, they use a similar provenance model to the one we use, in which provenance is represented as a causality graph. For that reason, provenance information differs from traditional data and, therefore, the existing security models used to protect "traditional information" do not apply to graphs and are not easy to extend. Thus, new solutions should be developed and specially designed. Their work focuses on access control and how each of the elements of a causality graph needs different levels of access control. In this paper, we have developed a new technique specially designed to protect the integrity of a provenance graph but focusing on the integrity property and not on access control. However, our work is compatible with access control techniques.

Chong *et al.* discuss the problem of confidentiality and privacy of provenance information from a semantic point of view in a "provenance traces" approach [23]. They develop semantic definitions and mechanism to enforce these security properties. They also mention that data and provenance have different security requirements and, therefore, special mechanism to protect provenance information should be designed. Although, in this paper we focus on the integrity of provenance information, we have also modelled and verified confidentiality and privacy of provenance information by using cryptographic and anonymisation techniques, respectively. This work is not presented due to space restrictions but we expect to publish it later.

Xu *et al.* present the secure provenance problem from the management point of view. Here, they present some desirable requirements for secure provenance management systems and propose a framework that satisfies these requirements [22]. Integrity is among those requirements for which they adopt a similar approach to ours: integrity of both data and provenance information is important. To ensure that, they propose the creation of a layer in their framework that maintains the integrity of data and provenance information during storage, transferring and processing. However, unlike us, they do not present any practical solution to support that property.

Finally, a set of approaches [25,26,27,28] used by the database community to support similar security properties as the ones presented in this paper can complement our work. Even these approaches were not created to specifically protect provenance information, the solutions presented to solve security issues (such as privacy) can be adapted to be implemented in the presented provenance model.

7   Conclusions

Securing provenance is critical for making systems accountable on the Open Provenance Vision, as described by Moreau [29]. This paper presents a solution for this. Initially, we have presented a framework that guarantees a set of security properties in a Provenance-based Auditing Architecture to increase the level of trust in provenance-based audit results. Due to space restrictions, we focus on the integrity property and only on one protocol of the architecture, Data Request. In this protocol, we can guarantee the integrity of the assertions created by the participant entities as well as the integrity of provenance query results. We secure them by including cryptographic elements to both that can later be verified. First, we define a secure communication protocol that ensures the integrity of the information exchanged between entities and of the assertions sent to the Provenance Store. This way, we secure the creation and storage of assertions. Second, to ensure that provenance query results have not been maliciously altered, we design the Secured Provenance Graph, which contains a specially designed hash-value in its nodes along with the Provenance Store signature. Later, with the Integrity Checking Algorithm, we can verify the integrity of this graph.

Finally, we present an automatic verification of the integrity property in the communication protocol presented in Section 3. This verification allows us to guarantee the integrity of the information exchanged and the created assertions. Although, just one property and one protocol have been presented, the complete architecture and more security characteristics have been verified. Our future work is focused on extending our Secured Provenance Graph to the Open Provenance Model [8]. We are also working on measuring the overhead generated by hash-values during the recording of process documentation and the querying process.

Acknowledgements. This research was partially supported by the Programme Alβan, the European Union Programme of High Level Scholarships for Latin America, (scholarship number E06D103956MX) and by the Mexican Council CONACyT (scholarship number 182546). Thanks to the anonymous reviewers for their useful comments.

References

1. Weitzner, D.J., Abelson, H., Berners-Lee, T., Feigenbaum, J., Hendler, J., Sussman, G.J.: Information accountability. Communications of the ACM 51(6), 82–87 (2008)
2. Groth, P., Moreau, L.: Recording process documentation for provenance. IEEE Transactions on Parallel and Distributed Systems (September 2009)
3. Miles, S., Groth, P., Munroe, S., Moreau, L.: PrIMe: A Methodology for Developing Provenance-Aware Applications. ACM Transactions on Software Engineering and Methodology (June 2009)
4. Groth, P., Miles, S., Moreau, L.: A Model of Process Documentation to Determine Provenance in Mash-ups. Transactions on Internet Technology (TOIT) 9, 1–31 (2009)
5. Miles, S.: Electronically querying for the provenance of entities. In: Moreau, L., Foster, I. (eds.) IPAW 2006. LNCS, vol. 4145, pp. 184–192. Springer, Heidelberg (2006)
6. Aldeco-Pérez, R., Moreau, L.: Provenance-based Auditing of Private Data Use. In: International Academic Research Conference, Visions of Computer Science (BSC 2008), London, UK, BCS, pp. 141–152 (2008)
7. Moreau, L., Groth, P., Miles, S., Vázquez, J., Ibbotson, J., Jiang, S., Munroe, S., Rana, O., Schreiber, A., Tan, V., Varga, L.: The provenance of electronic data. Communications of the ACM 51(4), 52–58 (2008)
8. Moreau, L., Clifford, B., Freire, J., Gil, Y., Futrelle, J., Kwasnikowska, N., Miles, S., Missier, P., Myers, J., Simmhan, Y., Stephan, E., Van Den Bussche, J., Pale, B.: The Open Provenance Model Core Specification (v1.1). Future Generation Computer Systems, 1–30 (2010)
9. Jürjens, J.: Secure Systems Development with UML. Springer, Heidelberg (2005)
10. Blake-Wilson, S., Nystrom, M., Hopwood, D., Mikkelsen, J., Wright, T.: Transport Layer Security (TLS) Extensions. RFC 3546 (June 2003)
11. Institute, N.S.: Trusted computer system evaluation criteria (5200.28-std). Technical report, Department of Defence Standard (1985)
12. HomeOffice: Data Protection Act (1998)
13. Kifor, T., Varga, L., Vazquez-Salceda, J., Alvarez, S., Willmott, S., Miles, S., Moreau, L.: Provenance in Agent-Mediated Healthcare Systems. IEEE Intelligent Systems 21(6), 38–46 (2006)
14. Dolev, D., Yao, A.: On the security of public key protocols. IEEE Transactions on Information Theory 29(2), 198–208 (1983)
15. Jürjens, J.: Using interface specifications for verifying crypto-protocol implementations. In: Foundations of Interface Technologies, FIT2008 @ ETAPS (2008)
16. Stenz, G., Wolf, A.: e-SETHEO: An Automated Theorem Prover. In: Dyckhoff, R. (ed.) TABLEAUX 2000. LNCS, vol. 1847, pp. 436–440. Springer, Heidelberg (2000)
17. Weidenbach, C., Brahm, U., Hillenbrand, T., Keen, E., Theobald, C., Topic, D.: S PASS Version 2.0. In: Voronkov, A. (ed.) CADE 2002. LNCS (LNAI), vol. 2392, pp. 275–279. Springer, Heidelberg (2002)

18. Shabalin, P.: Model Checking UMLsec Models. Master's thesis, Department of Informatics, TU München, Germany (2004)
19. Tan, V., Groth, P., Miles, S., Jiang, S., Munroe, S., Tsasakou, S., Moreau, L.: Security Issues in a SOA-based Provenance System. In: Moreau, L., Foster, I. (eds.) IPAW 2006. LNCS, vol. 4145, pp. 203–211. Springer, Heidelberg (2006)
20. Hasan, R., Sion, R., Winslett, M.: Introducing Secure Provenance: Problems and Challenges. In: Proceedings of the ACM Workshop on Storage Security and Survivability (StorageSS), pp. 13–18. ACM Press, New York (2007)
21. Braun, U., Shinnar, A., Seltzer, M.: Securing Provenance. In: Proceedings of the 3rd USENIX Workshop on Hot Topics in Security (HotSec 2008). USENIX Association (2008)
22. Xu, S., Ni, Q., Bertino, E., Sandhu, R.: A Characterization of the problem of secure provenance management. In: International Conference on Intelligence and Security Informatics, pp. 310–314. IEEE, Texas (2009)
23. Chong, S.: Towards semantics for provenance security. In: First workshop on Theory and practice of provenance (2009)
24. Hasan, R., Sion, R., Winslett, M.: The Case of the Fake Picasso: Preventing History Forgery with Secure Provenance. In: FAST 2009 7th conference on File and storage technologies, pp. 1–14. USENIX Association, Berkeley (2009)
25. Miklau, G., Levine, B.N., Stahlberg, P.: Securing history: Privacy and accountability in database systems. In: Conference on Innovative Data Systems Research (CIDR 2007), Asilomar, CA, USA, pp. 387–396 (2007)
26. Stahlberg, P., Miklau, G., Levine, B.N.: Threats to privacy in the forensic analysis of database systems. In: International Conference on Management of Data (SIGMOD 2007), pp. 91–102. ACM, New York (2007)
27. Vaughan, J.A., Jia, L., Mazurak, K., Zdancewic, S.: Evidence-based audit. In: 21st IEEE Computer Security Foundations Symposium (CSF 2008), pp. 177–191. IEEE Computer Society, Washington (2008)
28. Lu, W., Miklau, G.: Auditing a Database under Retention Restrictions. In: IEEE International Conference on Data Engineering (ICDE 2009), Washington, USA, pp. 42–53. IEEE Computer Society, Los Alamitos (2009)
29. Moreau, L.: The foundations for provenance on the web. Foundations and Trends in Web Science (in Press 2010)

System Transparency, or How I Learned to Worry about Meaning and Love Provenance!

Stephan Zednik, Peter Fox, and Deborah L. McGuinness

Rensselaer Polytechnic Institute, Troy NY 12180, USA

Abstract. Web-based science analysis and processing tools allow users to access, analyze, and generate visualizations of data without requiring the user be an expert in data processing. These tools simplify science analysis for all science users by reducing the data processing overhead for the user. The benefits of these tools come with a cost, the increased need for transparency in data processing. By providing a clear explanation of the science concepts and processing performed by the science analysis tool we can increase user trust, understanding, and accountability and reduce misinterpretation or generation of inconsistent results.

We will demonstrate knowledge provenance (processing lineage and related domain information) presentation capabilities applied to an existing web-based Earth science data analysis tool (e.g. Giovanni from NASA/GSFC). Our conclusion is that user accessible visual presentations of knowledge provenance are key to building meaningful user understanding of analysis and processing decisions and should be a key component of data analysis tools.

1 Introduction

Science communities are putting increasing emphasis toward sharing data and developing publicly accessible tools to support streamlined analysis and visualization of this data. These tools are of great benefit to the community, as the burden of dealing with downloading data, accessing specialized data formats, running analysis processes, and complicated plotting tools is lifted from the user, allowing them to get directly to the core of their research. These powerful user tools come with a hidden cost; while the barrier to entry is lowered since the user does not have to manually address system-specific behaviors of the analysis operations[1], the user may also be unaware of a multitude of system, science, and data lineage details that can negatively impact the scientific or statistical applicability of the results.

We aim to develop a multi-function provenance system geared toward enhancing user understanding of data products and information derived from science analysis tools. User-oriented visual presentations of science knowledge and processing provenance represent the key functional requirement to achieving our goal. To achieve a reasonable level of understanding regarding the fitness for purpose of science data, a user should be aware not just of what processes were run

---

[1] Data access, format translations, data calibrations and screenings, etc.

D.L. McGuinness, J.R. Michaelis, and L. Moreau (Eds.): IPAW 2010, LNCS 6378, pp. 165–173, 2010.

to produce the data product, but the science intent of the processing and science concepts associated with processing and data throughout the processing trace. We call this integration of processing history and science concepts, knowledge provenance, and we believe it is integral in developing transparent, open science applications. Beyond just attempting to capture this knowledge provenance, we must present it to the user in a manner designed for human consumption, yet thorough - with hooks that allow the user to dig into the web of knowledge and follow concepts to their definition and, ideally, provide understanding. It is our assertion that exposing rich knowledge provenance to the science tool user in a manner that is cognitively pleasing to use, easy to navigate and informative of meaning, will significantly enhance user understanding of science data and the processes used to develop it.

We illustrate our work toward knowledge provenance representation and presentation for operation of a test environment of the NASA Giovanni [1, 2] interactive online Earth science data visualization and analysis tool. Giovanni allows Earth scientists, interdisciplinary and other applications researchers to perform multi-sensor and model data analysis online, e.g., explore connections between atmospheric processes and sea or land surface properties. Giovanni is a publicly available production tool that is actively used by modelers, researchers, application users, policy makers, teachers, and students.

2   Use Cases

Our initial use case revolves around capturing and presenting Giovanni processing provenance with the specific goal of exposing this provenance for the user's visual consumption. Further use cases expand upon our presentation of the knowledge provenance to include highlighting potential differences in the knowledge provenance lineage of two compared products and advising the user on potential negative applicability factors in a data comparison by analyzing the knowledge provenance of the compared artifacts.

Provenance Visual Lineage/Proof Use Case: Provide a visual representation of processing and knowledge provenance for a time-averaged latlon map comparison of Aerosol Optical Depth from MODIS Terra and Aerosol Optical Depth from MODIS Aqua over the calendar period of 2008-01-01 to 2008-01-31.

Our basic provenance use case; capture and visually present the provenance to the end user. This scenario does not perform analysis of the provenance - just capture and presentation. Knowledge provenance is presented as a causality graph based on the provenance data lineage integrated with domain metadata.

Provenance-aware Advisor Use Case: Use Giovanni to compute a difference map of MODIS Daily Aerosols from Aqua and Terra Platforms, using knowledge provenance to

1. *understand the differences between the compared products*
2. *explain anomalies that may be present in the generated difference map.*

A more complex provenance use case; our system now provides applicability information, based on an analysis of the knowledge provenance, that a non-expert user would not necessarily glean from a raw visual presentation of the knowledge provenance. The basic flow for this use case scenario is:

System uses descriptive logic to determine when target domain concepts in the knowledge provenance are different in a manner that may affect a comparison

1. *System determines that the two datasets correspond to two different MODIS[2] sensors on two different satellites (Aqua (EOS PM-1) and Terra (EOS AM-1)).*
2. *System determines that the two satellites have different Nominal Equatorial Crossing Times (NEQCT) (13:30 for Aqua and 10:30 for Terra)*
3. *System determines that the two satellites have different daytime nodes[3] (Ascending vs Descending)*
4. *System uses these differences, together with the dataset DataDay definition[4] to infer that there is a difference in the local observation times included in grid cells in each product, with differences being greatest over the Central Pacific (see Figure 1.)*

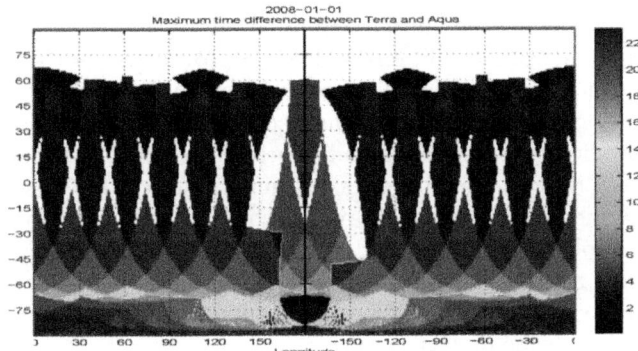

Fig. 1. Map of the time difference discrepancy between MODIS Aqua and MODIS Terra spatial coverage over the Pacific Ocean

We believe this is a critical provenance use case because it highlights how integrated provenance and domain information can be used by an intelligent system to discover highly-relevant information that would not be easily determinable if provenance and science domain metadata is disjoint.

3 System Requirements

The present production Giovanni service does not capture and retain provenance information, therefore, we developed a testbed Giovanni service based on the following architecture requirements

---

[2] Moderate-Resolution Imaging Spectroradiometer.
[3] Segment of the orbit transiting the Earth in daytime.
[4] A specification of how data are aggregated into daily data products, i.e., which pixels or scenes are included in a given day.

- develop test Giovanni environment to capture processing lineage
- encode processing lineage in a provenance interlingua
- encode domain metadata related to artifacts and processes referenced in the processing lineage in one or more domain interlinguas
- domain and provenance interlinguas must be integrable, that is to say the domain and provenance metadata should not be disjoint
- integrated knowledge base should be supported by standard query and rule systems
- visualization service should generate a user-orientated presentation of the knowledge provenance from the integrated metadata

To satisfy the provenance capture requirement our testbed Giovanni service produces a log of processes and inputs/outputs from processing. This log is translated to conform to an OWL[5] data lineage model. The artifact and processes identifiers in the log allow us to link the data lineage RDF graph with externally defined domain metadata encoded in OWL. By integrating the data lineage with the externally defined domain metadata we construct a knowledge base that supports mixed provenance / domain queries and reasoning (which can be used to infer domain or provenance information about entities in the knowledge provenance). Domain specific conditions related to provenance, such as highlighted in the provenance-aware advisor use case, can be checked by query or ruleset - with advisory or warning entities being declared in the knowledge provenance when the specific conditions are found. These rules and queries are engineered by domain experts but the advisories/warnings issued in the knowledge provenance contain descriptive metadata and become a part of the total knowledge provenance. Tools that support just the standard provenance OWL vocabulary can be used to generate a visualization of the data lineage; and tools that additionally support the integrated domain metadata can generate a visualization of the entire knowledge provenance.

4 Knowledge Provenance

We use the Proof Markup Language [3, 4] (PML) OWL ontology as a general-purpose provenance interlingua to encode a justification for the generation of Giovanni data visualizations. PML was chosen because it is a published provenance interlingua designed to encode justification metadata about general information or objects produced by an agent or decision mechanism. This generally scoped information-centric view of provenance lends itself well to our definition of knowledge provenance and we can make use of already-existing PML supported tools. Leveraging an OWL ontology as our provenance interlingua was also a supporting factor because OWL supports our requirement of using an interlingua system that supports the integration of multiple domain interlinguas and for which established query[6] and reasoning[7] mechanisms already exist.

---

[5] Web Ontology Language.
[6] SPARQL.
[7] SWRL, Jena Rules.

This mix of processing and science information in the provenance, which we call knowledge provenance, results in a very versatile knowledge base that supports a wide range of science-focused provenance reasoning. For example, in our provenance-aware use case, the applicability of a processing algorithm can be checked against the spatial and temporal resolutions of the service input dataset. Comparison integrity between two parameters or datasets can be checked based on a large number of factors, most encoded in the science metadata but reached by traversing the provenance lineage of the compared data products and their sources. These reasoning checks and queries would not be easy or straightforward if the science metadata and data lineage / processing provenance existed in disjoint knowledge bases.

5 Provenance Visualization

Probe-It! [5] is a provenance browser suited to graphically render provenance information encoded in PML. Probe-It! does not generate content, but renders an interactive visual representation of a provenance causality graph.

In Probe-It!, users can select nodes within the provenance trace to see a detailed view of the justification for the process/decision at that point. As of the time of this writing, Probe-It! only supports the presentation of information encoded in PML properties, so statements in the non-PML vocabulary are not visible to the user. Much of the science information in our knowledge provenance is not encoded in the PML interlingua, rather this information is stated in domain interlingua and related to the data lineage through entities common to both the PML graph and the domain graph. For the moment we are encoding the values of non-PML properties that capture important aspects of images, datasets, satellites, and processes into string description properties from the PML vocabulary. This gives us a basic mechanism to represent domain specific information (such as temporal and spatial resolutions of a dataset, or the orbital characteristics of the satellite an instrument operates on) from PML tools that do not support our domain interlinguas.

An early Probe-It! visualization of the provenance generated by our provenance visual lineage use case scenario is shown in Figure 2. The highlighted center node represents the process that extracts the requested data from the data source based on user selections of dataset, parameter, and spatial and temporal constraints. The output, or conclusion, of this process is a set of temporary data files listed in an XML fragment. This XML fragment can be viewed by the user using Probe-It! detail view of the node, or a human-friendly summary of the results of the process may also be shown. In this early representation of the knowledge provenance a fragment of the testbed Giovanni processing log detailing the output of the selected process are encoded in a PML string property as a representation for the conclusion of the process. This interface highlights the need for support of domain vocabularies in the visualization tools; both to support better domain presentation as well as to retain semantics of the domain interlingua and entities.

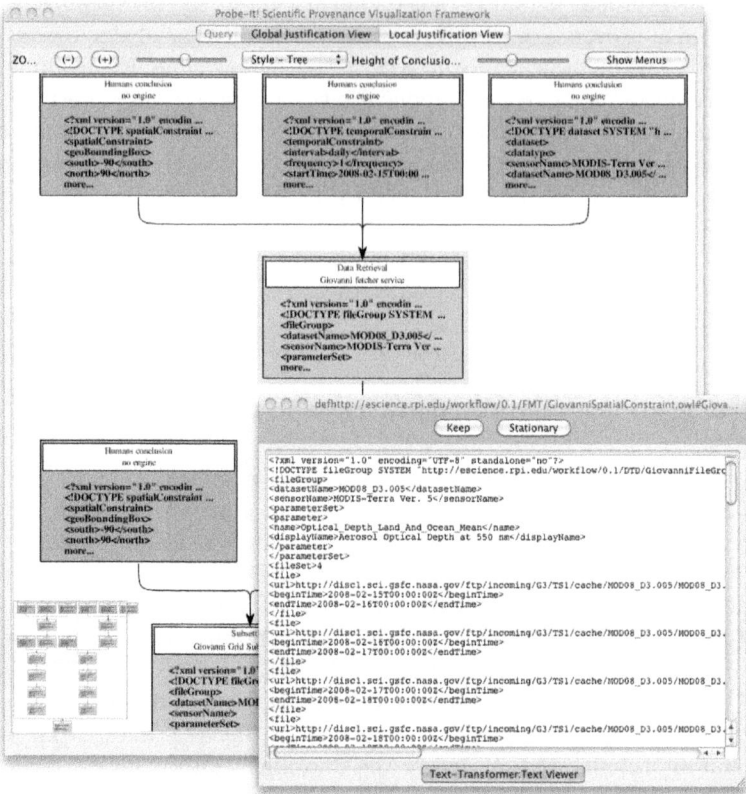

Fig. 2. Probe-It! visualizing the provenance of a data extraction process during a Giovanni data analysis comparison

We have been working with the Probe-It! team at UTEP[8] to determine the best way to present information from non-PML vocabularies (our domain interlinguas). Changes made to Probe-It! that support presentation of general vocabularies are folded back into the core Probe-It! browser.

The Probe-It! visualization is made accessible to the Giovanni user by way of a link that is available on the Giovanni results page. When the user clicks this link the Giovanni service invokes the Probe-It! web applet, passing to Probe-It! the entity URI of the final conclusion from the provenance trace, and Probe-It! automatically loads the provenance trace for the passed in information.

Internal use and informal evaluation of Probe-It! found that while processing provenance structure is clear and easy to follow, science information encoded as non-semantic text in the PML description properties can be hard to understand and difficult for users to act upon. User analysis of the provenance trace to

---

[8] University of Texas at El Paso.

determine the similarity of compared products or to discover potential applicability issues with processing actions was found to be especially difficult.

Subsequently, a visualization was defined by domain experts from the Giovanni team, whereby selected science information in the knowledge provenance is highlighted for the user in a concise table, geared towards the comparison and analysis scenarios for which a generic lineage presentation was found difficult to use. The table has a column for each data selection in a comparison analysis, to support a clear and simple presentation of differences in the knowledge provenance within the data selections. A set of simple semantic (Jena) rules was developed to search for semantically important differences in the knowledge provenance and if found, an advisory is generated in the model data displayed within the table with links to descriptive information regarding the posted advisory. These rules have been extended beyond simple semantic differences to include complex scenarios where multiple science aspects of the artifacts, along with certain processing actions, lead to anomalous results in the data visualizations. An example presentation of the domain differences found and advisory issued based on our provenance-aware advisor use case is shown in Figure 3.

The table representation of knowledge provenance has tested very well with our internal science group. Its ability to show, side-by-side, discrepancies between knowledge provenance of compared artifacts along with advisories and warnings about the comparison has proved to be an improved way to relate actionable information to the end user.

We plan to continue work on both (browse and table) visualizations of provenance. Both presentations have significant strengths, and both have areas where clarity or detail could be improved. At present, we do not know if these presentation scenarios will converge, but co-development should bring significant improvements to both.

6   Demonstration

We plan to demonstrate at IPAW 2010[9] execution of our provenance-capturing testbed Giovanni service and both visual presentations of the resulting provenance. We will show how Probe-It! is used to present a provenance trace of the Giovanni service execution and how Probe-it!'s local view can be used to access both processing and domain metadata about nodes within the provenance trace. We will also show how the Giovanni table view of knowledge provenance is used by domain experts to highlight differences in selected factors related to the provenance of compared data products and how the table view is used to inform users of comparison advisories and warnings in their data selection.

7   Discussion and Conclusions

To date, we have developed the ability to generate processing and science knowledge provenance for execution of a test environment of the NASA

---

[9] The Third International Provenance and Annotation Workshop,
http://tw.rpi.edu/portal/IPAW2010

Your Selected Options:

Spatial Area:	Longitude (-30, 150), Latitude (-10,60)
Parameters:	A: MYD08_D3.005 Aerosol Optical Depth at 550 nm
	B: MOD08_D3.005 Aerosol Optical Depth at 550 nm
Temporal Range:	Begin Date: Jan 01 2008
	End Date: Jan 31 2008
Visualization Function:	Lat –Lon map Time-averaged

About your selected parameters:

	Parameter A	Parameter B	Difference alert
Parameter Name :	Aerosol Optical Depth at 550 nm	Aerosol Optical Depth at 550 nm	
Dataset:	MYD08_D3.005	MOD08_D3.005	← Diff
Data-Day definition	UTC (00:00-24:00Z)	UTC(00:00-24:00Z)	The same but....
Temporal resolution	Daily	Daily	
Spatial resolution	1x1 degree	1x1 degree	
Instrument:	MODIS	MODIS	
Satellite:	Aqua	Terra	← Diff
EQCT	13:30	10:30	← Diff
Day Time Node	Ascending	Descending	← Diff
Pre-Giovanni Processes :	ATBD-MOD-30	ATBD-MOD-30	
Giovanni Processes:	Spatial subset Time average	Spatial subset Time average	

Known Issues:

The difference of EQCT and Day Time Node, modulated by data-day definition, caused the included overpass time difference, which makes the artifact difference. See sample images:

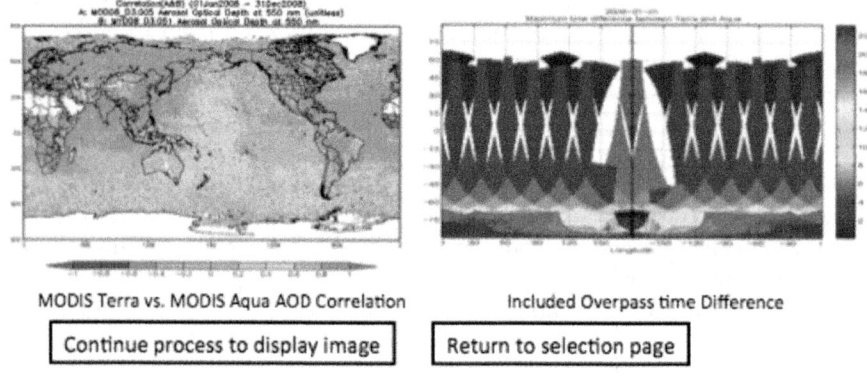

MODIS Terra vs. MODIS Aqua AOD Correlation   Included Overpass time Difference

| Continue process to display image | | Return to selection page |

Fig. 3. Knowledge provenance table, and advisories, for the visualization comparison from the use case scenario

Giovanni interactive online Earth science data visualization and analysis tool. This knowledge provenance captures both processing and science concepts involved in artifacts/information and processing within the system. Two user focused presentations of this provenance have been utilized.

- Probe-It! is used to browse the causality graph of Giovanni processing and contains a simple representation of science information for the artifacts and processes in the provenance trace.
- A Knowledge Provenance Table is used to show properties from the knowledge provenance side-by-side when Giovanni is used to generate an analysis comparison. This mode has been shown to be useful in showing the end user if the data selection comparison is potentially invalid.

The next stage of our work will be to increase and refine the expressiveness of our knowledge provenance, increase support and utility in Probe-It! for presentation of information from non-PML vocabularies, and further develop the knowledge provenance table presentation. The results of this work will eventually be incorporated into the production Giovanni analysis tool.

Acknowledgments

- This work was supported in part by the NASA ESTO AIST-08-071 project "Multi-Sensor Data Synergy Advisor" (PI: Gregory Leptoukh, NASA GSFC[10])
- The PML group at Inference Web
- The Probe-It group at UTEP/CyberShARE

References

1. Acker, J.G., Leptoukh, G.: Online Analysis Enhances Use of NASA Earth Science Data, 2007. Eos, Trans. AGU 88, 14–17 (2007)
2. Berrick, S.W., Leptoukh, G., Farley, J., Rui, H.: Giovanni: A Web Service Workflow-Based Data Visualization and Analysis System. IEEE Trans. Geoscience and Remote Sensing 46, 2788–2795 (2009)
3. da Silva Pinheiro, P., McGuinness, D., Fikes, R.: A Proof Markup Language for Semantic Web Services. Information Systems, 31(4-5), June-July 2006, pp 381-395. Prev. version, KSL Tech. Report KSL-04-01 (June 2006)
4. McGuinness, D., Ding, L., Pinheiro da Silva, P., Chang, C.: PML 2: A Modular Explanation Interlingua. In: ExaCt pp. 49-55 Also Stanford KSL Tech. Report KSL-07-07 (2007)
5. Del Rio, N., Pinheiro da Silva, P.: Probe-It! Visualization support for provenance. In: Bebis, G., Boyle, R., Parvin, B., Koracin, D., Paragios, N., Tanveer, S.-M., Ju, T., Liu, Z., Coquillart, S., Cruz-Neira, C., Müller, T., Malzbender, T. (eds.) ISVC 2007, Part II. LNCS, vol. 4842, pp. 732–741. Springer, Heidelberg (2007)

---

[10] Goddard Space Flight Center.

Pedigree Management and Assessment Framework (PMAF)

Kenneth A. McVearry

ATC-NY,
Cornell Business & Technology Park,
33 Thornwood Drive, Suite 500,
Ithaca, NY 14850
kmcvearry@atcorp.com

Abstract. The Pedigree Management and Assessment Framework (PMAF) is a customizable framework for writing, retrieving and assessing provenance and other metadata that reflects the quality of an information object (such as a document), the relationships between information objects and resources (such as people and organizations), etc. PMAF stores metadata in a volume-efficient format using RDF (Resource Description Framework), and can write and query metadata at a fine-grained level. Once metadata has been stored in PMAF, the user can run a variety of assessments (predefined queries) to reveal particular aspects of the metadata graph. We will demonstrate the PMAF browser interface, which can be used to view the existing metadata graph for an information object; the PMAF assessment interface, which allows the user to select and run predefined queries on the metadata; and the integration of PMAF with a standard document editor and content management system.

Keywords: information pedigree, provenance, RDF, metadata graph, assessment.

1 Introduction to PMAF

Modern information management systems are increasingly net-centric, making more information available more quickly. In this environment, the information consumer must distinguish decision-quality information from potentially inaccurate, or even conflicting, pieces of information from multiple sources. With knowledge of the information's pedigree, or provenance, the user can establish trust in information, ensure accountability, discover sources of errors, and correct propagated errors.

The Pedigree Management and Assessment Framework (PMAF) enables the publisher of information to record standard provenance metadata about the source, manner of collection, and the chain of modification of information as it passes through processing and/or assessment. In addition, the information publisher can define and include other metadata relevant to quality assessment, such as domain-specific metadata about sensor accuracy or the organizational structure of agencies. PMAF stores this potentially enormous amount of metadata compactly and presents it to the user in an intuitive graphical format, along with PMAF-generated assessments that enable the user to quickly estimate information quality.

D.L. McGuinness, J.R. Michaelis, and L. Moreau (Eds.): IPAW 2010, LNCS 6378, pp. 174–181, 2010.
© Springer-Verlag Berlin Heidelberg 2010

2 PMAF Background

PMAF was initially developed through SBIR (Small Business Innovation Research) funding provided by the Air Force Research Laboratory (AFRL) in Rome, NY. The Phase I SBIR was awarded in 2005, and the Phase II was awarded in 2006 and completed in 2008. PMAF was originally created for the Joint Battlespace Infosphere (JBI) program at AFRL, which implemented an information management environment. The original scenario for application of PMAF was the creation of Air Tasking Orders including the fusion of sensor data.

Follow-on work includes the Metadata Security Assertion Framework and Evaluation (MetaSAFE) system, which was a Phase II SBIR awarded in 2008 and completed in 2010. MetaSAFE securely manages and provides access to metadata used to validate security decisions, such as whether to release a document across a security domain. MetaSAFE added pedigree assurance features to PMAF including digital signatures and hashing; hashing provides strong binding of metadata to information objects, and digital signatures provide strong attribution of metadata to the people and/or processes that generate it.

3 Provenance Model

The PMAF model of pedigrees includes the following concepts.

3.1 Resource

A resource is any nameable object that can have an associated pedigree, or can be referred to in a pedigree. People, web sites, documents, programs, etc. are all considered resources.

3.2 Provenance Metadata

Provenance metadata is information about how a resource was created, transformed, or used.

3.3 Pedigree Fragment

Provenance metadata is stored in one or more provenance repositories in the form of pedigree fragments. Each pedigree fragment contains information about a resource. A pedigree fragment consists of one or more "local" claims about the provenance of a resource. A local claim is one that involves only a single step of the creation, transformation, or use of a resource. For example, the facts that a document was created (1) by a particular person, (2) at a particular time and place, (3) by running a particular program, and (4) using particular source documents are all local facts about that document. In contrast, if document A was created using document B as a source, then the sources of document B will be considered non-local facts about A.

The complete pedigree of a document is assembled from local statements about that document, its sources, the sources of those sources, etc. Typically, the pedigree fragments for a resource will be published by the same client application that created or modified the resource. However, "third party" contributions to a pedigree are also possible, i.e. created by an application that is neither the writer nor the reader of the associated resource document. Allowing such third-party contributions supports the handling of objects whose sources are unknown or partially known, such as web pages. Whether the pedigree fragments are published by the creating application, or by a third-party application, provenance metadata will typically be published through the PMAF publish API.

3.4 Root Pedigree

A provenance repository can be queried to obtain pedigree fragments associated with a given resource. These pedigree fragments are assembled into a root pedigree for a resource. A root pedigree is a complete (relative to the information available) collection of local information associated with a resource (where local is as defined above – within a single step – rather than non-remote). The complete root pedigree for a resource can be divided into two parts: source record and usage record. The source record for a resource is the local history of a creation or transformation step resulting in the current state of the resource. The usage record for a resource describes how that resource is used in the source pedigrees of other resources.

For example, if document A is produced using document B as a source, then this fact will be in the source record of A, but will be in the usage record of B. Typically, the usage records can be more difficult to assemble than the source records, because the source record only needs to be created once (when the resource is created), while the usage record can involve many different individual creation or transformation steps performed by different users at different locations and times.

3.5 Provenance Subgraph

A provenance subgraph is a collection of related provenance statements assembled for use by some assessment procedure. Like a root pedigree, a provenance subgraph is associated with a particular resource, but it may include information from several connected root pedigrees. For instance, a source pedigree subgraph for a resource A may include statements of the form "A has source B" as well as "B has source C". A provenance subgraph thus allows one to draw nonlocal conclusions about a resource, such as "foreign news reports contributed to this document."

There are two pure approaches to creating such provenance subgraphs: (1) create a complete pedigree, and then filter to get the desired provenance subgraph; or (2) build up the desired provenance subgraph by gathering pedigree fragments as needed. Because complete pedigrees can be huge and can be distributed among many different repositories, we consider it impractical to ever create a "complete" pedigree, so PMAF follows the latter approach. We use the word "subgraph" because these objects can be thought of as subsets of the complete pedigree, which in turn can be thought of as a potentially huge graph of relationships among resources. In PMAF we describe these relationships using RDF (discussed below).

PMAF uses a two-stage query system to assemble provenance information for use by assessments. The first stage involves querying the provenance repositories for pedigree fragments associated with a given resource; the results of this stage of the query are assembled into root pedigrees. The second stage of a query involves assembling appropriate root pedigrees together to make a required provenance subgraph.

4 Provenance Represented in RDF

In PMAF, pedigree fragments, root pedigrees and provenance subgraphs are all represented as graphs, described using the Resource Description Framework (RDF) specification. RDF supports: a) unique unambiguous identification of the entities mentioned in pedigree statements, b) exchange of machine-readable information for automated processing of pedigree, c) unlimited extensibility of terminology used to represent pedigree, and d) semantic tagging, logical inference and other automated processing of the pedigree information.

RDF represents information as a collection of statements, called triples. Each triple has three elements—the subject, predicate and object. Each element in the triple is specified by either a Universal Resource Identifier (URI) or a literal (a string, number, etc). A collection of RDF triples can be viewed as a graph, in which the subject and object are nodes and the predicate is a directed arc that points from the subject to the object.

URI's can be used to uniquely identify information that exists on the web, in a file-system, in a database, etc.; as well as concepts, persons, or objects that do not have an electronic representation. So if related pieces of information are stored in separate locations on a server or on the web, the relationships among them can be detailed using RDF, and a URI can be used instead of the full set of information that the URI refers to.

For example, a sensor may generate thousands of images an hour; the make and age of the sensor may help an analyst determine the quality or reliability of the images that were captured, but each image does not need to include a copy of the make/age metadata of the sensor in its pedigree. Instead, that sensor metadata can be stored in one unique location and only that location's URI will be incorporated into the pedigree metadata of each image. In addition, once an image has been transformed or fused with other information, the resulting image need not include another copy of the URI referring to that sensor metadata; instead, it will incorporate a URI to the earlier information's pedigree metadata, which in turn incorporates the sensor metadata URI. In this way, the volume of the metadata can be reduced to a linear function of the number of transformations.

5 PMAF Architecture

PMAF is intended for situations involving the following participants:

- One or more information object repositories. We assume that there is a unique naming system for objects obtained from each repository.
- One or more repositories of provenance metadata for the information objects. We do not assume that the provenance metadata is stored in the same repository as object information.

- A client application that reads and writes information objects and uses PMAF to read and write the corresponding provenance metadata.
- PMAF, which provides an API for both querying and publishing provenance metadata.

The design for PMAF and how it interacts with the various participants are shown in Figure 1.

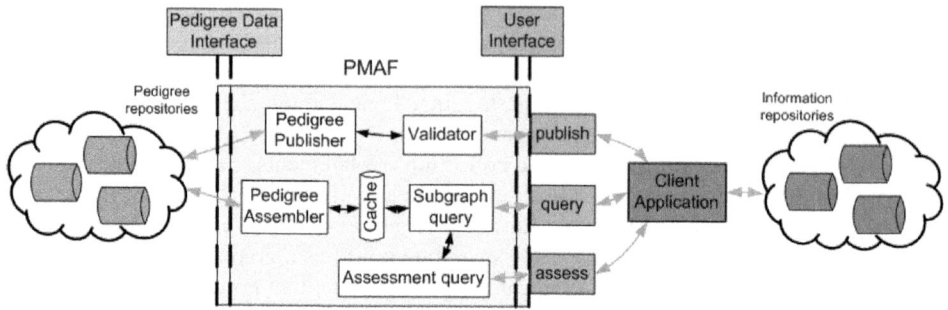

Fig. 1. PMAF Architecture

5.1 Pedigree Assembler

The pedigree assembler assembles the root pedigrees from pedigree fragments that it receives from one or more repositories of provenance metadata. It supports extensibility through the use of pluggable modules to handle system-specific operations that depend on the type of information repositories being used, and to use a standard framework for encoding provenance information, independent of the type of provenance storage in use.

The pedigree assembler can easily be adapted for different types of provenance storage, and for different granularities of provenance metadata. Provenance metadata can be stored in files, in a database, or as separate objects in an information object repository. Multiple sources of provenance metadata must be merged before full provenance can be assembled.

5.2 Assessment Query

A client application can invoke assessment queries on an object in its information repository(s) to help determine the quality and trustworthiness of the information.

5.3 Subgraph Query

Each assessment invokes one or more subgraph queries for the given object. The result of a subgraph query is a provenance subgraph, which is a data structure describing a particular aspect of the provenance of the object. Each request for a subgraph includes a specification for the type of subgraph desired, together with a URI that uniquely names the subject of the subgraph. The subgraph query component constructs the requested subgraph using root pedigrees that it receives from the pedigree assembler.

5.4 Pedigree Publisher

A client application can insert or modify objects in its information repository(s), and make calls on PMAF to publish corresponding additions to the provenance metadata in the appropriate pedigree repository.

5.5 Publish API

The mapping between information object names and the corresponding provenance metadata is a modular component that can be plugged into the PMAF framework to accommodate new types of information objects. The publish API allows client applications to publish provenance metadata for new objects without needing to know the format of the metadata or where it will be stored. It makes use of the modular mapping between object names and provenance metadata.

6 PMAF Interfaces

PMAF includes a variety of graphical interfaces; some support pedigree browsing and drill-down, and others enable users to quickly estimate information quality based on the assessments described in the next section.

PMAF's built-in pedigree browsers provide two distinct views of the pedigree. The tree browser depicts the ancestry of a given document (or, alternatively, its descendants) in hierarchical form, where each node in the tree represents a source (or descendant) document. Such hierarchal trees are familiar to computer users from file system browsers. The graph browser depicts the pedigree as a graph, with labeled arcs to source documents, publishers, and other pedigree metadata. The graph viewer enables the user to zoom out to a bird's eye view of the whole graph or zoom in (drill down) to sections of interest.

7 PMAF Assessments

In time-critical situations, users need to quickly evaluate information quality. To support assessment of the quality of information objects, PMAF offers quick, accurate, and focused analyses based on the pedigree. Documents and other objects and their relationships in the pedigree that have an immediate bearing on the quality of the information are evaluated and presented to the user. Other analyses estimate the trustworthiness of information publishers or the reliability of documents.

PMAF provides the user with five assessments for an information object that help to evaluate its quality:

- its influence or impact on other information objects (Source Impact)
- whether it has been superseded or deprecated by newer information (Source Deprecation)
- whether it derives from conflicting sources (Conflict Notification)
- publisher reputation (Feedback)
- source corroboration analysis (Unique Sources).

Based on the assessment analyses, the PMAF user can estimate the quality of the information. In addition, custom pedigree assessments can be created and plugged into PMAF that are specific to the information domain of a client application, provide additional dimensions of metadata analysis, etc.

8 PMAF Vocabularies

PMAF includes a baseline provenance ontology that extends the Dublin Core Metadata Initiative (DCMI) vocabulary, incorporating terms that support a decision-making process, the dependency of data in general, and the occurrence of conflicting data. In addition PMAF includes vocabulary from the Friend of a Friend (FOAF), DoD Discovery Metadata Specification (DDMS) and Intelligence Community Metadata Standard for Information Security Markings (IC-ISM) standards.

At its core PMAF is vocabulary-agnostic. PMAF does not require the use of any particular vocabulary or term, and is completely configurable to use any vocabulary – whether previously defined or newly created. Rather than requiring the use of a particular provenance model or vocabulary storage format, terms are recorded using the common denominator of RDF and need not be predefined by PMAF. Depending on the use case, an integrated approach combining PMAF with another ontology tool and/or model may be beneficial.

9 PMAF Applications

Our recent integration efforts for PMAF have focused on document processing and content management applications. However, we believe that the open architecture of PMAF is suitable for collection of provenance metadata from a variety of system and application types, such as:

- Workflow: collect provenance for information objects as they pass through processes that run within the workflow system
- Enterprise Service Bus: report message passing and transformations
- Web Services: collect provenance for web service processing of information objects, as well as of the web services themselves (e.g. versioning)

10 PMAF Demonstration

We will begin the PMAF demonstration by using the graph browser interface to view the existing metadata graph for an information object, in this case a document. Since the provenance metadata is stored in RDF format, it can be viewed as a graph with the subjects and object resources represented as nodes, and each predicate as a link between a subject node and object node. The links represent metadata such as the type of the object, the creator, the publisher, the create date, sources for the object (e.g. other documents), and if the object has subparts (each of which can have its own metadata, i.e. at a fine-grained level).

We will demonstrate interactively exploring the graph by reviewing the metadata for sources, sources of sources, etc (moving backward in time), and then understanding the impact of sources on downstream objects (moving forward in time). We will also demonstrate the results of running several of the built-in PMAF assessments on the sample provenance metadata, including the Unique Sources, Source Deprecation, Conflict Notification, and Source Impact assessments.

We will then demonstrate the integration of PMAF with a standard document editor (Microsoft Word), allowing the creation and publishing of provenance metadata as a side effect of copying and pasting information from existing files into a new document. Finally we will demonstrate the integration of PMAF with a Content Management System (Microsoft SharePoint), allowing the creation and publishing of new metadata for files based on standard CMS operations such as checking in, moving and renaming a file.

References

1. Gioioso, M.M., McCullough, S.D., Cormier, J.P., Marceau, C., Joyce, R.A.: Pedigree Management and Assessment in a Net-centric Environment. In: Proceedings of the SPIE Symposium on Defense and Security (2007)
2. Combs, V.T., Hillman, R.G., Muccio, M.T., McKeel, R.W.: Joint Battlespace Infosphere: Information Management within a C2 Enterprise. In: 10th International Command and Control Research and Technology Symposium (2005)
3. RDF Primer, http://www.w3.org/TR/rdf-primer
4. Berners-Lee, T.: Uniform Resource Identifiers (URI): Generic Syntax, http://www.ietf.org/rfc/rfc2396.txt
5. Dublin Core Metadata Initiative, http://dublincore.org
6. Chapman, A.: Industry Provenance State of the Art, presentation to the Information Assurance Metadata Community of Practice (IAM CoP) working group (2009)

Provenance-Based Strategies to Develop Trust in Semantic Web Applications

Xian Li[1], Timothy Lebo[1,2], and Deborah L. McGuinness[1]

[1] Rensselaer Polytechnic Institute, Troy, NY USA
[2] Air Force Research Laboratory, Information Directorate, Rome, NY USA
{lix15,lebot}@rpi.edu,
dlm@cs.rpi.edu

Abstract. Linked data and Semantic Web technologies enable people to navigate across heterogeneous sources of data thus making it easier for them to explore and develop multiple perspectives for use in making decisions and solving problems. While the Semantic Web offers benefits for developers and users, several new challenges are emerging that may negatively impact users' trust in Web-based collaborative systems.

This paper describes several use cases to illustrate potential trust issues faced by Semantic Web applications, and provides a concrete example for each using a specific system we built to investigate United States Supreme Court decision making. Provenance-based solutions are proposed to develop trust and/or minimize the distrust that is provoked by the situation. While these use cases address distinct situations, they are all described in terms of how a contradiction can arise between the user's mental model and the statements presented in the display. This commonality may be used to develop additional classes of trust-threatening use cases, and the proposed provenance-based solutions can be applied to many other Semantic Web Applications.

1 Introduction

As the amount of data available on the Web quickly increases, applications based on Semantic Web technologies are being developed to utilize information from multiple data sources. With a variety of visualization technologies, the advantages from heterogeneous sources of data are indicated by providing comprehensive views on a given problem, and gaining understanding of problems from a larger picture where different sources of data are interlinked. However, one essential growing challenge is related to diverse quality of the data. As more diverse data is used, user's distrust may increase, particularly when their prior knowledge and expectations are different from what the system appears to be presenting.

To address these emerging challenges, we propose provenance-based solutions using the Proof Markup Language (PML) [7] and apply them to representative use cases in Semantic Web Applications. The organization of the paper is as follows: in Section 2, we review related works in the area of provenance in the

D.L. McGuinness, J.R. Michaelis, and L. Moreau (Eds.): IPAW 2010, LNCS 6378, pp. 182–197, 2010.
© Springer-Verlag Berlin Heidelberg 2010

context of the Web. In Section 3, we give a brief introduction to the system with which we developed use cases to illustrate challenges and provenance solutions. Section 4 describes the principles used to generate use cases, the main cause behind different types of distrust risks, and the provenance used to develop trust. Section 5 concludes with a discussion of future work.

2   Related Work

In their multidisciplinary survey of trust research, Artz et al. [1] distinguish between policy- and reputation-based trust paradigms. While the former focuses on "hard security" that is determined through authentication, access control, and encryption, the latter combines personal experiences and experiences of others to determine a degree of trust. They identify the common theme that "trust is a willingness to be vulnerable to the actions of another." When making decisions based on information from the web, one can be vulnerable to distributed contributions that the system incorporates and displays. For example, Zhao et al. [14] describe risks to scientific users' trust in FlyWeb, a consolidation and alignment of three independent data sources related to the fruit fly. They note that asynchronous updates of component data sources can violate expectations of scientists working with older releases.

Vulnerability, however, is not necessary to gain trust, since trust may be imparted without vulnerability. To help qualify the notion of trust in an information system, it may be viewed as proportional to the characteristics of information quality. Naumann et al. [9] describe information quality using several components and incorporated them into query planning over multiple, distributed, and heterogeneous sources. Their approach strives to plan queries that select from good data sources based on their completeness, timeliness, uniqueness, availability, financial cost, and accuracy. Their approach uses rules at the granular level of attributes and queries instead of at the class or source level and relies upon a domain-specific global schema to which all contributing data sources are cast.

Data believability is similar to information quality. Prat and Madnick [10] reinforce its definition as "the extent to which data are accepted or regarded as true, real and credible." They propose the three dimensions of trustworthiness, reasonableness, and temporarily to measure data believability using provenance-based measurements and present computational approaches to combine the components of believability. They measure *trustworthiness of the data source* at a holistic level. *Reasonableness of data* measures the extent to which a data value is likely using possibility, consistency over sources, and consistency over time. *Temporality of data* measures the extent to which the query time overlaps with the data value's validity interval.

Provenance is an important aspect of information quality and believability. To track the lineage of changes between releases of FlyWeb, Zhao et al. proposed a provenance-based solution. Sillence et al. [11] describe several provenance factors important to users in a study of non-experts using the web to investigate health topics. Factors included the ability to cross-validate across information sources, recency of information updates, and citations to original sources. Buneman et al. [3] described primary issues for data provenance in the context of the web, including obtaining provenance information, citing components of a document in another context, and ensuring integrity of citations in situations where the cited items evolve. Hartig [5] proposes a general provenance model that incorporates both data creation and data access. Fox et al. [4] address the problem of identifying validity and origin of data on the web by modeling and maintaining information sources, information dependencies, and trust structures. Using four levels of provenance ranging from strong provenance (high certainty) to weak provenance (high uncertainty), they annotated web data to create islands of certainty among the wild uncertainty and incompleteness. Miles et al. [8] present use cases for process documentation in e-science experiments. For each use case presented, they present *provenance question* as an action that can be realized by processing recorded process documentation. In our use cases, we outline how trust can be developed by answering a provenance question.

Bizer and Cyganiak [2] present WIQA, a named graph query system that permits users to select policies to qualify the sets of characteristics to which they attribute a certain equivalent level of trust. These policies are then used to filter aggregated information to a contextually-trusted subset, and explanations for why information fulfills a policy are provided. Filtering policies may also contain explanation templates, which can be used to generate natural language as well as RDF explanations about filtering decisions. Their use of templates to specify what to show in the application is analogous to our subject-centric template approach. They use the Semantic Web Publishing Language to describe the provenance and signing of the aggregated named graphs, while we are using the Proof Markup Language. They are permitting the user to specify the templates, while our application currently imposes a fixed selection policy. Their use of explanation templates are also a convenient solution for producing explanations, which is not an aspect that we have fully addressed in our current work.

Tummarello et al. [13] present Sig.ma, a semantic integration mashup API and user browser. Based on a textual search, it presents data aggregated from multiple traditional and semantic web data sources and offers a highly interactive browsing experience permitting users to inquire for the source of a particular data item, reject or hide certain sources or data values, organize the arrangement of information, and capture their current view for sharing using a variety of popular representations such as RDF, JSON, permanent URLs, and HTML snippets. Sig.ma develops trust by allowing users to express their opinions of reliability on different data sources. This very flexible infrastructure and interaction methodology is useful for free-formed, user-driven exploration of content. However, this paradigm is not amenable to application developers attempting to communicate a particular, well structured story – as with the application we are evaluating for the use cases we describe in this paper. Although the system permits re-publishing of "customized views", the view type is limited to a single subject with traditional attribute-value listings and does not extend to visual depictions that may more effectively communicate such as the maps, faceted browsers, scatter plots, bar charts, tables, and timelines that we find in the system we evaluate. Although Sig.ma preserves provenance information by tracking the URL sources of data, it is not clear that it uses a common representation that can be reused by external applications. Our provenance-based proposals for addressing distrust events reuses the Proof Markup Language that is already used across a variety of applications. Using PML also permits comprehensive capture of the data incorporation and permits easy elaboration.

3   Supreme Court: Justices and Decision Making

3.1   Application Domain

Supreme Court scholars utilize data from each case and vote to analyze judicial decision-making. Scholars have made independent efforts to collect needed information, format them for easy processing, check their accuracy, and publish and maintain them in a reusable state. The U.S. Supreme Court Database (SCDB) [12] is regarded as a core dataset that encodes many aspects of Justices' votes since 1953. The SCDB is periodically released in formats accepted by most statistical applications. However, focusing on statistical aspects of these isolated data may result in a limited set of views and analytical directions, with missed opportunities to gain different perspectives and insights on existing data.

Besides the SCDB datasets, studies on judicial decision-making have relied on additional variables such as birth, education, party identification, and appointing presidents. These personal attributes are readily available from biographical directories and data collections of other scholars in the field. Due to the large amounts of data involved, manual encoding methods are time consuming and their limited visibility minimizes the chances for others to correct mistakes. The isolation of each data source may also limit insight into aggregate relationships.

3.2   Tools and Techniques: Advantages and Challenges

Linked Data and other Semantic Web technologies were proposed to improve this situation, demonstrated by an application *Supreme Court: Justices and Decision Making* [6]. The SCDB dataset was transformed into Resource Description Framework (RDF) and connected to linked data available from DBpedia. RDF represents data in a directed graph where a single labeled edge, known as a triple, has components known as the subject, predicate, and object. The SCDB and DBPedia data sources were bridged using data from a Semantic Media Wiki to reconcile different naming of Justices. The approach has many advantages. First, linked versions of SCDB datasets can easily be connected to many other datasets, enabling multiple perspectives on Supreme Court and Justices. Second, Linked Open Data covers much more factual information about Justices' personal attributes and career histories. Third, linked data is readily accessible.

Finally, a large community maintains linked data, which can reduce the bias and errors in the information.

However, challenges rise as data from different sources are incorporated to gain understanding, make decisions, and solve problems. The quality of the data from heterogeneous sources determines to what extent the data could be trusted and utilized. For certain information shown in the system, it is important to identify its quality such as the source of this information, author of the data, the update time, reliability and trustworthiness. The representative use cases described below address the most common scenarios in which users of *Supreme Court: Justices and Decision Making* encountered distrust.

4   Developing Trust through Provenance

When the user, based on their background knowledge and current context, identies either a surprise or a direct contradiction with the content of an information system, any part of the system is susceptible to blame. We refer to this situation as a *distrust event*. To develop trust, the system's role is to respond by identifying the sources and the processing leading to a particular conclusion. This is done by accepting a description of the issue contradiction and providing a subset of provenance to show the cause of the concern. We assume supplemental user interface elements that accept the user's concern and casts it into the appropriate URIs of an RDF subject and property.

Table 1 illustrates a simple taxonomy for the use cases described in this paper. The first dimension distinguishes among situations where the user believes that the system is either incorrect or has omitted some content. The second dimension distinguishes among the primary causes of the distrust event, whether it be the linked data, the application incorporating the linked data, or the application user. The use cases are further distinguished by three types of provenance that can be used to develop trust when faced with the distrust event. Each type of provenance is represented using the Proof Markup Language and is described further in the following sections with the use cases that they address. The composition of the three types of provenance represents the entire data flow from initial gathering of subjects, through multi-source incorporation as well as third-party APIs providing user interface components.

- **Provenance of subject scope** describes the actions taken by the application to determine the subjects that should be investigated. This includes a query, the web service providing a query response, and the web service parameters. The subject scope query may exist fully-parameterized or may be parameterized using user input.
- **Provenance of subject-centric queries** describes the actions taken by the application to gather information about the subjects within the available data sources. This includes the Uniform Resource Identifier for the in-scope subject, a query template parameterized for the subject, the web service providing a query response, and the web service parameters.

Table 1. Classification of five use cases that provoke distrust events, based on a simple taxonomy of the user response to the system and the primary cause of the situation.

	Linked Data is primary cause	Application is primary cause	User is primary cause
User believes that the System is Incorrect	1	4	2,3
User believes that the System Omitted Content		5	

- **Provenance of user interface invocation** describes the actions taken by the application to provide user interface elements using third-party APIs. This includes the API used and the subset of query results transferred.

4.1 Provenance of Subject-Centric Queries

The provenance solution proposed here is to show how answers were obtained for queries about specific subjects. It develops trust by displaying the source of the data and the steps taken to construct the query. The majority of use cases are addressed by this provenance type.

Use Case 1: User Belives That the System Is Incorrect, Incorrect Data

How distrust is generated. User trust is at risk when the system exhibits objective content that the user believes to be incorrect. Although it is the system's action to incorporate the data, the incorrectness of linked data is the primary cause. If the system attempts to display sources for its content along with the content, it may be difficult to ensure complete, granular coverage. The third factor leading to this event is an appropriate level of user background knowledge. Although common knowledge may lead to this potential conflict, greater user expertise will increase the likelihood of this type of distrust event. A conclusive resolution can be achieved because the conflict involves objective information. A corollary to this use case is where the user is not certain about the incorrectness, but is merely questioning his own interpretation due to unfamilarity with the content or the display design. Another corollary occurs when the application selects values of properties from multiple sources to find that they contradict.

How trust can be developed. Because the system relies upon external linked data sources, the objectively incorrect information can be traced to the source to identify whether it is the source that is incorrect or the application reads the source incorrectly. When the user inquires about the incorrect data, the subject's URI and one of its properties are used to search the provenance for the queries that were constructed for the subject using query templates that contain the property. It is important to note that the subject and property characterizing the distrust event need not be of the same RDF triple; they need only to co-occur within the provenance of an instantiated subject-centric template. Web services that responded to these queries would then be listed for the user as the source of contention. This strategy insulates the non-offending sources from blame and localizes the distrust to the appropriate linked data components. Higher granularities of source tracing would allow refined localization for offending sources. In the case where the same properties are selected from multiple sources, multiple subject/property pairs would be used to identify the appropriate provenance fragments for each.

Linked data can be used in a variety of ways. Dereferencable URIs may be crawled, and they may also be aggregated, indexed, and queried using SPARQL endpoints. Each technique offers benefits and tradeoffs. For lightweight clients accessing small portions of a large, curated dataset, use of a query endpoint is a good alternative. The application we evaluated used this approach, and the subject-centered provenance was identified to address its needs. Since the subject-centered provenance describes query construction and execution, the more straight forward "query" of dereferencing a URI could also be modeled in this fashion. Further, these two variants of subject-centered provenance are not mutually exclusive. A single application could perform both types depending on its data incorporation objectives.

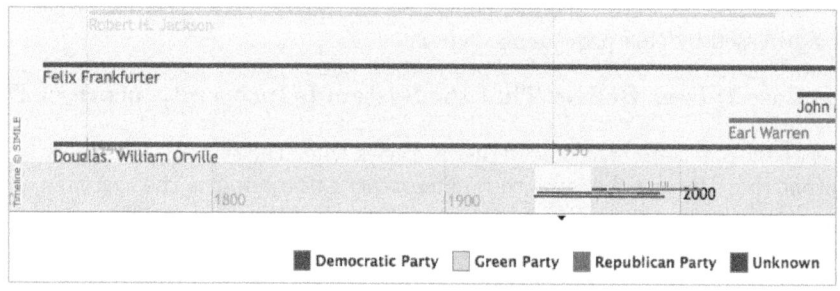

Fig. 1. User believes that no President was a member of the Green Party, and thus could not have nominated Robert Jackson to the Supreme Court of the United States

An example. As reproduced in Figure 1, the system reported that Robert H. Jackson was nominated by a President that was a member of the Green Party[1]. Only a moderate amount of common knowledge is needed to recognize that this nomination is impossible, since no President was a member of the Green Party. The commonality of this knowledge varies with the nationality and education level of the audience. Although the system is exhibiting a reasonable portrayal of the data by using the color green, this was done to handle the future possibility of the Green Party – the linked data is the primary cause of the distrust event.

Figures 2 and 3 show the structure of the provenance for query creation and execution, respectively. These form the subject-centric provenance that describes

---

[1] This use case assumes that the user correctly interprets the displayed content. The following use case describes a distrust event where the user misinterprets the display.

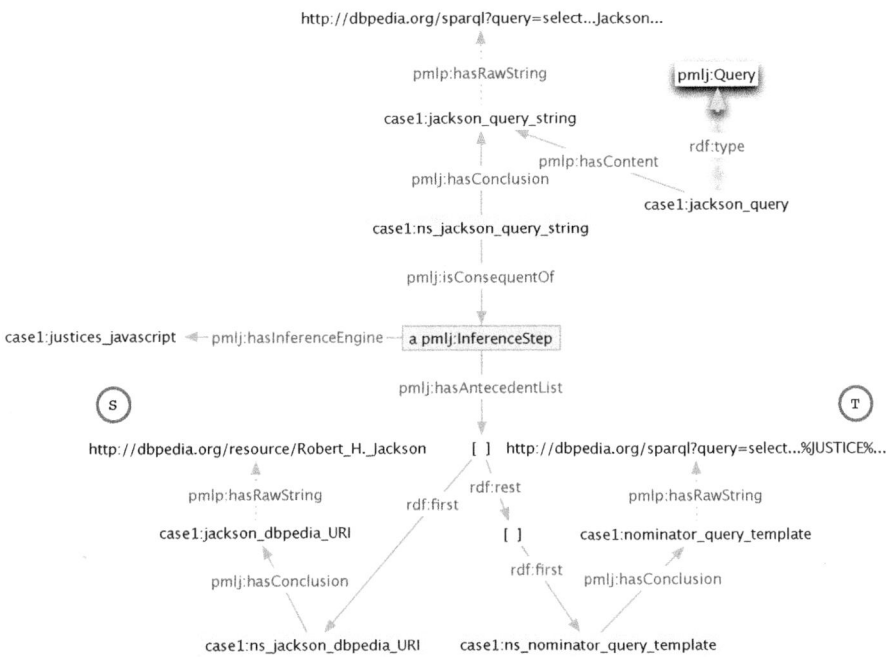

Fig. 2. Query creation half of the subject-centric provenance for the Green Party claim. Literal values are in blue font, `pmlj:NodeSets` have a yellow background, and `pmlj:InferenceSteps` have a gray background. The red S highlights the subject for which descriptions were gathered using the template highlighted by the red T, which contains the property that characterizes the Green Party distrust event. These are connected to the data source through the query `case1:ns_jackson_sparql_results`.

the cause of the Green Party claim. The URI for Jackson and the involved property "party" are used to identify the data source http://dbpedia.org/sparql. A `pmlj:NodeSet` augments the constructed query string `pmlp:Information` with an `pmlj:InferenceStep` to justify how the query was constructed. The `pmlj:InferenceStep` cites the application code as the `pmlj:InferenceEngine` and the subject and query template it used as input. The query string is also the content of a `pmlj:Query`, which is connected (in Figure 3) to the query result "Green" by a `pmlj:NodeSet` `case1:ns_jackson_sparql_results`. The `pmlj:InferenceStep` identifies the SPARQL endpoint proxy and the parameters used as a cause for the query result. The data source of the "Green Party" is found at the granularity of SPARQL query endpoint[2].

---

[2] Note that while we provide a portion of the detailed PML encoding, this is not intended to be displayed to the end user. Instead the fine grained encoding provides enough information for GUI application developers to provide details of the sources, query formation, and other reasoning on demand to end users in an appropriate format and context.

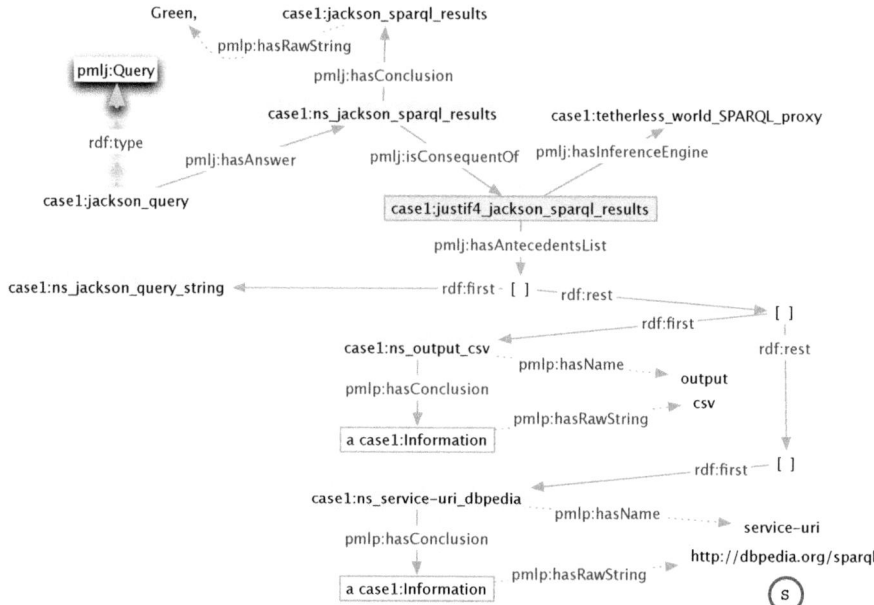

Fig. 3. Query execution half of the subject-centric provenance for the Green Party claim. Note that `case1:jackson_query` and `case1:ns_jackson_query_string` in this Figure are the same rdfs:Resources as shown in Figure 2. The red S highlights the data source responsible for descriptions involving the subject and property of the distrust event.

Use Case 2: User Doubts That the System Is Correct, User Misinterpretation

How distrust is generated. User trust is at risk when the user misinterprets content exhibited by the system. The system's role in this misinterpretation may contribute to this situation with varying degrees, depending upon the quality of its design. This situation occurs when either objective or subjective information is presented, where prior knowledge is correct, and linked data is correct. Both sides of this contradiction are based on factual information and the contradiction happens due to users misinterpretation of the data. This use case can apply in situations when the source data is correct or when it is incorrect.

How trust can be developed. Distinctions between objectivity and subjectivity and between incorrect or misinterpreted data rest with the user's perspective. In each case, the response to the distrust event is initiated by citing the subject and property of the data for which the user has a concern. In this way, the variety of distrust events are handled in a uniform manner. Because the system did not query for and did not receive this objectively incorrect information from external data sources, the system cannot blame the linked data. When the subject and

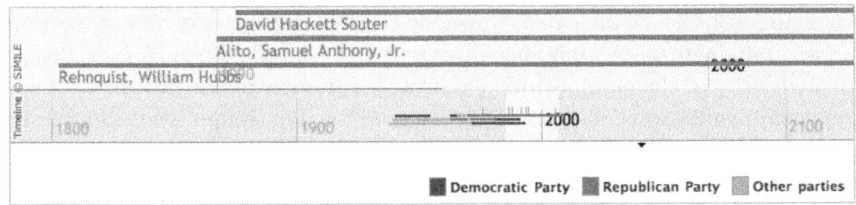

Fig. 4. The user misinterprets the content presented, thinking that the system is claiming David Hacket Souter was a Republican

property are questioned by the user, the provenance can be searched for the queries that were created using the subject's URI. Showing all of these using an interface appropriate for the user and context will inform the user that the property was not gathered by the application. Additionally, all query results may be searched for the property and value in question, and these can be shown to demonstrate that the subject is not included in these results. The graph patterns of SPARQL queries and the bindings structure of the results may present a challenge for a straight-forward solution.

An example. As reproduced in Figure 4, a user knows Justice David Souter is a Democrat while what she perceives from the interface is that Souter is Republican. The application is referring to the party of Souter's nominator, not of Souter himself. The system can develop trust by showing all queries involving Souter, none of which will involve his political party. The system could also show all query results involving "Republican" and show that Souter is not involved in these results. The same subject-centric provenance components are used as described in Use Case 1. But because no specific property is indicated in this scenario, the provenance process will search for all queries given Souter's URI, identifying a variety of templates where the actual queries come from. Alternatively, the provenance process could be searched for all query results mentioning "Republican," showing the queries that went into the results.

Use Case 3: User Is Certain That the System Is Incorrect, Subjective Content

How distrust is generated. This type of contradiction happens when the analytical results showed by the linked data contradicts with users subjective opinions instead of facts. The application is a source cause because it is aggregating data with subjective content. Linked data is a cause because the source is contributing data with subjective content. The user is a cause in this situation if their views disagree with the subjective content exhibited. Any subjective claims must be supported, but will not be conclusive as in the previous use cases that addressed objective content. This use case involves more complicated and ambiguous issues and can not be resolved conclusively because individuals disagree on interpretations of a set of facts.

How trust can be developed. A claim on its own is not a fact; it must be supported. The source of the claim can be provided using provenance of subject-centric queries, but instead of assigning blame of the source, the system is deferring the credibility of the claim. More elaborate solutions would incorporate how the analytical results were derived using source of data, computation mechanisms, and the people invoking the analysis.

An example. In the SCDB, each vote that a Justice makes is classified as reflecting a conservative or liberal position. The total conservative votes can be compared to the total liberal votes to quantify a Justice's stance. Figure 5 reflects the neutrality of David Hacket Souter because he voted approximately equally for conservative and liberal decisions. This contrasts with the general stereotype that he has a strong liberal stance[3]. Given Souter's URI and the property "decisionDirection," subject-centric provenance can be used to identify SCDB as the source of the vote tally for conservative and liberal votes.

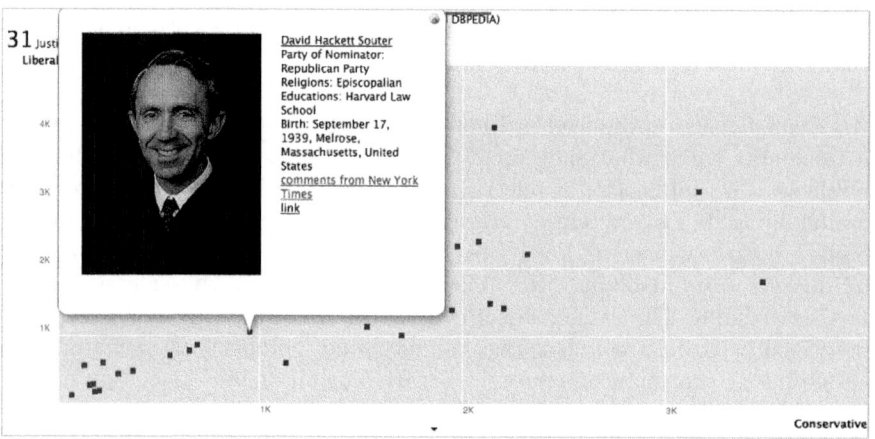

Fig. 5. A user with conservative political views considering David Souter to be a liberal disagrees with a claim that he served as a moderate Justice

4.2 Use Cases Addressed by Provenance of User Interface Invocation

Solutions for use cases in this category are based on an extension to the subject-centered query provenance described in the previous section. The content presented by a third-party user interface or visualization API is represented with an instance of pmlp:Information, and instances of pmlj:NodeSet provide justifications enumerating the content's antecedent query results. These query results

---

[3] http://topics.nytimes.com/top/reference/timestopics/people/s/
david_h_souter/index.html

are part of the subject-centered provenance already described. The use case addressed by this provenance solution involves the Exhibit framework. The incorporating web application is insulated from distrust when illustrating that it obtained correct data and transferred requests to the third-party API.

Use Case 4: User Is Certain That the System Is Incorrect, Rendering Distortion

How distrust is generated. Contradictions at this level may be caused by the inconsistency between two content elements depicting the same data property. Distrust in the system is generated because of its self-contradictory exhibition. Some user background knowledge may be required to fulfill the contradiction. The objective nature of the data can lead to a conclusive resolution of this distrust event.

How trust can be developed. Instead of reporting the source of incorrect or missing data as in the previous solutions, trust is developed by illustrating that correct data was incorporated and provided to a supporting API. Any distortions of content become the responsibility of the API and not of the web application. If the source data elements for the two contradictory content elements are the same, it is clearly a rendering distortion. However, if the same data property was provided by separate sources and the content is correctly portrayed, then the conflicting data sources should be shown and the third-party user interface APIs can be absolved.

An example. As reproduced in Figure 7, the system exhibited self-contradictory nativity information for David Hackett Souter, since the map is pointing to Quebec and the information box lists Melrose, Massachusetts. Users background knowledge about the uniqueness of a birthplace led to a contradiction. It is possible that "Quebec" came from SCDB and "Melrose, Massachusetts" came from DBpedia, but SCDB does not describe nativity. In this case, the same value "Melrose, Massachusetts" was provided to both display APIs. One simply displayed the text, while the other obtained incorrect latitude and longitude values for the string. Given Souter's URI and the property "Birthplace," the appropriate subject-centered queries could be found. Unlike in the previous section, conclusions derived from these results are found to identify the `pmlj:InferenceEngine` that used the query results to produce the visual display.

4.3   Use Case Addressed by Provenance of Subject Scope

Use Case 5: User Believes That the System Omitted Content, System Scoped

How distrust is generated. If the system is showing instances of a certain type, the user may reasonably expect all instances to be shown. The system is the primary cause of this distrust event, since it is scoped to show only certain data

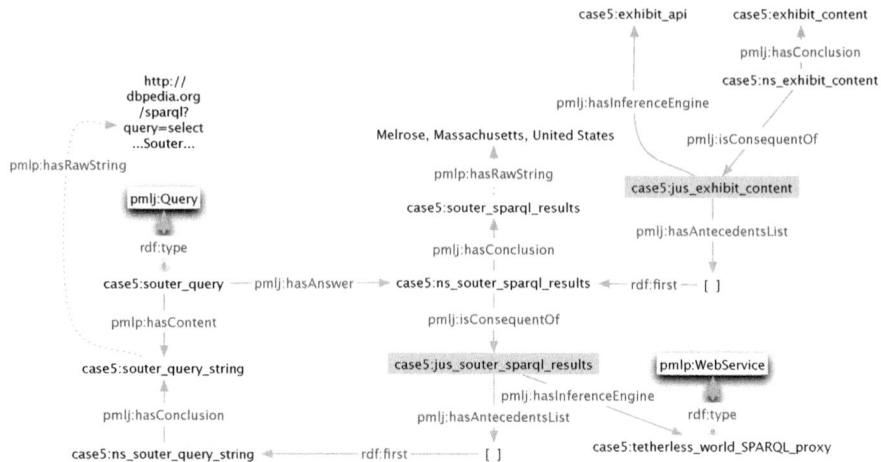

Fig. 6. With *provenance of user interface invocation,* subject-centered query provenance is extended to capture subsequent uses of the query result. An instance of `pmlp:Information` represents all content displayed by a third-party user interface API, and a `pmlj:NodeSet` provides justification for the information by citing that Exhibit was given the query results `case5:souter_sparql_results`

Fig. 7. User is certain that a person could not be born in two places. This incorrect content could be caused by several situations, each with varying degrees of blame for linked data and the application.

from certain sources. The linked data is not a cause because the system did not request the data. The user is a cause because of reasonable expectations for a comprehensive view. This use case differs from the previous because the system is subject-scoping, and thus not intending to show omitted data. A corollary to this use case is where the user not only knows an entity exists, but also knows it is described in the cited sources. An additional corollary occurs when the primary cause shifts from the applications subject-scoping to the lack of requested linked data. This would be classified into the first empty box[4] of the taxonomy shown in Table 1.

How trust can be developed. While principle data sources provide the entities that will be displayed, augmenting data sources provide supplemental properties. Searching the subject-centered query provenance for a URI from an augmenting source will not succeed because queries were only performed for URIs from primary sources. Without an appropriate subset of provenance, showing the overall flow of queries can distinguish among primary and secondary sources. Multiple subject-centered query provenance segments can be composed to capture the application's chaining of queries.

An example. As reproduced in Figure 8, search results for "white" do not show Edward Douglas White, whom the user knows was a Justice. The application is using SCDB as its primary data source and augmenting these descriptions using DBPedia. Since Edward Douglas White served before the period that SCDB describes (1953-2009), his descriptions are not available. Showing that the initial queries were constructed from entities in SCDB and not DBpedia will provide this explanation. DBpedia can be highlighted as containing descriptions of Edward Douglas White to indicate that if the system incorporated DBpedia as a primary source, it would have included it as content.

1 Justice filtered from 31 originally (Reset All Filters)

name	party	started from	left on▾
Byron Raymond White	Democratic Party	1962-04-16	1993-06-28

Fig. 8. The user knows Edward Douglas White was a Justice of the Supreme Court, but search results for "white" showing only Byron Raymond White leads to a contradiction

---

[4] The remaining empty box in the taxonomy would contain use cases where the user was the cause of the system's omission of content, where search terms or other data-filtering user elements are employed.

5 Conclusions

Our accumulation and analysis of use cases for an existing linked data application has established provenance of the subject-centric query as a primary type that can be used to address a variety of distrust events and help develop user trust in applications incorporating linked data by insulating non-offending sources from blame and localizing the distrust to the appropriate components. The two remaining provenance types reinforce its importance by demonstrating its basis for extension to address still other types of distrust events. We identified two types of user response that provoke a distrust event, three types of their primary cause, and a contradiction-based technique for identifying and developing distrust trust use cases. We propose these factors be considered when developing linked data applications and services.

We plan to use these use cases to guide implementation of provenance within the current implementation of *Supreme Court: Justices and Decision Making*. This will enable an evaluation of our proposed methodology, which should include the characteristics for information quality and believability. We plan to identify application-independent functionality that should be part of a provenance-enabled web application framework. Saving intermediate results that can be retrieved in response to distrust events will be an important aspect. Development of additional uses cases for the application may lead to a more sophisticated taxonomy and general understanding of distrust events, and approaches for accepting the user's concern to initiate provenance search and explanation will also be needed.

References

1. Artz, D., Gil, Y.: A survey of trust in computer science and the semantic web. Web Semantics: Science, Services and Agents on the World Wide Web 5(2), 58–71 (2007)
2. Bizer, C., Cyganiak, R.: Quality-driven information filtering using the wiqa policy framework. Web Semantics: Science, Services and Agents on the World Wide Web, The Semantic Web and Policy 7(1), 1–10 (2009)
3. Buneman, P., Khanna, S., Tan, W.-C.: Data provenance: Some basic issues. In: Kapoor, S., Prasad, S. (eds.) FST TCS 2000. LNCS, vol. 1974, pp. 87–93. Springer, Heidelberg (2000)
4. Fox, M., Huang, J.: Knowledge provenance in enterprise information. International Journal of Production Research 43(20), 4471–4492 (2005)
5. Hartig, O.: Provenance information in the web of data. In: Proceedings of the 2nd Workshop on Linked Data on the Web, LDOW 2009 (2009)
6. Li, X., Ding, L., Hendler, J.A.: Study supreme court justice decision making with linked data. Technical report, Rensselaer Polytechnic Institute (2010)
7. McGuinness, D., Ding, L., da Silva, P., Chang, C.: Pml 2: A modular explanation interlingua. In: Proceedings of AAAI, vol. 7 (2007)
8. Miles, S., Groth, P., Branco, M., Moreau, L.: The requirements of using provenance in e-science experiments. Journal of Grid Computing 5(1), 1–25 (2007)
9. Naumann, F., Leser, U., Freytag, J.-C.: Quality-driven integration of heterogeneous information systems. In: VLDB Conference, pp. 447–458 (1999)

10. Prat, N., Madnick, S.: Measuring data believability: A provenance approach. In: HICSS 2008: Proceedings of the Proceedings of the 41st Annual Hawaii International Conference on System Sciences, Washington, DC, USA, p. 393. IEEE Computer Society, Los Alamitos (2008)
11. Sillence, E., Briggs, P., Fishwick, L., Harris, P.: Trust and mistrust of online health sites. In: Proceedings of the SIGCHI conference on Human factors in computing systems, pp. 663–670. ACM, New York (2004)
12. Spaeth, H., Segal, J.: US Supreme Court Judicial Data Base: Providing New Insights into the Court, The. Judicature 83, 228 (1999)
13. Tummarello, G., Cyganiak, R., Catasta, M., Danielczyk, S., Delbru, R., Decker, S.: Sig.ma: live views on the web of data. In: WWW 2010: Proceedings of the 19th international conference on World wide web, pp. 1301–1304. ACM, New York (2010)
14. Zhao, J., Klyne, G., Shotton, D.: Provenance and linked data in biological data webs. In: Proceedings of the 17th International World Wide Web Conference WWW2008 (Workshop: Linked Data on the Web LDOW 2008), vol. 22 (April 2008) Citeseer

Reflections on Provenance Ontology Encodings

Li Ding[1], Jie Bao[1], James R. Michaelis[1], Jun Zhao[2], and Deborah L. McGuinness[1]

[1] Tetherless World Constellation, Rensselaer Polytechnic Institute
{dingl,baojie,michaj6,dlm}@cs.rpi.edu
[2] Image Bioinformatics Research Group, Department of Zoology, University of Oxford
jun.zhao@zoo.ox.ac.uk

Abstract. As more data (especially scientific data) is digitized and put on the Web, it is desirable to make provenance metadata easy to access, reuse, integrate and reason over. Ontologies can be used to encode expectations and agreements concerning provenance metadata representation and computation. This paper analyzes a selection of popular Semantic Web provenance ontologies such as the Open Provenance Model (OPM), Dublin Core (DC) and the Proof Markup Language (PML). Selected initial findings are reported in this paper: (i) concept coverage analysis – we analyze the coverage, similarities and differences among primitive concepts from different provenance ontologies, based on identified themes; and (ii) concept modeling analysis – we analyze how Semantic Web language features were used to support computational provenance semantics. We expect the outcome of this work to provide guidance for understanding, aligning and evolving existing provenance ontologies.

Keywords: provenance, ontology, semantic web.

1 Introduction

In distributed and open environments, such as the Web, consumers can access data without knowledge of its creation and expected use. Provenance plays an important role in supporting transparency and accountability of such data. In order to ensure data transparency, the corresponding provenance metadata should be made accessible for consumers through an effective environment for data management. Likewise, in order to evaluate the accountability of data, consumers need to correctly understand the provenance metadata. In both cases, the use of provenance ontologies can be helpful. We found it natural to use a Semantic Web-based approach in our work since semantic technologies have been integrated into the web and semantic web languages provide a means for encoding provenance concepts and their meanings.

A number of applications of provenance data management have benefited from the use of Semantic Web ontologies [1, 2, 3]. In these applications, provenance data is represented through RDF graphs serialized in an RDF syntax, such as RDF/XML, and can be published on the Web as Linked Data [4]. Likewise, to encode richer provenance data, either RDFS or OWL are used. Semantic Web tools, such as RDF APIs, triple stores and reasoners, are used to leverage the vocabulary defined by the provenance ontologies and make inferences accordingly. In particular, SPARQL can be used to express simple queries over provenance data.

D.L. McGuinness, J.R. Michaelis, and L. Moreau (Eds.): IPAW 2010, LNCS 6378, pp. 198–205, 2010.
© Springer-Verlag Berlin Heidelberg 2010

We selected a few representative Semantic Web provenance ontologies for analysis, and attempt to address two issues: (i) **Concept coverage**: what primitive provenance concepts are supported? What are the similarities and differences among the primitive concepts? (ii) **Concept modeling**: how are computational provenance semantics modeled? What are the expressivities? The outcome of our study not only provides guidance to provenance ontology users but also has the potential to promote best practices in collaborative provenance ontology development.

The rest of this paper is organized as follows: Section 2 reviews selected Semantic Web provenance ontologies; Section 3 analyzes primitive provenance concepts in these ontologies using theme-based grouping; Section 4 analyzes the use of ontology constructs in provenance ontologies; Finally, Section 5 provides concluding remarks.

2 Semantic Web Provenance Ontologies

Semantic Web provenance ontologies[1] have emerged in one of two ways: from scratch, or through the conversion of existing provenance vocabularies not based on Semantic Web technologies. Many of them focus on the provenance of digital objects (e.g. scientific data), using the Web as a data management infrastructure, and encoding computational provenance semantics using declarative ontology constructs. This paper focuses on the following representative ontologies[2].

Open Provenance Model (OPM) [5] originated from workflow trace sharing, and is also designed to support more general provenance representation and computation. It defines both provenance *entities* (e.g., "artifact") and provenance *relations* (e.g., an artifact "was generated by" a process). Starting from XML Schema-based encodings, OPM recently adopted an OWL-based encoding, which has evolved with the new OPM specification (OPM 1.1).

Proof Markup Language (PML) [6] originated from logical proof sharing, and has also been used in other information manipulation contexts such as information extraction and machine learning. It consists of three modules: (i) a taxonomy of primitive provenance entities with related properties; (ii) a representation of data derivation and acquisition trace using proof theoretic notation; and (iii) an encoding of trust and belief on data and agents. Since its inception in 2003, PML has consistently followed the linked data principle in publishing its data.

Dublin Core (DC) was originally developed in the digital library domain. It provides a provenance vocabulary which primarily covers generic binary provenance relations such as "source" and "creator". It leverages RDFS ontology constructs, and its provenance relations are typically binary without specifying domain/range restrictions. **Dublin Core Terms (DCTerms)** [3] is the current recommended version of Dublin Core, having more relations and concepts than the previous DC Element vocabulary[4].

Provenance Vocabulary (PRV) [7] was recently developed to track information manipulation. It consists of three modules: (i) the core module that defines basic concepts for tracking data creation and data access, (ii) a taxonomy specific to Web

---

[1] In the rest of this paper, the term "ontology" refers to semantic web provenance ontology.
[2] For more provenance related ontologies, see http://tw.rpi.edu/portal/Provenance.
[3] http://dublincore.org/documents/dcmi-terms/
[4] http://dublincore.org/documents/dces/

information transfer and (iii) a taxonomy specific to authentication of information. It uses OWL 2 constructs, e.g., property chain Axiom.

Provenir[5] [14] focuses on information manipulation. It is built on top of the OBO Relation Ontology (OBO-RO) [8], which covers generic binary relations frequently used in bioinformatics. This ontology defines new provenance entities, and it also uses the newly defined classes to extend the definition of OBO-RO by adding domain and range restrictions to existing OBO-RO properties.

Some of the above ontologies are modularized. Table 1 lists the selected ontologies as well as their key modules (with the corresponding namespace-prefix mappings). Every module can be retrieved by dereferencing the corresponding namespaces, except OPM[6].

Table 1. Selected semantic web provenance ontologies and their modules

Ontology	Namespace	Prefix
OPM 1.1	http://openprovenance.org/ontology#	opm
PML 2.0	http://inference-web.org/2.0/pml-provenance.owl#	pmlp
	http://inference-web.org/2.0/pml-justification.owl#	pmlj
Dublin Core Terms	http://purl.org/dc/terms/	dcterms
Provenance Vocabulary	http://purl.org/net/provenance/ns#	prv
Provenir Ontology	http://knoesis.wright.edu/provenir/provenir.owl#	provenir
OBO Relation Ontology	http://www.obofoundry.org/ro/ro.owl#	ro

Table 2 shows basic statistics about these ontologies: triples are counted using the JENA API[7]; class/property numbers are counted based on two criteria, i.e. (i) the terms are *defined as classes or properties* [9] and (ii) the terms use the module's namespace (we did not count redefined external concepts in PRV and Provenir); and OWL species and DL Expressivity were obtained using Pellet[8] online services.

Table 2. Basic statistics of selected semantic web provenance ontologies

	opm	pmlp	pmlj	dcterms	Prv	provenir	ro
# of triples	309	505	207	857	304	136	268
# of classes	20	30	8	22	14	8	0
# of properties	26	47	21	55	17	2	24
OWL Species	OWL DL	OWL DL	OWL DL	RDFS	OWL 2 DL	OWL DL	OWL Lite
DL Expressivity	ALCF(D)	ALCHIF(D)	ALHF(D)	ALH(D)	RI(D)	ALCH	$AL_{R+}HI$

3 Concept Coverage Analyses

We review concept coverage from two perspectives: (i) to group similar primitive concepts by their themes to see if different ontologies focus on similar themes; and (ii) to review semantics of primitive concepts for identifying the difference between similar

---

[5] http://wiki.knoesis.org/index.php/Provenir_Ontology

[6] http://github.com/lucmoreau/OpenProvenanceModel/raw/master/elmo/src/main/resources/opm.owl was used in this study as the current draft OWL profile for OPM 1.1 .

[7] http://jena.sourceforge.net/

[8] Pellet online demo at http://www.mindswap.org/2003/pellet/demo.shtml

primitive concepts. Due to their different design principles, primitive concepts in different ontologies are not necessarily the same even if they have the same name. Since the meaning of primitive concepts is primarily described in natural language in the annotations of ontology and the related publications, precise alignment is challenging. Therefore, we empirically identified several themes to use for grouping similar primitive concepts and further discuss their differences. We are not claiming comprehensive coverage with our provenance concept themes but we did find them instructive for provenance ontology comparison.

Table 3 lists the selected ontologies and compares their concept theme coverage. Due to space limitations, each table cell contains a few example terms from the corresponding ontology (see rows) on the theme (see columns). To support definition of themes, we use "entity" to refer to things that distinctly exist and "relation" to refer to relations among entities. A "theme" is used to group similar entities and relations reflecting one dimension of provenance metadata, and these themes have clear connection to the well-known five Ws (and one H)[9] in information gathering. Themes are identified based on an empirical study over the selected provenance ontologies[10], so it is not necessarily exhaustive. Themes are generally disjoint, but exceptions are permitted. For example, a robot could be considered as an agent in a car manufacturer factory, but an artifact (product) of a robot manufacturing factory.

Table 3. Provenance ontology theme coverage

	OPM 1.1	PML 2.0	DCTerms	PRV core	Provenir (+OBO-RO)
Agents	Agent	Agent	Agent	Actor	Agent
artifacts	Artifact	IdentifiedThing,Information	PhysicalResource	Artifact	Data
Events	WasGeneratedBy Process	pmlp:SourceUsage, pmlj:InferenceStep	ProvenanceStatement Source	Execution	provenir:process, ro:derives_from
methods		InferenceRule	Policy MethodOfAccrual	CreationGuideline	
time	OTime	hasCreationDateTime	PeriodOfTime	performedAt	temporal_parameter
space			Location		Spatial_parameter

- **Agents (Who):** Actionable entities that can take actions in an event. Organization and Person are two common types of agents. PML and PRV core additionally defined agent taxonomies. While opm:Agent is defined as a snapshot of an agent, the others define Agent as a continuant entity which is mutable over time.
- **Artifacts (Who):** Entities made by agents and involved in events. OPM explicitly emphasizes the immutable status of artifacts, such that an evolving entity could be related to multiple artifacts (each of which being a snapshot of the entity). While OPM and DCTerms consider both digital and physical entities, the other selected ontologies focus only on digital entities, especially data. opm:Artifact is defined to be disjoint with opm:Agent. Both PML and PRV additionally define artifact taxonomies. PML defines pmlp:Information (i.e. snapshot of data) and pmlp:Source (i.e. the container of information) to support differentiating inference steps (i.e., deriving data from data) from source usage (e.g., acquiring data from data containers).

---

[9] http://en.wikipedia.org/wiki/Five_Ws (Who, What, When, Where, Why, & How)
[10] Note: our study is based on the ontology and supporting documents. We are in discussion with ontology authors to confirm and refine our observations.

- **Events (What):** Observable occurrence(s), execution of action(s) (potentially including the past). Although not explicitly claimed, these ontologies contain entities and/or relations that record events, especially derivation, i.e., something was derived from something else. For example, opm:WasGeneratedBy captures an event where an artifact was generated by a process at a certain moment, and opm:Process is also a kind of event because *"processes also occurred in the past"*[5]. PML supports both data derivation events by pmlj:InferenceStep and data acquisition events by pmlp:SourceUsage. OBO-RO and DCTerms offer binary relations, e.g., ro:derives_from and dcterms:source, which obviously can be mapped to data derivation events and data acquisition events, respectively.
- **Methods (How):** Entities denoting the operations (or actions) used (or mentioned) in events. For example, a recipe exposes the instructions used in a cooking event, and a protocol shows the methods used in a biomedical experiment. PML uses pmlp:InferenceRule to annotate methods used in events so that users can find events reusing the same method. DCTerms and PRV also have similar concepts. An instance of method can be further declaratively annotated by declarative scripts such as list of instructions or program source code.
- **Time (When):** Temporal concepts, such as time and date when things were created (or updated), primarily used for annotating events. Most ontologies only defined temporal properties, while OPM and DCTerms define additional time classes. Unlike the other selected ontologies which only focus on time points, OPM additionally defines duration using *opm:noEarlierThan* and *opm:noLaterThan*.
- **Space (Where):** Geospatial concepts such as locations, GPS coordinates and regions. Only DCTerms and Provenir support this theme, and their definitions are remain general and avoid including detailed geospatial concept taxonomies.

A few additional observations arose with the theme analysis. First, similar concepts may still have different meanings, e.g., OPM and PML treat the concept "agent" as immutable and mutable, respectively. Second, feedback from the use of provenance ontologies in applications can lead to their evolution, e.g., a special concept pmlp:LearnedSourceUsage was added to better support explaining tasks in multi-agent learning contexts[10]. Third, some themes can be supported by dedicated ontologies, e.g., the OWL Time ontology[11], the WGS84 Geo Positioning Ontology[12] and Friend of a Friend (FOAF)[13]. Finally, it is important to represent the scope of a particular workflow, e.g., OPM defined opm:Account to associate entities with a workflow, and PML uses a recursive algorithm to determine the scope of a proof.

4   Concept Modeling Analyses

We now analyze the semantic structure and concept modeling patterns by comparing the use of ontology constructs in the ontologies (see Table 4). The ontology constructs are further grouped by the following four functional groups that were summarized from the manual analysis of the selected ontologies.

---

[11] http://www.w3.org/2006/time
[12] http://www.w3.org/2003/01/geo/wgs84_pos
[13] http://xmlns.com/foaf/0.1/

Table 4. How OWL/RDFS ontology constructs were used in provenance ontologies

		opm	pmlp	pmlj	dcterms	prv	provenir	ro
Concept	rdfs:subClassOf	X	X	X	X	X	X	
Taxonomy	rdfs:subPropertyOf		X	X	X	X	X	X
	owl:disjointWith	X	X			X	X	
	owl:unionOf	X				X	X	
	owl:equivalentClassOf					X		
Inference	owl:inverseOf		X			X		X
on relations	owl:TransitiveProperty							X
Constraints	rdfs:domain / rdfs:range	X	X	X	X	X	X	
	owl:allValuesFrom	X	X	X			X	
	Cardinality Restriction	X	X	X		X		
Concept	owl:imports		X	X				
Reuse	Reused ontology				foaf		ro	

Concept Taxonomy. Semantic ontology languages, e.g., RDFS and OWL, provide set-theoretic constructs (e.g. sub-set, union, equivalence, complement and disjoint) to support taxonomy definitions. These ontology constructs are observed in all selected ontologies in modeling class taxonomies and/or property taxonomies. A direct benefit of using OWL and RDFS is that those constructs are supported by corresponding reasoners that are capable of inferring additional information about taxonomies, e.g., transitive closure of sub-set relations and consistency validation using disjoint semantics. PML has a larger class taxonomy than some other provenance interlingua options (e.g. OPM). One reason for PML's growth was a direct consequence of application driven growth from reuse beyond its original scope (e.g., reuse in machine learning and text analytics applications although original constructor design was aimed at hybrid logical first order reasoning. Its growth also generated a redesign to create modules that could be used independently. We anticipate that other provenance ontologies, if they decide to grow in breadth, may also provide modularization options. The use of disjointness may be an issue in some ontologies. Overusing disjointness can limit reusability since for example an initial modeling might expect person and inference-engine to be disjoint but in a different context, a person might function as an inference engine and thus may be an instance of both classes.

Inference on Relations. A binary provenance relation can be defined as an OWL object property to carry additional computational semantics such as "inverse" and "transitive". Upon defining "part/whole" relation, OBO-RO additionally used both owl:TransitiveProperty and owl:inverseOf constructs in defining ro:has_part in comparison with a similar concept dcterms:hasPart from DCTerms. Besides the two constructs in table 4, PRV leverages the OWL2 construct owl:propertyChainAxiom to enable more complex inference on relations: if x is prv:serializedBy y and y is prv:createdBy z then x is prv:createdBy z. The OWL and OWL2 constructs discussed here are selected because they have obvious connection to provenance graph inference [5]. We should also note that SPARQL can also be used to enable some other kinds of provenance computation, such as converting binary relation from/to corresponding class instances.

Constraints. Upon sharing provenance metadata, users may also want to leverage provenance ontologies to assure the quality of provenance metadata. Integrity constraints, such as cardinality restrictions, may be encoded using the OWL syntax along with a non-standard semantics based on the Closed World Assumption (CWA) [11][14]. For example, an instance of opm:WasGeneratedBy needs to be associated with at least one instance of opm:Process via the opm:cause relation, and this can be encoded using owl:minCardinality.

Concept Reuse. Section 2 showed the trend of modularizing provenance ontologies, and raised issues on ontology reuse. In practice, ontology reuse can be done by using the owl:imports construct (i.e., explicitly copy the content of the other ontology, e.g., pmlj imports pmlp), or by directly using terms in the external ontology (i.e., users need to dereference the terms to get their definitions, e.g., PRV uses external terms to enrich its definition). It is notable that the meaning of imported terms may also be redefined during importing. For example, in Provenir, the meaning of ro:has_agent is beyond its original meaning in OBO-RO due to additional domain/range statements.

5   Conclusion

This study investigated a select group of Semantic Web provenance ontologies and yielded interesting observations: (i) provenance ontologies share common themes surrounding provenance research; (ii) similar terms in the same theme can carry different semantics, e.g. opm:Agent and pmlp:Agent; (iii) we observed the use of RDFS, OWL and OWL2 in encoding provenance ontologies and supporting provenance computation (e.g. transitive provenance graph inference); (iv) Some ontologies are fully self-contained while some others reuse external concepts.

   The above observations not only help users to review provenance ontologies via a side-by-side comparison, but also promote better collaborative provenance ontology development. First, modularization has been seen as a successful practice in ontology development for controlling the cost of development and reuse. It would be desirable to keep a minimal set of core concepts in one module and support extensions, such as detailed classification and domain specific concepts, in other modules. However, we should also avoid excessive modularization that may cause unnecessary overhead. Second, while provenance theme-level mapping provides general guidance for reusing ontologies, a concept-level mapping is still needed to keep the ontologies interoperable. Work on ontology mapping has been reported on the OPM-PML mapping [12] and the OPM-DCTerms mapping [13]. Additionally, mapping efforts are underway in the W3C Provenance Incubator[15]. Future research should also emphasize mapping different provenance ontologies as well as reusing concepts from other ontologies.

Acknowledgments. This work is supported in part by NSF #0524481, DARPA #FA8650-06-C-7605, #FA8750-07-D-0185, #55-002001, #F30602-00-2-0579, and ITA project W911NF-06-3-0001.

---

[14] Note that the standard semantics of OWL does not support the modeling of integrity constraints as it uses the Open World Assumption (OWA), c.f. [11].

[15] http://www.w3.org/2005/Incubator/prov/wiki/Provenance_Vocabulary_Mappings

References

[1] Zhao, J., Wroe, C., Goble, C., Stevens, R., Quan, D., Greenwood, M.: Using semantic web technologies for representing e-science provenance. In: McIlraith, S.A., Plexousakis, D., van Harmelen, F. (eds.) ISWC 2004. LNCS, vol. 3298, pp. 93–106. Springer, Heidelberg (2004)

[2] Golbeck, J., Hendler, J.: A Semantic Web approach to the provenance challenge. Concurrency and Computation: Practice and Experience 20, 431–439 (2008)

[3] Zednik, S., Fox, P., McGuinness, D.L., Pinheiro da Silva, P., Chang, C.: Semantic Provenance for Science Data Products: Application to Image Data Processing. In: Workshop on the role of Semantic Web in Provenance Management (2009)

[4] McGuinness, D.L., Pinheiro da Silva, P.: Explaining Answers from the Semantic Web: The Inference Web Approach. Journal of Web Semantics 1(4), 397–413 (2004)

[5] Moreau, L., Clifford, B., Freire, J., Gil, Y., Groth, P., Futrelle, J., Kwasnikowska, N., Miles, S., Missier, P., Myers, J., Simmhan, Y., Stephan, E., Bussche, J.: The Open Provenance Model Core Specification (v1.1), submitted to Future Generation Computer Systems (2009)

[6] McGuinness, D.L., Ding, L., Pinheiro da Silva, P., Chang, C.: PML 2: A Modular Explanation Interlingua. In: Proceedings of the 2007 Workshop on Explanation-aware Computing, ExaCt-2007 (2007)

[7] Hartig, O., Zhao, J.: Publishing and Consuming Provenance Metadata on the Web of Linked Data. In: Proceedings of the 3rd International Provenance and Annotation Workshop, IPAW (2010)

[8] Smith, B., Ceusters, W., Klagges, B., Köhler, J., Kumar, A., Lomax, J., Mungall, C., Neuhaus, F., Rector, A.L., Rosse, C.: Relations in Biomedical Ontologies. Genome Biology, 6:R46 (2005)

[9] Ding, L., Finin, T.: Characterizing the Semantic Web on the Web. In: Cruz, I., Decker, S., Allemang, D., Preist, C., Schwabe, D., Mika, P., Uschold, M., Aroyo, L.M. (eds.) ISWC 2006. LNCS, vol. 4273, pp. 242–257. Springer, Heidelberg (2006)

[10] McGuinness, D.L., Glass, A., Wolverton, M., Pinheiro da Silva, P.: Explaining Task Processing in Cognitive Assistants that Learn. In: AAAI 2007 Spring Symposium on Interaction Challenges for Intelligent Assistants (2007)

[11] Tao, J., Sirin, E., Bao, J., McGuinness, D.L.: Integrity Constraints in OWL, accepted by the 24th Conference on Artificial Intelligence (AAAI 2010)

[12] Michaelis, J.R., Zednik, S., Ding, L., McGuinness, D.L.: A comparison of the OPM and PML provenance models. Tetherless World Constellation Technical Report (2009)

[13] Miles, S., Moreau, L., Futrelle, J.: OPM Profile for Dublin Core Terms (v0.3) (July 2009),
http://twiki.ipaw.info/pub/OPM/ChangeProposalDublinCoreMapping/dcprofile.pdf

[14] Sahoo, S.S., Barga, R.S., Goldstein, J., Sheth, A.: Provenance Algebra and Materialized View-based Provenance Management, Microsoft Research Technical Report (MSR-TR-2008-170) (November 2008)

Abstract Provenance Graphs: Anticipating and Exploiting Schema-Level Data Provenance

Daniel Zinn and Bertram Ludäscher

{dzinn,ludaesch}@ucdavis.edu

Abstract. Provenance graphs capture flow and dependency information recorded during scientific workflow runs, which can be used subsequently to interpret, validate, and debug workflow results. In this paper, we propose the new concept of *Abstract Provenance Graphs* (APGs). APGs are created via static analysis of a configured workflow W and input data schema, i.e., *before* W is actually executed. They summarize *all* possible provenance graphs the workflow W can create with input data of type τ, that is, for each input $v \in \tau$ there exists a graph homomorphism $\mathcal{H}_v$ between the concrete and abstract provenance graph. APGs are helpful during workflow construction since (1) they make certain workflow design-bugs (e.g., selecting none or wrong input data for the actors) easy to spot; and (2) show the evolution of the overall data organization of a workflow. Moreover, after workflows have been run, APGs can be used to validate concrete provenance graphs. A more detailed version of this work is available as [14].[1]

1 Introduction

The ability to record, visualize, and query provenance information (in particular data lineage) is considered a key feature of scientific workflow systems and is becoming increasingly important, e.g., to help interpret, validate or debug runs of scientific workflows. So far, provenance information is provided, almost by definition, only *after* the execution of a workflow run. We propose a novel way of specifying, deriving, and exploiting a-priori (i.e., design-time) provenance information, i.e., which anticipates and summarizes the structure of workflow provenance graphs, based on (i) the given workflow specification, (ii) a description of the workflow input structure (e.g., XML DTDs), and (iii) declarative data scope expressions (i.e., actor configurations).

We focus on dataflow-oriented workflows with structured data models. Here, data is organized in nested, labeled collections much like XML data. The scientific data (*base data*) is handled opaquely by the workflow specification and the execution engine. *Actors*, which wrap external components or tools (*base functions*) use *configurations* to describe the interaction between the base data organized in nested collections and the base functions.

Example 1: Simple phylogenetics workflow. Fig. 1 shows a simple phylogenetics workflow. The input data, a set of amino acid sequences (of base type Seq) is stored inside the Project collection that will also contain the intermediary and overall output data.

---

[1] This work was supported in part by NSF awards IIS-0612326, OCI-0722079, DBI-0619060, DE-FC02-07ER25811, ATM-0619139, and IIS-0630033.

D.L. McGuinness, J.R. Michaelis, and L. Moreau (Eds.): IPAW 2010, LNCS 6378, pp. 206–215, 2010.

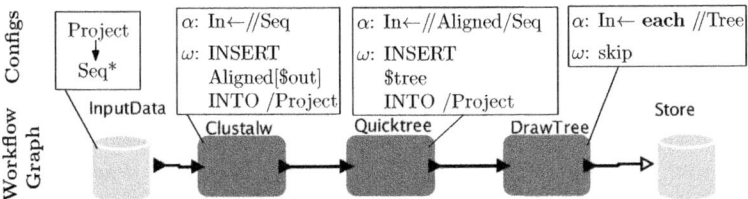

Fig. 1. A simple phylogenetics workflow consisting of three actors Clustalw, Quicktree, and DrawTree, together with a data source and sink. While the data (organized in nested, labeled collections) flows through the actors during workflow execution, each actor selects base data, calls external services, and places their results back into the stream. Actor configurations specify which base data is selected (α part of the configuration) and how results are written back into the stream (ω part of the configuration). Note that the write configuration ω of DrawTree is the no-operation skip since DrawTree should not have any effect on the collection data.

The actor Clustalw is configured to use all sequence objects (labeled with their type Seq) as input, and create a new sub-collection Aligned in the Project collection to put all output data in. Quicktree takes all Seq objects in the Aligned collection, passes the data to the Quicktree tool, and inserts the tool's output, a phylogenetic tree, directly under Project. DrawTree, which is used only for display purposes, draws each tree object found in the input data.   □

During workflow design, the scientist places actors on the workflow tool's canvas and subsequently provides actor configurations. The configurations play a significant role for the semantics of the workflow, and it is thus important that the designer does not introduce bugs. Our approach of providing the scientist with an abstract provenance graph during this crucial phase helps to detect errors in the configurations. Abstract provenance graphs make it obvious which base data is used and produced by which actor, and how the data organization evolves during the workflow execution.

    The main ideas and steps of our approach are as follows: We compute APGs *ahead of time*, i.e., before a workflow W executes, using *static analysis* (type inference) techniques. Specifically, we infer a *schema-level summary* of the *possible* concrete provenance graphs that W can generate for the given input structures and actor configurations. Since the information is provided at the schema-level, an APG can be seen as a compile-time summary of the scientific workflow itself.

    In particular, we make the following contributions: **(1)** We define abstract provenance graphs as summaries for the concrete provenance graphs a workflow can create for a given input schema. Concrete and abstract graphs are related via graph homomorphisms. **(2)** We introduce three kinds of abstract provenance graphs for workflows with a structured data model: flowgraph, time-collapsed and structure-collapsed flowgraph. **(3)** We provide examples to demonstrate the usefulness of APGs for workflow design.

2   Motivation

Recent work about scientific workflow design has demonstrated that constructing scientific workflows using an XML-like data model with XPath-like configurations leads to robust workflows with less shims and wires compared to approaches that do not deploy structured data models [10,13,12]. The key insight is that the XML data structure provides a level of indirection for actor communications and thus effectively removes the tight coupling between data flow, control flow, and the workflow graph.

Bugs introduced in the workflow configurations are hard to detect during designtime. The configurations determine which part of the input data of an actor is used as input to the wrapped component (base functions) and how the components output is incorporated back into the actors' XML output stream. Errors in input configurations α can cause actors to not call their base functions, simply because the XPath expressions do not match any data in the input stream. Further, even when input data is selected and base functions are called, a configuration error can cause a base function to be supplied with the wrong input data, i.e., data that the workflow designer did not intend to be input. We will now provide examples for these two kinds of errors.

Example 2: Configuration errors causing idle actors. Consider the phylogenetics workflow from Example 1 (Fig. 1). Imagine the input expression α of the QUICKTREE actor to contain a spelling error //Alinged/Seq instead of //Aligned/Seq. Then, no data would be selected from the actor's input, and consequently, its base function (here the QUICKTREE tool) would not be called; also none of the following actors would execute their base function. This bug of *idle* actors is hard to spot during design time.   □

Example 3: Configuration errors causing wrong input selections. Consider again the workflow in Fig. 1 with the input expression α of QUICKTREE changed to //Seq. Although the actor is not idle, the data provided to the base function comprises *all* sequence data. This includes the aligned sequences as well as the unaligned ones that were part of the global workflow input. Again, this configuration error is not evident without carefully inspecting the configurations and having the overall XML structure in mind. Note that this type of bug might even be hard to notice during runtime: the base function will simply be provided with more data, potentially not creating obvious fail-stop faults, but hard-to-detect semantic errors.   □

To summarize, although configurations allow us to construct flexible and adaptive workflows, they are also prone to typos and other errors that would cause the workflow to behave in ways not intended by the designer. However, once a workflow has been run, the data and its lineage (or provenance) can be visualized in several ways. A provenance *flowgraph* [3] shows how the nested collection structure and the data evolves from one workflow step to the next. The flowgraph of the workflow from Example 1 is shown in Fig. 2: the collection structure is laid out as a tree using black top-to-down edges; the green left-to-right edges show dataflow from the collection input to the actors and further to the output collection. The provenance flowgraph visualizes the detailed dataflow of a scientific workflow. It can thus be used to detect errors in the actor configurations. However, the following two reasons prevent the flowgraph being utilized during workflow design: **(i)** The provenance graph, by definition, is constructed *during* or *after* the workflow execution. **(ii)** The provenance graph provides too much detail. In fact, for realistic workflows, provenance graphs can easily contain thousands of nodes [3], making them impractical to find design-errors without explicitly querying the graph structure.

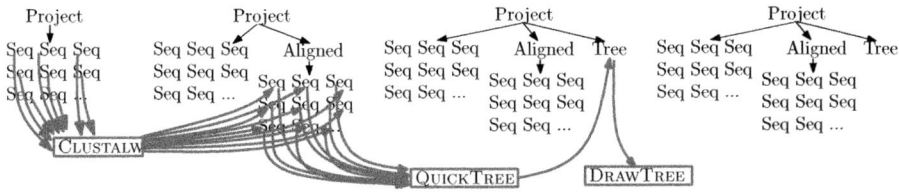

Fig. 2. Provenance flowgraph for the workflow of Fig. 1. It shows that the CLUSTALW actor reads in all Seq objects to create the Seq objects under the Aligned collection. These newly created aligned sequences are then used by QUICKTREE to infer a phylogenetic tree. DRAWTREE only displays the tree and not change the data stream; thus it is not connected to the last data-graph.

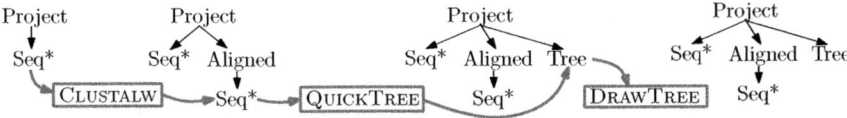

Fig. 3. Abstract provenance flowgraph for the phylogenetic workflow from Fig. 1. Similar to the concrete provenance graph (Fig. 2), a data-oriented view of the workflow is presented. However, the abstract graph uses a graphical representation at the schema-level to summarize the data involved in the computation and is thus more compact than the concrete flowgraph.

3   Abstract Provenance Graphs

Similar to concrete provenance graphs, abstract provenance graphs show the collection structure and dataflow. However, (1) the graph is computed as a static analysis before the workflow is run, and (2) the data and actors are shown at a *type level* and thus in a condensed yet informative way. Fig. 3 shows the abstract flowgraph for the phylogenetics workflow from Example 1. The relationship between workflow description W, a concrete flowgraph F_W, and an abstract flowgraph A_W is shown in the following diagram.

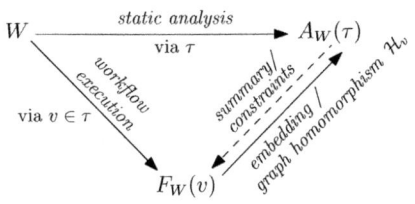

During the execution of a workflow W on an input value v, provenance information can be collected to create a concrete flowgraph $F_W(v)$. However, given a workflow W together with an input type τ, we can infer an abstract flowgraph $A_W(\tau)$ via abstract interpretation, a form of static analysis.

The abstract provenance graph summarizes possible concrete provenance graphs (i.e., one for each value $v \in \tau$) via an *embedding* that gives rise to a graph homomorphism[2] on the two graphs. Thus, the APG constrains the possible provenance graphs that can be created by the specific workflow W with input schema τ. Consider the APG

---

[2] A graph homomorphism is a mapping between two graphs that respects their structure. More concretely, it maps adjacent vertices to adjacent vertices.

in Fig. 3: Since there is no edge between the left Seq node in the second type graph to the QUICKTREE actor, there is *no* input value $v \in \tau$ for which QUICKTREE would use any of those sequence-data as input. The abstract provenance graph can therefore be used as a data-oriented view of the workflow specification itself. Since it is created at the type-level without actually executing the workflow, it can be used during workflow design time to provide immediate feedback to the designer upon configurations changes.

We use XML to represent nested, ordered collections that can contain base data, where B^v and C^v denote the set of base data nodes and collection nodes of a value v respectively. To simplify the presentation of the rest of the paper, we consider workflow pipelines, i.e., where a workflow W is a sequence of actors: $W = A_1 \to A_2 \to \ldots \to A_n$. We identify each actor with a function (or update) from values to values. The execution semantics of W on input data v_0 is then simply the composition of its actors.

Provenance flowgraph. A provenance *flowgraph* $F_W(v_0)$ shows the evolution of the XML data $v_0, \ldots, v_n$ during the execution of workflow W on the XML data v_0 (Fig. 2). In particular, the provenance of base data items $d \in B^v$ is illustrated. $F_W(v_0)$ is composed from (1) the individual graphs for each value, (2) nodes $i \in I$ representing actor invocations, and (3) provenance edges of the kind in, out, and copy with $in \subseteq B \times I$, $out \subseteq I \times B$, and $copy \subseteq B \times B$. Thus, our model closely ressembles the Open Provenance Model (OPM) [11]. Our in and out relations correspond to the inverses of OPM's used and genBy relations.

3.1 Abstract Provenance Flowgraphs

As an important step towards the creation of APGs, we now introduce the formalism for our types τ. We adapt regular expression types (RE types) [9] to *summarize* a set of values. Our RE types are similar to DTDs or XML-Schema, with two distinctions: (1) we disallow recursion, and (2) we restrict them to our data model, which contains no attributes. (3) As it is the case in XML Schema, we disallow ambiguous [6] RE types. Like XML Schemas, RE types can encode vertical context information (the sequence of labels from the root to the current node). Our non-recursive RE types are of the following form:

$$\tau ::= () \mid T \mid \tau, \tau' \mid \tau|\tau' \mid a[\tau] \mid \tau^* \qquad a \in \mathcal{L}, T \in \mathcal{T} \tag{1}$$

An RE type can either be the type of the empty sequence (); a base type T (e.g., string or Seq); a sequence of two already defined types; the alternative of two types; a collection type $a[\tau]$ with a label a from the label alphabet $\mathcal{L}$; or a repetition type τ^*. The set of values of a type τ (written $[\![\tau]\!]$) is recursively defined in the usual [9] way:

$$
\begin{aligned}
&(i) && [\![()]\!] = \{()\} \\
&(ii) && [\![T]\!] = \{d \mid d \text{ is a base data value of type } T\} \\
&(iii) && [\![\tau, \tau']\!] = \{x, y \mid x \in [\![\tau]\!], y \in [\![\tau']\!]\} \\
&(iv) && [\![\tau|\tau']\!] = [\![\tau]\!] \cup [\![\tau']\!] \\
&(v) && [\![a[\tau]]\!] = \{a[x] \mid x \in [\![\tau]\!]\} \\
&(vi) && [\![\tau^*]\!] = \{a_0, a_1, \ldots, a_n \mid n \in \mathbb{N}, \ 0 \leq i \leq n, \ a_i \in [\![\tau]\!]\}
\end{aligned}
\tag{2}
$$

Note, how the embedding $\mathcal{E}_1$ in Fig. 4(a) is a summary for the value v_1: regardless of how many A-labeled subtrees there are in v_1, they are all mapped to the single A symbol

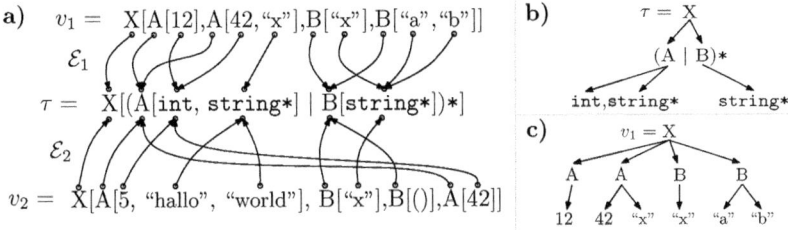

Fig. 4. (a) regular expression type τ and values $v_1, v_2 \in \tau$ with embeddings $\mathcal{E}_1$ and $\mathcal{E}_2$; (b) and (c) show the graphical representations of τ and v_1, respectively

in the type τ. In general, sequences in the value that are characterized by the repetition constructor "*" are collapsed in the type. Furthermore, since every $v \in \tau$ has a derivation that corresponds to an embedding, τ summarizes *all* its values. Fig. 4(a) highlights this fact by showing two different values v_1 and v_2 with their respective embeddings. We further group multiple invocations to one actor node via $\mathcal{A} : \mathtt{I} \rightarrow \mathtt{A}$. Due to space constraints, we refer to [14] for more details.

The abstract provenance flowgraph $A_W(\tau_0)$ is based on the intermediary types τ_i and the workflow output type τ_n (which are constructed via propagating τ_0 through the workflow) and provenance edges. This is similar to the concrete flowgraph, which is composed of the graphs for the individual values $v_0, \ldots, v_n$. Since there are embeddings $\mathcal{E}_i$ for each of the values into each of the types in the abstract graph, and since $\mathcal{A}$ is a mapping between the invocation nodes in $F_W(v_0)$ and the actor nodes in the abstract flowgraph $A_W(\tau_0)$, we have a complete mapping of all nodes in $F_W(v_0)$ to the nodes in $A_W(\tau_0)$. Similar mappings can be constructed for a different input value $v_0' \in \tau$. We now require that edges in $A_W(\tau_0)$ are placed such that for all input values $v \in \tau$ the resulting mapping $\mathcal{H}_v := \mathcal{E}_v \cup \mathcal{A}$ is a "tight" graph homomorphism as described below:

Property 1. The abstract flowgraph $A_W(\tau_0)$ has a provenance edge e (e.g., in, out, or copy edge) between two nodes N_1, N_2 iff there is an input value $v \in \tau_0$ such that the concrete flowgraph $F_W(v)$ contains two nodes n_1, n_2 with $\mathcal{H}_v(n_1) = N_1$ and $\mathcal{H}_v(n_2) = N_2$, such that n_1 and n_2 are connected with a provenance edge e of the respective kind[3].

Corollary 1. *If there is no* in *edge between a base type node T and an actor node A in the abstract flowgraph $A_W(\tau)$, then in* **no** *execution of W on* **any** *value $v \in \tau$ will* **any** *invocation of actor A use a data item b that would be mapped to T via $\mathcal{H}_v$. In particular, if an actor node A does not have any incoming edges in the abstract flowgraph, then its base function will never be called.*

This corollary is very useful in practice, as it helps to discover errors as in Example 2. The abstract provenance graph, which indicates that none of the actors QUICKTREE and DRAWTREE will be called is shown in Fig. 5.

Corollary 2. *If there is an* in *edge between a base type node T and an actor node A in the abstract flowgraph $A_W(\tau)$, then there is at least one input value $v \in \tau$ such*

---

[3] Note, that we have not drawn copy edges in our abstract provenance layouts (e.g., in Fig. 3) to avoid cluttering the graph.

Fig. 5. Abstract flowgraph for Example 2 showing idle actors QUICKTREE and DRAWTREE

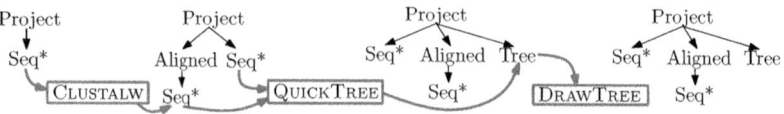

Fig. 6. Abstract flowgraph for Example 3 showing that QUICKTREE also uses the unaligned set of sequences as input and not just the aligned ones as was desired

that executing W on v will cause an invocation of actor A that uses a data item b that corresponds to T via $\mathcal{H}_v$.

This corollary helps to identify configuration errors as in Example 3, where too much data was selected as input for a particular component:

3.2   Variations of Abstract Provenance Graphs

Abstract provenance flowgraphs can be used as a starting point to create even more coarse-grained summaries:

Time-collapsed flowgraph.   Instead of showing the evolution of intermediary data from actor to actor in the workflow, we can collapse all nodes that are connected via copy edges into one single node. This *view* is especially interesting in workflows that only add data and collections from step to step, since here each node in the collapsed graph is also a node in the output type τ_n (since no actor deletes data or collections). Thus, the time-collapsed flowgraph for add-only workflows corresponds to a summary of the output data, explaining its provenance:

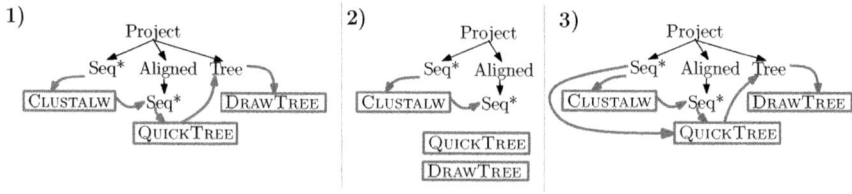

Fig. 7. Time-collapsed abstract flowgraphs for the workflows described in Examples 1-3. **1)** is the intended behavior, in **2)**, a configuration errors causes two actors to idle, and in **3)**, QUICKTREE also consumes the Seq data directly under the Project collection, which is a design error

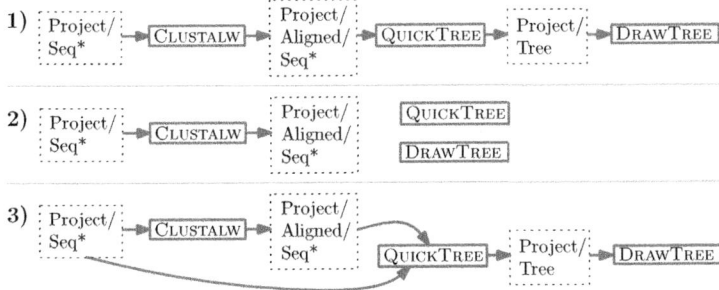

Fig. 8. Structure-collapsed flowgraphs for the workflows from Examples 1-3. The collection-structure is collapsed into the leaf nodes. This graph shows the explicit routing of data items through the set of actors. In this view, actors that work on data independently are drawn as parallel branches (not shown in these examples).

Structure-collapsed flowgraph. Starting from the time-collapsed flowgraph, we can additionally summarize the graph by collapsing XML nesting edges into their leaf nodes, i.e., into the data type nodes. The result (Fig. 8) shows how base data evolves.

4   Related Work

Our provenance model is closely related to the Open Provenance Model (OPM) [11]. OPM does not directly support nested data; although there is a proposal to handle collections in OPM [8]; we adopt the extensions of Anand et al. [3] for nested data here. Our concrete provenance flowgraph is also based on [3], which introduces a provenance model for workflows with XML-structured data models and actors with update semantics. In their work, they use a *combined structure* for efficient storage, which was the inspiration for our time-collapsed abstract graph versions. In [2], they propose summary techniques for provenance graphs along with a model to navigate between these different summaries. This work is similar to ours in the sense that it also addresses the problem of summarizing provenance graphs. However, their approach is based on actual provenance information that has been gathered during a workflow run. Their created views thus summarize only one specific workflow execution—not like our approach, which summarizes all possible executions based on the workflow's input data type. Furthermore, our approach is intended to be used during workflow design-time when no actual provenance information is available yet.

In a recent paper, Acar et al. [1] investigate the relationship between provenance graphs and the computation performed by the system. They extend DFL, a dataflow-oriented extension of the nested relational calculus, to produce concrete provenance graphs. This paper is close to ours in the spirit of computing provenance graphs from the language in which the workflow is defined rather than by collecting provenance information via a rather loosely linked provenance recording mechanism. Our paper demonstrates another advantage of linking provenance closely with the model of computation by showing the usefulness of computing schema-level graphs.

Related to the summarization goal of our abstract graphs is the work from Biton et al. [5,4], where groups of actors in a workflow are replaced by a module to simplify the provenance information. Our work here is orthogonal in the sense that the ZOOM groups can be used to further collapse multiple actors in our abstract graphs. In other words, we can further summarize abstract graphs by applying the ZOOM grouping to our grouping $\mathcal{A}$ of invocations.

Our work, suggesting to use abstract provenance graphs as feedback, aims at improving the workflow design process. Viewed from this perspective, there exists related work within the scientific workflow community. In [7], Gibson et al. present a "data playground" for intuitive workflow specification, in which users can focus on their data, rather than on the processes of the workflow. It would be interesting to investigate whether our concept of abstract provenance graphs can be utilized in this system. Using abstract provenance graphs inside a GUI to create workflow configurations by having the users interactively select nodes, and possibly groupings for multiple invocations, is also an interesting avenue for future work.

5 Conclusion

Abstract provenance graphs make explicit use of XML typing mechanisms to summarize potential provenance graphs. We generalized embeddings that occur while validating XML documents with DTDs to graph homomorphisms between concrete and abstract provenance graphs. Similar to how an XML document is validated against a DTD, our approach allows to validate a concrete flowgraph $F_W(v)$ (recorded by a scientific workflow system) against the abstract flowgraph $A_W(\tau)$ obtained from a configured workflow and input type τ. Furthermore, based on type propagation algorithms, abstract provenance graphs can be constructed without executing the workflow. Thus, they allow the designer to anticipate the high-level (XML) structure of the workflow result, together with a summary of the result derivation in terms of the workflow's active components (actors). To the best of our knowledge, this is the first attempt to exploit provenance information during the design process of scientific workflows.

Acknowledgements. The authors thank Timothy McPhillips, Lei Dou, Sean Riddle, Sven Köhler, and Shawn Bowers for their work on collection-oriented modeling and design in Kepler, as well as for the many fruitful discussions.

References

1. Acar, U., Buneman, P., Cheney, J., den Bussche, J.V., Kwasnikowska, N., Vansummeren, S.: A graph model of data and workflow provenance. In: Proceedings of the 2nd USENIX Workshop on the Theory and Practice of Provenance, TaPP 2010 (2010)
2. Anand, M.K., Bowers, S., Ludäscher, B.: A navigation model for exploring scientific workflow provenance graphs. In: Proceedings of the 4th Workshop on Workflows in Support of Large-Scale Science (WORKS 2009), pp. 1–10. ACM, New York (2009)
3. Anand, M.K., Bowers, S., McPhillips, T.M., Ludäscher, B.: Exploring scientific workflow provenance using hybrid queries over nested data and lineage graphs. In: SSDBM, pp. 237–254 (2009)

4. Biton, O., Cohen-Boulakia, S., Davidson, S.B.: Zoom UserViews: Querying relevant provenance in workflow systems. In: VLDB 2007, pp. 1366–1369 (2007)
5. Biton, O., Davidson, S.B., Khanna, S., Roy, S.: Optimizing user views for workflows. In: ICDT 2009: Proceedings of the 12th International Conference on Database Theory, pp. 310–323. ACM, New York (2009)
6. Bruggemann-Klein, A., Wood, D.: One-unambiguous regular languages. Information and Computation 142(2), 182–206 (1998)
7. Gibson, A., Gamble, M., Wolstencroft, K., Oinn, T., Goble, C., Belhajjame, K., Missier, P.: The data playground: An intuitive workflow specification environment. Future Generation Computer Systems 25(4), 453–459 (2009)
8. Groth, P., Miles, S., Missier, P., Moreau, L.: A proposal for handling collections in the Open Provenance Model (2009)
9. Hosoya, H., Vouillon, J., Pierce, B.C.: Regular expression types for XML. ACM Transactions on Programming Languages and Systems (TOPLAS) 27(1), 46–90 (2005)
10. McPhillips, T., Bowers, S., Zinn, D., Ludäscher, B.: Scientific workflow design for mere mortals. Future Generation Computer Systems 25(5), 541–551 (2009)
11. Moreau, L., Clifford, B., Freire, J., Gil, Y., Groth, P., Futrelle, J., Kwasnikowska, N., Miles, S., Missier, P., Myers, J., Simmhan, Y., Stephan, E., den Bussche, J.V.: The Open Provenance Model - core specification (v1.1). Future Generation Computer Systems (2010)
12. Zinn, D., Bowers, S., Ludäscher, B.: XML-based computation for scientific workflows. In: Intl. Conf. on Data Engineering, ICDE (2010); See also technical report CSE-2009-21, UC Davis, 2009
13. Zinn, D., Bowers, S., McPhillips, T.M., Ludäscher, B.: Scientific workflow design with data assembly lines. In: Deelman, E., Taylor, I. (eds.) Proceedings of the 4th Workshop on Workflows in Support of Large-Scale Science (WORKS 2009). ACM, New York (2009)
14. Zinn, D., Ludäscher, B.: Abstract provenance graphs: Anticipating and exploiting schema-level data provenance. Technical Report CSE-2010-14, UC Davis (2010)

On the Use of Semantic Abstract Workflows Rooted on Provenance Concepts

Leonardo Salayandia and Paulo Pinheiro da Silva

University of Texas at El Paso, Computer Science Department,
El Paso, Texas 79968, USA
{leonardo,paulo}@utep.edu
http://www.cs.utep.edu

Abstract. Two challenges related to capturing provenance about scientific data are: 1) determining an adequate level of granularity to encode provenance, and 2) encoding provenance in a way that facilitates end-user interpretation and analysis. A solution to address these challenges consists in integrating two technologies: Semantic Abstract Workflows (SAWs), which are used to capture a domain expert's understanding of a scientific process, and PML, an extensible language used to encode provenance. This paper describes relevant features of these technologies for addressing the granularity and interpretation challenges of provenance encoding and presents a discussion about their integration.

Keywords: Process, Provenance, PML, Semantic Abstract Workflows.

1   Introduction

Semantic Abstract Workflows (SAWs) are useful to encode process knowledge from the perspective of domain experts [1] and the Proof Markup Language (PML) is useful to encode justifications about how information is produced [2]. This paper describes the integration of SAWs and PML, which results in two benefits: 1) Given that determining an adequate level of granularity to encode provenance is challenging [3], i.e, provenance at a very fine level may not be scalable and provenance at a very coarse level may not be useful, process knowledge captured from the perspective of domain experts serves as a guide to determine an adequate level of granularity; 2) Provenance languages such as PML utilize specialized terminology that may be unfamiliar to end users. The integration of these technologies has the benefit of having domain-specific terminology used to refer to a domain expert's understanding of a process that can be propagated to refer to provenance knowledge as well.

This paper is organized as follows: Section 2 presents SAWs and PML, Section 3 presents how these technologies are integrated, Section 4 presents a discussion about the integration, and Section 5 concludes the paper.

D.L. McGuinness, J.R. Michaelis, and L. Moreau (Eds.): IPAW 2010, LNCS 6378, pp. 216–220, 2010.
© Springer-Verlag Berlin Heidelberg 2010

2 Background

2.1 Semantic Abstract Workflows

SAWs capture flows of information from information sources of a process, through information transformation activities, and finally to information sinks at the end of that process. An initial phase in creating a SAW is to have domain experts identify and name the types of information and types of activities involved in their processes. For example, the information type *Digital Elevation Map* is different from the information type *Gravity Map* for a geophysicist because each type of map models different properties of interest about a region of Earth. In contrast, both maps could be represented as PDF files, and therefore, be considered of the same information type from a programmer's point of view; however, this type classification would not yield a SAW that captures the point of view of the process' domain expert, i.e., the geophysicist. Activity types are similarly identified from the point of view of the domain expert, where Method is the preferred term used to refer to discrete activities included in processes that transform information, i.e., transform information from one type to another. Methods can be software driven, such as the type of application used to transform a dataset to a map, or human driven, such as the type of activity performed to analyze a model to obtain an interpretation.

SAWs do not contain constructs to represent control flow such as order of execution, selection, and iteration. As a result, one SAW can model different implementations of a process. Another characteristic of SAWs is that path traversals are suggestive in nature. Specifying an information type flowing from one method type to another means that it is conceivable, in the view of the domain expert, that such flow can occur. In executing a process implementation, however, that information flow may or may not happen.

2.2 Proof Markup Language

PML defines primitive concepts and relations for representing provenance about data. Two essensial modules of PML are: 1) The *provenance ontology* (PML-P) that defines concepts to represent identifiable things from the real world that are useful to determine data lineage; and 2) the *justification ontology* (PML-J) that defines concepts and relations to represent dependencies between identifiable things.

The foundational concept in PML-P is IdentifiedThing, which refers to an entity in the real world. These entities have attributes that are useful for provenance, such as name, description, create date-time, authors, and owner. Two key subclasses of IdentifiedThing motivated by provenance representational concerns are Information and Source. Information supports references to information at various levels of granularity and structure. Source refers to an information container, and it is often used to refer to all the information from the container. For example, things such as organization, person, agent, and service can be a Source. PML-P provides a simple but extensible taxonomy of sources.

PML-J provides concepts and relations used to encode information manipulation steps used to derive a conclusion. A justification requires concepts for representing conclusions, conclusion antecedents, and information manipulation steps used to transform or derive conclusions from antecedents. The justification vocabulary has two main concepts: NodeSet and InferenceStep. A NodeSet includes structure for representing a conclusion and a set of alternative InferenceSteps each of which can provide an alternative justification for a conclusion. Every NodeSet has a unique web-addressable identifier, i.e., a URI. Web-addressable NodeSets make it possible to construct justification trees in a distributed environment.

3   Integrating Process and Provenance Concepts

The ontology behind the encoding of SAWs is called Workflow-Driven Ontology (WDO) [4]. This ontology defines the generic concepts of Information and Method that domain experts specialize to capture the terminology about their processes. The ontology of provenance-related concepts used in PML is the PML-P ontology. PML-P includes the concepts of Information, MethodRule, and Source that are specializations of the more generic concept Identified Thing. The WDO and PML-P ontologies are aligned to take advantage of the process knowledge that domain experts capture through SAWs to encode provenance from a process implementation. The main alignment involves the merger of the WDO concept of Information with the PML-P concept of Information, and the substitution of the WDO concept of Method for the PML-P concept of MethodRule. The ontology alignment also includes the use of the PML-P concept Source as the sources and sinks used in SAWs. Sources and sinks as used in SAWs are conceptually equivalent, except for the flow of information, i.e., sources produce information and sinks receive information. Sources in PML, however, are used through another PML-P concept denominated SourceUsage, which records information about the date and time of source access. This is important in provenance encodings because sources, e.g., websites and documents, may change over time and the provenance encodings may lose validity. Date/time source access is not necessary for process knowledge.

4   Discussion

SAWs are designed to model a domain expert's understanding of a process. As such, SAWs can be used to identify provenance use cases that can be obtained from the implementation that the domain expert uses to carry out a process. This approach is offered by the WDO-It! tool, a Java-based editor for SAWs [5]. WDO-It! includes functionality to generate PML-encoding modules based on the activities identified in the process. These modules are used to instrument a process implementation to intercept and interlink intermediate results as a process is being executed, effectively capturing provenance in PML about the resulting artifact.

Abstract process knowledge encoded in SAWs is useful to present provenance at a manageable level of detail to the end user. For example, the execution of a process may involve many iterations of a cycle, and hence, the resulting provenance tree may be cumbersome to interpret and analyze. Given that SAWs do not contain control-flow information, SAWs are an effective canonical representation of a process with respect to the methods involved. What is more, since processes encoded in SAWs use the same ontological concepts used to encode provenance in PML, method and data types included in SAWs can be used to filter provenance trees with respect to specific parts of a process.

The integration of SAWs and PML results in controlled vocabularies created by domain experts to encode process knowledge that are also useful to formulate provenance-related queries and to present provenance for browsing by users familiar with the domain of discourse.

With respect to related work, [6] presents an approach that consists of inferring a schema-level summary of the possible concrete provenance graphs that could be generated from an executable workflow specification. The result is an abstract provenance graph that could be used to facilitate the analysis of data flow as it relates to a workflow specification. In this sense, abstract provenance graphs are similar in nature to SAWs. However, levels of abstraction provided by the two approaches differ. With SAWs, the approach consists in having the scientist model their understanding of a process as a graph and using the terminology that is specific to the problem domain. With abstract provenance graphs, the approach consists on creating an executable specification of the scientist's process first and then generating the abstraction from it. On one hand, abstract provenance graphs will result in a level of abstraction that is less close to the problem domain but that is tightly integrated to a specific execution environment. On the other hand, SAWs will result in a level of abstraction that closely relates to the problem domain, however, additional manual work is needed to map that level of abstraction to specific implementations of the process. An additional benefit of SAWs is that they can be mapped to multiple implementations of the same process, or even be mapped to manual systems where processes are human driven instead of software driven.

5   Conclusion

This paper presented an integration of technologies used to capture process and provenance knowledge through the alignment of their underlying ontologies. Two main benefits are that provenance is encoded at a granularity that suits the level of detail documented by domain experts, and that provenance is encoded using domain expert's defined concepts, which facilitates subsequent querying and analysis of provenance. The integration of these technologies is implemented through the WDO-It! tool [5], and an approach named CI-Miner [7] has been developed to guide domain experts to document their processes and to construct provenance-capturing modules that can be used to instrument process implementations. The latest version of the aligned ontology can be found at http://trust.utep.edu/2.0/wdo.owl.

This work was funded in part by the National Science Foundation (HRD-0734825) and the Department of Homeland Security (2008-ST-062-000007).

References

1. Pinheiro da Silva, P., Salayandia, L., Del Rio, N., Gates, A.Q.: On the Use of Abstract Workflows to Capture Scientific Process Provenance. In: 2nd Workshop on the Theory and Practice of Provenance (TaPP 2010), San Jose, CA (2010)
2. McGuinness, D., Ding, L., Pinheiro da Silva, P., Chang, C.: PML2: A Modular Explanation Interlingua. In: AAAI 2007 Workshop on Explanation-aware Computing, Vancouver, British Columbia, Canada (2007)
3. Stephan, E., Halter, T., Critchlow, T., Pinheiro da Silva, P., Salayandia, L.: Using Domain Requirements to Achieve Science-Oriented Provenance. Late Breaking Contribution Poster, to appear in IPAW (2010)
4. Salayandia, L., Pinheiro da Silva, P., Gates, A.Q., Salcedo, F.: Workflow-Driven Ontologies: An Earth Sciences Case Study. In: 2nd IEEE International Conference on e-Science and Grid Computing, Amsterdam, Netherlands (2006)
5. WDO-It!: An editor for Worflow-Driven Ontologies, http://trust.utep.edu/wdo
6. Zinn, D., Ludaescher, B.: Abstract Provenance Graphs: Anticipating and Exploiting Schema-Level Data Provenance. In: 3rd International Provenance and Annotation Workshop, Troy, NY (2010)
7. Pinheiro da Silva, P., Salayandia, L., Gandara, A., Gates, A.Q.: CI-Miner: Semantically Enhancing Scientific Processes. Earth Science Informatics 2(4), 249–269 (2009)

Provenance of Decisions in Emergency Response Environments

Iman Naja, Luc Moreau, and Alex Rogers

School of Electronics and Computer Science, University of Southampton
Southampton, SO17 1BJ, UK
{izn1g08,L.Moreau,acr}@ecs.soton.ac.uk

Abstract. Mitigating the devastating ramifications of major disasters requires emergency workers to respond in a maximally efficient way. Information systems can improve their efficiency by organizing their efforts and automating many of their decisions. However, absence of documenting how decisions were made by the system prevents decisions from being reviewed to check the reasons for their making or their compliance with policies. We apply the concept of provenance to decision making in emergency response situations and use the Open Provenance Model to express provenance produced in RoboCup Rescue Simulation. We produce provenance DAGs using a novel OPM profile that conceptualizes decisions in the context of emergency response. Finally, we traverse the OPM DAGs to answer some provenance questions about those decisions.

1 Introduction

Major disasters, like the 2004 Indian Ocean and the 2010 Haiti earthquakes cause deaths, injuries, and serious damage. To minimize the effect of such disasters, emergency responders must work in a maximally efficient way. They must make numerous decisions centered on prioritizing which civilians to rescue and they must make these decisions in unpredictable changing environments while racing against time and coordinating with different rescue agencies. As such, there is an increasing need to build information systems that organize the efforts of responders and improve their efficiency by automating many of the decisions they make on the ground. Most notably, recent efforts in research in the disaster management domain on the levels of developing infrastructure simulation and intelligent agent are being tested in the RoboCup Rescue Simulation league [1].

However, a critical shortcoming arises within current approaches through their inability to represent the causal factors that led certain decisions to be made. In turn, this makes it difficult to determine whether these decisions were compliant with policies and regulations, and to hold decision makers to account[1].

---

[1] We consider accountability of decisions to be analogous to Weitzner *et al.*'s [25] definition of information accountability, where the transparency of use of information enables ascertaining its appropriate use as per given rules. So, we perceive that transparency of actions and decisions, and how they influenced later actions and decisions, permits the checking of compliance with requirements or policies.

D.L. McGuinness, J.R. Michaelis, and L. Moreau (Eds.): IPAW 2010, LNCS 6378, pp. 221–230, 2010.

As such, there is a need to document how decisions were made and to refer to such documentation when the need arises to review the history of their making or to check compliance with rules and policies. This can done through recording and querying their provenance, where provenance describes the history of items, physical or immaterial, and how they came to be. Provenance has proven to be useful in a variety of domains including amongst others workflow re-enactment, inferring reasons for result differences in scientific experiments, and quality assurance of data [2,22,16]. To this end, we consider the provenance of decisions to include any data that affected their making as well as the processes that led to this data. We consider this provenance to be vital to understanding causality of events within a system and how decisions influence others in decision chains.

Thus, our work aims to exploit the provenance of decisions to understand how they were made and why. Being motivated by addressing problems in the emergency response domain, we proposed the use case "Provenance of Decision Making in Emergency Response" to the W3C Provenance Incubator Group. The work presented in this paper forms the first steps towards addressing the scenarios of the use case. Accordingly, we use RoboCup Rescue Simulation (RCRS) as a testbed to show how we can enable an automated decision-making system to record its provenance by applying the PrIMe methodology [14] to it. PrIMe assists in indicating what needs to be recorded so that the provenance questions, we are interested in, can be answered. Because answering the questions requires querying provenance graphs, we use the Open Provenance Model (OPM) [17] to produce provenance DAGs, making use of a novel OPM profile that specializes OPM and conceptualizes decisions in the context of emergency response.

In summary, the contributions of this paper are as follows:

1. Applying OPM to the decision making domain, a field in which it has not previously been used. We do so by proposing an OPM profile that specializes OPM and use it to represent decisions in the context of emergency response.

2. A prototype to be integrated with RCRS that generates OPM DAGs and answers provenance queries so as to handle the use case.

The rest of this paper is organized as follows. Section 2 presents our motivation and the use case. Section 3 briefly describes RCRS. Section 4 shows how PrIMe can be used to make RCRS provenance-aware. Section 5 details how provenance information of RCRS can be exposed using the OPM profile *RobocupProfile*. Section 6 presents related work and Section 7 presents future work and concludes.

2   Provenance of Decisions: Tracing Decisions Made by Emergency Responders

We are motivated by the need to interpret events in cases of floods where the police and fire brigade must evacuate casualties according to some prioritization scheme from buildings that are flooded or buildings under the threat of being flooded. Evacuees needing medical attention are taken to a triage area and examined by medics who prioritize their care and delivery to hospitals.

Consequently, we proposed the use case "Provenance of Decision Making: Tracing Decisions Made in Emergency Response Situations"[2] to the W3C Provenance Incubator Group[3] so as to address the need for information systems that not only organize efforts of emergency responders and improve their efficiency but also use the provenance of decisions to reveal how they were made and why. The goal of the use case is to suggest the use of provenance in the Justification for Decisions dimension[4]. This dimension is divided into three sub-dimensions [24]. Currently, we focus only on two: argumentation, where provenance is used to deduce what information affected the choice of a certain solution, and answering why-not questions, where provenance of decisions is used to capture why particular choices were *not* made.

3   Decisions in RoboCup Rescue Simulation

RCRS league is a competition aiming to stimulate research in multi-agent systems in the disaster management domain by inviting participants to devise state-of-the-art strategies that automate decision-making, prioritization, and coordination and cooperation [1]. The simulation models a city hit by an earthquake with fires erupting in various parts of the city and buildings collapsing blocking roads and trapping civilians. Three types of emergency response agents are initially spread across the city with only the knowledge of its map. They then move around learning about the world and performing their tasks. At each time step in the simulation, each agent 'thinks' about what it should do and submits an action to the simulator[5]. This computes the effect of all the agents' actions on the world's state and informs the agent about the effect of its action and what new entities or changes it should sense.

Due to space restrictions, we focus only on ambulance teams that remove civilians trapped in buildings and transport them to refuges[6].

Ambulance Agents. We utilize the platform's default ambulance agents after slightly improving them so they behave as follows. Each agent prioritizes civilians according to how far they are from it, irrespective of criticality of conditions of other civilians. So, it sorts the civilians, plans its path to the nearest one, heads to it, unburies it, loads it, plans its path to the closest refuge and moves there. Once at the refuge it unloads the civilian and repeats the previous steps for its next target. If it is not aware of any civilians, it wanders about until it finds one. Based on this scheme, when an agent heading to a civilian discovers another on its way, it re-prioritizes and chooses the closer one. Also, an agent informs other agents when it rescues a civilian or discovers that one has perished. This prevents cases where agents head to save civilians that have died or have already

---

[2] http://tiny.cc/Prov_Decision_Making
[3] www.w3.org/2005/Incubator/prov/wiki/Main_Page
[4] The use case includes additional propositions, see Future Work (§7).
[5] The simulator is composed of a mediator kernel and several specialized simulators.
[6] The other two types of agents are Fire Brigades which extinguish fires in buildings to prevent further damage to them and Police forces which clear blockages in roads.

been rescued and cases where agents wander about looking for civilians while others are aware of ones that need to be rescued.

4   Provenance-Aware RoboCup Rescue Simulation

We now show how to apply PrIME [14], a three-phase methodology that when applied to a system makes it provenance-aware, to enable RCRS to record its provenance. In the first phase of PrIMe, we identified the following questions as relevant to understanding events that usually take place in RCRS:

1. A civilian C1 was rescued by agent A. What were the steps (i.e. the sequence of actions) that A took to rescue C1?

2. A certain civilian C2 died. Why was C2 not rescued?

3. After A rescued C1, its prioritized target list had C2 on top. However, A rescued C3 next. What pieces of information influenced that change of goals?

4. What were the factors that led to the long delay in saving C4?

Note that PrIMe supports adding anticipated use cases at later stages. In the second phase of PrIMe, we decomposed RCRS into three actors representing the ambulance agent, kernel, and simulator. We then iterated the second phase to identify the actors within the ambulance agent that are responsible for the different decisions, and they are as follows. *(1) Thinker*: the component that decides what to do next based on the strategy and the state. It is further decomposed into two actors: the *State maintainer* maintains the agent's state and view of the world and the *Planner* decides what action to perform next. *(2) Path Searcher*: the component that uses a path search algorithm to plan the path from one place to another. *(3) Sorter*: the component that sorts the list of target civilians based on a prioritization scheme. In the third phase of PrIMe, we mapped actors and messages to OPM processes and artifacts respectively and created OPM edges corresponding to information flow between the actors.

Figure 1 shows an example of a decision reached with the involvement of some RCRS's actors and illustrates the flow of messages between them[7]. We trace the actors' decisions and their interactions and state what interesting process documentation they record. First, *Planner* checks the state of the agent by consulting *State Maintainer (message M1)*. *State Maintainer* asserts that the agent is currently carrying a civilian and that it is not at a refuge *(M2)*. Based on this state, *Planner* decides to move towards a refuge. It requests from *Path Searcher* the shortest path to the closest refuge *(M3)*. *Path Searcher* produces the path, asserts it, and returns it to *Planner (M4)*, which then informs the kernel that it wishes to execute a 'move' action *(M5)*. The kernel processes the action and replies to the agent with the updated state of the world, newly perceived entities, and agents' messages *(M6)*. Finally, *Planner* uses this response to asserts the new information and update *State Maintainer (M7)*.

---

[7] For an example involving all RCRS's actors check http://tiny.cc/iznMoveActors

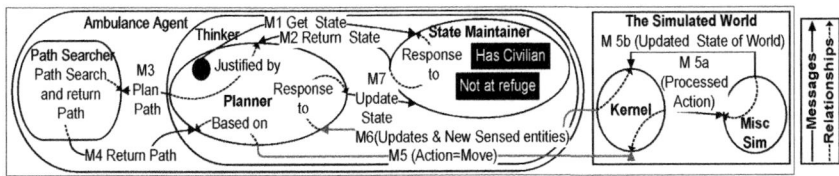

Fig. 1. Some RCRS Actors and their Interactions

5 OPM-Based RCRS Provenance Information

OPM is a model of provenance designed to, among other requirements, allow the exchange of provenance information between systems [17]. We assume that the reader is familiar with its basic concepts. We chose OPM because of the features it possesses, like controlled vocabulary, annotations, inference rules, and profiles. An OPM profile consists of a mandatory unique global identifier in addition to four optional elements as follows:

1. Controlled vocabulary for annotations, and their permitted subjects and values, specifying application-specific properties. These are used to subtype nodes and edges of OPM DAGs and to define application-specific properties.
2. General guidelines to how OPM graphs can be structured.
3. Profile expansion rules that show how nodes or edges can be derived.
4. Syntactic shortcuts and how they can be serialized.

We now present the OPM profile *RobocupProfile* that specializes OPM to represent provenance produced in RCRS. At this stage we only utilize the first two elements of OPM profiles. First, we specify two subtypes of the Agent node *(1) Ambulance*, corresponds to ambulance agents, and *(2) Kernel*, corresponds to the kernel. Also, accounts are classified into *(1) KernelAcct* - corresponds to the kernel's viewpoint, *(2) AgentAcct* - corresponds to the viewpoint of agents, and *(3) AgentDetailAcct* - corresponds to the nodes and edges pertaining to the internal processings of the agent. Finally, tables 1, and 2 display the controlled vocabulary of *RobocupProfile*.

RobocupProfile explicitly shows how processes and artifacts and the dependencies linking them can model how RCRS ambulance agents make their decisions.

Table 1. RobocupProfile Artifacts and Processes and the Accounts they belong to

	Sub-type	Account
Artifacts	*TaskResult* (rescuing a civilian succeeded or failed), *Agent-Perceptions, AgentMessage AgentState*, (e.g. agent's target list, position, whether it is carrying a civilian or not)	*AgentAcct* ∪ *KernelAcct*
	SortedListCivs, PlannedPath	*AgentDetailAcct*
Processes	*AmbulanceAction* (move, unbury, load civilian, unload civilain, rest), *PassMessages, ReceiveMessage*	*AgentAcct* ∪ *KernelAcct*
	DecideAction, PlanPath, SortCivilians	*AgentDetailAcct*
	ManageMessages, ManageActions	*KernelAcct*

Table 2. RobocupProfile Edges

Edge	Sub-type	Effect	Cause
Used	*ManagingMssgs*	*ManageMessages*	*AgentMessage*
Used	*ConstructingMssgs*	*PassMessage*	*AgentMessage*
WGB	*SortedListGeneration*	*SortedListCivs*	*SortCivilians*
WGB	*PathGeneration*	*PlannedPath*	*PlanPath*
WGB	*ResultOfAction*	*TaskResult ∪ AgentState*	*AmbulanceAction*
WGB	*ResultOfHandlingAction*	*TaskResult ∪ AgentState*	*ManageMessages*
WGB	*DecomposingMssgs*	*AgentMessage*	*ReceiveMessages*
WTB	*ActionHandling*	*ManageActions*	*AmbulanceAction*
WTB	*DecidingAction*	*AmbulanceAction*	*DecideAction*
WDF	*TargetDiscovery*	*AgentState*	*AgentMessage ∪ AgentPerceptions*
WDF	*SavedCivilian*	*TaskResult*	*AgentState*
WDF	*UpdatedState*	*AgentState*	*AgentState ∪ SortedListCivs*
WDF	*SortedCivs*	*AgentState*	*SortedListCivs*
WDF	*PathToPriority*	*PlannedPath*	*AgentState*

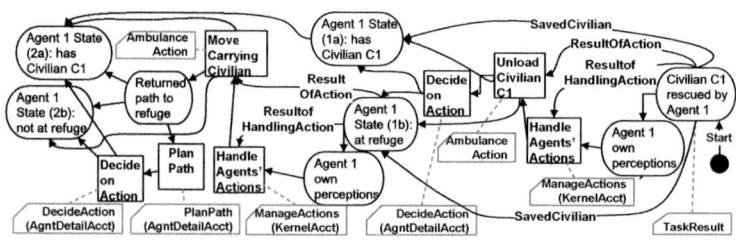

Fig. 2. Portion of OPM DAG

Specifically, the dependencies within each decision process on the different artifacts are explicitly stated. In turn, the dependencies of those artifacts on other artifacts are also declared. Further, the dependencies of those artifacts on previous decision process are stated, using subtypes of *was generated by* edges. Hence, chains of decisions, and how their results came out, can be expressed. Figure 2 shows a portion of an OPM DAG illustrating two *AmbulanceActions* (unload and move), the decisions that produced them, and the artifacts that influenced those decisions. In more detail, *TaskResult* 'Civilian C1 rescued by Agent 1' was derived from *AgentPerceptions* which were generated by the kernel managing agents' actions. This, in turn, was triggered by the agent unloading C1. The 'unload' action was triggered by *DecideAction* which used *AgentState* artifacts indicating that the agent 'has a civilian' and is 'at a refuge'. In turn, the *AgentState* indicating that the agent was at a refuge was generated by a 'move' action that used a path artifact generated by *PlanPath* that was triggered by *DecideAction*. Note that the kernel is required only in RCRS and not in the real world, as humans do not need a 'kernel' to tell them the results of their actions.

Querying RCRS Provenance. Understanding why events occurred in RCRS and how decisions affected them requires mapping provenance questions into provenance queries. Querying consists of traversing the OPM DAG to produce a provenance graph pertaining to the data items of interest. A query is formed of a *query data handle*, which identifies the entity for which the provenance is sought, and the *scope* of traversal [13], which identifies what forms a relevant answer to the query (i.e. what parts of the OPM graph are of interest to the querier).

Traversing a graph produced by RCRS should exploit *RobocupProfile*'s characteristics. For instance, the data handle can specify the type of artifact pertaining to the data item for which provenance is sought, e.g. for the query of question 1 in §4, the data handle is identified by the type of the artifact, namely *TaskResult*. Also, the scope can identify which paths to prune by discarding certain sub-types of nodes or edges, as well as stopping the traversal when certain types of nodes and edges are reached. Additionally, accounts can be used to prune nodes and edges that are not in the scope, e.g. nodes belonging to *KernelAcct* can be pruned when traversing the graph to address question 1.

We now briefly show how to address the questions in §4. Though all are queried based on the above, each has varied aspects and is handled distinctly.

Answering question 1 is done by finding and traversing a series of *Ambulance-Actions* where the last one generates a *TaskResult* concerning C1.

Question 2 requires checking why each agent did not save civilian C2, i.e. why C2 never became their priority on their sorted list of civilians. We use Chapman and Jagadish's algorithms which explore why certain data item were not returned by a query [5] and we find the *SortedListCivs* where C2 does not show.

Question 3 requires finding *AgentStates* concerning both civilians and their *UpdatedState* dependencies, and if needed the artifacts they were derived from.

Question 4 considers the activity of question 1 (sequence of actions taken to save a civilian) and analyzes its beginning, ending, and the number of steps between them. By showing the number of processes that took place within the activity, we point out the factors that contributed to its elongation.

6   Related Work

The Belief-Desire-Intention framework [20] is the best known and best studied model in the Agent Theories, Architectures, and Languages community [8]. However, it lacks mechanisms that allow agents to learn based on past experiences, thus it has been extended to allow the use of learning in [19]. Other recent work has aimed to make use of history and experiences by using an agent's past experiences and its history of interactions with other agents. While the aim of [12] is to improve organizational performance by presenting a structural adaptation method that is based on the history of interactions with agents to be used by an agent to self-organize and decide to drop relations with other agents; most of the other work is centered on using past interactions with other agents so that an agent can ultimately choose whether or not to trust, cooperate with, and rely on those other agents [23,7,4,10]. The aforementioned work does not treat past experiences as provenance data and so does not exploit any provenance framework or model nor does it utilize the history for the benefits of understanding what went on and why. This is done in [11,15] where distributed processes in an organ transplant management application are treated as agents and the provenance of their actions and interactions is recorded. Specifically, a provenance model that extends PrIMe to capture the goals and intentions of agents in distributed systems is presented in [15]. Although we apply our approach to multi-agent systems which fall under the umbrella of distributed systems, our focus is on how and why decisions were made; and *RobocupProfile* considers agents' goals and intentions through their influences on the decision making process.

Approaches to explanations in rule-based systems like the expert-system MYCIN included paraphrasing the system code; however, such expert-systems do not provide justifications for their rules [18]. On the other hand, the generation of explanations benefits from decision theory as a powerful tool for justifying decisions [18], commonly used in the contexts of decision trees and reasoning about preferences. Nevertheless, such approaches would be limited when reasoning about causality and chains of decisions; at least not to the extent that the application of provenance provides.

Additionally, addressing accountability of the autonomous entities forming distributed systems is a challenge [16]. For users to have confidence in them, these systems must be made accountable, i.e. be enabled to prove their compliance with policies [25]. Several approaches use provenance to make systems accountable, including [6] and [21]. Finally, the need to secure provenance is vital in many critical areas such as law, scientific data, and authorship [9] and would also be important in the decision making domain. Addressing this need includes securing provenance [3] and maintaining provenance integrity [9].

7   Conclusion and Future Work

In summary, our work provides a proof-of-concept for how provenance can be used to track decisions in automated emergency response systems. We presented the use case "Provenance of Decision Making in Emergency Response" as the motivation for our work. RCRS was used as a testbed application and PrIMe was applied to it to make it provenance-aware. Furthermore, OPM was used to produce provenance DAGs, making use of a novel OPM profile that specializes OPM and conceptualizes decisions in the context of emergency response. Thus, the presented work provides a means for justifying automated decisions in emergency response systems by capturing why and how they were made.

Our work shows how provenance of decisions can be exploited in an offline manner, after an application has terminated, to understand automated decisions in complex scenarios. We believe that provenance of decisions can also be used in an online manner for the purpose of making better decisions. This is especially true when previous decisions need to be revised because some new observation has invalidated or complemented previous knowledge. We have proposed these scenarios in our use case and our future work will aim to address these points.

Acknowledgements

This research was undertaken as part of the ALADDIN (Autonomous Learning Agents for Decentralised Data and Information Systems) Project and is jointly funded by a BAE Systems and EPSRC strategic partnership (EP/C 548051/1).

References

1. (RoboCup Rescue), http://www.robocuprescue.org/index.html
2. Bose, R., Frew, J.: Lineage retrieval for scientific data processing: a survey. ACM Computing Surveys 37(1), 1–28
3. Braun, U., Holland, D.A., Muniswamy-Reddy, K.K., Seltzer, M.I.: Coping with cycles in provenance. Technical report, Harvard University (2006)
4. Chalkiadakis, G., Boutilier, C.: Sequential decision making in repeated coalition formation under uncertainty. In: Proc. of AAMAS 2008, Estoril, Portugal, (2008)
5. Chapman, A., Jagadish, H.V.: Why not? In: Proc. of the 35th SIGMOD int'l conf. on Management of data
6. Chorley, A., Edwards, P., Preece, A., Farrington, J.: Tools for tracing evidence in social science. In: Third Int'l Conf. on e-Social Science (October 2007)
7. Fullam, K.K., Barber, K.S.: Dynamically learning sources of trust information: experience vs. reputation. In: Proc. of AAMAS 2007, (2007)
8. Georgeff, M., Pell, B., Pollack, M., Tambe, M., Wooldridge, M.: The Belief-Desire-Intention Model of Agency. In: Proc. of the 5th Int'l Workshop on Intelligent Agents V, Agent Theories, Architectures, and Languages (1998)
9. Hasan, R., Sion, R., Winslett, M.: The case of the fake picasso: Preventing history forgery with secure provenance. In: Proc. of 7th USENIX Conference on File and Storage Technologies, FAST 2009, pp. 1–14 (2009)
10. Khosravifar, B., Gomrokchi, M., Bentahar, J., Thiran, P.: Maintenance-based trust for multi-agent systems. In: Proc. of AAMAS 2009, Budapest, Hungary, (2009)
11. Kifor, T., Varga, L.Z., Vazquez-Salceda, J., Alvarez, S., Willmott, S., Miles, S., Moreau, L.: Provenance in agent-mediated healthcare systems. IEEE Intelligent Systems 21, 38–46 (2006)
12. Kota, R., Gibbins, N., Jennings, N.R.: Self-organising agent organisations. In: Proc. of AAMAS 2009, Budapest, Hungary, (2009)
13. Miles, S.: Electronically querying for the provenance of entities. In: Moreau, L., Foster, I. (eds.) IPAW 2006. LNCS, vol. 4145, pp. 184–192. Springer, Heidelberg (2006)
14. Miles, S., Groth, P., Munroe, S., Moreau, L.: Prime: A methodology for developing provenance-aware applications. ACM TOSEM (2010)
15. Miles, S., Munroe, S., Luck, M., Moreau, L.: Modelling the provenance of data in autonomous systems. In: Proc. of AAMAS 2007, (2007)
16. Moreau, L.: The foundations for provenance on the web. Foundations and Trends in Web Science (in Press 2010)
17. Moreau, L., Clifford, B., Freire, J., Futrelle, J., Gil, Y., Groth, P., Kwasnikowska, N., Miles, S., Missier, P., Myers, J., Plale, B., Simmhan, Y.L., Stephan, E., Van Den Bussche, J.: The Open Provenance Model Core Specification (v1.1). Future Generation Computer Systems (in Press 2010)
18. Papamichai, K.N., French, S.: Explaining and justifying the advice of a decision support system: a natural language generation approach. Expert Systems with Applications 24 (2003)

19. Phung, T., Winikoff, M., Padgham, L.: Learning Within the BDI Framework: An Empirical Analysis, pp. 282–288 (2005)
20. Rao, A.S., Georgeff, M.P.: BDI Agents: From Theory to Practice. In: Proceedings of the First International Conference on MultiAgent Systems (1995)
21. Ringelstein, C., Staab, S.: PAPEL: A Language and Model for Provenance-Aware Policy Definition and Execution. In: Hull, R., Mendling, J., Tai, S. (eds.) BPM 2010. LNCS, vol. 6336, Springer, Heidelberg (2010)
22. Simmhan, Y.L., Plale, B., Gannon, D.: A survey of data provenance in e-science. SIGMOD Rec. 34, 31–36 (2005)
23. Teacy, W.T., Patel, J., Jennings, N.R., Luck, M.: Travos: Trust and reputation in the context of inaccurate information sources. Autonomous Agents and Multi-Agent Systems 12, 183–198 (2006)
24. W3C Provenance Incubator Group: (Provenance dimensions) http://www.w3.org/2005/Incubator/prov/wiki/Provenance_Dimensions (last accessed March 01 2010)
25. Weitzner, D.J., Abelson, H., Berners-Lee, T., Feigenbaum, J., Hendler, J., Sussman, G.J.: Information accountability. Commun. ACM 51, 82–87 (2008)

An Approach to Enhancing Workflows Provenance by Leveraging Web 2.0 to Increase Information Sharing, Collaboration and Reuse

Aleksander Slominski

Department of Computer Science, Indiana University
Bloomington, IN, 47405, USA
{aslom}@cs.indiana.edu

Abstract. Web 2.0 promises a more enjoyable experience for creating content by users by providing easy-to-use information sharing and collaboration tools, and focusing on user-centered design. Provenance in Scientific Workflow Management is one kind of user-generated data that can benefit from using Web 2.0. We propose a simple set of Web 2.0 technologies that is simple to implement and can be immediately leveraged by scientific users. Using Atom Syndication Protocol to represent workflow state and its provenance users can easily disseminate their scientific results. Collaboration and authoring can be facilitated by using Atom Publishing Protocol and standard Web 2.0 blogging tools to publish and annotate provenance. Users can search stored provenance by using search engines. If search results are in standard Atom Syndication Protocol, for example when search engines support OpenSearch standard, then Atom feeds can be used to monitor provenance changes increasing the likelihood of discoveries. By using those Web 2.0 standards, the value of scientific provenance data increases by making it a natural part of growing a variety of user-generated scientific (and non-scientific) content.

Keywords: scientific workflow provenance, user-generated content, scientific notebook, atom syndication format, atom publishing protocol.

1 Introduction

Web 2.0 promises greater control over user-generated content and a more enjoyable experience for users by improving information sharing and collaboration capabilities, and focusing on user-centered design. Those benefits should not only be enjoyed by end-users but enterprise and scientific users as well.

There is an increasing interest in trying to leverage Web 2.0 benefits in science with the ultimate goal to create something that may be called "Science 2.0" [4]. Scientific Workflow Management (SWFMS) [14] is one of such areas of science that may benefit to leverage Web 2.0 (e.g. [6][7]). In particular, we believe that one of the areas where the biggest gains can be obtained from using Web 2.0 standards is to apply it to provenance in Scientific Workflow Management Systems. That will help to solve one of the biggest problems that scientists have when working on scientific workflows: how to collaborate and disseminate results. To collaborate scientists need

D.L. McGuinness, J.R. Michaelis, and L. Moreau (Eds.): IPAW 2010, LNCS 6378, pp. 231–235, 2010.
© Springer-Verlag Berlin Heidelberg 2010

to have a shared environment (Web 2.0 is a good candidate) and to disseminate results they need to be able to not only send output files but allow other scientists to reproduce them (that is why provenance is important).

2 Web 2.0 and Scientific Workflow Provenance

Web 2.0 does not have one clear definition [16] but key characteristics of Web 2.0 around user-generated data can be identified [1]:

- Search: the ability to find useful information in ever- increasing amounts of data is a key feature of Web 2.0 for users. Making data and metadata generated in scientific workflows searchable by search engines is the simplest approach to accomplish it. Moreover, by using OpenSearch 1.1 [8] more customized search queries and results in formats required by scientists can be provided. For example, search results in standard Atom Syndication Protocol [10] can represent provenance and its metadata (as in examples below).

- (Hyper) Links are the key ingredient to the Internet experience. If scientific content is not linked, it is as if did not "exist" on the Internet. The ability to cite and reference is an integral part of scientific process and scientific papers – the same concept in Science 2.0 is implemented by using links.

- Authoring has been the enabling factor in making Web 2.0 successful. In particular, blogs provide easy-to-use platforms that ordinary users can leverage with minimal computer-science experience. Scientific Workflows are managed by scientific users (such as scientists) that, in majority, prefer to concentrate on their science than to become proficient in computer-science. Leveraging well-tested Web 2.0 authoring tools in scientific environments, therefore, can lead to quicker dissemination of results as well as easier sharing and collaboration.

- Tags are a very easy-to-use tool for organizing information without the need for users to learn and understand taxonomies. Tags provide bottom-up taxonomy and should significantly help scientific users organize quickly increasing amounts of data produced in science.

- Syndication and publication of content is made easy with standards such as The Atom Publishing Protocol [9]. The pull model of publishing works well to broadcast scientific results to interested subscribers and facilitate collaboration.

We believe that the Scientific Workflow Provenance can benefit from network effect by making it a natural part of a variety of Web 2.0 user-generated content. To achieve this there are several proposed solutions. A leading approach is to build on a larger framework of Semantic Web and in particular Linked Data [11] with HTTP URIs and combination of RDF and SPARQL as machine readable data format and query language. However Semantic Web requires a layer of sophisticated middleware to achieve its goals - it is much more than a simple extension of World Wide Web and using it for provenance require additional work [13][15].

As a simple alternative to full stack of Semantic Web one could use The Atom Syndication Format [10] as it is an extensible entry data format that can embed any XML data (including XHTML) and metadata about it (including links). That extensibility can be leveraged to encode scientific workflow provenance. In particular, the Open Provenance Model [2] may be good target to assure that provenance data is not locked inside SWFMS. The query part can be fulfilled by search engines indexing pages generated from ATOM entries and feeds. For more targeted searches Open-Search can be leveraged.

Even though ATOM provides only a subset of capabilities available in fully featured Semantic Web solution, ATOM entries can be easily transformed into RDF and can be fully integrated into evolving Semantic Web middleware.

3 Using the Open Provenance Model with ATOM

In the Open Provenance Model (OPM) [2] there are several types of nodes, including Artifact, Process, Agent and OPM nodes and edges:

•   Artifact is an "immutable piece of state, which may have a physical embodiment in a physical object or a digital representation in a computer system";

•   Process is defined as an "action or series of actions performed on or caused by artifacts, and resulting in new artifacts";

•   Agent is a "contextual entity acting as a catalyst of a process, enabling, facilitating, controlling, or affecting its execution";

•   OPM also describes relations between nodes, edges in a graph. Typical edges are "used," "wasGeneratedBy," and "wasDerivedFrom."

OPM nodes and edges could be naturally represented as ATOM entries, edges translated to links in ATOM entries, and an OPM graph becomes an ATOM feed. There are already existing proposals to do it. In this paper we show a very simple encoding of OPM into ATOM. Each ATOM entry has atom:link to give URL to retrieve HTML representation and a unique atom:id that works well as an graph node ID. Moreover, any part of XML representation of OPM (such as [3]) can be embedded:

```
<entry>
   <title>Workflow 1 in Foo Version  1.1 </title>
   <link href="http://example.org/foo/1.1/w1 "/>
   <id>urn:uuid:...-888888888</id>
   <updated>2010-03-13T17:00:03Z</updated>
   <summary>Workflow 1 was executed by system Foo
Version  1.1.</summary>
   <opm:Agent id="urn:uuid:...-888888888" />
</entry>
<entry>
   <title>Input file bar.dat</title>
   <link href="http://example.org/f/bar.dat"/>
   <id>urn:uuid:...-9999999999</id>
   <updated>2010-03-13T17:01:03Z</updated>
   <summary>Input file bar.dat</summary>
   <opm:Artifact id="urn:uuid:...-9999999999" />
   <category scheme="http://..." term="bar" />
</entry>
```

User actions will naturally correspond to blog postings, with the "agent" doing work (or becoming an author)

```
<entry>
  <title>Running Xyz Processing</title>
  <link href="http://example.org/w/AAAA "/>
  <id>urn:uuid:...-AAAAAAAA</id>
  <updated>2010-03-13T17:11:03Z</updated>
  <summary>Xyz processed bar.dat </summary>
  <opm:Process id="urn:uuid:...- 888888888" />
  <oprel:used id="urn:uuid:...-9999999999" />
  <link rel="http://.../opm/rel#used"
     href="http://example.org/f/bar.dat" />
</entry>
```

4 Use Case Scenario

To illustrate how scientific workflow users can benefit from Web 2.0 integration, we describe a scenario where Alice is monitoring workflows that are run by Bob. Bob either manually or by using a job scheduler runs large weather forecast workflows using his custom code. The workflow system Foo used by Bob is running a process that Bob designed and that leverages Bob's experience. In particular, he has designed a special Xyz processing used in his workflows. For each new process started, the Foo system creates a new ATOM feed (OPM graph) and publishes workflow progress as ATOM entries to this feed. The system also publishes ATOM entry to public ATOM feed when a new process starts. Alice is using specialized software to monitor this feed (it could be a slightly modified commercial blog reader). If Bob used PubSub-Hubbub protocol [12] then Alice could get near-instant notifications about changes in Bob workflows.

When results of Xyz processing are published, they are automatically downloaded to Alice's desktop (standard function of blog software) and analytics code is executed (additional software required). The analytics could also be a workflow process that publishes results as ATOM feed so Bob (and other scientists) can monitor it and verify provenance of results. When analytics detects interesting conditions (such as a strong possibility of a tornado), an alarm is published to high priority ATOM feed to which Alice is subscribed (by email, SMS, etc.).

When Alice finds something interesting about Bob's results, she can publish it to her blog or post a comment to Bob's workflow feed to let Bob know that his workflow produced something that may be incorporated in Alice's future publications.

5 Summary

We hope that we demonstrated that provenance publishing and collaborating on scientific results can be facilitated by using Atom Publishing Protocol and standard Web 2.0 blogging tools. With easy migration path for data stored in ATOM format to future Semantic Web and Provenance standards additional benefits can be leveraged in the future as Web 2.0-related technologies mature and become attractive to scientists.

References

1. McAfee, A.P.: Enterprise 2.0: The Dawn of Emergent Collaboration. MITSloan Management Review 47, 21–28 (2006)
2. The Open Provenance Model Core Specification (v1.1),
   http://eprints.ecs.soton.ac.uk/18332/1/opm.pdf
3. http://github.com/lucmoreau/OpenProvenanceModel/blob/master/opm/src/main/resources/opm.1_1.xsd
4. Waldrop M.: Science 2.0: Great New Tool, or Great Risk? In Scientific American (May 2008)
5. Harrison, A., Taylor, I.: Web enabling desktop workflow applications. In: SC-WORKS 2009 (2009)
6. De Roure, D., Goble, C.: myExperiment: A Web 2.0 Virtual Research Environment for Research using Computation and Services. In: Workshop On Integrating Digital Library Content with Computational Tools and Services at JCDL 2009, Austin, Texas, USA (19-06-2009)
7. De Roure, D., Goble, C., Bhagat, J., Cruickshank, D., Goderis, A., Michaelides, D., Newman, D.: myExperiment: Defining the Social Virtual Research Environment. In: 4th IEEE International Conference on e-Science, Indianapolis, Indiana, USA, December 7-12 (2008)
8. OpenSearch 1.1 Specification,
   http://www.opensearch.org/Specifications/OpenSearch/1.1
9. The Atom Publishing Protocol. Internet Official Protocol Standards, RFC 5023 (October 2007), http://tools.ietf.org/html/rfc5023
10. The Atom Syndication Format. Internet Official Protocol Standards, RFC 4287 (December 2005), http://tools.ietf.org/html/rfc4287
11. Berners-Lee, T.: Linked data,
    http://www.w3.org/DesignIssues/LinkedData.html
12. PubSubHubbub Core 0.3 – Working Draft,
    http://pubsubhubbub.googlecode.com/svn/trunk/pubsubhubbub-core-0.3.html
13. Hartig, O.: Provenance Information in the Web of Data. In: Proceedings of the Linked Data on the Web (LDOW) Workshop at the World Wide Web Conference (WWW), Madrid, Spain (April 2009)
14. Yu, J., Buyya, R.: A Taxonomy of Workflow Management Systems for Grid Computing. Technical Report GRIDS-TR-2005-1, Grid Computing and Distributed Systems Laboratory, University of Melbourne (2005),
    http://www.gridbus.org/reports/GridWorkflowTaxonomy.pdf
15. Moreau, L.: The Foundations for Provenance on the Web. Foundations and Trends in Web Science, http://eprints.ecs.soton.ac.uk/18176/ (submitted)
16. Sharma, P.: Core Characteristics of Web 2.0 Services. (Published 28 November 2008),
    http://www.techpluto.com/web-20-services/

StarFlow: A Script-Centric
Data Analysis Environment

Elaine Angelino, Daniel Yamins, and Margo Seltzer

School of Engineering and Applied Sciences, Harvard University,
33 Oxford St., Cambridge, MA 02138
{elaine,margo}@eecs.harvard.edu, yamins@fas.harvard.edu
http://www.eecs.harvard.edu/~margo/

Abstract. We introduce StarFlow, a script-centric environment for data analysis. StarFlow has four main features: (1) extraction of control and data-flow dependencies through a novel combination of static analysis, dynamic runtime analysis, and user annotations, (2) command-line tools for exploring and propagating changes through the resulting dependency network, (3) support for workflow abstractions enabling robust parallel executions of complex analysis pipelines, and (4) a seamless interface with the Python scripting language. We describe real applications of StarFlow, including automatic parallelization of complex workflows in the cloud.

Keywords: automatic parallelization, automatic updating, computational workflows, control flow, data-flow, data analysis, dependency tracking, provenance, Python, workflow abstraction.

1 Introduction

Many people analyze data by writing pipelines of scripts: short programs written in high-level languages such as Python that parse input, call numerical analysis routines, and write output.

Scripts plus data files are powerful because they are very flexible: they allow users to mix and match many kinds of data formats and analysis routines, output files where convenient, write code that performs complicated computational tasks, re-use code in different places, and put related functions into the same file. While script pipelines are less rigid than databases, they are more prone to disorganization. Scripts and data live in conventional file systems, where dependency relationships are exposed only at runtime, and provenance of data is easily lost.

The data analysis work cycle consists of basic actions: create an analysis pipeline and execute its initial run, modify input data or an analysis function and propagate the change, add an analysis function and re-execute the pipeline, and create related pipelines based on an abstract workflow. In this context, it is difficult and annoying to remember what functions were called with what parameters to produce what files, to re-run a long chain of downstream scripts when an upstream data file or script is modified, to capture repeated patterns of analysis, to parallelize execution, and to communicate or replicate analyses.

D.L. McGuinness, J.R. Michaelis, and L. Moreau (Eds.): IPAW 2010, LNCS 6378, pp. 236–250, 2010.
© Springer-Verlag Berlin Heidelberg 2010

Data analysts who write scripts are thus confronted by fundamental data management challenges: identifying dependencies, propagating changes, parallelizing work, sharing data and code, and archiving relevant information. Dependency tracking and workflow management tools would help them by making recomputation automatic and efficient and by making sharing easier.

These programmers are an important and unique user group. They are comfortable with and depend on writing code, and as a result are unwilling to depend on tools that depart from the scripting environment. At the same time, they are not sophisticated software engineers; they write code as a means to produce analytic results, not to produce code as an end result.

A workflow tool for these users must integrate in a simple way with the existing scripting environment. By focusing on these users in this environment, we have designed a dependency tracking system and workflow engine with novel features. A key observation is that scripts plus data files already contain workflows in the sense that they implicitly describe a dependency graph. This insight motivates both design constraints and a unified and flexible framework for managing dependencies across multiple workflows that may exist separately or overlap within a user's file system.

Dependency tracking systems can explicitly capture the provenance of data analysis and enable workflow tools for managing, generating and executing analysis pipelines. Existing tools track dependencies by combining dynamic runtime analysis, static analysis, and/or user annotations; their specific choices restrict when and what dependencies can be extracted and thus when and how they can be used to drive actions. User annotations plus static analysis extract control flow prior to runtime execution, enabling automatic parallelization. Even without annotations, dynamic analysis extracts both information and control flow. Whether dynamic or static, control flow dependency tracking at the level of *functions* facilitates incremental recomputation.

StarFlow strategically uses all three methods of dependency tracking while integrating seamlessly with a script-based programming environment[1]. This unique combination of features makes StarFlow widely applicable, from single-purpose analysis pipelines written "on the fly" to complex workflows in a high-performance computing environment.

Below, we introduce a design framework for data analysis workflow engines and describe existing implementations (§2). Next, we describe StarFlow's implementation (§3), user scenarios (§3.4), workflow abstraction and automatic parallelization of complex workflows in the cloud (§4).

2   Features of a Workflow Engine for Data Analysis

A workflow engine for data analysis can be evaluated by: (1) how and at what level of granularity it tracks dependency relationships between data and analysis functions, (2) what user actions it supports using those dependencies, (3)

---

[1] See http://bitbucket.org/dyamins/starflow/ for StarFlow source code and documentation.

whether and how it supports workflow abstraction, and (4) how it integrates with a programming environment. We use this framework to describe our design and to classify existing workflow tools (Table 2).

2.1   Tracking Dependencies

A set of scripts implies a dependency network of links between data and functions. A function may **depend on** file inputs, **create** file outputs, and **use** other functions (Fig. 1). There are three complementary sources of dependency information: user annotations, static code analysis, and dynamic runtime analysis. Each technique has strengths and weaknesses (Table 1).

User annotation of dependencies allows a workflow tool to be aware of dependencies without having to extract them, and is a widely used technique. The familiar Unix `make` utility requires that a user create a `Makefile`, explicitly specifying file targets, their dependencies, and commands transforming one to another. Although `Makefiles` are notoriously difficult to maintain, they are still the de facto standard way to specify source code dependencies. Workflow management systems also ask users to explicitly describe both information and control flow; there are many in the scientific (e.g. Galaxy[26], GenePattern[16], Kepler[18], Knime[3], Pegasus[9], Taverna[22], Vistrails[4]) and business (e.g. clario[5], Pentaho Data Integration [8]) communities. Their users construct workflows by connecting functional "nodes" with well-defined input/output types.

Static analysis of code can automate some of this manual annotation, but in the general case cannot completely capture information or control flow; these

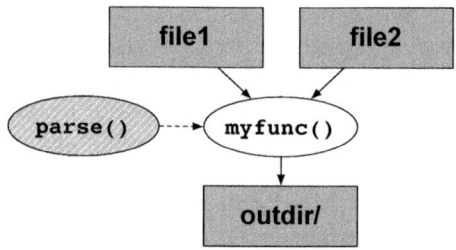

Fig. 1. The function `myfunc()` depends on input files 'file1' and 'file2', creates output directory 'outdir/', and uses the function `parse()`. Arrows are in the direction of information flow.

Table 1. Three complementary methods for tracking information flow and control flow: dynamic runtime analysis, static analysis of code, and user annotation

	Runtime analysis	Static analysis	User annotation
Information flow data dependencies	Accurate, but sometimes too late	Difficult	Acceptable if lightweight
Control flow functional dependencies	Accurate, but mostly unnecessary	Usually possible	Very annoying

Table 2. Comparison of data tracking implementations

	Runtime analysis	Static analysis	User annotation
`make`			Specify file targets, their file dependencies & executable commands in a `Makefile`
`make + Automake`	`depcomp` determines source file dependencies during compilation	When `depcomp` fails, `makedepend` determines source file dependencies	Specify C/C++ source files in a simplified `Makefile`
Workflow management systems			Specify node parameters & data flow in a GUI or flow language
`IncPy`	Modified Python interpreter tracks file I/O & function calls; memoizes function returns		
`StarFlow`	File I/O interception & stack trace inspection in the Python interpreter	Abstract syntax tree analysis of Python code tracks **function**-level control flow	Specify data flow & non-Python control flow directly in function definition lines

are Turing-undecidable problems. In practice, static analysis can often extract a highly accurate description of control flow. For example, `makedepend` augments the standard `make` utility by using static analysis to automatically extract C source code file dependencies. Static analysis can even extract dependencies at the level of functions because their syntax makes them easy to parse from the abstract syntax tree. Data-flow dependencies are difficult to extract because they are not explicit in the abstract syntax tree, e.g. they may be implicit in a concatenation of strings.

Dynamic analysis captures the actual information and control flow generated during runtime execution of scripts. File input/output interception captures data file dependencies, and stack trace inspection captures functional dependencies. Pure runtime systems use only dynamic runtime analysis. For example, provenance-aware storage systems (PASS) automatically track provenance at the level of files and processes dynamically at runtime [21], while `IncPy` is a modified Python interpreter that dynamically tracks file I/O and computational results at the level of function calls [13]. `Automake` is another dynamic analysis tool that automates the construction of `Makefiles` [24].

The **granularity** of dependency tracking determines what actions it can support. Notably, `make`-like tools track control flow at the level of *files*, but practical incremental recomputation requires tracking at the level of *functions*.

2.2 Using the Dependency Network

Knowing the dependency network supports three activities: dependency exploration, automatic change propagation, and pipeline extraction and sharing.

Dependency exploration involves querying the dependency network to understand where files and functions come from and their upstream and downstream dependencies. A query might concern only dependency structure (e.g., "On what Python modules does this output depend?") or could take into account other information, such as the file modification times of dependency targets relative to their sources (e.g., "Do I need to rerun this analysis?").

Automatic change propagation involves the use of a "smart" updating engine that queries the dependency network to support incremental recomputation; it updates targets by (re-)executing the minimal set of control flow components necessary. When the user invokes make, it examines the file modification times of targets relative to their dependencies to determine those in need of updating and executes the minimal sequence of necessary commands. The Panda project is developing a formalism and algorithms for provenance-based refresh in data-oriented workflows [14]. IncPy's dynamic analysis and memoization facilitates fine-grain incremental recomputation.

Extraction and sharing of an analysis pipeline between users is facilitated by knowing its dependency network.

2.3   Workflow Abstraction

Once a user develops an analysis pipeline, she often needs to apply it to a potentially large number of similar analyses. If we view the overall pipeline as an abstract workflow, then each of these pipelines becomes an instance of that abstract workflow. Workflow environments differ in whether and how they allow users to represent abstract workflows, concrete instances or both. Those that do support workflow abstraction additionally differ in whether they support programmatic instantiation of concrete pipelines from abstract workflows. Scripting environments support but do not typically come with ready tools for workflow abstraction, while workflow management systems emphasize workflow abstraction but not necessarily programmatic instantiation.

2.4   Integration with the Programming Environment

There are two fundamental approaches to providing dependency tracking capabilities: make the workflow management system the center of the system or integrate dependency tracking into the programming environment. Workflow management systems tend to do the former while integrated development environments (IDEs) do the latter. It is often a design goal of workflow management systems to support novices who do not want to write programs [18]. For example, Taverna replaces a regular programming environment with a GUI for manipulating an XML-based flow language, Scufl [20]; users can also directly write in Scufl to annotate dependencies. IDE-based systems provide a unified interface for code developement that decreases the distance between where a user edits and executes scripts. Eclipse's C/C++ Development Tooling (CDT) IDE includes standard make build, plus a GUI for writing Makefiles and invoking make [12]. While the Chimera virtual data system is script-based, it requires use of a virtual data language (VDL) [11].

An important extension of a workflow engine's integration with the programming environment is its support for distributed computing on a grid or in the cloud. Users often have computational needs at multiple scales, from jobs they want to run a personal computer to high performance computing (HPC) problems; many of the scientific and business workflow tools mentioned already can be deployed in a variety of environments. Other workflow management solutions are specifically for distributed systems, such as Azkaban and Oozie for Apache Hadoop by LinkedIn and Yahoo!, respectively [7,15]. Some tools, including Pi-Cloud and pomsets, specialize in workflow management for cloud services, e.g., Amazon's EC2 [10,23].

3   StarFlow

StarFlow is a data analysis environment that is script-centric, has make-like tools, tracks dependencies at the level of functions rather than files, and is constrained in scope to the level of a scripting language. Our implementation of the StarFlow workflow engine has four main features: (1) dependency tracking of both information and control flow via a novel combination of static analysis, dynamic analysis, and user annotations, (2) command-line tools supporting dependency exploration, automatic updating, and pipeline extraction and sharing, (3) workflow abstractions and concrete analysis pipeline instances, and (4) a seamless interface with Python. Although our initial implementation is for Python, our design principles and algorithms are broadly applicable. Sections §3.2 and §3.3 describe how StarFlow tracks and uses dependencies, and section §3.4 presents various usage scenarios.

3.1   Design Principles

A few basic principles guide StarFlow's design. First, users express dependencies only in their code. This design choice makes sharing dependency information a consequence of sharing code, and so these actions do not have to occur separately. Second, StarFlow is designed to place a minimal burden on the user, implying that any required annotations must be lightweight. Finally, StarFlow is for programmers who aren't software engineers, and so it is script-centric and simple.

3.2   Tracking Dependencies

StarFlow uses a combination of dynamic analysis, static analysis and user annotations to track data and functional dependencies.

User annotations. Although user annotations in StarFlow are purely optional, they enable parallelization and dependency querying before a script has ever been run. They also make sharing dependency provenance a side effect of sharing code. Such annotations are simple declarations within Python functions that expose the inputs and outputs of the function. For example,

```
def myfunc(depends_on=('file1','file2'), creates='outdir/'):
```

indicates that ('file1','file2') and 'outdir/' are the file names of the inputs and output of myfunc, respectively. The user can also annotate non-Python functional dependencies, e.g. a Perl script, with an analogous parameter, uses.

When functions specify input and output file namess via parameters, the user can write a simple one-line annotation to describe information flow. It is a Python decoration, indicated by @activate, consisting of two lambda expressions, one representing the inputs (depends_on annotations) and the other representing the outputs (creates annotations). Upon function invocation, the decoration maps the parameters to the appropriate lambda expression. For example, in

```
@activate(lambda x: (x[0], x[1]), lambda x: x[2])
def myfunc(infile1, infile2, outdir):
```

the first lambda represents the depends_on values, mapping to the first two parameters (x[0] and x[1]), while the second lambda represents the creates values, mapping to the third parameter x[2]. Thus, like in the previous example, (infile1, infile2) are the inputs and outdir is the output of myfunc(). This is particularly useful for workflow abstraction (§4) but also for any function whose inputs and/or outputs are specified at runtime.

Static analysis. StarFlow uses static code analysis to determine most control flow prior to runtime execution. First, it examines import statements to determine what external modules a script depends on. Then, it uses Python's built-in compiler.ast module to access the abstract syntax tree to determine the functional dependencies within a module. Static analysis cannot determine conditional control flow, and StarFlow has different methods for approximating dependencies in different scenarios. For example, it extracts control flow in all conditional clauses, but never extracts control flow in an eval statement.

Dynamic analysis. During runtime, for each function executed at the top of the Python stack, StarFlow uses sys.settrace to set a trace function. StarFlow walks the stack and examines all function calls to extract control flow and intercepts file I/O functions to extract information flow. This produces a trace of all function calls specifying the stacks where they were invoked, as well as what I/O operations were performed and what files they involved. By setting an environment variable, the user can control how StarFlow uses runtime dependencies: they can be simply logged, or they can be compared to the results of static analysis and user annotations to check for consistency.

Dependency representation. As a result of using the three methods of dependency tracking, StarFlow determines the dependency network; we describe its representation here.

`LoadLiveModules()` takes a set of directories and recursively determines all the Python modules inside those directories. The user can pass `LoadLiveModules()` a set of regular expression filters to conditionally select modules and functions and can maintain a `LiveModules` configuration file to set the default input.

`LinksFromOperations()` determines the dependency network corresponding to a list of Python modules. It uses static code analysis and extracts user annotations to construct the dependency list including both information and control flow. `LinksFromOperations()` caches the compiled bytecode of user-generated functions so that irrelevant changes, such as edits to comments or changes to unrelated functions in the same module, do not result in changes to the dependency network. It returns the `LinkList`, a table whose records correspond to dependency links and whose columns describe the links. For example, this `LinkList` describes the dependencies in Figure 1:

Link Type	Link Source	Source File	Link Target	Target File	Update Script	Update ScriptFile
DependsOn	file1	file1	`myfunc()`	mymodule.py	None	mymodule.py
DependsOn	file2	file2	`myfunc()`	mymodule.py	None	mymodule.py
CreatedBy	`myfunc()`	mymodule.py	outdir/	outdir/	`myfunc()`	mymodule.py
Uses	`parse()`	mymodule.py	`myfunc()`	mymodule.py	None	mymodule.py

There are four files: 'file1', 'file2', 'mymodule.py', and 'outdir/'. The four links represent that: (1-2) the `myfunc()` function depends on the files 'file1' and 'file2', and is inside of the Python module 'mymodule.py', (3) the 'outdir/' directory is created by the function `myfunc()` inside of 'mymodule.py', and (4) the `myfunc()` function uses the function `parse()`, and both are in 'mymodule.py'.

The `LinkList` is stored on-disk in a serialized format. The `LinkList` can trivially be represented in a tabular format (CSV) or XML or RDF consistent with the Open Provenance Model (OPM) [6]. We could easily allow users to edit pipelines by directly editing the `LinkList`, but do not currently do so.

3.3   Exploring, Updating and Sharing

StarFlow includes a set of Python command-line tools for exploring dependencies, propagating changes, and extracting and sharing analysis pipelines.

Exploring dependencies. `DownstreamLinks()` takes a list of source dependencies and propagates down through the dependency network to return a list of downstream dependencies. Its default behavior uses file time stamps to propagate only through dependencies in need of updating, i.e., dependencies whose targets' time stamps are older than those of their sources. When `Forced = True`, it ignores time stamps and instead propagates through all downstream dependencies. `UpstreamLinks()` is an analogous function for upstream dependencies.

`ShowUpdates()` uses `DownstreamLinks()` to determine and print a readable report describing what Python functions to execute, and in what order, to update dependency targets relative to their sources, without actually calling them.

Propagating changes. StarFlow's automatic updating engine supports two styles of change propagation. `Update()` uses `ShowUpdates()` to implement **downstream updating**, so changes to the dependency network trigger execution of downstream functions. `Make(Targets)` implements **upstream updating** in the spirit of `make`, so targets are made by executing upstream functions that have changed or whose upstream dependencies have changed. For both functions, the user can force re-execution by passing `Forced = True`. Both can propagate changes through a restricted dependency network, i.e., a filtered `LinkList`. The user can pass a list of regular expression filters mapping to a list of Python functions and specify default filters from a configuration file.

StarFlow's automatic updating engine combines change propagation with a set of optional "smart" features: (1) consistency checking that can issue an error or warning if user annotations contradict runtime file I/O, (2) Unix-style `diff` checking between each round of updates, so that if a set of updates produces no changes, unnecessary downstream updates are cancelled, (3) data archiving and managed exception handling so that if user scripts throw errors, downstream updates are cancelled and previous versions of data restored, and (4) storing of sha-1 checksums after each round of computation to detect corrupt data.

Extracting and sharing. `Extract(Targets)` uses `UpstreamLinks(Targets)` to find all code modules and data sources required to recompute `Targets` and then extracts them into a zipped archive. The result of `Extract(Targets)` can then be integrated into another user's StarFlow environment with `Integrate()`.

3.4   Basic Use Case

StarFlow enables a highly organized real-time data analysis development cycle where the user can automatically update her pipelines every time she edits scripts or data. Consider a user-generated Python module containing several parameterized functions for basic data processing and analysis:

```
def Parser(infile, outfile):
  X = open(infile)
  Y = remove_header(X)
  Z = pivot(Y)
  save(Z, outfile)

def Cluster(infile, outfile, distfunc, param=None):
  X = open(infile)
  C = hcluster(X, distfunc, param)
  save(C, outfile)

def PCA(infile, outfile):
  X = open(infile)
  Y = pca(X)
  save(Y, outfile)
```

```
def Compare(PCAfile, Clusterfile, outfile):
X1 = open(PCAfile)
X2 = open(Clusterfile)
Y = compute_error(X1, X2)
save(Y, outfile)
```

These functions read input data files, process their contents, and write output data files. They depend on other functions located either in the same module or imported from elsewhere. Regular user interaction at the Python interpreter, without StarFlow, might look like this:

```
>> from my_module import *
>> Parser('raw_data.csv', 'data.csv')
>> PCA('data.csv', 'pca.csv')
>> Cluster('data.csv', 'euc.csv', EuclideanDistance)
>> Compare('pca.csv', 'euc.csv', 'error1.csv')
>> Cluster('data.csv', 'geo.csv', GeometricDistance)
>> Compare('pca.csv', 'geo.csv', 'error2.csv')
```

StarFlow enables the user to track the dependencies of these sorts of operations. Suppose the user wants to use the depends_on and creates annotations to record the first four function calls from the above interpreter session. She could add the following lines to my_module.py:

```
def ParseBigInput(depends_on='raw_data.csv', creates='data.csv'):
  Parser(depends_on, creates)

def DoPCA(depends_on='data.csv', creates='pca.csv'):
  PCA(depend_on, creates)

def ClusterEuclid(depends_on='data.csv', creates='euc.csv'):
  Cluster(depends_on, creates, EuclideanDistance)

def Comp(depends_on=('pca.csv', 'euc.csv'), creates='error.csv'):
  Compare(depends_on[0], depends_on[1], creates)
```

With the information flow annotated, StarFlow can determine the complete dependency network prior to runtime (Fig. 2). The user opens the Python terminal and initializes StarFlow by importing its modules.

```
>> from starflow.interactive import *
```

Before executing anything, the user can type ShowUpdates() to see what functions will run and in what order:

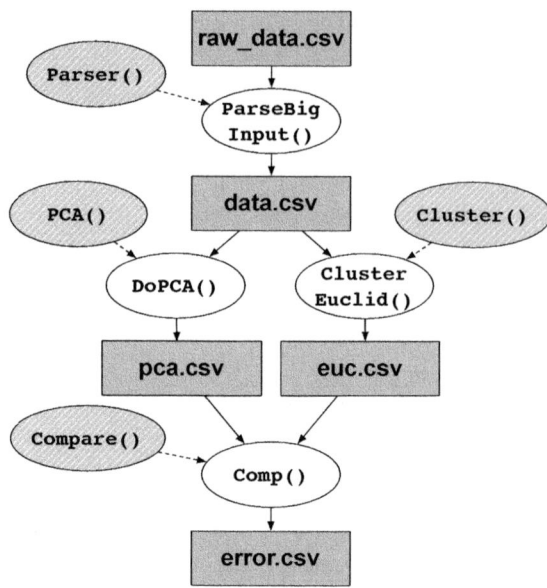

Fig. 2. Dependency graph extracted by StarFlow. Arrows are in the direction of information flow. Files are rectangles and functions are ovals. For example, the function DoPCA() depends on the file data.csv, creates the file pca.csv, and uses the function PCA().

```
>> ShowUpdates()
Round 1:   my_module.ParseBigInput
Round 2:   my_module.DoPCA, my_module.ClusterData
Round 3:   my_module.Comp
```

The output of ShowUpdates() corresponds to the breadth-first parallelization scheme that StarFlow can implement automatically. As before, the user can make edits to data or functions and propagate incremental changes by calling Update() or related tools. When using StarFlow with the depends_on and creates annotations, the user may find that she only needs to type two commands at the prompt – ShowUpdates() and Update() – to review and propagate changes as she develops her analysis pipelines.

Later, the user edits her scripts and data, and wants to propagate these changes. First, she makes a small change to the file raw_data.csv. She types Update(), and StarFlow re-executes each of the function calls she typed at the prompt because they are all downstream of the raw_data.csv file. Next, she makes a small change to the hcluster function. Now when she types Update(), StarFlow re-executes only the function calls to Cluster, because it depends directly on hcluster, and Compare, because it is downstream of Cluster.

4   Workflow Abstraction

StarFlow supports a simple metaprogramming syntax that allows the user to construct abstract workflows and then instantiate concrete analysis pipelines from them. The user represents a workflow by a simple data model for a list of concrete workflow steps, the OpList. Each step corresponds to a concrete function call with inputs and outputs and is represented as a three-tuple: a unique string name, a function, and a tuple of function parameters. Actual concrete workflows are instantiated by passing the OpList to the Actualize() templating engine. Actualize(OpList, 'path.py') writes out a Python module, 'path.py' where each step corresponds to a hard-coded function with depends_on and creates annotations. For example, this script:

```
def instantiator(creates='instances.py'):
  L = []
  for i in ['a', 'b', 'c']:
      L += [('step_'+i, myfunc, ('in1_'+i, 'in2_'+i, 'out_'+i))]
  Actualize(L, 'instances.py')
```

instantiates three concrete instances of a one-step workflow, where myfunc is @activate decorated, as in §3.2. Each workflow step is automatically written out as a separate function in 'instances.py':

```
def step_a(depends_on=('in1_a', 'in2_a'), creates='out_a')
  myfunc('in1_a', 'in2_a', 'out_a')

def step_b(depends_on=('in1_b', 'in2_b'), creates='out_b')
  myfunc('in1_b', 'in2_b', 'out_b')

def step_c(depends_on=('in1_c', 'in2_c'), creates='out_c')
  myfunc('in1_c', 'in2_c', 'out_c')
```

By combining workflow abstraction with automatic updating, we have developed a parallelization engine. Users can exploit this engine by writing an abstract workflow that generates many concrete instances. When configured for parallelization, StarFlow's Update() command materializes these instances, computes their dependency network and partitions them into parallelizable groups. We then use a grid scheduler to dispatch the parallel jobs on available machines. The next section shows how we have integrated StarFlow with Amazon's Elastic Compute Cloud (EC2) [17] to perform automatically, parallelized web download and analysis.

Applying parallelization to abstract workflows. We combine StarFlow with StarCluster [25] to enable automatic parallelization of workflows in a high performance cloud setting. StarCluster manages the creation and adminstration of clusters hosted on Amazon's EC2, connecting to SunGrid Engine for job scheduling and load balancing.

Below we illustrate a representative and simple scenario; it is embarrassingly parallel and contains just one of many possible analyses of interest. Suppose the user wants to download data from the U.S. Environmental Protection Agency about facilities or sites subject to environmental regulation [2]. There is one downloadable file for each of 50 states, and the user wants to call the function `pairwise_comparison()` for each pair of states. She writes this module, using Actualize to automatically produce 'EPA_instances.py':

```
01 urlroot = 'http://www.epa.gov/enviro/html/frs_demo/'
02 urlroot += 'geospatial_data/state_files/state_combined_'
03
04 def EPA(depends_on='states.txt', creates='EPA_instances.py'):
05
06     L = []
07     statelist = open('states.txt','r').read().strip().split(',')
08
09     for S in statelist:
10         L += [('get_'+S, wget, (urlroot+S+'.zip', S+'.zip'))]
11         L += [('unzip_'+S, unzip, (S+'.zip', S+'/'))]
12
13     for i in range(0, 49):
14         S1 = statelist[i]
15         for j in range(i+1, 50):
16             S2 = statelist[j]
17             L += [('compare_'+S1+'_'+S2, pairwise_comparison,
18             (S1+'/data.csv', S2+'/data.csv', S1+'_'+S2+'.csv'))]
19
20     Actualize(L, 'EPA_instances.py')
```

In the first `for` loop (lines 9-11), the user downloads and unzips the data, producing two rounds of 50 function executions that, within a round, can be run in parallel. For each state, a large CSV file ($\approx$100 MB) is unarchived. Next, she analyzes all pairs of states, generating a third round of 1225 parallelizable function executions.

The user starts a 10-node cluster on EC2 with StarCluster, opens a Python terminal and initializes StarFlow. When she runs `Update()`, StarFlow executes `analyze.EPA()`, which writes out 'EPA_instances.py'. StarFlow automatically detects the functions inside of this new module, determines their dependencies and how to run them in parallel on 10 nodes, and then does so.

5   Future Directions

Although Starflow is currently Python-specific, we'd like to take the underlying principles and design and apply them to other scripting languages, such as

Perl and R, to determine how generally applicable the ideas are. We also would like to to extend StarFlow to the interactive shell in two ways: (i) given a variable, automatically update its value in response to upstream changes, and (ii) given a sequence of commands, automatically generate a script from the minimal sequence needed to produce a set of targets. We have developed and plan to improve a GUI for StarFlow that integrates browsing of files, dependencies, data and metadata. We are working on more comprehensive parallelization and workflow tools. We will integrate StarFlow's dependency tracking infrastructure with a version control system such as Mercurial [19].

6   Conclusion

StarFlow provides a powerful, script-centric environment for data analysis. It strategically combines dynamic runtime analysis, static analysis of code, and user annotations to provide fine-grain propagation. StarFlow enables workflow abstraction and automatic parallelization, and we have implemented StarFlow in the cloud.

Acknowledgments. We thank P. C. Sabeti (Harvard), who supported our initial effort, and whose students and collaborators provided us with a valuable case study. In particular, I. Shlyakhter, a member of the Sabeti Lab, provided us with valuable insight on workflow abstraction. Finally, we thank the reviewers, members of the PASS group (Harvard), and P. J. Guo (Stanford) for many helpful comments on this manuscript.

References

1. Proceedings of the 2010 USENIX Workshop on the Theory and Practice of Provenance, San Jose, CA, USA. USENIX (February 22, 2010)
2. United States Environmental Protection Agency. Epa frs facilities state combined csv files download,
   http://epa.gov/enviro/html/frs_demo/geospatial_data/
   geo_data_state_combined.html
3. Berthold, M.R., Cebron, N., Dill, F., Gabriel, T.R., Kotter, T., Meinl, T., Ohl, P., Thiel, K., Wiswedel, B.: Knime - the konstanz information miner: version 2.0 and beyond. SIGKDD Explor. Newsl. 11(1), 26–31 (2009)
4. Callahan, S.P., Freire, J., Santos, E., Scheidegger, C.E., Silva, C.T., Vo, H.T.: Vistrails: visualization meets data management. In: SIGMOD 2006 Proceedings of the 2006 ACM SIGMOD International Conference on Management of Data, pp. 745–747. ACM, New York (2006), General Chair-Yu, Clement and General Chair-Scheuermann, Peter and Program Chair-Chaudhuri, Surajit
5. clario Analytics. clario, http://clarioanalytics.com
6. Clifford, B., Freire, J., Gil, Y., Groth, P., Futrelle, J., Kwasnikowska, N., Miles, S., Missier, P., Myers, J., Simmhan, Y., Stephan, E., den Bussche, J.V.: The open provenance model core specification, v1.1 (2009), http://eprints.ecs.soton.ac.uk/18332/1/opm.pdf

7. LinkedIn Corporation Azkaban, http://sna-projects.com/azkaban/
8. Pentaho Corporation, Kettle: Pentaho data integration,
   http://kettle.pentaho.org
9. Deelman, E., Blythe, J., Gil, A., Kesselman, C., Mehta, G., Patil, S., Su, M.-h.,
   Vahi, K., Livny, M.: Pegasus: Mapping scientific workflows onto the grid, pp. 11–20
   (2004)
10. Elkabany, K., Staley, A., Park, K.: Picloud - cloud computing for science. simplified.
    In: SciPy 2010 Python for Scientific Computing Conference, Austin, TX (July 2010)
11. Foster, I., Vckler, J., Wilde, M., Zhao, Y.: Chimera: A virtual data system for
    representing, querying, and automating data derivation. In: Proceedings of the
    14th Conference on Scientific and Statistical Database Management, pp. 37–46
    (2002)
12. The Eclipse Foundation. Eclipse c/c++ development tooling project,
    http://www.eclipse.org/cdt
13. Guo, P.J., Engler, D.: Towards practical incremental recomputation for scientists:
    An implementation for the python language. In: TaPP 2010 [1] (2010)
14. Ikeda, R., Widom, J.: Panda: A system for provenance and data. In: TaPP 2010
    [1] (2010)
15. Yahoo! Inc., Oozie, http://yahoo.github.com/oozie/
16. Kuehn, H., Liberzon, A., Reich, M., Mesirov, J.P.: Using genepattern for gene
    expression analysis. Curr. Prot. in Bioinformatics, 7.12.1–7.12.39 (2008)
17. Amazon Web Services LLC. Amazon elastic compute cloud (ec2),
    http://aws.amazon.com/ec2
18. McPhillips, T., Bowers, S., Zinn, D., Ludaschera, B.: Scientific workflow design for
    mere mortals. Future Generation Computer Systems 25(5), 541–551 (2009)
19. Mercurial. Mercurial, http://mercurial.selenic.com
20. Missier, P., Belhajjame, K., Zhao, J., Roos, M., Goble, C.: Data lineage model for
    taverna workflows with lightweight annotation requirements. In: Freire, J., Koop,
    D., Moreau, L. (eds.) IPAW 2008. LNCS, vol. 5272, pp. 17–30. Springer, Heidelberg
    (2008)
21. Muniswamy-Reddy, K.-K., Holland, D.A., Braun, U., Seltzer, M.I.: Provenance-
    aware storage systems. In: USENIX Annual Technical Conference, General Track,
    pp. 43–56. USENIX (2006)
22. Oinn, T.M., Addis, M., Ferris, J., Marvin, D., Senger, M., Greenwood, R.M.,
    Carver, T., Glover, K., Pocock, M.R., Wipat, A., Li, P.: Taverna: a tool for the
    composition and enactment of bioinformatics workflows. Bioinformatics 20(17),
    3045–3054 (2004)
23. Pan, M.J.: pomsets: workflow management for your cloud. In: SciPy 2010 Python
    for Scientific Computing Conference, , Austin, TX (July 2010)
24. The GNU Project, Gnu automake, http://www.gnu.org/software/automake
25. Riley, J.: Starcluster - numpy/scipy computing in the cloud. In: SciPy 2010: Python
    for Scientific Computing Conference, Austin, TX (July 2010)
26. Taylor, J., Schenck, I., Blankenberg, D., Nekrutenko, A.: Using galaxy to perform
    large-scale interactive data analyses. Curr. Prot. in Bioinformatics, 10.5.1–10.5.25
    (2007)

GExpLine: A Tool for Supporting Experiment Composition[*]

Daniel de Oliveira[1], Eduardo Ogasawara[1], Fernando Seabra[1], Vítor Silva[1],
Leonardo Murta[2], and Marta Mattoso[1]

[1] COPPE, Federal University of Rio de Janeiro, Rio de Janeiro, Brazil
[2] Fluminense Federal University, Niterói, Brazil
{danielc,ogasawara,fernando_seabra,silva,marta}@cos.ufrj.br,
leomurta@ic.uff.br

Abstract. Scientific experiments present several advantages when modeled at high abstraction levels, independent from Scientific Workflow Management System (SWfMS) specification languages. For example, the scientist can define the scientific hypothesis in terms of algorithms and methods. Then, this high level experiment can be mapped into different scientific workflow instances. These instances can be executed by a SWfMS and take advantage of its provenance records. However, each workflow execution is often treated by the SWfMS as independent instances. There are no tools that allow modeling the conceptual experiment and linking it to the diverse workflow execution instances. This work presents GExpLine, a tool for supporting experiment composition through provenance. In an analogy to software development, it can be seen as a CASE tool while a SWfMS can be seen as an IDE. It provides a conceptual representation of the scientific experiment and automatically associates workflow executions with the concept of experiment. By using prospective provenance from the experiment, GExpLine generates corresponding workflows that can be executed by SWfMS. This paper also presents a real experiment use case that reinforces the importance of GExpLine and its prospective provenance support.

1 Introduction

Scientific workflows are a prominent solution to model scientific experiments [1]. One fundamental problem is representing and tracking the composition process. Composing a scientific workflow involves many trials. Scientists usually execute different tasks during composition, such as: establishing the logical sequence of activities, planning variations that have to be explored, and defining the types of input and output data for each activity. All these actions are taken before using a SWfMS and are not registered.

Since scientists need to draw conclusions from a scientific experiment. During the experiment life cycle, many different workflow executions need to be evaluated by choosing different parameters, alternative data sets, programs, or even algorithms and

[*] This work was partially sponsored by CNPq and CAPES.

D.L. McGuinness, J.R. Michaelis, and L. Moreau (Eds.): IPAW 2010, LNCS 6378, pp. 251–259, 2010.

methods [2]. Additionally, some activities may be optional in the workflow, *i.e.*, scientists should explore the experiment by choosing to use (or not) a particular activity in order to model the entire workflow in a suitable way for the experiment being conducted. The exploration of all these different workflows represents trials that are performed to evaluate the initial hypothesis. Nevertheless, existing approaches are not conceived to relate two or more workflow trials as part of a single experiment. For instance, a SWfMS such as VisTrails [3] offers a framework for controlling workflow versions, which represent several modifications of the same executable workflow over the time. In VisTrails, different versions of an executable workflow are related and represented in an evolution version tree. Although these versions share common characteristics, they do not necessarily represent alternatives for the same experiment. For example, a new version of a workflow is generated by simply removing a specific activity from the workflow. The reason for this removal could be a bug fix or the exploration of a different type of result for the same experiment. Unless some annotation is used to represent which actions are allowed to be performed over a workflow (*e.g.*, removing some specific activities), the decision regarding removing or choosing activities can be extremely error prone and counterproductive.

These several composition tasks should be registered in addition to producing an executable workflow. These composition tasks represent a significant amount of effort for the scientists. Representing a workflow in hierarchical abstract levels can help the process of analyzing the experiment, but this kind of representation is an open issue [4]. A conceptual workflow is a workflow where scientists define what they want to do without specifying how to do it.

Representing a workflow at hierarchical levels of abstraction presents several advantages. For example, it is possible to add semantics to the executable level by registering the main algorithms and software that originated the concrete workflow. It is also possible to group different concrete workflows as alternative (similar) solutions to one experiment. Thus, provenance from workflow trials is registered as part of one single experiment. Workflow reuse and generation of executable workflows from conceptual representations become simpler than browsing executable workflow repositories or querying workflow provenance databases.

GExpLine is a tool for supporting experiment composition. GExpLine is complementary to existing SWfMS, thus offering extra representation layers to be coupled to the existing workflow systems. Its goal is to provide a high abstraction level representation environment for scientists to model their scientific experiments and to automatically generate corresponding executable workflows in pre-defined SWfMS specification languages.

Provenance data is a key concept used to link the experiment of GExpLine to the SWfMS workflow executions. GExpLine provides mechanisms to gather prospective provenance data from the experiment definition. This prospective provenance data is related to the retrospective provenance data produced by the SWfMS. In addition, by coupling GExpLine to workflow ontologies, the experiment representation is boosted with ontology concepts, such as algorithms or methods inherent to scientific experiments, and the provenance may also be analyzed based on these concepts. The GExpLine representation is based on the concept of experiment lines [2].

The use case presented in this paper is based on a real experiment of the deep water oil exploitation domain to reinforce GExpLine's representation of experiments at higher abstraction levels, supporting workflow composition and the derivation [2] to different SWfMS with prospective provenance support. This paper is organized in four sections besides this introduction. Section 2 presents GExpLine architectural features. Section 3 presents details of the use case that demonstrates how to model a real experiment of deep water oil exploitation using GExpLine. Section 4 brings the related work and Section 5 concludes the paper.

2 GExpLine

The concept of experiment lines [2] is an innovative approach to represent a scientific experiment. It is based on the successful concept of software product lines [5]. An experiment line may be defined as a conceptual workflow that is capable to derive multiple workflows at the concrete level. It is a flow of activities where each activity behaves like an independent component [6]. When an activity of the flow can be implemented by any activity from a list of alternative activities, it is called a variation point. It means that there is more than one alternative program, algorithm or method to implement the variation point. Also, when an abstract activity can be suppressed when deriving a concrete workflow, in order to represent a different type of result or analysis, and not due to its incorrectness, it is defined as an optional activity. On the other hand, a mandatory activity is an activity that must be present in all derived concrete workflows. Experiment lines follow the optional, mandatory, and variant activities. In addition, GExpLine presents a powerful configuration management mechanism that allows the versioning of workflow elements to model the experiment.

The GExpLine tool is based on five main components: (i) *Experiment Line Modeler:* designs experiment lines, (ii) *Derivation:* derives concrete workflows based on abstract ones. The derivation process is based on the concept of cartridges, *i.e.* when scientists are deriving their conceptual workflows (represented in our object model) into concrete ones they have to choose one cartridge in a set of available cartridges, where each cartridge of this set generates concrete workflows for different representation language and also in XPDL [7] which is agnostic from SWfMS, (iii) *Import:* imports concrete workflows from Kepler [8], Taverna [9], and VisTrails [3]. This import process is also based on the concept of cartridges. There is a different cartridge implemented for each type of workflow language, and (iv) *Version Control:* controls versions of abstract/concrete workflows [10]. (v) *Query:* queries prospective provenance data using abstract/concrete information. In the current version, provenance queries are executed directly in SQL using DBMS functionalities. The following section explains in detail the GExpLine conceptual model that allows scientists to extract prospective provenance data from the modeled experiments.

3 GExpLine Prospective Provenance Model

The GExpLine prospective provenance model defines the experiment, abstract and concrete workflows, workflow components such as ports and relations, version identification and organization, as well as operations for retrieving existing versions and constructing new versions [10]. The GExpLine prospective provenance model is composed by three main parts: (i) workflow classes, in which workflow concepts are represented; and (ii) version classes, which represent the way that versions are organized. Figure 1 presents the GExpLine prospective provenance model as UML class diagram. Classes were colored differently since they represent different perspectives on the model. The white classes, which are *Experiment, Workflow, Activity, Relationship, Port, AbstractActivity, ConcreteActivity, Derivation* and *MetaArtifact* represent the workflow classes, which is actually the workflow meta-model. Finally, light gray classes, which are *Version, Transaction, ConfigurationItem, User,* and *Project,* represent the version classes. Workflow classes represent, in configuration management terminology [11], the product space. The version classes are called, in configuration management terminology, the version space [10]. The linking between the product space and version space is defined by the *VersionedElement* class, which acts as an interface between both spaces. All classes that are part of the workflow meta-model just need to inherit from the *VersionedElement* class to be versioned and managed by the configuration management mechanism.

A workflow (class *Workflow*) is composed of activities (class *Activity*) and relationships (class *Relationship*). The class *Workflow* may be specialized into conceptual abstract workflows (class *AbstractWorkflow*) and concrete workflows (class *ConcreteWorkflow*). An activity in a workflow has input and output ports (class *Port*). The relationship between activities is a directed edge that establishes the dependency between activities and also defines the workflow activity chaining. In addition, the class *Activity* presents a self-relationship that indicates variability, *i.e.*, the choices that scientists make when modeling a workflow. There are two specializations for the *Activity* class. The *AbstractActivity* class represents activities modeled in the abstract level while *ConcreteActivity* represents activities modeled in the executable level. Both *AbstractActivity* and *ConcreteActivity* inherit from the class *Activity*. Each *Activity* that is part of a *Workflow* produces and consumes a specific *MetaArtifact*. A *MetaArtifact* is a type of artifact in a prospective provenance model. A generated artifact obtained during workflow execution is actually an instance of a *MetaArtifact*. The derivations performed by scientists are registered in the class *Derivation*. This way, the activities and workflows derived are registered and provide important information for future backtracking information.

It is possible to relate the GExpLine workflow meta-model with Open Provenance Model (OPM) [12] nodes. For example, the class *MetaArtifact* is mapped to the *Artifact* OPM node. Indeed, a *MetaArtifact* is a conceptual representation of an artifact node in OPM. The class *Activity* is mapped to the *Process* OPM node, since both of them are performed on artifacts. The class *User* is mapped to the *Agent* OPM node. This way it is possible to discover which entity composed and derived the activity. The composition and derivation actions can be mapped to the OPM *Role*, which in this case are *compose* and *derive,* since they designate an artifact's or agent's function in a process.

The version space is decoupled from the product space, allowing both spaces to evolve independently. The version space is composed by six main classes: *ConfigurationItem, Version, Transaction, User, VersionedElement,* and *Project.* Each configuration item (class *ConfigurationItem*) is composed by versions (class *Version*). Each version has relationships to the next and previous versions, which can be null for the first and last versions of a configuration item, respectively. A specific attribute differentiates versions that were deleted by the user. Additionally, there is a relationship to branched versions, which allows non-sequential development. Versions are queried or created by transactions (class *Transaction*) made by users (class *User*). Finally, versions have relationships to the versioned elements (interface *VersionedElement*).

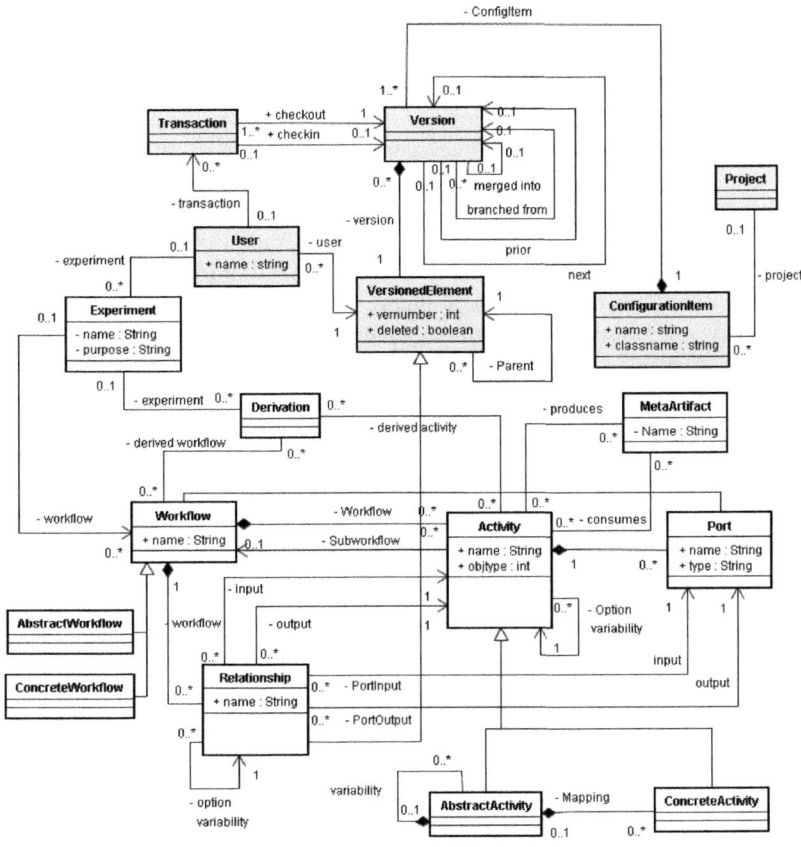

Fig. 1. GExpLine Prospective Provenance Model

VersionedElement interface is not exclusive for the version space. It is also part of the product space, since it connects the versioning space with the product space, as presented in Figure 1. Although a configuration item does not know more than the type and the hierarchy of one of the versioned element in the product space, it is used to retrieve the product information. Also, from the project (class *Project*), which is a representation of a compound object, it is possible to obtain the configuration item that is actually associated with the whole workflow. The conceptual model of Figure 1 was instantiated in a relational schema in the PostgreSQL DBMS and it is used as the prospective provenance schema for GExpLine. While using the information presented in this model, scientists are able to extract and analyze provenance data and draw important conclusions about the entire experiment. The next section presents a real experiment of the deep water oil exploitation scientific workflow modeled in GExpLine.

4 Modeling a Deep Water Oil Exploitation Experiment

The scientific experiment used in this GExpLine demonstration is based on the Deep Water Oil Exploitation Domain. Although the experiment is more complex and with many alternatives, for sake of simplicity, we present a small fraction of the experiment, which is composed by four conceptual activities that are sequentially connected: (i) Pre-Processing (implemented by PreProc program); (ii) Intermediate Processing (implemented by SigProc program), (iii) Structural Analysis (implemented by StruCAD or S-Analyst programs), and (iv) Generation of tension histogram (implemented by Histogram program). In this experiment, the fourth activity of the flow is optional, which means that it can be suppressed in some derived workflows, and the third activity is a variation point, which means that scientists have alternatives (StruCAD and S-Analyst) as presented in Figure 2. When using a SWfMS directly, these two workflows from Figure 2 would be managed independently by the SWfMS. Querying provenance corresponding to all executions of the same experiment line would require a significant effort through the SWfMS provenance support. It is not simple to gather and combine the provenance results of these specific executions.

Based on the experiment definition, the initial step is to set up the versioning mechanism in GExpLine. The scientist must create a workspace for this new experiment line. A workspace in the GExpLine context is an environment where scientists are able to model their experiment lines, isolated from the outside world, *i.e.*, isolated from each other's work. The scientist is able to choose an experiment line version to work with if there is any committed version available.

The second step to be performed is to model the experiment line. It may be created from scratch (top-down) or by importing multiple concrete workflows and generalizing them (bottom-up). The experiment line is modeled just once and scientists may derive or make annotations any time after that.

From the modeled experiment line, scientists may conduct experiments by deriving concrete workflows associated to that experiment. In this demonstration, the first concrete workflow is composed by the programs PreProc, SigProc, StruCAD, and Histogram. Let us suppose that the scientists were not satisfied with the obtained results, and want to experiment a different method or algorithm. GExpLine can derive an alternative concrete workflow. In this second trial, the optional activity was suppressed and the concrete workflow has three activities, represented by the programs PreProc, SigProc, and S-Analyst. This change is part of the experimentation process and all this information is gathered and stored in the prospective provenance schema of GExpLine.

It is important to notice that the experiment line composition is highly dependent on the expertise of senior scientists and is a knowledge intense activity. However, using an existing experiment line to derive workflows is a less error prone activity and can be performed even by novice scientists. This occurs due to the effective use of composition rules (already adopted in software product lines) [13]. The essence of experiment lines is the systematic and efficient composition of experiments. This composition is made by chaining a series of programs in a coherent manner. However, not all programs are compatible. Composition rules are commonly used to define the legal combinations of programs in an experiment line. In addition to domain constraints, there are low level implementation constraints that must also be satisfied.

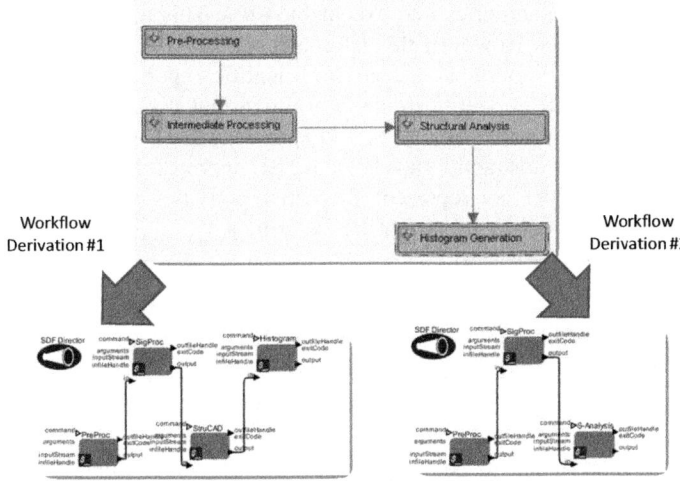

Fig. 2. Derivation in GExpLine

The demonstration ends with queries on prospective provenance data related to the experiment line using DBMS features. This query service allows analyzing information about concrete workflows associated with one experiment. Using the provenance query directly from the SWfMS, the user would have to gather the set of independent workflow executions corresponding to the experiment line. Let us take the example explained in this subsection. There are many generated concrete workflows for the same experiment. Particularly, the activity Structural Analysis has two different programs that implement it (StruCAD and S-Analyst) where each one produced different artifacts. If scientists want to discover which workflow produces the "tension amplitude histogram", using existing SWfMS, scientists are not able to discover the available workflows in the provenance schema (retrospective provenance is not available since the query is prior to execution). A demonstration video can be found at *http://gexp.nacad.ufrj.br/news/gexpline-demo-ipaw*.

5 Related Work

We have analyzed the literature and SWfMS support for workflow representation in different abstraction levels. Current SWfMS are restricted to one workflow execution at a time. In this way, the knowledge of which activities can be linked to each other is still tacit, since there is no conceptual representation of the experiment as happens in

GExpLine. Currently, projects in many SWfMS force scientists to redefine, almost from scratch, scientific workflows previously developed by other scientists, incurring in the same composition trial and error. This occurs due to the absence of a systematic approach for composition and lack of a conceptual workflow representation.

Ludäscher *et al.* [14] present an approach to relieve the scientists from directly designing executable workflows. It represents an abstract workflow based on directed acyclic graphs. It proposes to use database mediation techniques that automatically map abstract workflow activities into executable ones. This mapping is powerful and independent of SWfMS. However, this approach does not add represent optionalities or variabilities that are important concepts for scientific experiments. Using those concepts, scientists are able to identify similar workflows that share a common ancestor.

The task specification language (TSL) [15] is an initiative to represent scientific workflows in different abstraction levels. The TSL approach is coupled to the VIEW [16] SWfMS, but it does not represent alternative activities and it does not concern about representing the concept of scientific experiment.

6   Conclusion

GExpLine allows scientists to model their experiments in a high abstraction level, improving the management of the scientific experiment. GExpLine provides features to associate different concrete workflows to a single conceptual definition of the experiment. This experiment to concrete workflow mapping is fundamental for scientific experiment management. It produces conceptual prospective provenance data for analysis together with provenance data from SWfMS concrete workflow instances. This prospective provenance data is thus complementary to the SWfMS provenance data. Ongoing work includes developing a lightweight interface for querying provenance data and incorporating composition rules in GExpLine.

References

[1] Taylor, I.J., Deelman, E., Gannon, D.B., Shields, M. (eds.): Workflows for e-Science: Scientific Workflows for Grids, 1st edn. Springer, Heidelberg (2007)

[2] Ogasawara, E., Paulino, C., Murta, L., Werner, C., Mattoso, M.: Experiment Line: Software Reuse in Scientific Workflows. In: 21th SSDBM, New Orleans, LA, pp. 264–272 (2009)

[3] Callahan, S.P., Freire, J., Santos, E., Scheidegger, C.E., Silva, C.T., Vo, H.T.: VisTrails: visualization meets data management. In: Proc. SIGMOD 2006, USA, pp. 745–747 (2006)

[4] Shoshani, A.: The Scientific Data Management Center: Providing Technologies for Large Scale Scientific Exploration. Scientific and Statistical Database Management, 1–2 (2009)

[5] Northrop, L.: SEI's software product line tenets. IEEE Software 19(4), 32–40 (2002)

[6] Szyperski, C.: Component Software: Beyond Object-Oriented Programming. Addison-Wesley Professional, Reading (1997)

[7] I. WfMC, Binding, WfMC Standards, WFMC-TC-1023 (2009),
http://www.wfmc.org (2000)

[8] Altintas, I., Berkley, C., Jaeger, E., Jones, M., Ludascher, B., Mock, S.: Kepler: an extensible system for design and execution of scientific workflows. In: SSDBM, Greece, pp. 423–424 (2004)

[9] Hull, D., Wolstencroft, K., Stevens, R., Goble, C., Pocock, M.R., Li, P., Oinn, T.: Taverna: a tool for building and running workflows of services. Nucleic Acids Research 34(Web Server issue), 729–732 (2006)

[10] Ogasawara, E., Rangel, P., Murta, L., Werner, C., Mattoso, M.: Comparison and Versioning of Scientific Workflows. In: CVSM 2009, Vancouver, Canada, pp. 25–30 (2009)

[11] Conradi, R., Westfechtel, B.: Version Models for Software Configuration Management. ACM Computing Surveys 30(2), 232–282 (1998)

[12] Moreau, L., Freire, J., Futrelle, J., McGrath, R., Myers, J., Paulson, P.: The Open Provenance Model: An Overview. In: Provenance and Annotation of Data and Processes, pp. 323–326 (2008)

[13] Garg, A., Critchlow, M., Chen, P., Westhuizen, C.V.D., Hoek, A.V.D.: An Environment for Managing Evolving Product Line Architectures. In: Proceedings of the International Conference on Software Maintenance, pp. 358–366 (2003)

[14] Ludascher, B., Altintas, I., Gupta, A.: Compiling abstract scientific workflows into web service workflows. In: Proceedings of the 15th International Conference on Scientific and Statistical Database Management, Cambridge, MA, pp. 251–254 (2003)

[15] Lin, C., Lu, S., Fei, X., Pai, D., Hua, J.: A Task Abstraction and Mapping Approach to the Shimming Problem in Scientific Workflows. In: Proc. Services 2009, pp. 284–291 (2009)

[16] Lin, C., Lu, S., Lai, Z., Chebotko, A., Fei, X., Hua, J., Fotouhi, F.: Service-Oriented Architecture for VIEW: A Visual Scientific Workflow Management System. In: Services, pp. 335–342 (2008)

Data Provenance in Distributed Propagator Networks

Ian Jacobi

Computer Science and Artificial Intelligence Laboratory
Massachusetts Institute of Technology
Cambridge, MA 02139
jacobi@csail.mit.edu

Abstract. The heterogeneous and unreliable nature of distributed systems has created a distinct need for the inclusion of provenance within their design to allow for error correction and redundancy. Many traditional distributed systems have limited provenance tracing abilities, usually included in generic workflow generation or in an application-specific way. The novel programming paradigm of distributed propagator networks allows for the inclusion of provenance from the ground up.

In this paper, I present the concept of propagator networks and demonstrate how provenance may be easily integrated into programs built using them. I also demonstrate the possibility of converting non-provenance-aware applications built using propagator networks into provenance-aware applications by simply performing a transformation of the existing program structure.

1 Introduction

Data provenance, that is, the derivation history of a piece of data [1], is an integral need of distributed systems like Google's MapReduce algorithm [2], or BOINC [3]. In distributed systems such as these, it is difficult to infer provenance of a particular result as the result may be generated by any one of thousands of systems. As a result, provenance handling must be explicitly factored into distributed system design.

Depending on how well an existing distributed architecture is designed, it may be difficult to support many use cases of provenance in applications that use the architecture. Such programs may need to explicitly include provenance in the design of the application. It would be far easier for developers of distributed applications not to need to worry about how provenance is handled in their distributed system; this would reduce complexity of program design. Data propagation, a model of concurrent [4] and distributed computation [5], allows for the transformation of programs that use it so they may track provenance.

2 Propagator Networks

Propagator networks, developed by Radul [4], are a general-purpose concurrent programming paradigm. These bipartite networks are constructed by connecting

D.L. McGuinness, J.R. Michaelis, and L. Moreau (Eds.): IPAW 2010, LNCS 6378, pp. 260–264, 2010.
© Springer-Verlag Berlin Heidelberg 2010

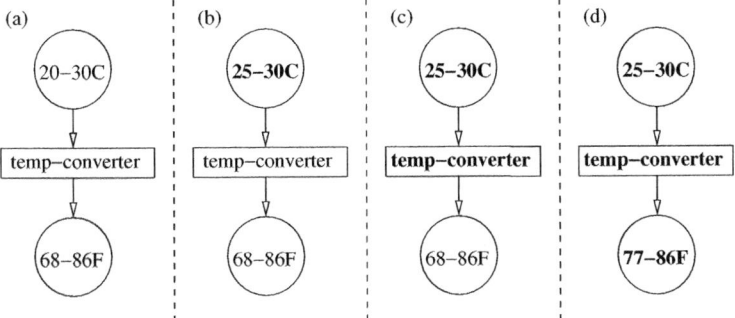

Fig. 1. A refinement of the contents of the top cell in (b) causes `temp-converter` to fire in (c), which then refines the bottom cell in (d)

"cells" that permanently store state and stateless propagators which perform computation and update the cells they are connected to.

Cells are a form of memory which may be assigned a partial value that can be refined. Upon receiving an update to this value, a cell accumulates knowledge of the value by applying a user-defined merge operation to unify the information contained in the update with the partial value currently stored there.

After a cell has changed its state by merging an update, any propagators that have registered an interest in the cell wake up and begin to process, as in (c) in Figure 1. These propagators may then send updates to other cells (d) and cause another cycle of cell merging and notification of propagators; this drives continued computation.

Networks of propagators have no constraints on their topology and may contain cycles. The order of operations in propagator networks is undefined other than the ordering enforced by propagation itself (i.e. a cell must update before propagators attached to it may fire). This, along with the separation of state and computation makes propagation a flexible framework for concurrency.

2.1   Propagators in a Distributed System

The modularity of propagator networks makes it relatively simple to extend their use to distributed systems. [5] In order to push updates across a network, we may bridge the network with propagators that duplicate cells on different computers. By implementing a "synchronization propagator" on each host to forward updates between copies of cells, local updates can trigger remote ones, effecting remote computation. This computation may update other cells that then cause cell synchronization and update more remote cells.

To ensure that no inconsistencies arise due to network issues, we require four properties of a cell merge operation: idempotency, associativity, commutativity, and monotonicity. We also require all cell copies to have the same merge operation. Although the only operations that adhere to these constraints may be the operations of logical conjunction and disjunction or comparable operations

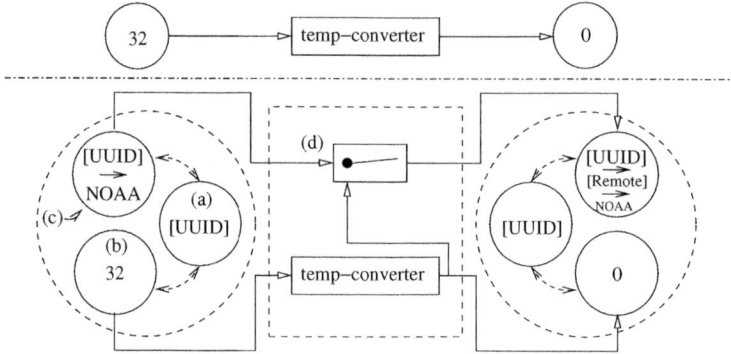

Fig. 2. We transform a propagator `temp-converter` (top) into a provenance-aware propagator network (bottom). Solid arrows indicate the flow of computation in the propagator network. Note that the provenance (c) and data (b) cells contain pointers to the main identifier cell (a) (and vice versa), marked with dashed arrows.

over alternate domains, merge operations that do not adhere to these principles may be modified into operations that do. Standard distributed database implementations account for the transitivity and implicit monotonicity of network communications when performing non-transitive and non-monotonic deletions [6]. Similar adaptations of other merge operations may be possible.

3   Adding Provenance to Propagator Networks

Provenance may be easily implemented on top of existing propagator networks without adding any additional mechanisms or basic primitives to the propagator paradigm. Rather than treating a cell as a single object with a number of simple propagators attached to it, we may apply a simple transformation that adds the cells and propagators needed to make the propagator provenance-aware.

We choose to separate provenance from the data itself, as in Figure 2. In that example, a cell containing a measurement of 32 (degrees Fahrenheit) made by the National Oceanic and Atmospheric Administration (NOAA) is divided into three sub-cells. One cell contains the data (b), another the provenance (c), and a third (a) that points to both sub-cells and contains a Universally Unique Identifier (UUID) along with associated metadata, linking the three cells together.

Separating the sub-cells in this way allows these separate aspects of the data to be refined separately. It also allows for separate access control of provenance and data, as the auditors allowed to view provenance may be different from general users. [7] Each of these three components, data, provenance, and metadata, are placed into one of three sub-cells where they may be refined.

Transforming a propagator to be provenance-aware is even simpler; it requires the propagator to be modified with an additional sub-propagator for each input/output cell pair (d). This sub-propagator will only allow the provenance of an input to be sent to the output cell when data has been sent by the main propagator to the output, effectively acting as a switch.

Provenance may be constructed by gradually aggregating the graph of provenance stored in each provenance sub-cell. Contents of new provenance updates may be added to an existing provenance graph, and then propagated through other provenance-aware propagators. Changes to existing provenance will also be forwarded through a provenance-aware propagator, and these changes may be merged into the existing knowledge of the provenance sub-cell. Thus, data propagation may be used for both computation and provenance construction.

4   Related Work

The work of Moreau, et al. [8] features the automatic construction of provenance, much as provenance-aware data propagation does. However, Moreau focuses on querying the provenance after its construction rather than detailing its generation. Moreau also assumes that provenance may be general in his system, able to document the *purpose* of an action. Although propagator networks may be able to do so, we make no claims about the creation of subjective provenance.

Altintas, et al.'s extension of the Kepler Scientific Workflow System [9] is also similar to the work presented here. Just as we may extend existing propagator networks to support provenance, Altintas demonstrates an extension of an existing framework, Kepler, to support provenance. Altintas's centralized approach for collecting provenance is not suitable for propagator networks however, as propagator networks are inherently decentralized. Adapting Altintas's approach would scale poorly with the propagator network as the number of messages sent to the propagator server grows.

The Matrioshka system presented by da Cruz, et al [10] proposes another mechanism for provenance tracking in distributed workflows. Unlike provenance propagation, Matrioshka requires a single centralized provenance store rather than distributing the provenance with the data. Matrioshka is also somewhat more brittle than the system proposed here, as it assumes that logging is aleady performed, and relies on the generation of a log prior to constructing provenance.

5   Contributions and Future Work

The power of data propagation may resolve many of the difficulties encountered in concurrent and distributed processing, and we should consider the role of integrating provenance into systems that make use of this technique. In this paper I have demonstrated the value of the data propagation paradigm not only by allowing for the distribution of provenance, but also by permitting the extension of existing programs to support provenance.

I have currently implemented the system described in this paper on top of a distributed propagator framework (DProp) that I have designed. While the implementation of both DProp and the provenance-aware component are Python-based, the more generic nature of propagators allows this design to be useful more generally. I hope to eventually test the system across a number of hosts to ensure that the system is fully scalable.

Acknowledgements

I would like to thank Joe Pato of HP Labs, and Gerry Sussman and other members of the Decentralized Information Group at MIT for their advice and criticism. I would like to extend particular thanks to Alexey Radul for his assistance with the architectural design of distributed propagation. Finally, I would also like to acknowledge that this work was supported in part by the National Science Foundation under NSF Cybertrust Grant award number CNS-0831442 and by IARPA under Grant FA8750-07-2-0031.

References

1. Simmhan, Y.L., Plale, B., Gannon, D.: A survey of data provenance in e-science. ACM SIGMOD Record 34(3), 31–36 (2005)
2. Dean, J., Ghemawat, S.: MapReduce: Simplified data processing on large clusters. In: Proceedings of the 6th Symposium on Operating System Design and Implementation (OSDI 2004), USENIX Association (2004)
3. Anderson, D.P.: BOINC: A system for public-resource computing and storage. In: Proceedings of the 5th IEEE/ACM International Workshop on Grid Computing, pp. 4–10. IEEE Computer Society, Los Alamitos (2004)
4. Radul, A.: Propagation Networks: A Flexible and Expressive Substrate for Computation. PhD thesis, Massachusetts Institute of Technology (2009)
5. Jacobi, I., Radul, A.: A RESTful messaging system for asynchronous distributed processing. In: Proceedings of the First International Workshop on RESTful Design, Raleigh, NC, USA. ACM, New York (2010)
6. Birrell, A.D., Levin, R., Needham, R.M., Schroeder, M.D.: Grapevine: An exercise in distributed computing. Communications of the ACM 25(4), 260–274 (1982)
7. Braun, U., Shinnar, A.: A security model for provenance. Technical Report TR-04-06, Computer Science Group, Harvard University (2006)
8. Moreau, L., Groth, P., Miles, S., Vazquez-Salceda, J., Ibbotson, J., Jiang, S., Munroe, S., Rana, O., Schreiber, A., Tan, V., Varga, L.: The provenance of electronic data. Communications of the ACM 51(4), 52–58 (2008)
9. Altintas, I., Barney, O., Jaeger-Frank, E.: Provenance collection support in the kepler scientific workflow system. In: Moreau, L., Foster, I. (eds.) IPAW 2006. LNCS, vol. 4145, pp. 118–132. Springer, Heidelberg (2006)
10. da Cruz, S.M.S., Barros, P.M., Bisch, P.M., Campos, M.L.M., Mattoso, M.: Provenance services for distributed workflows. In: Proceedings of the 2008 Eighth IEEE International Symposium on Cluster Computing and the Grid, pp. 526–533. IEEE Computer Society, Los Alamitos (2008)

Towards Provenance Aware Comment Tracking for Web Applications

James R. Michaelis and Deborah L. McGuinness

Tetherless World Constellation
Rensselaer Polytechnic Institute
Troy, NY 12180
{michaj6,dlm}@cs.rpi.edu

Abstract. Provenance has been demonstrated as an important component in web applications such as mashups, as a means of resolving user questions. However, such provenance may not be usable by all members of a given applications user base. In this paper, we discuss how *crowdsourcing* could be employed to allow individual users to get questions answered by the greater user base. We begin by discussing a technology-agnostic model for incorporating Provenance Aware Comment Trackers (PACTs) into web applications. Following this, we present an example of a PACT-extended application with accompanying two accompanying use cases.

1 Introduction

On the Web, applications are continuously being created to serve communities of users. These applications are capable of generating browsable content via an interface for users to review and browse. In reviewing this content, users may have questions about the content they see, which could impact their trust in the application [1].

Provenance can provide information on the creation and history of artifacts, such as web-based resources [8] and be used as an aid in question answering. However, for someone to work effectively work with the provenance of web content, certain kinds of background are necessary. Examples of such background include understanding how the individual components of an application's workflow (e.g., code, supporting technologies) are supposed to function [7]. Personalized views of provenance can help with this [2][12]. Yet these approaches are not guaranteed to produce understandable provenance for a given user in all cases. While such a user may be unable (or unwilling) to review this provenance, other members of a web community may be able to it for them. The use of collective intelligence, or *crowdsourcing*, has been applied previously in web applications [3]. Due to differences in the backgrounds of individuals (i.e., different knowledge and experiences), certain users may understand application output that a particular user doesnt. As such, access to the insights of a greater community of users for a web application could be a valuable aid to any single community member. Here, it

D.L. McGuinness, J.R. Michaelis, and L. Moreau (Eds.): IPAW 2010, LNCS 6378, pp. 265–273, 2010.

is important to emphasize the role of provenance in crowdsourcing driven question answering. For web applications based on data and services that continually change (e.g., an application that pulls in content from Wikipedia), what one user sees in the interface may be quite different from what other users see. As such, provenance can provide context to user questions on web applications, such that other users can make sense of them.

1.1   Deliverables

This work discusses the idea of crowdsourcing provenance evaluation as a means of addressing user questions on web application outputs, and is intended as a starting point upon which more applied work can later follow. To help convey our current views, three deliverables are provided in this paper:

- A model for extending web applications with provenance-based comment tracking, known as the Provenance Aware Comment Tracker (PACT) model. In the PACT model, users may comment on sections of a web application interface, known as *outputs*. In turn, other web community members may reply to this user, forming discussion threads in the process.
- An example of a PACT-extended web application, titled US Global Aid. This application presents a mashup of user foreign aid contributions made to individual countries by the US Agency for International Development (USAID) with supplementary country facts provided by DBPedia.
- Based on this example application, two use cases are presented to illustrate PACT usage.

Additionally, it is important to mention what this work doesn't attempt to cover:

- User interface or usability issues for accessing a PACT from a web application, or presenting provenance and presenting previously made comments to end users.
- The usage of specific technologies for implementing PACTs in web applications. However, some recommendations on promising technologies are provided for this purpose at the end of the paper.

The outline of the remainder of the paper is as follows: Section 2 discusses related work; Section 3 introduces the PACT model; Section 4 introduces the US Global Aid mashup, and discusses corresponding use cases; finally, Section 5 provides our discussion and concluding remarks.

2   Related Work

The use of provenance in mashups has received significant recent attention. For instance, the documenting of application activities, based on models such as the p-structure [5], has been explored. Additionally, frameworks for tracking the provenance of mashup evolution, such as VISMASHUP [10], have been developed. Here, users can view multiple instances of a mashup, distinguished by the provenance of their development by an end user. This work builds on the VisTrails [4] approach of tracking the provenance of workflow evolution.

Likewise, the application of crowdsourcing toward problem solving has received significant attention [3]. Examples of the kinds of problem solving explored include reviewing the quality of Wikipedia articles [6] and linguistic annotation [13]. In both of these particular cases, communities of users are assigned tasks, and complete them through the Amazon Mechanical Turk[1] service. To our knowledge, little work has been explored on applying crowdsourcing of any kind toward provenance evaluation.

3   The Provenance Aware Comment Tracker (PACT) Model

In this section, we discuss the PACT model model and its relationship to web applications. Here, we assume the existence of:

- An application A consisting of a workflow $W = \{N, C, I\}$ with:
  - **N:** A set of all input parameters to the application, where $|N| \geq 0$.
  - **P:** A set of all processing stages carried out by the application, where $|P| \geq 0$.
  - **I:** The interface of the application, consisting of a set of *outputs* viewable by a user[2], where $|I| > 0$.
- A user community U, where $|U| \geq 0$.

Additionally, we assume that each user $u \in U$ is capable of running A, resulting in an execution of W. For each execution of W:

- The same set of input parameters is used, with possibly changing values (e.g. if one of the parameters is an RSS feed).
- The same set of processing stages P are used, with possible variability in execution sequence (based on factors such as variability in the input parameters).
- The same set of interface outputs are displayed, with possible variability based on the execution sequence.

What this means is that while each execution of the application will follow a common plan, different users may end up seeing different information in the application outputs. With these assumptions in mind, we define the components of a PACT based on the activities an end user can do for each application output:

- **Inspect Provenance:** A provenance trace detailing all activities managed by the application to generate the output should be accessible (i.e. the trace goes from the output to input parameters), should a user want to inspect provenance themselves.

---

[1] https://www.mturk.com/

[2] Here, we are not attempting to define what constitutes an application output. For the purpose of this paper, it is some discrete entity whose provenance is logged.

- **Make a comment:** Additionally, for each application output, a user should be able to make a comment based on what they see. For each comment made, the PACT should register the following things, in addition to the comment itself: (i) information on the commenting user (e.g., name and email address), (ii) a provenance trace of the output they saw, going from the output to inputs, and (iii) an *glimpse* of the output as the user saw it, which could either be an image or a fully functional output reproduced for others to look at. These materials can help establish the context of a given user's comments for the greater web community.
- **Review comments:** Here, members of the web community can review comments made by given users. For each comment, the users will be able to see the comments, as well as three types of information described above.
- **Reply to a comment:** Upon reviewing a comment, users can reply to comments - yielding child comments or to the children of comments yielding discussion threads based on an original comment.

4   Exemplar Application: US Global Aid

Mashups are a kind of web-based application designed to integrate data and web services from different sources, yielding new functionality in the process. These kinds of web applications are particularly good candidates for provenance usage as it can often be unclear what data sources used to create the information presented in the interface [8]. To illustrate the use of PACTs in web applications, we present a basic mashup called US Global Aid[3]. This mashup, shown in Fig. 1, is designed leverage Semantic Web based resources to display two kinds of information:

- Foreign aid contributions made to individual countries in 2008 by the US Agency for International Development (USAID), derived from data hosted by the US Government website Data.gov[4]
- Facts for individual countries obtained from DBPedia.org. Here, population, Human Development Index (HDI) and Failed State Index (FSI) are presented[5].

To ensure the user community views this mashup as reliable, it needs to have mechanisms to preserve transparency, as well as the accountability of data it uses. This helps address two general issues: first, flaws may be present in mashup workflow itself that misrepresent content; second, the mashup output may change regularly due to changes in data sources.

---

[3] This mashup is a simplified version of the foreign aid mashup *US Global Aid*, hosted at http://www.data-gov.tw.rpi.edu/

[4] Specifically, Dataset 1554 is referenced: http://www.data.gov/raw/1554

[5] On DBPedia, these may be referenced for individual countries through the RDF properties dbpprop:populationEstimate, dbpprop:hdi and dbpprop:fsi respectively, where the namespace dbpprop is defined as http://dbpedia.org/property/

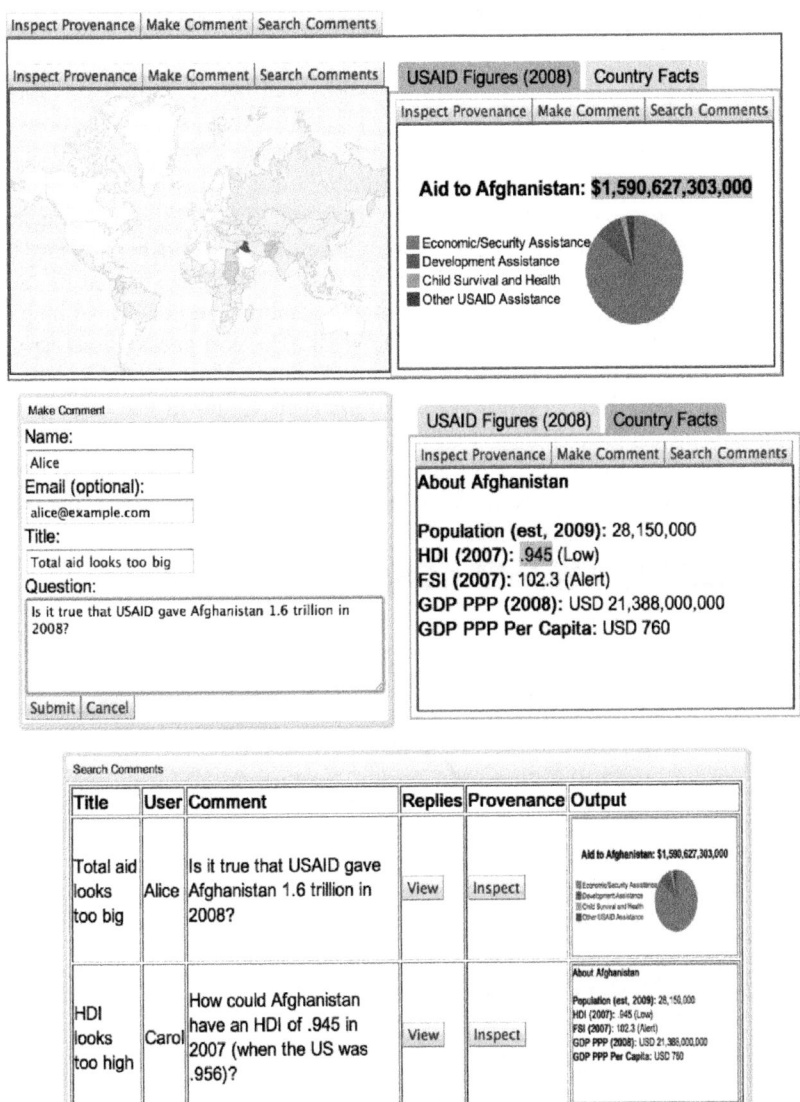

Fig. 1. Screenshots from the mashup US Global Aid. *Top:* A world map, shaded according to the amount of aid received by individual countries, along with aid figures for Afghanistan. This are the outputs seen by Alice in Use Case 1, in which Afghanistan is shown as receiving about 1.6 trillion from USAID. *Middle Left:* The "Make Comment" form that Alice uses to make her comment in Use Case 1 *Middle Right:* Country facts for Afghanistan that Carol Sees in Use Case 2, in which an HDI value of .945 is given. *Bottom:* The "Search Comments" interface used by Bob to find, and reply to, Alice and Carol's comments in Use Cases 1 and 2. Here, the search interface is displaying comments for the two different outputs that were commented on.

4.1   Use Case 1: Problem in Mashup

Here, a user Alice runs the mashup and sees that Afghanistan received about 1.6 trillion in 2008 - an amount which would constitute a significant portion of the US national debt [6]. Alice has little background with what provenance is, so she decides to simply make the comment: "Is it true USAID gave Afghanistan 1.6 trillion in 2008?". Following this, another user Bob decides to search for comments made on the Afghanistan figures and finds Alice's comment. Bob looks at the glimpse of the output Alice viewed, which is exactly what he sees on his execution of the application, and agrees the figure is suspicious. Since he has some background in the structure of this mashup, he decides to inspect the provenance of this output (Fig. 2). In doing this, he compares data retrieved as the result of a SPARQL query to a version of the data formatted for use in the visualization itself. Here, he notices the numerical values in the data record for Afghanistan are multiplied by 1,000, following the process *Format Data*. Bob concludes that the problem lies with this process, likely due to a unit conversion error, and replies accordingly to Alice that it is an application-specific problem.

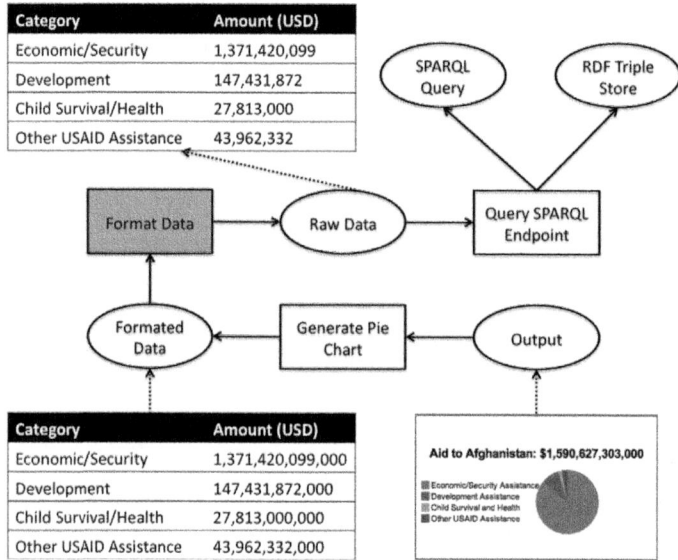

Fig. 2. An OPM-based[9] diagram of the provenance that Bob inspects in Use Case 1, with artifact values illustrated. Here, Bob isolates the problem to the "Format Data" process.

4.2   Use Case 2: Problem with Data

Here, another user Carol runs the mashup and sees that Afghanistan had an HDI value of .945 in 2007, which would place it among the world's most developed

---

[6] Approximately 13 trillion, as of June 2010.

countries. Like Alice from Use Case 1, Carol decides against viewing the provenance of this output, instead leaving the comment "How could Afghanistan have an HDI value of .945 in 2007?" Following this, Bob decides to search for comments made on the Afghanistan country facts and finds Carol's comment. Bob looks at the glimpse of the output Carol viewed, but it is different from what he sees - on his screen, Afghanistan's HDI is shown as .345, making it one of the least developed countries. He inspects the provenance of this output (Fig. 3), comparing data retrieved as the result of a SPARQL query to a version of the data formatted for use in the visualization itself. However, the HDI values in both data records are the same - meaning that the HDI value of .945 was obtained as a result of the SPARQL query to DBPedia[7]. Bob concludes that the problem most likely was with the data on DBPedia, possibly due to a typo or vandalism that was subsequently corrected, and replies to Carol that it is a data-specific problem. [9]

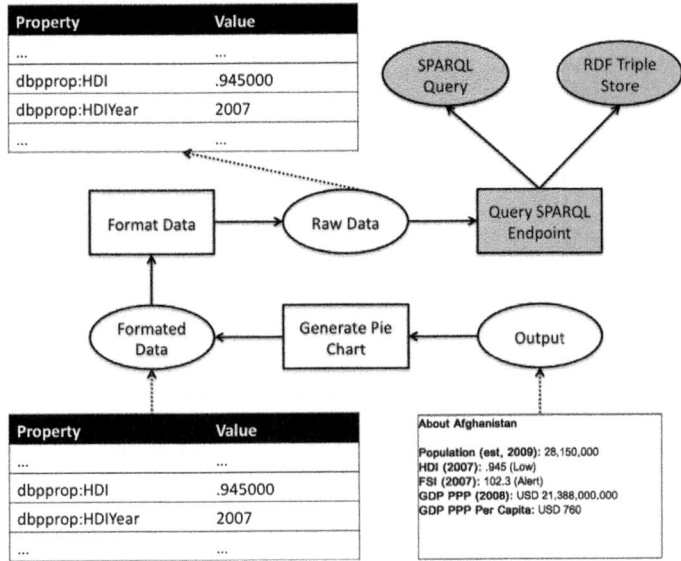

Fig. 3. An OPM-based diagram of the provenance that Bob inspects in Use Case 1, with artifact values illustrated. Here, Bob determines the problem lies before the "Raw Data" artifact.

5   Discussion and Conclusion

Currently, the PACT model is defined to express functionality similar to Amazon Mechanical Turk, and therefore faces similar requirements to effectively coordinate the crowdsourcing of tasks. Some of these requirements are discussed in[6], and include:

---

[7] Here, the mention of any specific error in the DBPedia corpus is hypothetical and done only for illustrative purposes.

- A need for constrained, verifiable problems for crowd members to solve. Else, answers provided by crowd members could simply be a matter of opinion, or guesses as to the answer.
- Determining the incentives for members of a web community to answer questions provided by other users.
- Mechanisms for preventing ineffective or malicious users from registering comments (or replies to comments).

While this paper doesn't discuss the implementation of specific technologies for a PACT, some recommendations are made

- *Information Structuring:* The goal of this would be to categorize users, as well as the comments/replies they make. Semantic Web languages, such as RDF and OWL, provide such functionality, and can be used in the creation of ontology-based classifications of information. In doing this, functionality
- *Viewing Provenance:* At present, a number of tools exist for reviewing provenance. Among these are Probe-It and IWBrowser [11], which are designed to view provenance encoded using the OWL-based Proof Markup Language (PML).

Achieving these goals will be important future work for refining the PACT model, as well as for implementing PACT instances in web applications.

References

1. Berners-Lee, T.: Cleaning up the User Interface (1997),
   http://www.w3.org/DesignIssues/UI.html
2. Biton, O., Cohen-Boulakia, S., Davidson, S., Hara, C.: Querying and managing provenance through user views in scientific workflows. In: Proceedings of ICDE (2008)
3. Brabham, D.: Crowdsourcing as a model for problem solving: An introduction and cases. Convergence 14(1), 75 (2008)
4. Freire, J., Silva, C., Callahan, S., Santos, E., Scheidegger, C., Vo, H.: Managing rapidly-evolving scientific workflows. Provenance and Annotation of Data, 10–18 (2006)
5. Groth, P., Miles, S., Moreau, L.: A model of process documentation to determine provenance in mash-ups. ACM Transactions on Internet Technology (TOIT) 9(1), 3 (2009)
6. Kittur, A., Chi, E., Suh, B.: Crowdsourcing user studies with Mechanical Turk. In: Proceeding of the Twenty-Sixth Annual SIGCHI Conference on Human Factors in Computing Systems, pp. 453–456. ACM, New York (2008)
7. Miles, S., Groth, P., Deelman, E., Vahi, K., Mehta, G., Moreau, L.: Provenance: The bridge between experiments and data. Computing in Science and Engineering 10(3), 38–46 (2008)
8. Moreau, L.: The Foundations for Provenance on the Web. Foundations and Trends in Web Science (2009)
9. Moreau, L., Clifford, B., Freire, J., Futrelle, J., Gil, Y., Groth, P., Kwasnikowska, N., Miles, S., Missier, P., Myers, J., Plale, B., Simmhan, Y., Stephan, E., den Bussche, J.V.: The open provenance model — core specification (v1.1). Future Generation Computer Systems (July 2010)

10. Santos, E., Lins, L., Ahrens, J., Freire, J., Silva, C., et al.: VisMashup: Streamlining the Creation of Custom Visualization Applications. IEEE Transactions on Visualization and Computer Graphics 15(6), 1539–1546 (2009)
11. Pinheiro da Silva, P., McGuinness, D., Del Rio, N., Ding, L.: Inference web in action: Lightweight use of the proof markup language. In: Sheth, A.P., Staab, S., Dean, M., Paolucci, M., Maynard, D., Finin, T., Thirunarayan, K. (eds.) ISWC 2008. LNCS, vol. 5318, pp. 847–860. Springer, Heidelberg (2008)
12. Simmhan, Y., Plale, B., Gannon, D.: Query capabilities of the Karma provenance framework. Concurrency and Computation: Practice and Experience 20(5), 441–451 (2008)
13. Snow, R., O'Connor, B., Jurafsky, D., Ng, A.: Cheap and fast—but is it good?: evaluating non-expert annotations for natural language tasks. In: Proceedings of the Conference on Empirical Methods in Natural Language Processing, pp. 254–263. Association for Computational Linguistics (2008)

Browsing Proof Markup Language Provenance: Enhancing the Experience

Nicholas Del Rio, Paulo Pinheiro da Silva, and Hugo Porras

The University of Texas at El Paso, Computer Science,
500 W. University Ave. El Paso TX 79968 USA

1 Introduction

Probe-It! is a browser that allows users to navigate through Proof Markup Language (PML) based provenance traces by interacting with a number of different perspectives or *views* [1]. These views provide specific renderings or presentations for the different kinds of provenance information defined in the PML ontology [2]. Throughout our three year experience with Probe-It! we have gathered requirements from users who have a need for browsing PML captured from theorem provers in the Thousands of Problems for Theorem Provers (TPTP) and Homeland Security domains as well as from scientific processes in areas such as solar astronomy, seismology, and environmental science. This paper briefly describes the enhancements made to Probe-It! to improve usability and performance with regards to visualization.

2 Usability

Probe-It!'s *global justification* view grants users visual access to a PML based provenance trace in its entirety. The global justification view renders PML justifications as a DAG, where nodesets are represented as graph nodes and the *hasAntecedent* relationships are represented by the arcs connecting nodesets. The nodesets composing the proof DAG are each represented as a box that contains a nodeset's conclusion. These DAGs have the potential to be very large, especially in the Thousands of Problems for Theorem Provers (TPTP) domain, where many of the proofs consist of hundreds of nodesets. In these cases providing users with options on how to navigate around these large provenance traces becomes essential. In fact, it was noted by a member of the TPTP community that his instinct was to "drag" around the global view justification canvas, which Probe-It! was not capable of. Probe-It! now addresses this limitation by now supporting *Google Earth-like* navigation capabilities rather than relying solely on a scrollable pane to move the DAG around. In addition users now have the ability to zoom in/out, abstract the information shown in the nodesets, a feature found in [4], or move around the graph by dragging on the canvas or using the *panner*.

D.L. McGuinness, J.R. Michaelis, and L. Moreau (Eds.): IPAW 2010, LNCS 6378, pp. 274–276, 2010.
© Springer-Verlag Berlin Heidelberg 2010

Another enhancement to Probe-It!, that we hope will increase the quality of users' experience, was the adoption of the Inference Web [3] group's *local* view. The local view presents both data transformation trace information (PML-J) and transformation trace metadata (PMP-J) associated with a single nodeset, where as the global justification view hides much of the PML-P information and puts more emphasis on presenting the structure of a justification as a whole. The information presented to users in the local view is categorized by: the selected nodeset's conclusion, how the selected nodeset was derived (antecedents, rule), what its conclusion is used to derive (consequents of), and what it is used to finally derive (final conclusion of proof). It is also possible to navigate to any other nodesets that were used to derive or are derived from the currently selected nodeset, through the use of *links*. Upon selection of new nodeset, the information presented in the local view is updated to reflect the newly selected nodeset. We are currently devising scenarios in which to measure the effectiveness of the local view in a scientific context, where nodeset conclusions are visualizable datasets rather than logical statements.

3   Performance: Preprocessed Views

In cases where PML traces are documenting derivations of scientific products rather than derivations of logical conclusions, Probe-It! may be required to transform nodeset conclusions captured in their raw form into a complex visualization that a scientist is familiar with or expecting. Because performing these transformations in viewing time can really slow down the global justification browsing experience, we have employed a preprocessing system that caches any visualization that can be generated from nodeset conclusions. In fact, as soon as any PML nodeset is written to our file system, the cacher can be initiated and thus can be run in parallel with the execution of the workflow being audited.

The importance of such a caching system was first realized when we attempted to browse the PML capturing a run of Hole's code (an iterative process used for modeling the Earth's crust by seismologists) in the global view. In this case, Probe-It! was required to generate a Visualization Toolkit (VTK) based visualization for each of the 300 nodesets composing the trace. From our experiences, we have learned that seismologists prefer to inspect Hole's code datasets visually, and so it is not useful for them to have access to provenance when verifying if their models have converged, if they cannot visualize them.

References

1. del Rio, N., da Silva, P.P.: Probe-it! visualization support for provenance. In: Proceedings of the Second International Symposium on Visual Computing (ISVC 2), Lake Tahoe, NV, pp. 732–741. Springer, Heidelberg (2007)
2. McGuinness, D., Ding, L., da Silva, P.P., Chang, C.: PML2: A Modular Explanation Interlingua. In: Proceedings of the AAAI 2007 Workshop on Explanation-aware Computing, Vancouver, British Columbia, Canada, July 22-23 (2007)

3. McGuinness, D.L., da Silva, P.P.: Inference Web: Portable and Sharable Explanations for Question Answering. In: Proc. of the AAAI Spring Symposium Workshop on New Directions for Question Answering, Stanford, CA, USA, March 2003, pp. 67–71. AAAI Press, Menlo Park (2003)
4. Trac, S., Puzis, Y., Sutcliffe, G.: An interactive derivation viewer. In: Proceedings of the 7th Workshop on Workshop on User Interfaces for Theorem Provers, 3rd International Joint Conference on Automated Reasoning. Electronic Notes in Theoretical Computer Science, vol. 174, pp. 109–123 (2006)

Towards a Threat Model for Provenance in e-Science

Luiz M.R. Gadelha Jr.[1], Marta Mattoso[1], Michael Wilde[2], and Ian Foster[2]

[1] Computer and Systems Engineering Program
Federal University of Rio de Janeiro, Brazil
{gadelha,marta}@cos.ufrj.br
[2] Computation Institute
University of Chicago / Argonne National Laboratory, USA
{wilde,foster}@mcs.anl.gov

Abstract. Scientists increasingly rely on workflow management systems to perform large-scale computational scientific experiments. These systems often collect provenance information that is useful in the analysis and reproduction of such experiments. On the other hand, this provenance data may be exposed to security threats which can result, for instance, in compromising the analysis of these experiments, or in illegitimate claims of attribution. In this work, we describe our ongoing work to trace security requirements for provenance systems in the context of e-Science, and propose some security controls to fulfill them.

1 Introduction

As an important paradigm of scientific research, computer simulations are increasingly being used to perform computational scientific experiments. As the scale of these experiments increase, scientific workflow management systems become a relevant tool to specify, execute, and analyze them. These systems can collect provenance information, often distributed in grids or remote clusters, that is useful in the analysis and reproduction of such experiments. If the appropriate security controls are not in place, provenance systems may be exposed to threats that may compromise the integrity, confidentiality, or availability of provenance data. In this work, we describe our ongoing work to trace security requirements for provenance systems in the context of e-Science, and propose some security controls to fulfill them. The study of security issues in provenance systems is relatively recent. However, some important security requirements, described in section 2, were not yet identified in related academic works, to our knowledge. In section 3, we conclude describing subsequent steps in our provenance security research.

2 Security Requirements for Provenance Systems

The typical execution of a workflow involves specifying its flow using some mechanism, such as a parallel scripting language or a GUI-based workflow specification tool. Later on, it can be executed by a workflow management system, this involves selecting appropriate computational resources, submitting tasks to these resources, and transferring data. After the experiment is executed, scientists typically face the challenge of analyzing a large number of output data files to understand the outcome of the

D.L. McGuinness, J.R. Michaelis, and L. Moreau (Eds.): IPAW 2010, LNCS 6378, pp. 277–279, 2010.

experiment, provenance systems are useful in this context since they can help to determine, for instance, which tasks where executed to generate a particular data object, and which parameters were used for these tasks. This provenance data is usually collected and stored during workflow execution, to describe causal relationships between tasks and data (retrospective provenance); or during workflow specification, to describe the planned tasks, and data flow (prospective provenance). In general, provenance data is accessed and analyzed by scientists using a query language, such as SQL. In our ongoing threat modeling effort, we are enumerating threats to each of these components of a provenance system. Many of these are already taken into account by security frameworks for underlying technologies used by provenance systems, such as databases and grids. Provenance security is a relatively recent research issue [12] [7] [14], found in different areas such as scientific workflows, databases, and storage systems. Provenance data is useful in security audits [1], and there are cases in which the subject of provenance data may lead to privacy concerns [3]. Braun et al. [2] analyze the problem of providing adequate access control techniques to provenance data, observing that it describes causal relationships, that are not adequately protected by commonly used access control techniques. Hasan et al. [9] [8] propose a security solution with the goal of protecting confidentiality and integrity of provenance data. They use asymmetric cryptography for achieving confidentiality and signature-based checksums for achieving integrity. Nagappan et al. [10] present a model for sharing provenance data that uses role-based access control techniques where the user dynamically select its confidentiality level. A common approach for protecting provenance information [2] [10] [11] is to use access control mechanisms to prevent unauthorized access to this information. None of these approaches allow for non-restricted dissemination of provenance information with maintenance of correct attribution, a requirement in the context of e-Science. Scientists, specially in the life sciences, often avoid sharing details of experiments prior to publishing their results in some academic journal or event, to assure correct attribution of scientific results. During this interval, scientific collaboration is prevented. Therefore, security controls that prevent illegitimate claims of attribution are an important security requirement for provenance systems. These controls must allow the verification of not only who executed an experiment but also when it was executed. A combination of digital signatures and cryptographic timestamps [6] were used in the Kairos [5] security architecture for provenance systems to provide these properties. Another desirable security property is fine-grained access control, where scientists can delegate to their collaborators access to provenance data, so it can be read or modified.

3   Concluding Remarks

This work describes our progress in defining a threat model and proposing security controls for provenance systems in the context of e-Science. We identify the assurance of correct attribution of scientific results as an important security requirement for these systems. For this purpose, we proposed Kairos [5], a security architecture for provenance that uses cryptographic timestamps [6] and digital signatures. We are working with the Swift [13] parallel scripting system to extend its provenance system [4] with appropriate security controls. As future work, we will investigate fine-grained access control techniques, and a data model to store and query security properties.

Acknowledgement

This work was supported in part by CAPES, CNPq, NSF grant OCI-0944332, and the Office of Advanced Scientific Computing Research, Office of Science, U.S. Department of Energy, under Contract DE-AC02-06CH11357.

References

1. Aldeco-Pérez, R., Moreau, L.: Provenance-based Auditing of Private Data Use. In: Proc. of the BCS International Academic Research Conference, Visions of Computer Science (2008)
2. Braun, U., Shinnar, A., Seltzer, M.: Securing Provenance. In: Proc. 3rd USENIX Workshop on Hot Topics in Security, HotSec 2008 (2008)
3. Davidson, S., Khanna, S., Roy, S., Cohen-Boulakia, S.: Privacy Issues in Scientific Workflow Provenance. In: Proceedings of the 1st International Workshop on Workflow Approaches to New Data-centric Science, WANDS 2010 (2010)
4. Gadelha, L., Clifford, B., Mattoso, M., Wilde, M., Foster, I.: Provenance Management in Swift. Future Generation Computer Systems (2010) (in press, accepted manuscript)
5. Gadelha, L., Mattoso, M.: Kairos: An Architecture for Securing Authorship and Temporal Information of Provenance Data in Grid-Enabled Workflow Management Systems. In: Proc. 4th IEEE International Conference on e-Science (e-Science 2008), pp. 597–602 (2008)
6. Haber, S., Stornetta, W.: How to Time-Stamp a Digital Document. Journal of Cryptology 3(2), 99–111 (1991)
7. Hasan, R., Sion, R., Winslett, M.: Introducing Secure Provenance: Problems and Challenges. In: Proc. 2007 ACM Workshop on Storage Security and Survivability (StorageSS 2009), pp. 13–18 (2007)
8. Hasan, R., Sion, R., Winslett, M.: Preventing history forgery with secure provenance. ACM Transactions on Storage 5(4), 1–43 (2009)
9. Hasan, R., Sion, R., Winslett, M.: The Case of the Fake Picasso: Preventing History Forgery with Secure Provenance. In: Proc. 7th USENIX Conference on File and Storage Technologies (FAST 2009), pp. 1–14 (2009)
10. Nagappan, M., Vouk, M.: A Model for Sharing of Confidential Provenance Information in a Query Based System. In: Freire, J., Koop, D., Moreau, L. (eds.) IPAW 2008. LNCS, vol. 5272, pp. 62–69. Springer, Heidelberg (2008)
11. Ni, Q., Xu, S., Bertino, E., Sandhu, R., Han, W.: An Access Control Language for a General Provenance Model. In: Jonker, W., Petković, M. (eds.) Secure Data Management. LNCS, vol. 5776, pp. 68–88. Springer, Heidelberg (2009)
12. Tan, V., Groth, P., Miles, S., Jiang, S., Munroe, S., Tsasakou, S., Moreau, L.: Security Issues in a SOA-Based Provenance System. In: Moreau, L., Foster, I. (eds.) IPAW 2006. LNCS, vol. 4145, pp. 203–211. Springer, Heidelberg (2006)
13. Wilde, M., Foster, I., Iskra, K., Beckman, P., Espinosa, A., Hategan, M., Clifford, B., Raicu, I.: Parallel Scripting for Applications at the Petascale and Beyond. IEEE Computer 42(11), 50–60 (2009)
14. Xu, S., Ni, Q., Bertino, E., Sandhu, R.: A Characterization of The Problem of Secure Provenance Management. In: Proc. IEEE International Conference on Intelligence and Security Informatics (ISI 2009), pp. 310–314 (2009)

Provenance Support for Content Management Systems: A Drupal Example

Aída Gándara and Paulo Pinheiro da Silva*

University of Texas at El Paso, Computer Science Department,
El Paso, Texas 79968, USA
agandara1@miners.utep.edu, paulo@utep.edu

Abstract. Provenance helps with understanding data but without proper tools to share and access content, its reusability is limited. This paper describes the CI-Server framework currently being used to help scientific teams seamlessly share data and provenance about scientific research. CI-Server has been built using Drupal, a content management server workbench, with a focus on publishing and understanding the semantic content that is now available over the Web. By focusing on an open framework, scientists publish provenance related to their scientific research then leverage the semantic knowledge to understand and visualize the information.

1 Introduction

Regardless of how useful provenance is for capturing knowledge related to scientific research, how provenance is managed, e.g. how to access provenance-related information, can greatly affect its reusability. For example, for some scientists, research is performed on a single workstation and the results, data and data-related provenance, are stored on the same system. Consequently, most information including provenance is restricted to only scientists with specific privileges to access that workstation. As a result of such isolated environments, data and provenance are not shared. Web portals, Web sites focused on collecting and sharing data and resources, normally within a particular domain, provide a solution for scientists to share their data and make it available to other scientists. For example, the Earthscope Data Portal[3] is a Web portal built to enable sharing and discovery of geological data. One drawback to portals is that in many cases publishing data on them is a manual process; a user interactively uploads directly to a portal location or requests administrative support from the portal's webmaster. Portals can be quite unique in their presentation and usage, i.e. the management of resources and the process of uploading files is different for every portal. As searches span across multiple Web portals, scientists are forced into understanding the multiple cultures of different Web portals. The GEO portal[4], for example, has a similar focus as the Earthscope portal, yet the interface and

---

* This work was supported in part by DHS grant 2008-ST-062-000007 and by NSF grant HRD-0734825.

D.L. McGuinness, J.R. Michaelis, and L. Moreau (Eds.): IPAW 2010, LNCS 6378, pp. 280–282, 2010.

structure of the site is quite different. The distinct steps of understanding the culture of the portal and manually uploading information can be distracting to scientists' needs to share and discover information. One proposed solution is to unify several related data archives onto one, e.g. the Earthscope portal. Our solution is to focus more on building a structure into content management servers so tools can access the needed information, data and provenance-related data, without having to access one portal or understand the nuances of each portal's interface.

2   Provenance Support for Drupal

Drupal is an open source content management server framework used to build Web sites and Web portals. The tool supports user security and multiple levels of configuration, e.g. menu calls, forms, and event hooks. The Drupal Development Community is currently a very active component of Drupal because developers share software solutions that can be enabled in different Drupal implementations.[2] We have built additional functionality in Drupal, providing provenance support based on the PML notation[5] in an open-portal based infrastructure we call the CI-Server. Our implementation uses and extends various modules provided by the Drupal Development Community in an effort to facilitate the sharing of information and reuse of provenance for scientific research.

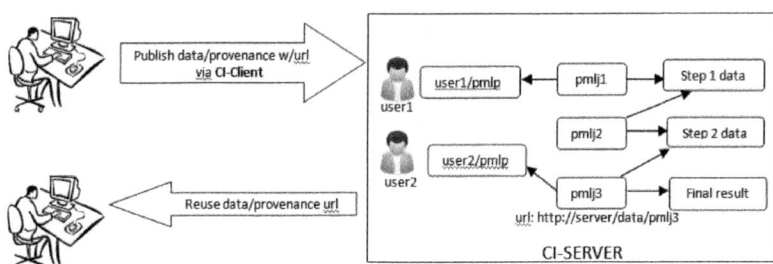

Fig. 1. The CI-Server Framework enables sharing of provenance

Figure 1 illustrates the provenance support enabled by the CI-Server framework. Via a CI-Client module and CI-Client API that extend and expose internal server functionality, scientific tools can be enabled to seamlessly publish data and provenance (pmlj) files, moving data from the scientist's workstation to any Drupal based CI-Server. This avoids the manual step of file uploads or the nuances of understanding different portal interfaces. In Figure 1, the top scientist has published pmlj1, pmlj2, pmlj3, called a PML nodeset, and some corresponding data. The pmlj documents are semantic documents, written in OWL. These documents are built with knowledge about how a scientific process occurred and they rely on links to available resources, e.g. data. The CI-Server uses modules to support file management and url aliasing, enabling users to upload content and then access it via url links. Since the pmlj documents contain references to entities that it is capturing provenance about, provenance knowledge is immediately available to traverse as a knowledge set. Furthermore, the CI-Server manages content and information that is often useful in capturing provenance. For example, user content on Drupal can be used to document source related information, e.g. who published a data file. The CI-Server builds pmlp nodes for users on the system. To see a user's public information, the user's pmlp page would be accessed via a dynamically created OWL-based pmlp node. Building provenance dynamically with internal CI-Server knowledge, aids in the collection of provenance and avoids scientists from having to supply that information repetitively. Figure 1 shows that pmlj1 captures the knowledge that user 1 was involved in creating Step 1 data and that pmlj2 captures the knowledge that Step 1 data was an input to create Step 2 data and finally that pmlj3 captures the knowledge that user 2 and Step 2 data were used to create the Final result. Because pmlj3 is identified with an URL, the scientist reusing the information can use the url link to access the entire provenance nodeset and visualize it using context-related scientific tools. A PML nodeset, for example, can be visualized via Probe-It[1] by simply providing the nodeset's URI.

References

1. Del Rio, N., da Silva, P.P.: Probe-it! visualization support for provenance. In: Bebis, G., Boyle, R., Parvin, B., Koracin, D., Paragios, N., Tanveer, S.-M., Ju, T., Liu, Z., Coquillart, S., Cruz-Neira, C., Müller, T., Malzbender, T. (eds.) ISVC 2007, Part II. LNCS, vol. 4842, pp. 732–741. Springer, Heidelberg (2007)
2. Drupal community innitiatives, http://drupal.org/community-initiatives
3. Earthscope data portal, http://earthscope.data.porta
4. Geo-portal, http://geoportal.org
5. McGuinness, D., Ding, L., da Silva, P.P., Chang, C.: PML2: A Modular Explanation Interlingua. In: Proceedings of the AAAI 2007 Workshop on Explanation-aware Computing, Vancouver, British Columbia, Canada, July 22-23 (2007)

ProvenanceJS: Revealing the Provenance of Web Pages

Paul Groth

VU University Amsterdam
De Boelelaan 1081a, 1081 HV, Amsterdam, The Netherlands
pgroth@few.vu.nl

Abstract. Web pages are regularly constructed through combining content from multiple providers (e.g. photos from Flickr, quotes from the New York Times). As a result, it is often difficult for users and programmers to retrieve the provenance of a web page. Here, we present a JavaScript library, ProvenanceJS, that allows for the retrieval and visualization of the provenance information within a Web page and its embedded content. A key contribution is to demonstrate that provenance can be supported using widely deployed browser-based technologies.

There has been a rapid proliferation of content sharing on the Web. Sites such as Flickr, Slideshare.net, and YouTube make it easier to find and then integrate images, video, and documents into web pages. Additionally, the cultural of the Web, in particular the blogsphere, thrives on quoting and re-quoting information. Because of this mash-up culture and infrastructure, most web pages consist of content originating from multiple sources. Thus, when viewing a web page it is often difficult to determine where its content came from and how it was produced. This lack of provenance is seen as a critical issue in both the provenance and Web communities as highlighted by the start of the W3C Provenance Incubator Group and its recently produced report on requirements for provenance on the Web [3]. In particular, provenance is one of the most import features users rely on when determining whether to trust a Web page [4]. Indeed, Tim Berners-Lee envisioned an "Oh, yeah?" button within Web browsers that when clicked on would produce reasons why the user should trust the web page based on its provenance [1].

To move towards the realization of such an "Oh, yeah?" button that is widely distributed, we have developed a library, ProvenanceJS[1], that allows for the retrieval and visualization of the provenance of a web page. There are two key contributions stemming from ProvenanceJS:

1. Browser-based technologies are capable of retrieving and rendering provenance information without the need for additional software installation.
2. Embedding provenance information within content is a viable approach for ensuring that the provenance information is available.

---

[1] Source available at: `http://code.google.com/p/opmv/source/browse/#svn/trunk/js`

D.L. McGuinness, J.R. Michaelis, and L. Moreau (Eds.): IPAW 2010, LNCS 6378, pp. 283–285, 2010.
© Springer-Verlag Berlin Heidelberg 2010

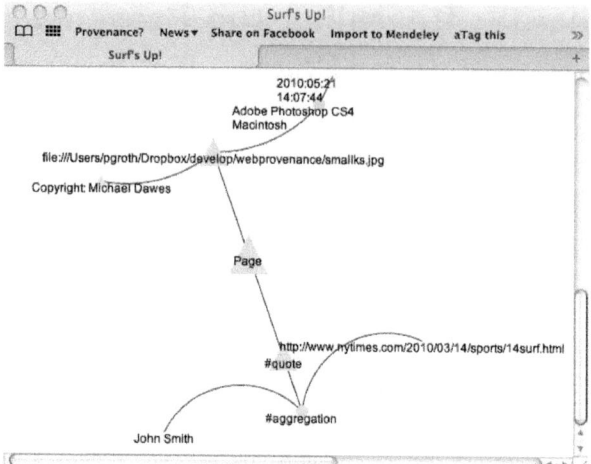

Fig. 1. A visualization of the provenance of a Web page

1   Provenance Metadata and Implementation

In order to make provenance apparent to the user, ProvenanceJS must retrieve provenance information from a Web page. It can acquire this information either from interrogating the page's metadata, extracting the metadata of the embedded content (e.g. an image), or by consulting an outside service that maintains the provenance. Because our aim was to develop a browser-based solution, we chose to focus on the first two sources.

From a page's markup, ProvenanceJS extracts RDFa metadata. RDFa is a widely adopted standard for embedding structured data within web pages. ProvenanceJS recognizes RDFa published using the Open Provenance Model Vocabulary [9]. This vocabulary is an RDF realization of the Open Provenance Model (OPM) [8] with a number of extensions and is being actively developed to help address the needs of data.gov.uk. Using this vocabulary, publishers can markup their data with explicit statements about the provenance of the various parts of their page.

While explicit provenance metadata within Web pages is advantageous, many times it is not practically feasible to provide it explicitly. To address this concern, ProvenanceJS aims to extract provenance metadata from a page's content. For example, ProvenanceJS can extract information from the EXIF metadata found within JPEG images.

ProvenanceJS is implemented entirely in Javascript using the Javascript Info-Vis Toolkit, rdfQuery, and exif.js. In addition to the extraction of the metadata described above, it provides an API for building and manipulating OPM Graphs and visualizing those graphs. A bookmarklet ('Provenance?') is included, which visualizes the current web page's provenance. An example is shown in Figure 1. Triangle nodes are artifacts. Circle nodes are processes. It shows how the quote on a page was generated by an aggregation process controlled by John Smith. In addition, it depicts that the image was modified by Adobe Photoshop and that the copyright of the image belongs to Michael Dawes. The bookmarklet is a first step towards a true "Oh, yeah?" button.

2   Related Work and Conclusion

Moreau provides an extensive review of the provenance literature from the perspective of the Web [7]. A number of authors have considered provenance on the Semantic Web. In particular, Bizer et al. present a Semantic Web based policy framework for information quality [2]. It included an implementation of the "Oh, yeah?" button. However, this implementation required a browser plug-in. We see ProvenanceJS as building on-top of such existing Semantic Web approaches. Margo and Seltzer showed how by treating user interaction with a Web browser as provenance, novel search functionality could be realized [6]. The closest work to ProvenanceJS is the Provenance-Embedding Document approach [5]. This approach uses Javascript to extract provenance from RDFa metadata. Our work differs in that we support the extraction of provenance from embedded content and use a community driven provenance vocabulary.

ProvenanceJS can be used to retrieve and visualize the provenance of a web page using only browser-based technology, namely Javascript. Additionally, provenance metadata from page markup and embedded content can be integrated to provide a full view of provenance.

References

1. Berners-Lee, T.: Cleaning up the User Interface (1997), http://www.w3.org/DesignIssues/UI.html
2. Bizer, C., Cyganiak, R.: Quality-driven information filtering using the WIQA policy framework. Web Semantics: Science, Services and Agents on the World Wide Web 7(1), 1–10 (2009)
3. Cheney, J., Gil, Y., Groth, P.E., Miles, S.: Requirements for Provenance on the Web (2010), http://www.w3.org/2005/Incubator/prov/wiki/User_Requirements
4. Gil, Y., Artz, D.: Towards content trust of web resources. Journal of Web Semantics 5(4), 227–239
5. Jones, H.C.: XHTML documents with inline, policy-aware provenance. M. eng., Massachusetts Institute of Technology (2007)
6. Margo, D.W., Seltzer, M.: The Case for Browser Provenance. In: 1st Workshop on the Theory and Practice of Provenance, TaPP 2009 (2009)
7. Moreau, L.: Foundations of Provenance on the Web. Foundations and Trends in Web Science (2009) (submitted)
8. Moreau, L., Clifford, B., Freire, J., Futrelle, J., Gil, Y., Groth, P., Kwasnikowska, N., Miles, S., Missier, P., Myers, J., Plale, B., Simmhan, Y., Stephan, E., den Bussche, J.V.: The open provenance model — core specification (v1.1). In: Future Generation Computer Systems (July 2010)
9. Zhao, J.: Guide to the Open Provenance Model Vocabulary (2010), http://purl.org/net/opmv/guide

Integrating Provenance Data from Distributed Workflow Systems with ProvManager[*]

Anderson Marinho[1], Leonardo Murta[2], Cláudia Werner[1], Vanessa Braganholo[1],
Eduardo Ogasawara[1], Sérgio Manuel Serra da Cruz[1], and Marta Mattoso[1]

[1] Federal University of Rio de Janeiro
[2] Fluminense Federal University
{andymarinho,werner,ogasawara,serra,marta}@cos.ufrj.br,
leomurta@ic.uff.br, braganholo@dcc.ufrj.br

Abstract. Running scientific workflows in distributed environments is moti-
vating the definition of provenance gathering approaches that are loosely coupled to the workflow execution engine. This kind of approach is interesting because it allows both storage and access to provenance data in an integrated way,
even in an environment where different workflow systems work together.
Therefore, we have proposed a provenance gathering strategy that is independent from the workflow system technology. This strategy has evolved into a
provenance management system named ProvManager. In this paper we show
how provenance data is captured along in a distributed execution environment
with ProvManager and we show its web interface, in which scientists can register experiments, monitor workflow execution, and query provenance data.

Keywords: provenance, scientific workflows, distributed environment.

1 Introduction

Provenance provides historical information about data manipulated in a workflow [1].
This historical information tells us how data products were generated, showing their
transformation processes from primary input and intermediary data. The management
of provenance information provides to the scientists a variety of data analyses, such as
data quality, audit trails, and experiment documentation [2]. Provenance gathering
becomes more complex when the workflow is executed among distributed and heterogeneous execution environments, such as clusters, P2P, grids and clouds.

One can foresee several scenarios of workflow execution in a distributed environment [3]. Each one has its own characteristics that contribute to the complexity of
provenance management. In this paper we focus in a scenario where pre-existing
workflows were conceived independently, using different scientific workflow management systems (SWfMS). However, these independent workflows needed to be
integrated into a complex experiment, which entail some additional manual activities
that link such workflows. In this scenario, each SWfMS may manage provenance
information in a decentralized and isolated way, meaning that each system considers

---

[*] This work was partially sponsored by CNPq and CAPES.

D.L. McGuinness, J.R. Michaelis, and L. Moreau (Eds.): IPAW 2010, LNCS 6378, pp. 286–288, 2010.

provenance in a specific granularity, stores the information on a specific language, or even worse, some SWfMS may not even provide a provenance solution at all.

Therefore, a solution to this heterogeneity is to transfer the responsibility of provenance management to an independent provenance system. This system would be responsible for capturing, modeling, storing, and providing queries to an integrated provenance management system of an experiment. The main difficulty of the SWfMS agnostic strategy is that the SWfMS and the provenance management system need to communicate to exchange information. In order to make this communication possible, some solutions [4,5] propose a series of manual activity adaptations over the workflow specification. However, this solution introduces additional overhead to scientists. Some workflow activities used by scientists are third-party codes, which make their adaptation more complex. In many cases, these activities cannot be altered, but only wrapped by other activities.

For that reason, in our previous work [3] we have proposed a strategy for gathering provenance information in a distributed environment. This strategy is independent of workflow system technology and tries to address some problems discussed here. This strategy has evolved into a provenance management system named ProvManager. In addition to the gathering mechanism, ProvManager provides means for modeling, storing, and querying an integrated provenance repository.

2 ProvManager

The main focus of ProvManager system is to manage provenance in distributed environments. The main idea is to work as a central repository that stores all the provenance data generated from an experiment. The provenance data are collected by automatically adapting the workflow. Workflow activities are thus configured to send this information via a web services API during the workflow execution.

Figure 1.a illustrates the experiment structure that we use as an example for describing the ProvManager's functionalities. This experiment is segmented in two workflows: one workflow is instantiated in VisTrails, and the other in Kepler. Fig. 1.b shows a fragment of the workflow in VisTrails with more details. The fragment is composed by three activities: *GetData*, *Validate*, and *Simulate*, running on a remote host with IP address 192.168.0.5. In order to capture provenance data from this workflow, the scientist has to publish it in ProvManager, uploading the workflow specification (in the VisTrails case, a .VT file). At this moment, ProvManager configures the workflow, automatically adding special activities that will be responsible for capturing and publishing provenance data in ProvManager (this process is described in [3]) during workflow execution. This process of adding provenance components in the workflow is called instrumentation. At present moment, ProvManager can instrument only workflows executed in Kepler and VisTrails. However, ProvManager works with the concept of plugin to be able to support future extensions of other SWfMS instrumentation mechanisms. Finally, at the end of the instrumentation, a new .VT file is returned to the scientist to be reloaded in VisTrails. During both the instrumentation and execution of the workflow, ProvManager captures provenance data from the workflow and publishes this data in the repository. This repository is a Prolog database, so provenance data are mapped into Prolog predicates. Fig. 1.c shows the .VT file mapped into prolog predicates.

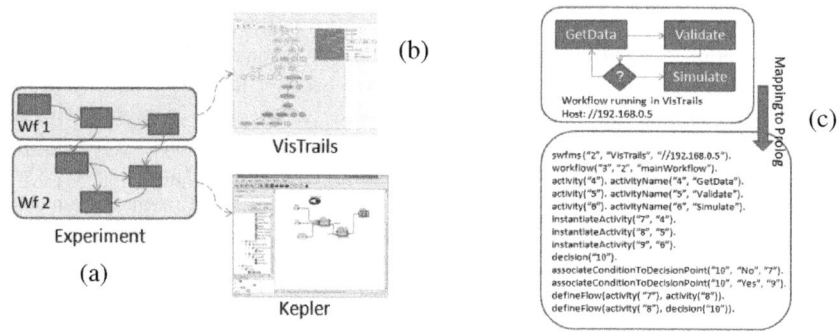

Fig. 1. Experiment example (a), and VisTrails workflow (b) mapped to Prolog predicates (c)

With all the provenance data collected from the experiment, ProvManager makes the experiment analysis process simpler to the scientist since it works as an integrated place for accessing the provenance data, avoiding scientist to visit individually each system responsible for gathering provenance (in our example, Kepler and VisTrails) in a distributed execution environment. Besides, ProvManager provides functionalities to help the scientist manipulate the experiment provenance data, such as high-level provenance query interface, and workflow execution monitoring (Fig. 2).

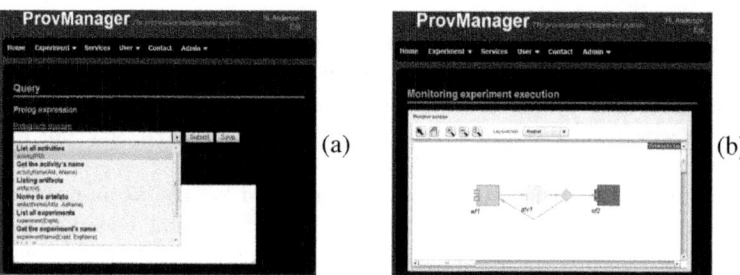

Fig. 2. ProvManager's screens: (a) Query interface; (b) Execution monitoring

References

[1] Freire, J., Koop, D., et al.: Provenance for Computational Tasks: A Survey. Computing in Science and Engineering 10(3), 11–21 (2008)
[2] Simmhan, Y.L., Plale, B., Gannon, D.: A survey of data provenance in e-science. ACM SIGMOD Record 34(3), 31–36 (2005)
[3] Marinho, A., Murta, L., et al.: A Strategy for Provenance Gathering in Distributed Scientific Workflows. In: IEEE International Workshop on Scientific Workflows, Los Angeles, California, United States (2009)
[4] Simmhan, Y., Plale, B., Gannon, D.: A Framework for Collecting Provenance in Data-Centric Scientific Workflows. In: ICWS, pp. 427–436 (2006)
[5] Groth, P., Jiang, S., et al.: An Architecture for Provenance Systems (2006), http://eprints.ecs.soton.ac.uk/13216/ (Visited in: July 19, 2010)

Using Data Lineage for Sub-image Processing

Johnson Mwebaze[1,2], John McFarland[2], Danny Boxhoorn[2],
Hugo Buddelmeijer[2], and Edwin Valentijn[2]

[1] Makerere University, P.O. Box 7062, Kampala, Uganda
[2] University of Groningen, Landleven 12, 9700 AV Groningen, The Netherlands

Abstract. In the paper, we show that lineage data collected during the processing and analysis of datasets can be reused to perform selective reprocessing (at sub-image level) on datasets while the remainder of the dataset is untouched, a rather difficult process to automate without lineage.

1 Introduction

In some scientific applications, most often users are interested in a source (e.g., moving, variable, or extreme in some colour index) that lies on a few pixels of an image. The approach adopted by most observation systems is processing the entire image or set of images even when the sole source of interest may exist on only a few pixels of one or a few images [6] [1]. Accordingly, out of millions of images in a survey, it is nearly impossible and wasteful to process the whole data volume. Instead of processing the whole dataset, a user should only select, retrieve and process only relevant pixels on an image where the source exists. However pipelines have been written and designed for instruments with fixed detector properties (e.g.,image size, calibration frames, overscan regions, etc.). All metadata and processing parameters are based on an instruments or a detector, moreover some image operations can not be done on a sub-image level.

Therefore, to perform processing at sub-image level, we make use of lineage data to assemble the sub-image processing pipeline and to select all necessary inputs to the pipeline. By matching and retrieving existing pre-processed information in the system and knowing the relationship between what we want to process and what has been processed before, we are then able to determine the difference between pipelines (and objects). We can then modify any new pipelines/objects/parameters so that the new processing follows the new user processing requirements for a particular region on the image.

Data lineage (provenance) is a well-defined problem with known solutions as pointed out in recent workshops [4] and surveys [5]. The use of provenance has also gained significant attention [4]. Several workflow management systems (e.g [2,3,7,9]) do exploit provenance information for different purposes. To the best of our knowledge, this is the first work that leverages lineage information to support sub-image processing to simplify and automate the reprocessing of objects. Since we are working with pixels, this framework required lineage at pixel level. We extended our lineage model presented in [8] to trace lineage at pixel level and then used pixel lineage for sub-image processing.

D.L. McGuinness, J.R. Michaelis, and L. Moreau (Eds.): IPAW 2010, LNCS 6378, pp. 289–291, 2010.

2   Sub-image Processing

Sub-image processing requires the ability to store and mine provenance data. Since no input data, metadata and parameters exists for sub-images, we use data from previous runs to enable sub-image processing. The underlying assumption is that the target has been processed before as part of a full image and probably a user would like to carry out a detailed analysis or a computation to a target that lies on few pixels of an image (or sub-image). The pipeline for sub-image processing is thus built based on lineage data. Likewise all input data, attributes and parameters to be used in the subimage pipeline is selected from the same lineage data. However, since we are processing a sub-image, some of the input data, parameters and parts of the pipelines have to be modified. When such changes occur then the part of pipeline affected by the changes must be re-run. The rerun will take data dependencies into account and only execute those parts of the workflow affected by the changes.

The starting point of sub-image processing is the selection of the target. i.e. set of sky positions. The system then builds a directed graph representing the data dependencies with nodes representing objects and edges representing all dependencies attached to an object. The graph begins with the topmost node, which is the target to be made. New edges are added starting at this trigger and expanding outward, using the dependency logic derived from lineage data. The dependency graph is built and checked recursively till the last dependency (in this case raw data from the telescope).

Each node in the graph is associated to an object. Each object is identified with a unique ID. Using this unique ID, we can query for all data that went into the processing of the object. The queried data is modified and used as input to the sub-image pipeline. This data also includes the software code and version that was used. If a unique ID is associated with an image, a cutout is made of the pixels of interest from this image and used as input to the module. The pixels extracted as a cutout are determined through pixel lineage.

However, in some cases input to the sub-image pipeline might be selected from any other related processing. For example, a critical step for astronomical processing is deriving an astrometric solution. This is derived by fitting distortion polynomials to images, taking into account the objects seen. For accurate results, several reference stars are used to derive the final solution. For the case of sub-image processing, such a process would fail since reference stars on the sub-image will be very few. Therefore, in such cases, we use the astrometric solution of another set of images of the same field, processed using the same parameters as needed to process the sub-image. The solution is then modified and fitted to the pixels of the sub-image.

After assembling the pipeline and collecting all necessary input data, the sub-image is processed. Source extraction is then run on the sub-image resulting in a new catalog of sky positions, and/or any other user specific processing done on the sources extracted.

3   Use Case: Analyzing Transitioning Galaxies

We demonstrate the use of provenance using a usecase of analyzing transitioning galaxies. These are galaxies that fall into galaxy clusters that interact with their environment. Initially a full image is processed and an initial photometric catalog of the sources on the image is extracted. The density of galaxies around each source is calculated using the galaxy position. The magnitudes and densities of galaxies that undergo a transitional phase can be identified. During processing of the full image the system records all lineage for this task and therefore a provenance graph can be queried and displayed for this image. Out of hundreds of galaxies that were observed in this processing only transitioning galaxies will then be further analyzed by extracting sub-images from the raw images where these galaxies lie and reprocessing only these sub-images to estimate more complex and time consuming parameters such as quantifications of the internal structure of the galaxy. To identify the images required for this task and the position of the galaxy in all images, we work backwards from the galaxy through all the dependencies. The other inputs (any other sub-images, calibration objects, processing parameters, etc) to the sub-image pipeline are also selected from the initial lineage recorded during the initial processing of the full image. By performing selective processing we save hours/days/weeks of computational time.

References

1. Astro-wise portal, http://www.astro-wise.org/portal/aw_prompt.shtml
2. Anderson, E.W., Ahrens, J.P., Heitmann, K., Habib, S., Silva, C.T.: Provenance in comparative analysis: A study in cosmology. Computing in Science and Engg. 10(3), 30–37 (2008)
3. Ellkvist, T., Koop, D., Anderson, E.W., Freire, J., Silva, C.: Using provenance to support real-time collaborative design of workflows, pp. 266–279 (2008)
4. Freire, J., Koop, D., Moreau, L. (eds.): Provenance and Annotation of Data and Processes: Second International Provenance and Annotation Workshop. Springer, Heidelberg (2008)
5. Freire, J., Koop, D., Santos, E., Silva, C.T.: Provenance for computational tasks: A survey. Computing in Science and Engineering 10(3), 11–21 (2008)
6. Greenfield, P.: Reaching for the stars with python. Computing in Science and Engg. 9(3), 38–40 (2007)
7. Groth, P., Miles, S., Fang, W., Wong, S.C., Zauner, K.P., Moreau, L.: Recording and using provenance in a protein compressibility experiment. In: HPDC 2005 Proceedings of the High Performance Distributed Computing, pp. 201–208. IEEE Computer Society, Washington (2005)
8. Mwebaze, J., Boxhoorn, D., Valentijn, E.: Astro-wise: Tracing and using lineage for scientific data processing. In: International Conference on Network-Based Information Systems, pp. 475–480 (2009)
9. Scheidegger, C., Vo, H., Koop, D., Freire, J., Silva, C.: Querying and creating visualizations by analogy. IEEE Transactions on Visualization and Computer Graphics 13(6), 1560–1567 (2007)

I Think Therefore I Am Someone Else: Understanding the Confusion of Granularity with Continuant/Occurrent and Related Perspective Shifts

James D. Myers

National Center for Supercomputing Applications,
1205 W. Clark St, Urbana, IL 61801
jimmyers@illinois.edu

Abstract. Managing multiscale and multi-witness provenance is often assumed to involve relatively straight-forward matters of matching identifiers and recognizing composite processes and aggregate artifacts. However, the issue is much more complex and related to millennia of debate over the nature of objects and processes in the world. This work develops a set of concrete examples where such issues arise in provenance, discusses the core conceptual distinctions involved, and postulates a basic mechanism for extending provenance models to enable integration across granularities and process types, recognizing the OPM 'agent' concept as a special case.

Keywords: provenance, multiscale, semantic integration.

1 Introduction

Over the past few years, there has been a broad effort to define common requirements for provenance, to outline real-world use cases, to define core models of provenance, and to assess interoperability of existing systems. In these discussions, there has been recognition that there are a variety of levels of granularity and a variety of types of processes for which provenance is important, as well as recognition that many use cases of interest require integration of provenance information across these dimensions. The issues involved in such integration have mostly been viewed as simple matters of aggregation, i.e. requiring concepts such as 'collections' of artifacts and composite processes. However, the need for constructs such as agents (as in the Open Provenance Model) hint at deeper issues related to the concepts of identity and distinctions between continuant and occurrent (or endurant and perdurant respectively), and of versions and replicas.

Consider the use case hinted at in the title: a person engages in a thought process (or attends a class or participates in a discussion to include cases where the process is external to the person). In OPM and similarly expressive languages, one could model this as

NaiveArtifact ←(used) EduProcess ←(wasGeneratedBy) InformedArtifact,

or

Person ←(wasControlledBy) EduProcess

D.L. McGuinness, J.R. Michaelis, and L. Moreau (Eds.): IPAW 2010, LNCS 6378, pp. 292–294, 2010.

but neither is satisfactory. The first ignores the persistent identity of the person involved (and indeed only talks about what we could call the frozen state of a person) while the later fails to describe the effect of the process (why pay for education if you are not changed by it in explicit ways?). One can see versions being edited (that we would like to consider as being states of an evolving book), bits being moved through storage hierarchies and network locations (that we would like to consider as a single persistent logical 'file'), and even workflows producing files (which we would like to consider as discoveries made by a team, financed by sponsors, and leading to Nobel prizes) as additional examples where the nominal notion of granularity of description in fact obscures a perceptual shift in the nature of the artifacts (and processes) involved. It is conceptually incorrect, for example, to consider a person and their naïve state as aliases: combined with provenance that the person was issued a driver's license one would erroneously conclude that driving home from class would be illegal.

The core of this issue has been debated for thousands of years and the question is basically one of identity – what constitutes an object (artifact) – and the relationship between state and change, object and process, continuant (a thing outside time) and occurrent (an event in time). Much of the philosophical debate appears to center on how far one can drive either perspective as a way to model the world, but at least some groups [1,2] have attempted to define a practical view that is very relevant for the development of a provenance model capable of handling multi-granularity, multi-process-type use cases. Specifically, Galton and Mizoguchi [1] propose a definition of objects (object identity) in terms of which processes are considered internal and which external to that object; the chemical processes holding a rock together are internal to it whereas the processes that move it (falling under gravity, throwing) are external to it, and, critically, it is this separation of processes that enables us to identify what we mean by the rock.

In this view, it is easy to recognize that the examples above, and many of the issues involved in integrating accounts from different witnesses, involve perspectives where the process being described in the provenance record is internal to objects in one view and external in the other. This is not an issue of granularity in the sense of simply ignoring intermediate states and processes. Consequently, the relationships needed to provide crosswalks between these views are ones that connect one type of objects (A) with another type (B) than can be considered as aspects/states of an A object that can be used and generated by processes considered internal to A objects. Examples of such relationship vocabularies include versioning (versions are states, connected by editing processes, of a mutable (editable) book), copying (copies are physical instantiations, connected by replication processes, of logical entities), and, less obviously, collecting (a specific set of pictures, created by insert/delete processes, can be considered part of a living collection).

How does this affect provenance models? It suggests that a minimal model capable of integrating accounts from witnesses observing at different granularities or who are concerned with different processes, should include a construct to identify artifacts as 'aspectsOf' other types of artifacts that are 'engagedIn' a given process. I.e. a witness could add to a statement that

B was 'usedBy' process P

that

B is an 'aspectOf' a (different type of) artifact A that is 'engagedIn' P where A is a type of artifact for which processes of type P are part of their normal lifecycle.

In the spirit of profiles in OPM, these relationships could be specialized to address versioning, copying, etc. The current notion of Agent in OPM can be seen as a start in this direction in which 'engagedIn' is specialized to represent control. In addition to clarifying the need for Agent (Agents are minimally a different type of artifact that has a different relationship with a process than its inputs and outputs, whose identity is unaffected by participation in the process, and for whom participation in such processes is part of their normal lifecycle). The line of argument presented here suggests that Agents in OPM should be allowed to have an additional relationship with artifacts that are 'aspectsOf'/states of the Agent that enable a finer level of detail on how Agents control processes.

A scalable provenance model sufficiently powerful to model real-world use cases involving multiple type of processes and multiple granularities must include a mechanism that recognizes when the notion of identity has shifted due to assumptions about the set of processes that can change identity. Such a mechanism could be along the lines of the "aspectOf"/"engagedIn" bridging vocabulary given here, which defines artifact-to-artifact and artifact-to-process relationships but may also need to include process-to-process relationships (Agents 'live' and processes they engageIn are part of their overall 'life' process) and could potentially include inference rules (in the spirit of OPM's use of timestamps to validate/refute causality claims) that would support assessment of the validity of integrated provenance claims.

References

1. Galton, A., Mizoguchi, R.: The water falls but the waterfall does not fall: New Perspectives on objects, processes, and events. Applied Ontology 4, 71–107 (2009)
2. Grenon, P., Smith, B.: SNAP and SPAN: Towards Dynamic Spatial Ontology. Spatial Cognition & Computation: An Interdisciplinary Journal 4(1), 69–104 (2004)

A Multi-faceted Provenance Solution for Science on the Web

Edoardo Pignotti, Peter Edwards, and Richard Reid

School of Natural and Computing Sciences, University of Aberdeen
{e.pignotti,p.edwards,r.reid}@abdn.ac.uk

Abstract. To support the interface between scientific research and the wider public policy agenda it is essential to make the provenance of research processes and artefacts more transparent and subject to scrutiny. We outline the requirements for a multi-faceted approach to provenance and present a Web-based virtual research environment (ourSpaces) to demonstrate how research artefacts, projects, geographical locations and online communications can be linked in order to facilitate collaborative research.

Keywords: provenance, VRE, collaboration.

1 Introduction

The PolicyGrid project[1] is exploring how novel e-Science technologies can be used to support researchers; in particular, the provision of support for evidence-based policy research. De Roure [1] has argued that in order to assist collaboration among researchers it is necessary to go beyond basic e-Science infrastructure and to develop technologies to facilitate the discovery and interpretation of knowledge generated by others and to allow connections between people, places, organisations, ideas, and data. The Web has drastically improved this exchange. Scientists can now utilise social networking tools as a way to convey ideas much like a person may want to "Tweet" about his or her day. Similarly, virtual research environments enable users to share scientific resources in much the same way as Facebook might be used to share photos. However, provenance information is essential to enable researchers to assess the accuracy, timeliness, reliability, and trustworthiness of information available on the Web. To support science on the Web we require a representational framework for provenance which goes beyond simple metadata descriptions of artefacts and processes. Based upon interactions over a number of years with several research groups and communities, we have identified the following requirements for such a provenance fabric:

1. It should describe and uniquely identify a range of entities: artefacts (digital & physical); processes (services & human activities); people; organisational structures/membership; social networks.

---

[1] http://www.policygrid.org

D.L. McGuinness, J.R. Michaelis, and L. Moreau (Eds.): IPAW 2010, LNCS 6378, pp. 295–297, 2010.

2. It should situate entities in time and space.
3. It should incorporate online communication (e.g. instant messaging, blog entries, email) into the provenance record.
4. It should allow relationships (e.g. causal, social, organisational) to be defined between entities.
5. It should make explicit goals and constraints associated with processes and associated artefacts, in order to capture the 'why?' aspect of provenance.
6. It should facilitate reasoning about access control; documentation policies; completeness of the provenance record; trust and reputation.

While many of the existing provenance solutions [4,5] have focused on specific technologies to support narrow scientific domains, some recent research has focused on interoperability of provenance information across different systems. Most notably the Open Provenance Model was developed to address issues in managing provenance information in science, independent from technology and domain. The aim of OPM is to provide a technology-agnostic model supporting the digital representation of provenance describing any "thing" that is produced by a computer system (or not). OPM is based on three primary entities namely *Artefact*, *Process* and *Agent* and associated causal relationships namely *used*, *wasGeneratedBy*, *wasTriggeredBy* and *wasControlledBy*. OPM also defines a core set of rules that specify inferences that can be made on a provenance record (e.g. *wasDerivedFrom, wasTriggeredBy*).

In order to meet the much broader requirements of our provenance fabric an approach is required which integrates organisations, people, domains, technologies, systems and the physical and digital worlds. The Open Provenance Model has made an important step towards realising this vision by allowing the provenance of individual systems to be expressed in a coherent fashion. However, in order to realise a true *provenance fabric* we need to go beyond just descriptions of agents, artefacts and processes.

2 ourSpaces - Supporting Provenance on the Web

ourSpaces (www.ourspaces.net) [6] has been developed as a working realisation of various elements of the *provenance fabric*. Built using a number of Semantic Web technologies [2], users are able to perform various activities such as uploading and describing digital artefacts, maintaining personal profiles, initiating instant messaging (IM) conversations, creating blog posts and calendar events, tagging and commenting on other resources and forming groups (in the form of projects) with other researchers. At the heart of ourSpaces is an OWL representation of the Open Provenance Model [3], used to express metadata regarding digital artefacts and processes. However, additional ontologies (including FOAF SIOC, GeoNames)[2], are used to capture information regarding people, organisations, social networks, geographical context and online communications.

Through a system demonstration, we will present the following: (a) Resource management including resource upload and description; (b) How OPM can be enriched by social context; (c) Project creation and management features; (d) Use of maps; (e) Multiple approaches to metadata querying and browsing.

---

[2] http://xmlns.com/foaf/spec/, http://rdfs.org/sioc/spec/, http://www.geonames.org/ontology/

Fig. 1. ourSpaces VRE home page

References

1. De Roure, D.: The new e-Science presentation (2008),
   http://www.slideshare.net/dder/the-new-science-bangalore-edution
2. Berners-Lee, T., Hendler, J., Lassila, O.: The Semantic Web. Scientific American 284(5), 34–43 (2001)
3. Moreau, L., Clifford, B., Freire, J., Gil, Y., Groth, P., Futrelle, J., Kwasnikowska, N., Miles, S., Missier, P., Myers, J., Simmhan, Y., Stephan, E., Van den Bussche, J.: The Open Provenance Model - Core Specification (v1.1). In: Future Generation Computer Systems (2009) (submitted)
4. Simmhan, Y., Pale, B., Gannon, D.: A Survey of Data Provenance in e-Science. SIGMOD Record 34(3), 31–36 (2005)
5. Bose, R., Foster, I., Moreau, L.: Report on the International Provenance and Annotation Workshop (IPAW 2006). Sigmod Records (September 2006)
6. Reid, R., Pignotti, E., Edwards, P., Laing, A.: ourSpaces: Linking Provenance and Social Data in a Virtual Research Environment. In: Proceedings of the World Wide Conference (2010)

Social Web-Scale Provenance in the Cloud

Yogesh Simmhan[1] and Karthik Gomadam[2]

[1] Microsoft Research
yoges@microsoft.com
[2] University of Southern California
gomadam@usc.edu

Abstract. The lower barrier to entry for users to create and share resources through applications like Facebook and Twitter, and the commoditization of social Web data has heightened issues of privacy, attribution, and copyright. These make it important to track the provenance of social Web data. We outline and discuss key engineering, privacy, and monetization challenges in collecting and analyzing provenance of social Web resources.

Keywords: Provenance, social web, scalability, privacy, Cloud.

1 Introduction

The pervasiveness of social networks as an intrinsic part of users' online presence allows easy sharing of information among peers and the public at large. Social network services such as Facebook allow sharing of *free form* comments, *semi-structured* hashtags, and *resources* like images with other users. External applica-tions can query these user relationships and content through APIs, and publish feeds.

The ease of such portals that cause their success also masks privacy issues that have unintended consequences for the users [1,4], ranging from plagiarism to misrepresentation. Tracking the provenance of shared social network resources becomes crucial, yet challenging, given the *ad hoc* nature of the sharing model and the scalability needed [6]. For e.g., an indie artist who shares a soundtrack on Facebook may like to find out which of her friends or friends of friends (FOAFs) downloaded the music or published "similar" albums on finding remixed versions of her work [2].

Provenance in social networks pose additional challenges to those in workflows and databases, viz. (1) Identifying resources, relationships, and semantics from unstructured information, (2) Online scaling with social network size, frequency of feed updates, and popularity, (3) Ensuring privacy of aggregated provenance, and (4) Incentivizing service use and revenue given the expectations of free online services.

Provenance information for resources on the social web can be characterized as:

1. **Resource provenance:** This traces the creation, publishing, reuse, and deletion of social data artifacts like media and documents identified by URI/URLs.
2. **Social provenance:** This describes social operators such as "Like", "Comment", and "Share" applied to resources to track activities beyond its creation and reuse. Recording social relationships like Friends and FOAFs, over time, is also needed.
3. **System provenance:** This includes access statistics, download history and site metrics of the resource automatically and passively tracked by the social network.

D.L. McGuinness, J.R. Michaelis, and L. Moreau (Eds.): IPAW 2010, LNCS 6378, pp. 298–300, 2010.
© Springer-Verlag Berlin Heidelberg 2010

1.1 Engineering and Scalability Challenges

A provenance system for the social Web involves: (1) *Integration* of provenance from social networks, and (2) *Subscription* to query provenance features of interest.

Architecture: Our proposed architecture employs a publish-subscribe model for aggregating social network feeds from users based on *Pubsubhubbub* [7]. The aggregator identifies resource entities and relationships in the feed using unstructured and structured content – a challenging research problem, and integrates it with prior provenance that is enhanced with specific resource metadata pulled from the network.

Provenance is accessed through user queries performed either on the feeds in near-realtime, or on the aggregated provenance and metadata. The former standing queries [9] have timeliness but restrict query attributes. The latter provide richer query terms but is performed once or triggered on a schedule. The queries may be as broad as requesting all updates to a resource or use heuristics to identify similar resources in a FOAF network. The query results can themselves be pushed as feeds.

Scaling: Pubsubhubbub is a scalable protocol for publishing feeds and query results. However, storage and query over the aggregated provenance has to scale too. *Cloud computing* provides a model for scaling the aggregator and querying hubs. SQL Azure [8] databases hosted in Virtual Machines (VMs) can store provenance metadata and scale on demand as the number of users increase. The metadata is partitioned across VM instances based on tight linkages in the friend network to ensure metadata locality – trading better query performance within closely linked friends for costlier access to distant friends or the public. Using a carousel approach that batches scheduled queries across users and scans tables can also achieve load balancing. Scaling with the rate of feeds and the number of queries is also key as service or resource popularity increases (e.g. a leaked music video). On demand scale-out by Clouds combined with dynamic repartitioning of stored provenance can address this.

1.2 Privacy and Monetization

Tracking provenance benefits privacy preservation and in determining its compromise. Awareness of who is *actually* viewing your resource can help detect incorrect privacy configurations, and bridge perceived and actual privacy. One challenge is to collect the provenance *transparently* with user opt-in, rather than giving the sense of yet another privacy invasion and harvest of personal information.

Another aspect of privacy is the *social granularity* of collected provenance. The provenance service can be a private service for groups of friends who sign up and track resources they publish. The group can even own the hosted provenance service and data in the Cloud using their own account – paying for the *private provenance service* and Cloud resources and ensuring no third party mines it. The diminished cost per user for the Cloud service as more users join is an incentive for FOAFs to join.

The above approach can create disconnected provenance repositories for each user group. These can be linked by exporting provenance through standards like Open Provenance Model [5] and those evolving in the W3C Provenance Incubator [3]. Else, third parties can provide a more connected, shared service across users in exchange for payment, or for a free, Ad supported model that mines accumulated provenance.

1.3 Related Work

Social networks provide users with system provenance on resource creation and use to popularize their access. Tools studied to reuse data in social networks and blogs enhance the metadata of republished resources with semantic annotations on their provenance to support accountability and enforce usage right policies [2]. Others have combined provenance of user assertions with their social network links to gauge the trust rating of the assertion, used in movie recommendation systems [1]. The W3C Provenance and Social Web Incubator groups have identified requirements of provenance for social networks and surveyed technologies that can address them [3].

2 Conclusion

The commoditization of social Web data increases concerns about privacy and resource sharing in social networks that can be addressed through tracking provenance of social Web resources. The issues around such provenance has a different quality from provenance collection for workflows and databases, both due to the fungible nature of the data and the scales involved. Our article highlights some of these issues and proposes an architecture for addressing this in part. These form the basis for further investigation into this important and emerging area of research.

Acknowledgments. The authors thank members of the W3C Provenance Incubator and Social Web Incubator groups for discussions that motivated some of these issues.

References

1. Golbeck, J.: Combining Provenance with Trust in Social Networks for Semantic Web Content Filtering. In: Moreau, L., Foster, I. (eds.) IPAW 2006. LNCS, vol. 4145, pp. 101–108. Springer, Heidelberg (2006)
2. Wagner, C., Motta, E.: Data Republishing on the Social Semantic Web. In: Workshop on Trust and Privacy on the Social and Semantic Web (2009)
3. Requirements for Provenance on the Web. In: Cheney, J., Gil, Y., Groth, P., Miles, S. (eds.) Working Report by the W3C Provenance Incubator Group, April 9 (2010)
4. Dwyer, C., Hiltz, S.R., Passerini, K.: Trust and privacy concern within social networking sites. In: Americas Conference on Information Systems (2007)
5. Moreau, L., Clifford, B., Freire, J., Gil, Y., Groth, P., Futrelle, J., Kwasnikowska, N., Miles, S., Missier, P., Myers, J., Simmhan, Y., Stephan, E., Van den Bussche, J.: The Open Provenance Model - Core Specification (v1.1). Future Generation Computer Systems (in press 2010)
6. Moreau, L.: The Foundations for Provenance on the Web. Foundations and Trends in Web Science (2009) (submitted)
7. Pubsubhubbub: A simple, open, web-hook-based pubsub protocol (June 4, 2010), http://code.google.com/p/pubsubhubbub/
8. Microsoft SQL Azure, (June 4, 2010), http://www.microsoft.com/windowsazure/sqlazure/
9. Data Stream Query Processing. Nick Koudas and Divesh Srivastava. In: International Conference on Data Engineering, ICDE (2005)

Using Domain Requirements to Achieve Science-Oriented Provenance

Eric Stephan[1], Todd Halter[1], Terence Critchlow[1], Paulo Pinheiro da Silva[2], and Leonardo Salayandia[2]

[1] Pacific Northwest National Laboratory, Richland WA, USA
[2] University of Texas at El Paso, El Paso TX, USA

Abstract. The US Department of Energy (DOE) Atmospheric Radiation Measurement Program (ARM) is adopting the use of formalized provenance to support observational data products produced by ARM operations and relied upon by researchers. Because of the diversity of needs in the climate community provenance will need to be conveyed in a domain-oriented context. This paper explores a use case where semantic abstract workflows (SAW) are employed as a means to filter, aggregate, and contextually describe the historical events responsible for the ARM data product the scientist is relying upon.

1 Introduction

What is the right level of provenance, disseminated to the right audience, in the right scientific context? This is a continual question facing the Department of Energy's Atmospheric Radiation Measurement (ARM) Program [1], especially as a diversity of audiences such as climate modelers, and researchers use the ARM data products in new and innovative ways. ARM is currently advancing the way day-to-day tasks relating to data capture, processing, and reprocessing, error detection, and troubleshooting in analytical methods by formally adding a provenance component to preserve the workflow history of tasks. This year the ARM Data Management Facility will manage the data flow for over 420 sensors located around the world, and will be ingesting one half terabyte of observations daily. As sensor data is collected, ARM transforms the ingested data into a uniform format, performs quality control, reprocessing, and transfers the finished products to the ARM Archive. From an operational standpoint it is foreseen that the number of ARM data products will continue to increase significantly, dwarfing today's complexity of algorithm interdependency. As demands on data increase the need for provenance is challenging our capability of properly supporting data and product attribution.

2 Issues with Scientific Outreach

For ARM sensor data stream processing and reprocessing, a standard Integrated Software Development Environment (ISDE) workflow has been adapted that is

D.L. McGuinness, J.R. Michaelis, and L. Moreau (Eds.): IPAW 2010, LNCS 6378, pp. 301–303, 2010.

comprised of all or a subset of the following steps: Initialize, Get, Translate, Scientific Analysis, Translate, and Put. While on the surface these steps seem trivial each step relies upon detailed algorithms for processing the data, and each algorithm must iterate through the stream to operate on each sample. Part of the provenance challenge is retaining knowledge about how the data was processed that meets the needs of both operational staff and downstream researchers.

Provenance at multiple tiers [2] is required to provide relevant information for operations and researchers. Each tier has a different focus and resolution. The first tier that represents the lowest resolution of provenance depicts lineage because ARM data products are highly interdependent. This information is not only invaluable to the researcher in terms of knowing what went into making a product, it is vital to addressing cascading errors produced when erroneous products are relied upon by downstream data processes. The underlying tiers depict provenance as a "hedge" or forest of ordered acyclic graphs. The hedge tier provides provenance and referential information common to all samples being processed at the component level within the ISDE workflow, and each acyclic graph within the context of the hedge represents the third tier that we refer to as the "branch". The current approach is to capture provenance for every step within the ISDE workflow, analyze the provenance from an operational standpoint, and retain a subset of provenance to be used by researchers. A challenge is that of only retaining provenance useful for scientific understanding as data products are archived for future dissemination to researchers.

3   Developing Domain-Oriented Provenance Requirements

One approach to retain provenance most useful for scientific means is to restrict its capture to knowledge with a well-defined usage. Because provenance needs will be diverse, a knowledge-driven strategy is suggested to identify provenance in support of ARM's diverse research community.

A common understanding of the ISDE workflow by domain experts and computer scientists is a requirement to understand where and how provenance needs to be permanently archived. For instance, many steps (and sub-steps) of the workflow are required to support the execution of the workflow, and from an operational standpoint need to verify datasets being pre-staged for translation. However, from a scientific perspective, this information needs to be conveyed in an aggregate perspective. In other cases, scientists need a high resolution perspective of the samples being translated, but need a filtered view of what actually occurred. In both cases, scientists need to be able to describe the ISDE workflow in terms of scientific steps, and of using these scientific steps to identify the ones that they need provenance.

Our strategy is to have different domain expert focus groups to describe their understanding of the ISDE workflow through the use of semantic abstract workflows (SAW) [3] and for the computer scientists to map the SAW steps (i.e., SAW methods) into concrete ISDE workflow tasks. One immediate benefit of this approach is that the workflow would be described in scientific terms. Another benefit is that non-scientific steps are going to be abstracted away from the workflow. From the ISDE SAW, domain experts should be able to identify (and rank) the steps of the workflow that require provenance. From the SAW, it is possible to identify feasible provenance use cases and, by using the mappings between SAW methods and workflow tasks, to anticipate the content of the provenance for each task of the workflow. Moreover, the SAW can be use to determine provenance use cases that cannot be implemented because of unintentional uses of ARM data requiring knowledge not captured in the current provenance encoding.

References

1. Atmospheric Radiation Measurement Climate Research Facility: ARM Annual Report. U.S. Department of Energy, DOE/SC-ARM-0706 (2007)
2. Stephan, E.G., Halter, T.D., Ermold, B.D.: Leveraging The Open Provenance Model as a Multi-Tier Model for Global Climate Research. In: Proc. of 3rd International Provenance and Annotation Workshop, IPAW 2010 (2010)
3. Pinheiro da Silva, P., Salayandia, L., Gandara, A., Gates, A.Q.: CI-Miner: Semantically Enhancing Scientific Processes. Earth Science Informatics 2(4), 249–269 (2009)

Author Index

GPSR Compliance

The European Union's (EU) General Product Safety Regulation (GPSR)
is a set of rules that requires consumer products to be safe and our
obligations to ensure this.

If you have any concerns about our products, you can contact us on
ProductSafety@springernature.com

In case Publisher is established outside the EU, the EU authorized
representative is:

Springer Nature Customer Service Center GmbH
Europaplatz 3
69115 Heidelberg, Germany

Batch number: 09490872

Printed by Printforce, the Netherlands